CITE THIS BOOK

THUS:

first tuesday

The §1031 Reinvestment Plan

4th Edition

Cutoff Dates:
Legal editing of this book was
completed November 2005

Copyright ©2006 by first tuesday
P.O. Box 20069, Riverside, CA 92516

Printed in the United States of America

Editorial Staff

Legal Editor/Publisher:
Fred Crane

Managing Editor:
Ai M. Kelley

Project Editor:
Sheena Wong

Contributing Editors:
Melissa L. Clayton
Connor P. Wallmark

Senior Editorial Assistant:
Joseph Duong

Editorial Assistant:
Sylvia Rodemeyer

Comments or suggestions to:
first tuesday, P.O. Box 20069, Riverside, CA 92516
e-mail: editorial@firsttuesday.us
www.firsttuesdayonline.com

Table Of Contents

Section A

**General
Introduction**

Section B

**§1031
Fundamentals**

Section C

**Reinvestment
Scenarios**

Table of Forms

Introduction

The objective of this study is to fully develop the real estate professional's knowledge on all aspects of the §1031 investment planning and his application of the concepts underlying §1031 reinvestment planning in real estate sales. The concepts that drive §1031 tax-exempt sales and exchange transactions are as unique as the IRS regulations regarding them are obtuse. The writing in this book uses plain language that can be adopted by a broker or agent to skillfully advise clients and persuade their other advisors on the tax avoidance decisions that are most beneficial for the client.

The objective of this material is to develop the understanding and background of a §1031 reinvestment so brokers or agents can gain the confidence needed to advise an investor at any stage of a §1031 reinvestment plan, whether it is a sale or an exchange, a concurrent or a delayed reinvestment.

Brokers and agents can and do advise clients on the §1031 aspects of reinvesting. More importantly, all real estate brokers and most agents know that the §1031 tax avoidance scheme does exist, though few know much about its internal mechanics. Any broker or agent who has ever thought about advising clients on the tax aspects of their transactions will realize §1031 tax advice always includes two properties and two fees.

This material provides a hands-on application of the §1031 reinvestment plan. Every student of this material will carry away profit-making ideas and be equipped to put them to work immediately.

SECTION A

General Introduction

Chapter 1

An investor's §1031 motivation

This chapter sets out the benefits of the §1031 profit tax exemption, and discusses how a broker coordinates real estate transactions comprised of buyers and sellers with differing motivations.

The tax-exempt sale by reinvestment

Numerous benefits and advantages are available to sellers of §1031 like-kind properties who, rather than "cash out" on the sale of their property, **couple the sale** with the purchase of replacement property(ies). Thus, a reinvestment is arranged that establishes the seller's **continuing investment** in the ownership of like-kind real estate, a requirement to qualify the sale for profit tax exemption under Internal Revenue Code (IRC) §1031.

One or more of these benefits and advantages becomes the **motivating factor** influencing an investor's decision to sell one property and buy replacement property in a tandem transaction called a *§1031 reinvestment plan*.

If a broker knows the advantages of buying and selling under §1031 rules, the broker:

- can undertake the duty to determine how his client might benefit from §1031 tax treatment by advising his client about the benefits [See Chapter 2];

- can arrange a reinvestment where the motives of opposing parties to buy or sell may differ; and

- can be rewarded by receiving two fees for giving advice and assistance in the negotiations of the two transactions.

Determining the investor's needs

A workable §1031 reinvestment environment exists when an investor's motivation for selling property includes his ability to avoid reporting profit on the sale by buying replacement property.

A broker who knows the investor intends to buy replacement property with the net proceeds from the sale of his property to qualify the sale and reinvestment as a §1031 tax-free reinvestment plan, is in a position to:

- **negotiate the sale** of the investor's property to a buyer who will enter into a purchase agreement containing a cooperation provision calling for the buyer to accommodate the investor's transfer of funds in a §1031 reinvestment plan; and

- coordinate the investor's **use of the net proceeds** from the sale of his property to purchase replacement property from a seller who enters into a purchase agreement containing a cooperation provision calling for the seller to accommodate the investor's §1031 reinvestment plan.

A broker working with an investor who has an interest in acquiring other real estate with the net proceeds from a sale should prepare a **client profile sheet** as the result of a counseling session with the investor.

The client profile sheet documents the investor's needs and expectations in a replacement property the investor would like to acquire to complete a §1031 reinvestment with his net sales proceeds, which are also called *§1031 money*. [See Form 350 accompanying this chapter]

§1031 cooperation provision

An investor's future depends on for the buyer cooperating in the investor's reinvestment of the net proceeds of a sale and is best negotiated

CLIENT PROFILE
Confidential Personal Data Sheet

DATE:_____, 20_____, at_____, California

> Use of the form assists in collecting information about an individual's personal traits, family obligations, composition of wealth, community integrity and accomplishments to better inform the Broker/agent about the individual's wants and needs.

1. Personal information:

1.1 Name: _____

    a. Address: _____

    b. City:_____ State:_____ Zip: _____

    c. Phone:_____ Fax:_____ Email: _____

    d. Age:_____ General health: _____

    e. Length of time in the community:_____

    f. Personal achievements: _____

1.2 Occupation: _____

    a. Professional designations & licenses: _____

    _____

    b. Business address:_____

    c. City:_____ State:_____ Zip: _____

    d. Business phone:_____ Fax:_____ Email:_____

1.3 Marital status: _____

    a. Spouse's name: _____

    b. Spouse's occupation:_____

    c. Children – names & ages: _____

    _____

1.4 Membership in cultural or civic organizations: _____

    a. Religious preference/time dedicated: _____

2. Financial information:

    a. Gross annual income: . . . . $_____

    b. Interest income:. . . . . $_____

    c. Dividend income: . . . . $_____

    d. Spendable income (real estate): . . . . $_____

    e. Approximate net worth
       (excluding home, car and furnishings): . . . . $_____

       Cash on deposit: . . . . $_____

       Liquid stocks & bonds:. . . . . $_____

       Net equity in real estate:. . . . . $_____

    f. Investor can make additional capital
       contributions in the annual amount of:. . . . . $_____

       Source of funds: _____

    g. Cash value of life insurance:. . . . . $_____

3. Investment background:

    a. Stocks, bonds or commodities: _____

    _____

    _____

    b. Real estate owned other than residence: _____

    _____

    _____

    c. Investor involvement in partnership(s): _____

    _____

    _____

4. Investment needs (explain briefly):

a. Tax benefits: _____

_____

_____

b. Spendable income, loan reduction or increased value: _____

_____

_____

c. Short-term investment goals (less than 5 years): _____

_____

_____

d. Long-term investment goals: _____

_____

_____

5. Investor's advisors:

a. Accountant: _____

b. Insurance broker: _____

c. Banker: _____

d. Attorney: _____

e. Stockbroker: _____

f. Real estate broker: _____

6. Educational background:

a. Degrees and majors: _____

_____

b. Real estate or law courses studied: _____

_____

_____

7. Investor's special interests (hobbies, clubs, etc.):

_____

_____

_____

8. Personality traits:

a. Positive and decisive? ☐ Yes ☐ No

b. Negative and evasive? ☐ Yes ☐ No

c. Passive and follows? ☐ Yes ☐ No

9. Relationship with broker:

a. Brief description of previous relationships (business, social, civic) with investor: _____

_____

_____

_____

FORM 350   06-05   ©2005 **first tuesday**, P.O. BOX 20069, RIVERSIDE, CA 92516 (800) 794-0494

by using a purchase agreement that contains a §1031 cooperation provision. [See Figure 1 accompanying this chapter]

Purchase agreements designed to document the sale of a single-family residence by an investor who occupies the property to a buyer who will occupy the property do not usually contain provisions that implement tax avoidance.

Most buyers will agree to a cooperation provision as long as the price and terms of purchase are agreeable, since they too appreciate the benefits of avoiding the tax on profit.

§1031 benefits by reinvestment

The benefits and advantages available to real estate investors, one or more of which may influence the investor's decision to enter into a §1031 reinvestment plan, include:

- an **exemption** from reporting all or a portion of the profit on the sale;

- an increase in **debt leverage** and **income yield** by replacing the property being sold with a higher-priced, more efficient and more productive property;

- an increase in the **depreciation deduction** schedules by assuming (or originating) larger amounts of debt on higher-priced replacement property as part of a fresh start for allocation of basis between land and depreciable improvements;

- the **avoidance of costs** incurred to originate new financing by assuming or taking title subject to the existing loans on the properties sold or acquired;

- an **inflation and appreciation hedge** to take maximum advantage of an anticipated rapid increase in cyclical property values by acquiring highly leveraged property to replace a lower-leveraged property;

- the voluntary **elimination of a partner** from the co-ownership of a property by acquiring multiple replacement properties for an "in-kind" distribution the following year;

- a **consolidation of the equities** in several properties (by one or more owners) into a single, more efficient property;

- the acquisition of several lesser-valued replacement properties to **diversify the investment** and reduce the risk of loss inherent in the ownership of one high-value property, or, alternatively, to facilitate an **orderly liquidation** of a single, high-value property over a period of years;

- the receipt of **tax-free cash** through the execution of a purchase-money carryback note on acquisition of the replacement property;

- the replacement of a management-intense property with a **more manageable property**;

- the **avoidance of profit taxes** on foreclosure of a property with little if any equity by adding cash to an exchange for replacement property with equal or greater debt which is financially more manageable and owned by someone interested in taking on a seemingly over-encumbered property which may require a pre-foreclosure workout with the lender;

Figure 1   *Excerpted from* **first tuesday** *Form 171*

4.4 Both Parties reserve their right to assign, and agree to cooperate in effecting an Internal Revenue Code §1031 Exchange prior to close of escrow on either Party's written notice.

- the **relocation** of an equity in property, undiminished by taxes, by an investor who himself moves to a new geographic location;

- the **creation of a job** for the investor who desires to undertake the management or rehabilitation of a replacement property;

- the coupling of a **carryback note** retained on a sale with the reinvestment of the cash down payment from the sale in a replacement property; and

- the $250,000 individual §121 homeowner's profit **exclusion** on the sale of a principal residence coupled with the §1031 profit **exemption** on reinvestment of any sales proceeds remaining after withdrawing the amount of profit excluded under §121, in a tandem effort to avoid profit taxes on any long-term capital gains not excluded under §121 or taxed as unrecaptured depreciation gains.

Improper tax avoidance motivation

The primary tax advantage for an investor selling one property and buying another in a §1031 reinvestment plan is the ability to "shift" the **cost basis** remaining in the property sold into the replacement property, without a tax on the **profit**, called *nonrecognition of gain* by the Internal Revenue Service (IRS). The §1031 exemption implicitly allows the profit or loss on the sale to be carried forward to the replacement property without consequence, to be reported (profit or loss) in a later sale of the replacement property.

As a result, family members or family-owned corporations are motivated to collaborate with a second family member (or related corporation) in an attempt to **reduce the profit tax** on the sale of a property which has a very low cost basis.

For example, before closing a sale of a property, family members enter into an exchange of properties between themselves. A first family member who owns a low-basis property that he wants to sell, first exchanges it for a high-basis property owned by a second family member that is nearly equal to or greater than the value of the low-basis property.

The second family member acquires title to the low-basis property before it is sold in a cash-out sale to an unrelated buyer. As a result of the prior exchange, the second family member carries forward — shifts — to the low-basis property he receives and resells, the very high cost basis he has in the property he owns and transfers to the first family member.

On the further transfer of the now high-basis property in a sale to an unrelated buyer, the family will have "cashed out" of the property. With the second family member's high cost basis shifted into the property sold, little, if any, profit exists to be reported and taxed on the sale. As always, "price minus basis equals profit."

The shift of the high cost basis into the property on the exchange between family members is designed to eliminate the profit the family member who originally owned the property would have reported had he sold it directly to the buyer. Hence, the family saved hugely on its wealth by reducing their profit taxes.

Now consider a wealthy grandfather who owns an income property he has held for decades. He has received a purchase agreement offer from an unrelated buyer at a price 15 times greater than his depreciated cost basis. His very low cost basis will produce a huge profit: combined state and federal taxes will be nearly 25% of the price offered for the property.

A grandson of means acquired developable land during a recent real estate boom. The land, while valuable for future development, is now worth less than he paid for it due to current market conditions. Thus, his cost basis is greater than the property's value. If sold, the sale would generate a loss, not a profit.

The land is of similar value to the income property his grandfather is contemplating selling. Further, the grandson needs cash; the grandfather does not.

The family decides the grandfather should not cash out on a sale of the property. He should agree to sell the property contingent on his acquiring suitable replacement property and completing a §1031 reinvestment of the cash proceeds.

Since the grandson needs cash and the land will be unable to be developed for four or five years, the grandson will first exchange his land for his grandfather's income property. Then, the grandson will immediately resell his grandfather's property to the prospective buyer.

Thus, on the cash sale to the unrelated buyer, the grandson would pocket the cash proceeds while the grandfather becomes the owner of the land. The grandson is unconcerned that his exchange will not qualify for a §1031 exemption due to his immediate cash out of his investment in the grandfather's real estate. The grandson has a high cost basis and will be reselling the replacement property at a reportable loss.

The family engages a person as a **qualified intermediary**, using a procedure established by the IRS under the alternative *safe harbor rules* for avoiding the receipt of sales proceeds, to facilitate the exchange, since the grandfather would be barred from qualifying for the §1031 exemption under the §1031 *related persons rule* if the exchange of the property to be sold was directly between himself and his grandson and a qualified intermediary who will acquire title from the grandfather is an unrelated person.

By a series of agreements, the intermediary takes title to both properties and conveys them on to the opposing family members, called *sequential deeding*. Within a few weeks, the grandson further conveys the income property he now owns to the cash buyer and receives the proceeds from the sale.

The grandfather reports the exchange of his income property into the land as a §1031 tax exempt transaction. However, the IRS challenges the exemption.

The IRS claims the qualified intermediary used to comply with the safe harbor rules for avoiding the receipt of cash proceeds on a sale directly to a cash buyer, cannot be "sandwiched" into contracts and conveyancing as an unrelated person to avoid the *§1031 related person rule*.

An exchange between **related persons**, such as lineal descendants and ancestors, does not qualify for the §1031 exemption should either property be resold within two years after closing the exchange. [Internal Revenue Code §1031(f)(1)]

The grandfather claims the qualified intermediary is not acting as his agent and that he did acquire replacement property in exchange. Thus, he has demonstrated his commitment to a "continuing investment" in like-kind real estate as required to qualify his profit for the §1031 exemption.

The IRS claims that even if the exchange is not collapsed (to eliminate the sequential and transitory conveyancing) and is recast as a single, direct exchange between two family members (or controlled entities), that the transactions resulting in the sale had as **one of its purposes** the **intent to avoid** federal income taxes. Thus, the §1031 profit exemption would also be disallowed under the related persons rules. [IRC §1031(f)(4)]

Was the exchange between family members by use of an intermediary and resale of one of the properties a tax avoidance scheme which disqualifies the grandfather's use of the §1031 exemption to avoid the tax on the profit he realized on the exchange with his grandson?

Yes! The series of transactions involving related persons included as **one of its purposes** the avoidance of income taxes, an avoidance permitted only between unrelated persons. The exchange reduced the amount of the profit tax the grandfather would have paid had he cashed out on a direct sale of the property to the unrelated buyer.

The family members exchanged a low-basis property owned by one family member for a high-basis property owned by another family member. If the §1031 exemption applied, each family member would retain his basis in the property he exchanged and would carry it forward — shifted — to the property he acquired.

Thus, the exchange by the grandfather was intended to allow the grandson to resell the grandfather's property and report a significantly lesser amount of profit (due to the grandson's high basis) than the grandfather would have reported had the sale of the property occurred directly between the grandfather and the cash buyer. [**Teruya Brothers, Ltd. & Subsidiaries** v. **Commissioner of Internal Revenue** (2005) 124 TC No. 4]

Further, related persons who exchange property directly between themselves, or indirectly through any type of facilitator, must each retain the property they acquired for a **two-year holding period** before either one may sell or further exchange the property they received. If they fail to meet the two-year, post-exchange holding period, the §1031 profit tax exemption is disallowed. Thus, the profit on the original exchange is taxed at the time of the further disposition of either property as though an exchange had never occurred. [IRC §1031(f)(1)]

Related or disqualified persons

Individuals and entities are classified as *persons*. Thus, an investor selling a property as the owner is either an individual or an entity comprised of two or more associated individuals.

When the investor sells a property and reinvests the sales proceeds in a replacement property, the replacement property he acquires also is owned by a **person**, specifically, an individual or an entity co-owned by two or more individuals.

Also, when the investor's acquisition of the replacement property is delayed until after escrow closes on his sale, the net sales proceeds by design will be rerouted and received by a person other than the investor.

Further, the individual or entity who receives the net proceeds on the closing of the investor's sale of a property in a §1031 reinvestment plan act as either:

- a facilitator under the *general rule* or the *safe harbor rule* employed by the investor to avoid actual and constructive receipt of the cash proceeds; or

- an escrow opened for the investor's acquisition of the replacement property with the cash proceeds of the sale.

The person acting as the facilitator will receive the sales proceeds under one of two rules allowing the investor to avoid actual and constructive receipt of the sales proceeds. Both rules for avoidance deal with related persons, but each rule is based on different qualifying standards for the related persons.

Thus, the facilitator (buyer's trustee) and the seller of the replacement property must be *unrelated* persons to the investor when the investor's property is being cashed out to a third-party buyer. If the facilitator holding the sales proceeds is a person related to the investor, or the seller of the replacement property is related and further transfers the investor's property in a cash out sale, the §1031 exemption is lost on the sale (or exchange) and the profit is taxed. [IRC §1031(f)(1), (3); Revenue Regulations §§1.1031(k)-1(f)(2), 1.1031(k)-1(k)(3)]

An individual or entity who acts as a facilitator established under the general rules for avoidance of receipt, or as the seller of the replacement property, is a **related person** if he bears any of the following family or business relationships with the investor:

- *family members*, limited to the investor's brothers and sisters, his spouse, his ancestors (parents, grandparents) and his lineal descendants (children, grandchildren) [IRC §267(b)(1)]; and

- *entities*, such as a corporation, LLC or partnership, in which the investor owns, directly or indirectly, **more than 50%** of the value, outstanding stock, capital interest or share of profits in the entity, sometimes called a *controlled entity*. [IRC §§267(b)(2), 707(b)(1)]

Based on the use of an unrelated person to facilitate a §1031 reinvestment of sales proceeds, the general rule for the avoidance of receipt of the sales proceeds is the classic method for avoiding receipt in a §1031 reinvestment plan. The general rule for avoiding receipt permits **direct deeding** of property to whomever is actually acquiring it. [IRS Revenue Ruling 90-34; see Chapter 16]

An **alternative method**, which may be used in place of the general rule to avoid receipt of sales proceeds, has been recently established by the IRS, called the *safe harbor rules*. [Rev. Regs. §1.1031(k)-1(g)]

The **safe harbor rules** for avoiding receipt of the cash proceeds from a sale require the person who holds the funds to meet the criteria of a *qualified intermediary*. The intermediary will receive the sales proceeds and take title in the transitory, **sequential deeding** required for the conveyancing of all properties involved in a safe-harbor §1031 reinvestment plan.

The persons who may qualify for the role of the **qualified intermediary** under the alternative safe harbor rules are far more limited than the persons who may act as an **unrelated person** under the general rules for using facilitators to avoid receipt of the sales proceeds. Further, direct deeding is not permitted under the safe harbor rules as title must pass sequentially through the qualified intermediary. [See Chapter 21]

When following the safe harbor rules and selecting a qualified intermediary, limitations establish **disqualified persons** who may not act as a qualified intermediary by excluding:

- *family members* limited to the investor's brothers and sisters, his spouse, his ancestors and lineal descendants [IRC §267(b)(1)];

- *entities* in which the investor owns, directly or indirectly, **more than 10%** of the value, outstanding stock, capital interests or share of profits [Rev. Regs. §1.1031(k)-1(k)(3); IRC §§267(b)(2), 707(b)(1)]; and

- *any agent* of the investor who has, within two years prior to closing out the §1031 reinvestment plan, acted as an employee, attorney, accountant, investment banker/broker or real estate agent/broker on behalf of the investor in any transaction or service rendered, unless the professional services rendered were solely with respect to §1031 exchanges or were routine services of a financial institution, title company or escrow company. [Rev. Regs. §1.1031(k)-1(k)(2)]

Chapter 2

Duty to advise on the tax aspects

This chapter clarifies the extent of the broker's duty to inform his client about the tax aspects of a proposed real estate transaction.

Disclosure of known consequences

The seller of an income-producing parcel of improved real estate intends to hire a broker to market his property and locate a buyer. But before hiring an individual to represent him, the seller interviews a few brokers and sales agents to determine who he will employ to list the property for sale.

The seller's primary concern is to hire a broker who is most likely to produce a prospective buyer who will purchase the property. Thus, the seller's interviews include an inquiry into:

- the contents of the listing package the broker or sales agent will prepare to market the property;

- the scope of the advertising the broker will provide to locate prospective buyers; and

- the professional relationship the broker or sales agent has with other brokers, agents and property owners.

One broker interviewed by the seller inquires about the seller's intended use of the proceeds from the sale. The seller indicates he would like to reinvest the funds in developable land, to hold for profit on a later resale to a subdivider or builder. On further inquiry, the seller provides the broker with data on the price he paid for his property, the debt now encumbering the property and his depreciated cost basis remaining in the property. These three key pieces of data are needed for an agent to assist the seller in his tax planning for a sale.

The broker does some quick mental math (sales price minus basis equals profit) to approximate the amount of profit the seller will realize on a sale. He immediately determines the seller would pay profit taxes at *recapture* (25%) and *long-term* (15%) rates that will equal nearly one fifth of his net proceeds from a sale (plus one twelfth for state taxes). The seller is informed of the broker's initial opinion about the seller's tax liability on a sale.

The broker then informs the seller he can avoid reporting his profit and paying income taxes on the sale by buying the land he would like to acquire now. Thus, the sale of his income property and his purchase of land can be linked together to form a **continuing investment** in real estate.

Also, the purchase agreements, entered into for the sale of the income property and the purchase of the land will contain a **contingency provision** conditioning the closing of the sale on the seller's purchase of other property.

So as not to mislead the seller about the extent of the broker's experience handling §1031 reinvestment plans for clients, the broker informs the seller he has not personally handled a §1031 transaction. However, he lets the seller know he has taken courses on §1031 transactions and has discussed §1031 funding procedures with brokers and escrow officers who have experience handling §1031 reinvestments.

The broker tells the seller he believes he can properly market the property and locate suitable land for the seller's reinvestment as well as follow up on procedures for §1031 tax avoidance, should the property be listed with him.

Conversely, another broker contacted by the seller is reticent about becoming involved in a review of the tax aspects of selling property.

The other broker hands the seller a written statement attached to a proposed listing agreement advising the seller that the broker:

- has disclosed the extent of his knowledge of the tax consequences on the sale of real estate;

- is unable to give further tax advice on the rules and procedures involved in a §1031 transaction; and

- has advised the seller to seek the advice of his accountant or tax attorney on how to properly avoid the tax on profit from the sale and purchase of real estate.

Did both brokers comply with their agency duty to make proper disclosures to the seller about their knowledge and willingness to give tax advice?

Yes! Both brokers met the **agency duty** undertaken when soliciting employment, since each broker:

- determined the tax consequences of the sale might affect the seller's handling of the sales transaction, called a *material fact*;

- disclosed the extent of his knowledge regarding the possible tax consequences of the sale; and

- advised on the need for a professional who would further investigate and advise on the §1031 tax aspects.

The question then remains, "Must a broker, employed by a seller of real estate, give tax advice to the seller?"

The answer lies in the type of real estate involved and the seller's intended use of the sales proceeds.

An affirmative duty to advise

Consider a listing broker who determines that information about the tax aspects of a sale are *material* to a sales transaction entered into by his client since tax information might affect the client's handling of the transaction. Accordingly, the broker has a duty owed to his client to disclose the extent of his knowledge on the transaction's tax aspects, called an *agency duty* or *fiduciary duty*.

Further, a concerned listing broker will go beyond disclosure of mere tax information and assist his client in structuring the sales arrangement to achieve the best possible tax consequences available.

However, a **statutory exception** to the disclosure duties exists. On one-to-four unit residential dwellings, a broker acting as the listing agent for a client, has **no duty to disclose** his knowledge of possible tax consequences, even if the tax consequences are known by the broker to affect the client's decision on how to handle the sale of his property, unless the topic becomes the subject of the client's inquiry. [Calif. Civil Code §2079.16]

Advice and disclosure exemption

Consider a seller of a one-to-four unit residential rental property who enters into a client-agent relationship with a broker, employing the broker to sell the property under a listing agreement.

The listing agreement form used by the broker contains a boilerplate clause stating a real estate broker is a person qualified to advise on real estate, a statement that is consistent with the training and knowledge of agents. However, the clause goes on to state that if the seller desires legal or tax advice, he should consult an appropriate professional.

The boilerplate clause appears as nothing more than an *advisory disclaimer* that, by definition, imposes no obligation on the seller to take steps to act in response to the clause's suggestion to seek other professional advice. No reason is given as to why such advice is necessary. The clause does not disclose anything about the legal or tax aspects of the transaction **as known** by the broker to affect the seller.

The broker also hands the seller a statutorily mandated **agency law disclosure** form that states: "A real estate agent is a person qualified to advise about real estate. If legal or tax advice is desired, consult a competent professional." This further *advisory disclaimer* contains no advice from the broker regarding the necessity or desirability known to the broker as to why the seller should respond to the advisory. Further, the disclaimer does not obligate the seller to employ the other professional to advise on the tax aspects of the transaction before closing escrow. [CC §2079.16]

The broker locates a buyer who enters into a purchase agreement with the seller to buy the rental property. The purchase agreement also states the seller should consult his attorney or accountant for tax advice, but does not say whether or why the broker believes he should do so.

Prior to closing the sale of the seller's property, the broker also negotiates the seller's purchase of another one-to-four unit residential rental property, which involves the broker's preparation of a purchase agreement.

Before the separate escrows close on the sale and the purchase transactions, the seller asks the broker about the number of days he has after the sale closes to purchase the replacement property and avoid paying profit tax on the sale. The seller has never been involved in a §1031 reinvestment.

The broker informs the seller he is not sure of the number of days and orally advises the seller to consult a tax accountant. The seller does not do so.

Ultimately, the seller is taxed on the profit from the sale, but not because of the time constraints on his closing of escrow that he inquired about. The profit is taxed because the seller failed to avoid actual and constructive receipt of the sales proceeds by either directly transferring the sales proceeds to the purchase escrow or impounding the sale proceeds with a third party facilitator until the proceeds were needed to fund the purchase escrow for the replacement property.

The seller seeks to recover his losses from the broker. He claims the broker breached the agency duty owed to the seller by failing to disclose that the structure of the seller's transfer of net sales proceeds from the sales escrow to the purchase escrow for the replacement property might result in adverse tax consequences due to his actual receipt of the reinvestment funds.

The broker claims he has no duty to advise the seller on the tax consequences of the one-to-four unit sale since the listing agreement, the agency law disclosure and the purchase agreement all clearly state:

- the broker does not advise on tax matters; and

- the seller should look to other professionals for advice.

Did the listing broker have a duty to advise the seller on the tax consequences of the sale as known to the broker?

No! On the sale of one-to-four unit residential property, sellers (and buyers) are expected, as a matter of public policy, to obtain tax advice from competent professionals other than the real estate brokerage office handling the transaction. [CC §2079.16]

Further, a broker has no duty to voluntarily disclose any tax aspects surrounding the sale of a one-to-four unit residential property, even if the information is known to the broker or the sales agent, so long as the listing agreement specifies the broker and his agents do not **undertake the duty** to advise the seller on the tax aspects of the transactions. However, on a direct inquiry from the seller (or buyer), the agent must respond honestly and to the best of his knowledge. [**Carleton** v. **Tortosa** (1993) 14 CA4th 745]

The agency law disclosure addendum attached to listing agreements and purchase agreements eliminates the duty of a broker and his agents to disclose their knowledge about the tax aspects of a sale when a one-to-four unit residential property is involved.

Editor's note — California statutes state sellers and buyers of one-to-four unit residential properties should consult a competent professional for tax or legal advice since a real estate agent is qualified to advise about real estate.

*However, even if brokers deal only in owner-occupied, single-family residences and are not especially knowledgeable about the details of §1031 reinvestment plans, brokers know a seller of investment property can avoid profit reporting by following §1031 exemption procedures. Thus, a broker could **undertake the duty** to advise his seller.*

If a broker is willing to let his seller face tax consequences without disclosing his knowledge about the benefits of a §1031 reinvestment, perhaps it would be wise for the broker to refer the seller to another broker who is known to be competent and willing to share his tax knowledge with a client.

The irony of mandated disclosures

The tax consequences of sales transactions involving the subsequent purchase of replacement property are as *material* to a seller as is the structuring of carryback financing. Carryback financing arrangements require the broker to make extensive mandated disclosures regarding documentation of the carryback and the rights

of the carryback seller. However, carryback arrangements are less frequently encountered than §1031 reinvestment opportunities.

Further, the financial damage of avoidable taxation often exceeds the risk of loss on an improperly structured carryback note and trust deed transaction. Unlike the agency duty of a broker in §1031 transactions, however, the agency duty a broker owes to his seller includes full disclosure of information necessary for the seller to make an informed decision about the **financial suitability** of a carryback sale, before the seller enters into the transaction. [**Timmsen** v. **Forest E. Olson, Inc.** (1970) 6 CA3d 860]

Avoiding misleading disclaimers

The boilerplate statement included in some listing agreements and purchase agreements used by unionized real estate brokers incorrectly implies real estate brokers and their agents are not qualified to give tax advice. These statements are wrong!

If a broker is not fully qualified to handle the sale and purchase aspects of a §1031 transaction, he is at least aware of its beneficial tax aspects available to a seller of property.

Further, real estate brokers and their agents with tax knowledge are duty bound to advise their client about their knowledge concerning the tax consequences of the real estate transaction their client is about to enter into — unless a one-to-four unit residential property subject to agency law disclosure statutes is involved.

However, a savvy broker **capitalizes** on the tax knowledge he has spent time acquiring by advising clients on the tax results of their real estate transactions, regardless of the type of property involved. When a broker uses his knowledge to **voluntarily counsel** his client on the transaction's tax consequences, the decision made by the client will be the result of more relevant information.

However, the broker who advises a client on a transaction's tax consequences has a duty to not mislead the client by intentional or negligent misapplication of the tax rules. [**Ziswasser** v. **Cole & Cowan, Inc.** (1985) 164 CA3d 417]

To avoid misleading the client, the broker should disclose to his client:

- the full extent of his tax knowledge regarding the transaction;

- how he acquired his tax knowledge; and

- whether the broker intends to further investigate the matter or whether the client should seek further advice from other professionals.

When a broker does give tax advice, he should take steps to involve other advisors of the client in the final decision. Input from others who know the client help the broker eliminate future claims arising out of adverse tax consequences due to the **client's reliance** on the broker's (incorrect) opinion. The most practical (and effective) method for shifting reliance to others or to the client himself when the broker gives a client his opinion on a transaction's tax consequences, is to insert a *further approval contingency* in the purchase offer or counteroffer.

The contingency requires the client to initiate his own investigation by obtaining additional tax advice and further approval of the transaction's tax consequences from his attorney or accountant before allowing escrow to close. An oral or written warning, or general advice to further investigate, is not sufficient since it does not require the client to act nor does it explain why the broker believes the client should act to protect himself. [**Field** v. **Century 21 Klowden-Forness Realty** (1998) 63 CA4th 18]

Tax advisor's further approval

In an exchange agreement (or purchase agreement), the purpose for including a further approval contingency regarding the transaction's tax consequences is to allow the client to confirm that the transaction does qualify for §1031 tax-exempt status as represented by his broker. If the tax status cannot be confirmed, the client may terminate the transaction by delivery of a notice of cancellation. [See **first tuesday** Form 171 §5.2j]

In other words, the client is **not relying** on the broker's opinion if he decides to enter into an exchange agreement with the intent to close escrow with further confirmation of the tax consequences.

However, a purchase agreement or exchange agreement that contains a written contingency provision calling for a third party's approval of some aspect of the transaction, such as the transaction's qualification as an Internal Revenue Code (IRC) §1031 reinvestment plan, also contains an unwritten *implied covenant* provision. Under the implied covenant provision, before a client can cancel a transaction, he is required to "act in good faith and with fairness" in his efforts to obtain a third party's approval, such as submitting data on the transaction for confirmation from his attorney or accountant.

Thus, the implied covenant provision compels the client to seek the third party's further approval (from an accountant or attorney) to actually submit documentation on the transaction to the third party, and to do so within the time period called for after the date of acceptance.

Here, the broker usually steps into the chain of events by contacting the third party and providing the paperwork sought to review the transaction for its §1031 tax-exempt status. On review, procedural changes may need to be made to meet the client's objectives and satisfy objections of the third party. In response, the broker sees to it the changes are made, unless the changes would be inconsistent with the intent of his client regarding his acceptance of the replacement property.

Since fair dealing and reason are implied in every agreement and applied to the conduct of all parties, a termination of the exchange agreement due to the disapproval of an activity or occurrence subject to a contingency provision must be based on a **justifiable reason**.

On a potential disapproval and possible termination due to reasons expressed by the client or his advisor, the broker may well be able to cure the defect that gave rise to the reason for disapproval or demonstrate that the third party's concern is not well founded, i.e., if it is in fact or law an erroneous conclusion. [**Brown** v. **Critchfield** (1980) 100 CA3d 858]

Tax aspects: a material fact

All real estate in the hands of a seller is classified as either his principal residence, like-kind (§1031) property or dealer property.

An inquiry as to what the seller of property other than a personal residence or dealer property intends to do with the sales proceeds often opens a window of opportunity, allowing the agent to review his tax knowledge with the seller.

When representing sellers of real estate that, on a sale, would qualify for the §1031 profit reporting exemption, a broker should use a purchase agreement containing a §1031 cooperation provision. [See **first tuesday** Form 159 §10.6]

A §1031 cooperation provision is not an advisory disclaimer by which a broker attempts to relieve himself of his responsibility to give tax advice. Instead, the provision puts the seller on notice he is able to avoid profit reporting on the sale and has bargained for the buyer's cooperation should the seller decide to act to qualify his profit for a §1031 exemption.

Again, a broker who is not knowledgeable about the handling required for a §1031 reinvestment can initially avoid a discussion of tax aspects by including the §1031 cooperation provision in the purchase agreement. The §1031 cooperation provision conveys to the seller the seller's need to consider, plan for and inquire about the tax consequences of the sale.

Knowledge of basic tax aspects

Technical questions posed by a seller that go beyond a listing broker's knowledge or expertise require a truthful response from the broker. In response, the listing broker has several ways he can respond, including:

- disclose the extent of his knowledge to the seller and advise the seller to seek any further advice they may want from another source;

- associate with a more knowledgeable broker, a tax attorney or accountant who provides the seller with the advice; or

- learn how to handle §1031 reinvestments and give the advice himself.

Escrow officers are of great assistance in a private discussion with a broker who is aware he has a potential §1031 transaction. Some escrow officers and brokers advertise their expertise in handling §1031 tax-deferred reinvestments to broadcast their competitive advantage over other escrow officers and brokers.

Ideally, every broker handling the sale of real estate used in the seller's business or held for investment (like-kind property) should, as a **matter of basic competency**, possess an understanding of several fundamental tax concepts:

- the principal residence owner-occupant's $250,000 profit exclusion;

- the separate income and profit categories for each type of real estate;

- the §1031 profit reporting exemption;

- interest deductions on real estate loans;

- depreciation schedules and deductions;

- the $25,000 deduction and real-estate-related business adjustments for rental property losses;

- tracking rental income/losses separately for each property;

- profit and loss spillover on the sale of a rental property;

- standard and alternative reporting and tax bracket rates; and

- installment sales deferred profit reporting.

All of these tax aspects are basic to the sale or ownership of real estate commonly listed and sold by agents. When applicable, they have significant financial impact on sellers and buyers of real estate. Any broker with a working knowledge of the tax aspects of real estate can and should consider offering a wider range of services, including tax advice, when competing to represent buyers and sellers.

Also, giving a seller tax advice concerning a §1031 reinvestment plan when the seller follows the advice always leads to a second fee for negotiating the purchase of the replacement property and coordinating the transfer of funds.

Initiating a §1031 discussion

Before a broker or agent can close a §1031 reinvestment plan, i.e., take an investor out of one investment or business property and place him in another, the broker or agent must start where he first finds the prospective §1031 investor. Further, to initiate a §1031 reinvestment, the investor must possess a keen desire to move his equity into property that has a significantly greater or lesser value than the property being sold.

Most brokers and agents, when soliciting investors to list their income property or land for sale, will find the status of a prospective §1031 investor to be highly predictable, such as:

- the investor is one who should sell his property, but either does not realize he should sell or has not made the decision to do so; or

- the investor wants to sell, but has been restrained for some reason from listing the property for sale.

A common thread among investors who have not committed themselves to the sale of their property is the lack of understanding about the analytical process they must go through, along with the personal commitment they must make to **sell property and reinvest**, including:

- **evaluating** the property to be sold to establish its worth to buyers;

- determining the amount of **wealth loss** on a sale due to taxes and transactional costs;

- preparing the **property disclosures** for a marketing (listing) package to be handed to prospective buyers and the release of information and data during a buyer's due diligence investigation;

- selecting **replacement property** that will best suit the investor; and

- identifying the **motivation required** to make a commitment to sell and reinvest.

The task of educating an investor on the worth of his property as an investment in an income-producing parcel of real estate, must be undertaken by the broker even if the investor is already predisposed to selling it. The evaluation of ownership requires the broker or sales agent to give the investor a step-by-step presentation, designed to bring the investor to a decision as to whether he should keep the property or sell it.

Thus, the initial approach used by the broker or agent is to deal with the investor as though the broker or agent is soliciting employment limited to the sale of the property under a listing.

The **listing stage** in an agent-client relationship includes, by necessity, an inquiry by the agent into all the property's fundamentals needed to successfully market the property. The primary focus is on the evaluation of the operating income and expenses of the listed property.

An Annual Property Operating Data Sheet (the APOD form) is handed to the investor with a request to fill out as accurately as possible. Alternatively, the investor could provide the agent with a printout of the past 12 months of the property's operating income, expenses and principal and interest payments so the agent can fill out the form. [See Form 352 accompanying this chapter]

When completed, the agent will review the contents of the APOD form with the investor. Since the objective of the APOD form is to determine the worth of the investor's position, APOD for comparable properties that have recently sold (or been listed) need to be produced by the agent. The APOD for each comparable property, as well as the investor's APOD, will be spread on a worksheet designed to compare the investor's property to other properties.

Comparative analyses of the respective properties made with the investor will help the agent reach an agreement with the investor about the property's likely value to prospective buyers. [See Form 353 accompanying this chapter]

After setting the property's fair market value for a sale under a listing, called the *listing price*, the agent prepares a **seller's net sheet** for review with the investor. The purpose of the net sheet is to determine the amount of net proceeds a sale of the property will generate at the listed price. Thus, the broker discloses the transactional costs the investor will incur on a sale of the property.

Regardless of the investor's equity in the property, the transactional costs to close escrow on a sale or exchange will be approximately 8% of the price received for the property. Any costs incurred to fix up the property for sale will be added to that figure. [See **first tuesday** Form 310]

The release of property information

A large part of the process for selling an income-producing property falls on the seller as his **duty to cooperate** with his listing broker in the marketing of the property and with the prospective buyer during the buyer's due diligence investigation. It is the seller who must come forward with information about the property that he is aware of and that might have an adverse affect on the property's value in the hands of a prospective buyer.

The procedure established for the seller to provide property information begins at the listing stage as a matter of good brokerage practice. Out of commercial necessity, the listing broker must have the seller's assistance to develop a **marketing (listing) package** that will contain sufficient, fundamental operating information for a buyer to analyze the property and establish a value. Yet, the disclosures need not be too intrusive to publicly disclose data and information on occupancies and management operations that, if the property does not sell, were prematurely released. [See **first tuesday** Form 107]

On entering into a purchase agreement to sell the property, the buyer's **due diligence investigation** includes a routine expectation that the seller will cooperate in order to close escrow. A due diligence investigation usually is most intrusive, calling for the buyer's inspection of the seller's income and expense (operating) records on the property, the property's improvements, leases, permits, loan conditions, tenant security deposits, maintenance records, service contracts, inventory and like matters of concern to prudent buyers.

To be able to properly market the property on behalf of the seller, the broker needs the seller's **cooperation** to provide adequate and timely disclosures. To initiate the marketing process and develop the seller's appreciation for his need to cooperate in the preparation of disclosures, the listing broker can again turn to forms.

Forms are used as checklists for property conditions and due diligence contingencies the seller can reasonably be expected to comply with in a sale. The **seller's compliance** can be either *affirmative and voluntary*, as is required of property conditions known to the seller which have an adverse effect on value, or **in response** to an inquiry by the buyer. An offer made by a buyer on a standard purchase agreement form for income property provides such a checklist. [See **first tuesday** Form 159 §§11, 12]

The more information the broker can obtain from the seller and place in the marketing package to be handed to a prospective buyer before entering into a purchase agreement, the less information will be required to be delivered later which may trigger a cancellation of the purchase agreement and escrow. Thus, surprises experienced by the buyer during the due diligence investigation to confirm his expectations about the property's conditions and its value can be avoided.

Also, an early review of purchase agreement provisions concerning **disclosure provisions** clears the way for the broker to limit later reviews of an exchange agreement to the terms of the exchange. An early review eliminates the need for later review of the due diligence provisions for each party's investigation into the other's property. [See **first tuesday** Form 171 §3]

Profit taxes provide the motivation

The shift in a broker's focus and analysis now turns to providing reasons, and thus incentive, for an investor to use the net proceeds from a sale — or the equity in the property itself — as a down payment to purchase property which will be called a *replacement property*.

Before alluding to any reinvestment of the net sales proceeds from a sale, a discussion of the tax consequences of the proposed sale sets the stage for considering a reinvestment of the net sales proceeds. A tax discussion will naturally lead to a review of methods to reduce or eliminate the profit tax under Internal Revenue Code (IRC) §1031.

The profit on a sale will be taxed at 25% and 15%, respectively, for gains produced by depreciation deductions and an increase in property value during the investor's holding period. The task for an agent in any tax analysis is to gather tax-related data from the investor and use it to prepare a worksheet to estimate the tax consequences of the sale. Accordingly, the agent asks the investor for information from his tax return for the previous year.

To analyze the investor's tax liability on a sale, the agent needs only the total amount of **depreciation**, taken in deductions by the investor during his ownership, and the amount of his remaining **cost basis** in the property. By subtracting the cost basis from the property's market value, the agent calculates the amount of **profit** the investor will realize on a sale.

The agent prepares an Individual Tax Analysis form (INTAX) by filling out only the "profit batching" section to break down the profit into its component gains:

- the *unrecaptured gain* amounting to the previous depreciation deductions taken from income by the investor and taxed on a sale at a 25% rate; and

- the *long-term capital gain* that is the increase in the dollar value of the property over the investor's original cost to acquire (and improve) the property and is taxed on a sale at a 15% rate. [See Chapter 6]

APOD
Annual Property Operating Data

Date:_____, 20_____, at _____, California

1. PROPERTY TYPE: _____

    1.1 Location: _____

    1.2 APOD figures are estimates reflecting:

        a. ☐ Current operating conditions.

        b. ☐ Forecast of anticipated operations.

        c. Prepared by:_____

2. INCOME:

				%
2.1 **Scheduled Rental Income** . . . . $_____				**100%**
a. Less: Vacancies, discounts and uncollectibles. . – $_____				%
Credit card charges . . . . – $_____				%
2.2 **Effective Rental Income** . . . . $_____				%
a. Other income . . . . + $_____				%
2.3 **Gross Operating Income** . . . . $_____				%

3. EXPENSES:

		%
3.1 Electricity . . . . $_____		%
3.2 Gas . . . . $_____		%
3.3 Water . . . . $_____		%
3.4 Rubbish . . . . $_____		%
3.5 Insurance . . . . $_____		%
3.5 Taxes . . . . $_____		%
3.6 Management Fee . . . . $_____		%
3.7 Resident Manager . . . . $_____		%
3.8 Office expenses/supplies . . . . $_____		%
3.9 Advertising . . . . $_____		%
3.10 Lawn/Gardening . . . . $_____		%
3.11 Pool/Spa . . . . $_____		%
3.12 Janitorial . . . . $_____		%
3.13 Maintenance . . . . $_____		%
3.14 Repairs and Replacements . . . . $_____		%
3.15 CATV/phone . . . . $_____		%
3.16 Accounting/Legal Fees . . . . $_____		%
3.17 _____ . . . . $_____		%
3.18 _____ . . . . $_____		%
3.19 **Total Operating Expense** . . . . – $_____		%

4. NET OPERATING INCOME: . . . . $_____   %

5. **SPENDABLE INCOME** (annual projection):

   5.1 **Net Operating Income** (enter from section 4)................... $_____ ____%

5.2 Loan	Principal Balance Amount	Monthly Payment	Rate	Due Date
a. **1st**	$_____	$_____	____%	_____
b. **2nd**	$_____	$_____	____%	_____
c. **3rd**	$_____	$_____	____%	_____

   5.3 Total Annual Debt Service .... − $_____ ____%

   5.4 **Spendable Income** .... $_____ ____%

6. **PROPERTY INFORMATION:**

   6.1 Price $_____; Loan amounts $_____; Owner's equity $_____

   6.2 Current vacancy rate or vacant space: _____%

   6.3 Assessor's allocations for depreciation schedule:
   Improvements _____%; Land _____%; Personal property _____%.

   6.4 Property disclosures:

      a. ☐ Rent roll available; ☐ need confidentiality agreement.

      b. ☐ Rent control restrictions.

      c. ☐ Condition of improvements available: ☐ by owner, ☐ by inspector.

      d. ☐ Environmental report available.

      e. ☐ Natural hazard disclosure available.

      f. ☐ Soil report available.

      g. ☐ Termite report available.

      h. ☐ Building specification available.

      i. _____

      j. _____

7. **REPORTABLE INCOME/LOSS** (annual projection): | For Buyer to fill out. |

   7.1 **Net Operating Income** (enter from section 4).................. $_____

      a. Annual interest expense .... $_____

      b. Annual depreciation deduction (ft Form 354.5) .. $_____

   7.2 Total deductions from NOI................................ − $_____

   7.3 **Reportable Income/Loss** (annual projection): .... $_____

Broker: _____

Address: _____

_____

Phone: _____ Cell: _____

Fax: _____

Email: _____

I have reviewed and do approve this information.

Date: _____, 20_____

Owner's name: _____

Signature: _____

Signature: _____

Collectively, the federal profit tax on these gains amounts to approximately 18% to 21% of the profit taken on a typical sale. California state profit taxes are approximately 1/3 of the federal profit taxes.

Thus, an investor selling property which is encumbered by a trust deed loan balance equal to 40% of the sales price will experience a reduction in his net sales proceeds of approximately 20 to 22% for payment of profit taxes on the sale. The increase in the percentage of the investor's net equity consumed by taxes as compared to the average tax rate on all his profit is due to the fact the cost basis is usually reduced faster (and further) by straight-line depreciation deductions than is the reduction of principal on the loan by payments amortized over 25 or 30 years.

With the investor now aware he will suffer a huge loss of wealth by the payment of taxes on a sale, the agent presents the investor with an option: avoid any liability for profit taxes by reinvesting the net sales proceeds in a replacement property more suitable to the investor than the listed property.

The simulated §1031 exchange

To develop a seller's understanding and commitment to the concept of totally avoiding any taxes on a sale, a broker needs to present the seller with a *simulated §1031 reinvestment* before beginning any selection, much less analysis, of suitable replacement property.

Thus, the momentary focus is to demonstrate no more than the notion that the equity in the seller's property can be used as a down payment, directly by exchange or indirectly by reinvesting the cash from a sale, without suffering any reduction of net worth due to taxes on a sale.

The only **financial data** needed to present a complete picture of a tax-free sale includes:

- the seller's remaining *cost basis* in the property;

- the amount of *debt* and *equity* in his property; and

- the amount of debt and equity in three to five properties which are presently on the market and somewhat comparable to the listed property.

The simulated replacement properties chosen by the broker should be of significantly greater value than the value of the seller's property. Also, each property must have a greater amount of debt and a larger equity than the seller's property so a fully tax-free trade-up situation can be readily presented.

The seller will be shown these **estate building** examples, an introduction to the typical motivation of investors who enter into §1031 reinvestment plans. The examples of tax-free sales implicitly suggest the use of an equity in one property as a cash down payment to purchase other, more desirable property.

Again, the broker turns to a form, the **§1031 profit and basis recapitulation worksheet**, to make his point. The form will be filled out once for each property selected to demonstrate the §1031 tax result. Sections 1, 3 and 4 are the only portions of the form which need to be used for the limited simulated exchange purpose (debt, adjustment by purchase money note and basis in the seller's property). [See **first tuesday** Form 354]

Should the seller need to "generate cash" for personal needs, one simulated exchange drawn up on the recap form can demonstrate a reinvestment of the net sales proceeds remaining after withdrawing the cash. The remaining cash will be the down payment on a replacement property and the seller will execute a purchase-money note for the balance due on the purchase of the replacement property.

COMPARATIVE ANALYSIS PROJECTION (CAP)

DATE:_____, 20_____

CLIENT:_____

Client's Property: _____

_____

Prepared by:_____

	This sheet contains confidential information for clients who own or are acquiring income property.

This sheet contains confidential information for clients who own or are acquiring income property.
For owners: illustrates the effect of different loan amounts, or projects the tax benefits and rate of return.
For Buyers: compares available properties to one another.
The conclusions and projections developed on this form depend on the accurate preparation of backup sheets.

A. PURPOSE:
a. ☐ Property selection/comparison
b. ☐ Ownership projection for years
c. ☐ Debt leverage by refinance
d. ☐ Equity performance review

B. BACKUP SHEETS ATTACHED:
a. ☐ APOD for each property [ft Form 352]
b. ☐ Seller's net sheet [ft Form 310]
c. ☐ Other:_____

	– A –	– B –	– C –	– D –
1. PROPERTIES ANALYZED:	_____	_____	_____	_____
1.1 Year analyzed:	20_____	20_____	20_____	20_____
2. PROPERTY VALUATION				
2.1 Fair market value (FMV)... $	_____	$_____	$_____	$_____
2.2 Less loan – $	_____	– $_____	– $_____	– $_____
2.3 Less sales costs – $	_____	– $_____	– $_____	– $_____
2.4 NET EQUITY (total) $	_____	$_____	$_____	$_____
3. SPENDABLE INCOME/DEFICIT (annual)				
3.1 Gross operating income $	_____	$_____	$_____	$_____
3.2 Operating expense – $	_____	$_____	$_____	$_____
3.3 NOI (subtotal) $	_____	$_____	$_____	$_____
3.4 Loan payments – $	_____	$_____	$_____	$_____
3.5 SPENDABLE INCOME/DEFICIT (total) $	_____	$_____	$_____	$_____
4. INCOME-TO-VALUE (annual)				
4.1 Fair market value (§2.1) $	_____	$_____	$_____	$_____
4.2 Net operating income (§3.3) $	_____	$_____	$_____	$_____
4.3 RATE OF RETURN (§4.2 ÷ §4.1) _____ %		_____ %	_____ %	_____ %
5. REPORTABLE INCOME/LOSS (annual)				
5.1 NOI $	_____	$_____	$_____	$_____
5.2 Interest – $	_____	$_____	$_____	$_____
5.3 Depreciation – $	_____	$_____	$_____	$_____
5.4 REPORTABLE INCOME/LOSS +or– $	_____	$_____	$_____	$_____
6. CLIENT INCOME TAX ASPECTS				
6.1 Reportable income/loss (§5.4) +or– $	_____	+or– $_____	+or– $_____	+or– $_____
6.2 Client's tax bracket (x) _____ %		_____ %	_____ %	_____ %
6.3 TAX LIABILITY OR REDUCTION +or– $	_____	$_____	$_____	$_____
7. RETURN ON EQUITY (annual)				
7.1 Spendable income/deficit +or– $ (§3.5 above)	_____	$_____	$_____	$_____
7.2 Loan principal reduction + $ (§3.4 - §4.2)	_____	$_____	$_____	$_____
7.3 Income tax liability +or– $ (§6.3 above; reverse the +or–)	_____	$_____	$_____	$_____
7.4 Annual FMV adjustment (____%) + $ (estimated appreciation/inflation)	_____	$_____	$_____	$_____
6.5 DOLLAR RETURN ON EQUITY (after taxes) $	_____	$_____	$_____	$_____
6.6 Percent return on net equity _____ % (§7.5 ÷ §2.4)		_____ %	_____ %	_____ %

Thus, the cash the seller needs to withdraw from the sales proceeds will be withdrawn at the time of the reinvestment. No profit taxes will be paid on the cash withdrawn if the terms of the purchase of the replacement property include the execution of a carryback note.

Alternatively, the seller may decide not to sell, but would like to acquire more real estate. This keep-and-buy situation suggests the equity in the property owned by the seller could be the security for a no-cash, down payment-note executed to purchase additional property. [See **first tuesday** Form 154]

In the actual selection of a replacement property, the combined sale-and-purchase environment requires two significant decisions to be wrapped into one §1031 reinvestment plan. This sale-and-purchase concept may cause the seller to experience some anxieties which are not normally present in a single analysis and decision to either sell or buy.

Analyzing a change in position

The motivation needed by a client to move out of one property and into another must be developed by consensus between the broker and his client.

The client's particular motivation does affect the yield the client can expect from the replacement property as a return on the investment. Factors that may influence the client's motivation to sell include:

the *proximity* of the replacement property to the client's residence, viewed in terms of how "geographically bound" the client might be and the rate of return available on nearby properties versus more distantly located properties;

- the *loan-to-value* ratio the client can tolerate depending on the client's risk aversion and the durability of the property's income based on leases;

- the *future inflation* and *appreciation* in property values anticipated as an additional source of earnings in the next real estate business cycle, i.e., a seller's market or a buyer's market with higher or lower prices than the projected historic *equilibrium trend price* of real estate;

- the *level of management* required of the client to generate spendable income that either decreases the client's time and effort by reason of greater efficiency in the operations of the replacement property or increases his personal involvement to step up the earnings from the reinvestment;

- the *type of property*, be it industrial, residential, commercial or office, to suit the client's desires more than the property he owns; and

- any other point of comparison between conditions existing in the property owned and those sought in a replacement property.

When the selection of a suitable replacement property has been made by the client, the profit tax analysis is again prepared on the §1031 recap form. [See **first tuesday** Form 354]

Further, the **annual depreciation deduction** for the proposed replacement property is estimated on the basis allocation worksheet form. [See Chapter 26; see **first tuesday** Form 355]

The annual depreciation is then entered on the APOD form, which has been prepared to reflect the annual income tax impact that the acquisition of the proposed replacement property will have on the client's tax return. [See **first tuesday** Form 352]

The final, detailed tax analysis, to demonstrate the amount of tax liability increase or decrease the replacement property will likely bring about, is estimated on an INTAX form. [See **first tuesday** Form 351]

Lastly, an **economic analysis** of all aspects which contribute to an anticipated future yield for the client due to ownership of the replacement property is calculated on the CAP form. [See **first tuesday** Form 353]

With a review of the worksheets completed, the agent switches his concern from the sales listing to a solicitation of employment to locate suitable replacement property. Thus, the agent's approach becomes that of a buyer's selling agent, with a quest to determine if the client is at all interested in the actual purchase of other real estate.

Chapter 3

The formal exchange agreement

This chapter presents an exchange agreement form used to initiate a §1031 transaction where the ownership of properties is exchanged between two persons.

Structuring a comprehensible transaction

An **exchange of properties** is an arrangement structured as an agreement and entered into by owners of two or more parcels of real estate who agree to transfer the ownership of their properties between themselves in consideration for the value of the equity in the properties received. Economic adjustments are made for any difference in the valuations given to the equities in the properties exchanged.

Thus, the owners of real estate, on entering into a written exchange agreement, agree to **sell and convey** their property to the other party. However, unlike a sale under a purchase agreement, the down payment is not in the form of cash. Instead, the down payment is the **equity in property** each owner will receive. The dollar amount of the down payment is the value given to the equity in the property to be received in exchange.

In an exchange of equities, as in the sale of property with a cash down payment, the **balance of the price** agreed to must be paid in some form of consideration. If a sales price is to be paid in cash, the balance of the price after the down payment is typically funded by a purchase-assist loan.

Conversely, in a sale calling for a cash down payment and an assumption of the loan of record, any balance remaining to be paid on the price is usually deferred, evidenced by a carryback note. The carryback note in a cash down payment sale presents no different a situation than the carryback note in an "equity down payment" situation, such as occurs in an exchange of an equity in one property as a down payment toward the purchase of a larger equity in another property, called an *adjustment* or *balancing of equities*.

Also, unlike a cash sale which "frees up" the capital investment in real estate by converting the equity to cash proceeds on closing, an exchange is a clear manifestation of the owner's desire to **continue his investment** in real estate. In an exchange, the owner disposes of a property he no longer wants.

The owner might use his equity in an estate building plan to move up into property of greater value (and greater debt leverage), or simply to consolidate several properties the owner has that he exchanges to acquire a single, more efficiently operated property.

The **hallmarks of an exchange transaction**, in contrast to the common features of a sales transaction, include:

- the **exchange of equities** in real estate in lieu of a cash down payment;

- no **good-faith deposit** as cash is rarely used in an exchange of equities, except for prorations, adjustments (such as security deposits), transactional expenditures or as a "sweetener" to encourage an acceptance of the exchange offer, since the signature of each party commits them to perform on the exchange agreement and is the only consideration needed from each party to form a binding contract;

- a take-over of **existing financing** by an assumption of the loans or a transfer of title subject to the loans, rather than refinancing and incurring expenses that greatly increase the cost of reinvesting in real estate;

- **adjustments** brought about by the difference in the value of the equities exchanged, a balancing that requires the owner with the lesser valued equity to cover the difference in cash installments evidenced by the execution of a promissory note or the contribution of additional personal property or real estate of value;

- joint or **tandem escrows**, interrelated due to the conveyance of one property as consideration for the conveyance of the other property, similar in effect to a cash sale of a property when the closing is contingent on the sale of other property to obtain the funds needed to close escrow, a contingency that does occur in some delayed §1031 reinvestment plans;

- two sets of **brokerage fees**, one for each property involved in the exchange, rather than the receipt of a single fee as occurs in a cash-out sale of property;

- one party simultaneously selling and buying, a **coupling of two properties** consisting of a sale of one and purchase of the other, motivated primarily by the tax compulsion to remain invested in business or investment real estate, called *like-kind properties*, rather than cash out on the sale of one and later separately locate, analyze and purchase a replacement property with the cash proceeds of the sale, as occurs in a delayed "sell now/buy later" §1031 reinvestment plan; and

- **tax advice** from a real estate broker counseling on the profit tax avoidance of a coordinated, simultaneous reinvestment of the owner's equity in business or investment category real estate in a replacement property, thus avoiding the need to first locate a cash buyer to convert the equity to cash and then scramble to locate property and reinvest the sales proceeds within specific time periods while avoiding receipt of the proceeds.

Commonality with a sale

The **common features** found in the acquisition of real estate by either a cash purchase or an exchange of equities include:

- a **disclosure** by the owner and listing broker of the conditions known to them about the property improvements, title, operation and natural hazards of the location which adversely affect the property's market value or the buyer's intended use of the property; and

- a **due diligence investigation** by the buyer acquiring title concerning his ownership, use and operation of the property.

As in all real estate transactions, a form is used to **prepare the offer** and commence written negotiations. The objective of a written agreement is to provide a comprehensive checklist of boilerplate provisions for the parties to consider in their offer, acceptance and counteroffer negotiations.

Also, the terms of an exchange agreement must be sufficiently complete and clear in their wording to prevent a misunderstanding or uncertainty over what the parties have agreed to do should the agreement require enforcement by one or the other party.

Once the brokerage process of locating a suitable replacement property has produced a property the owner is willing to acquire in exchange for the property he wants to dispose of, the broker prepares an exchange agreement on a preprinted or computer generated form. When prepared, the terms are reviewed with the owner, signed by the broker and the owner, and submitted to the owner of the replacement property for acceptance. [See Form 171 accompanying this chapter]

An exchange agreement form will only be used when an owner's equity in a property is offered as a **down payment** in exchange for replacement property. An owner who has already en-

EXCHANGE AGREEMENT

(Other than One-to-Four Residential Units)

DATE:_____, 20_____, at _____, California

Items left blank or unchecked are not applicable.

PROPERTIES TO BE EXCHANGED:

1. The FIRST PARTY, _____ will deliver
   the FIRST PROPERTY, located in the City of _____
   County of _____, State of _____
   described as _____.

   1.1 The equity valuation for the property is...$_____
   1.2 The loans of record presently encumbering the property total ....$_____
       a. A first loan of $_____ payable $_____ monthly
       including _____% interest ☐ ARM, due _____, 20_____.

       b. A second loan of $_____ payable $_____ monthly
       including _____% interest ☐ ARM, due _____, 20_____.

   1.3 The market value of the First Property is ....$_____
   1.4 The market value includes delivery of personal property described as:
   _____

2. The SECOND PARTY, _____will deliver
   the SECOND PROPERTY, located in the city of_____
   County of _____, State of _____,
   described as _____.

   2.1 The equity valuation for the property is...$_____
   2.2 The loans of record presently encumbering the property total ....$_____
       a. A first loan of $_____ payable $_____ monthly
       including _____% interest ☐ ARM, due _____, 20_____.

       b. A second loan of $_____ payable $_____ monthly
       including _____% interest ☐ ARM, due _____, 20_____.

   2.3 The market value of the Second Property is...$_____
   2.4 The market value includes delivery of personal property described as:
   _____

3. **TERMS OF EXCHANGE:**

   3.1 The First Party to acquire the **Second Property** on the following terms:
       a. Transfer the First Property with an equity valuation in the amount of ....$_____
       b. Payment of cash, as an adjustment for the First Party's receipt of a larger equity
       in the Second Property, in the amount of ....$_____
       c. Payment of additional cash, to fund the payoff by the Second Party of the loans
       of record on the Second Property, in the amount of ....$_____
       d. ☐ Take title subject to, or ☐ assume, the loans of record encumbering
       the Second Property in the amount of..$_____
       e. Execution of a note in favor of the Second Party in the amount of.............$_____
       Secured by a trust deed on the Second Property, junior to the loans of record,
       payable $_____ monthly, or more, beginning one month after
       closing of escrow and including interest at _____% from closing, due _____
       years after closing. This note to include terms and conditions set out in § 3.3.
       f. Deliver additional property with an equity value in the amount of..............$_____
       described as_____,
       encumbered by a loan in the amount of $_____, payable_____
       _____.

       g. Receipt of consideration from the Second Party provided for in §3.2b, §3.2e
       and §3.2f.
       as compensation for First Party conveying a larger equity, for an offset of ......(-)$_____
       h. **TOTAL CONSIDERATION** given the Second Party as the market value paid
       by the First Party for the Second Property is the amount of...................$_____

    i. Obtain a ☐ first or ☐ second trust deed loan to be secured by the Second Property in the amount of $_____, payable approximately $_____ monthly including interest not to exceed _____%, ☐ ARM, type_____, with a due date of _____ years or more.

3.2 The Second Party to acquire the **First Property** on the following terms:

    a. Transfer the Second Property with an equity valuation in the amount of. . . . . $_____

    b. Payment of cash, as an adjustment for the Second Party's receipt of a larger equity in the First Property, in the amount of . . . . $_____

    c. Payment of additional cash, to fund the payoff by the First Party of the loans of record on the First Property, in the amount of. . . . . $_____

    d. ☐ Take title subject to, or ☐ assume, the loans of record encumbering the First Property in the total amount of . . . . $_____

    e. Execute a note in favor of the First Party in the amount of . . . . $_____ secured by a trust deed on the First Property, junior to the loans of record, payable $_____ monthly, or more, beginning one month after close of escrow and including interest at _____% from closing, due _____ years after closing. This note to include terms and conditions set out in §3.3.

    f. Deliver additional property with an equity value in the amount of. . . . . $_____ described as_____, encumbered by a loan in the amount of $_____, payable_____ _____.

    g. Receipt of consideration from the First Party provided for in §3.1b, §3.1e and §3.1f as compensation for Second Party conveying a larger equity, for an offset of . . . . (-)$_____

    h. **TOTAL CONSIDERATION** given the First Party as the market value paid by the Second Party for the First Property is the amount of. . . . . $_____

    i. Obtain a ☐ first or ☐ second trust deed loan to be secured by the First Property in the amount of $_____, payable approximately $_____ monthly including interest not to exceed _____%, ☐ ARM, type_____, with a due date of _____ years or more.

3.3 The terms and conditions of any note and trust deed executed by one party in favor of the other under sections §3.1e or §3.2e include:

    a. ☐ Grantor/payee's carryback disclosure statement attached as an addendum to the agreement. [**ft** Form 300]

    b. Provisions to be provided by the grantor/payee for ☐ due-on-sale, ☐ prepayment penalty, ☐ late charges, ☐ _____.

    c. ☐ Grantee/payor to provide a request for notice of delinquency to senior encumbrances. [**ft** Form 412]

    d. ☐ Grantee/payor to hand Grantor/payee a completed credit application on acceptance. [**ft** Form 302]

    e. Within _____ days of receipt of Grantor/payee's credit application, Grantor/payee may terminate the agreement based on a reasonable disapproval of Grantor/payee's creditworthiness. [**ft** Form 183]

    f. Grantor/payee may terminate the agreement on failure of agreed terms for priority financing. [**ft** Form 183]

    g. As additional security, Grantee/payor to execute a security agreement and file a UCC-1 financing statement on any personal property Grantee/payor acquires under this agreement by Bill of Sale.

4. ACCEPTANCE AND PERFORMANCE:

4.1 This offer to be deemed revoked unless accepted in writing within _____ days after date, and the acceptance is personally delivered or faxed to the First Party or the First Party's Broker within the period.

4.2 After acceptance, Brokers are authorized to extend any performance date up to one month.

4.3 On the failure of either party to obtain or assume financing as agreed by the date scheduled for closing, that party may terminate the agreement.

4.4 Any termination of the agreement shall be by written Notice of Cancellation timely delivered to the other party, the other party's broker or Escrow with instructions to Escrow to return all instruments and funds to the parties depositing them. [**ft** Form 183]

4.5 Both parties reserve their rights to assign and agree to cooperate in effecting an Internal Revenue Code §1031 exchange prior to close of escrow on either party's written notice. [**ft** Forms 172 or 173]

4.6 Should either party breach this agreement, that party's monetary liability to the other party is limited to $_____.

5. DUE DILIGENCE CONTINGENCIES:

5.1 Prior to accepting delivery of the First Property, the Second Party may, within _____ days after receipt or occurrence of any of the following checked items, terminate this exchange agreement based on the Second Party's reasonable disapproval of the checked item.

    a. ☐ Income and expense records, leases, property management and other service contracts, permits or licenses affecting the operation of the property, which documents First Party will make available to Second Party on acceptance.

    b. ☐ A Rental Income Statement itemizing, by unit, the tenant's name, rent amount, rent due date, delinquencies, deposits, rental period and expiration and any rental incentives, bonuses or discounts signed by First Party and handed to Second Party on acceptance. [ft Form 380]

    c. ☐ Seller's Natural Hazard Disclosure Statement to be signed by First Party and handed to Second Party on acceptance. [ft Form 314]

    d. ☐ A Seller's Condition of Property (Transfer) Disclosure to be signed by First Party and First Party's Broker and handed to Second Party on acceptance.

    e. ☐ Itemized inventory of the personal property included in the sale to be handed to Second Party on acceptance.

    f. ☐ Inspection of the property by Second Party, his agent or consultants within _____ days after acceptance for value and condition sufficient to justify the purchase price.

    g. ☐ Preliminary title report for the policy of title insurance, which report First Party will cause escrow to hand Second Party as soon as reasonably possible after acceptance.

    h. ☐ An estoppel certificate executed by each tenant affirming the terms of their occupancy, which certificates First Party will hand Second Party prior to seven days before closing. [ft Form 598]

    i. ☐ Criminal activity and security statement prepared by the First Party and setting forth recent criminal activity on or about the First Property relevant to the security of persons and their belongings on the property and any security arrangements undertaken or which should be undertaken in response.

    j. ☐ Submission of the exchange agreement, escrow instructions and any other documentation related to this transaction to the Second Party's attorney or accountant within _____ days after acceptance for their further approval of this transaction as qualifying, in its entirety or partially, as an IRC §1031 tax exempt transaction reportable by the Second Party.

    k. ☐ _____

5.2 Prior to accepting delivery of the Second Property, the First Party may, within _____ days after receipt or occurrence of any of the following checked items, terminate this exchange agreement based on the First Party's reasonable disapproval of the checked item.

    a. ☐ Income and expense records, leases, property management and other service contracts, permits or licenses affecting the operation of the property, which documents Second Party will make available to First Party on acceptance.

    b. ☐ A Rental Income Statement itemizing, by unit, the tenant's name, rent amount, rent due date, delinquencies, deposits, rental period and expiration and any rental incentives, bonuses or discounts, signed by Second Party and handed to First Party on acceptance. [ft Form 380]

    c. ☐ Seller's Natural Hazard Disclosure Statement to be signed by Second Party and handed to First Party on acceptance. [ft Form 314]

    d. ☐ A Seller's Condition of Property (Transfer) Disclosure to be signed by Second Party and Second Party's Broker and handed to First Party on acceptance.

    e. ☐ Itemized inventory of the personal property included in the sale to be handed to First Party on acceptance.

    f. ☐ Inspection of the property by First Party, his agent or consultants within _____ days after acceptance for value and condition sufficient to justify the purchase price.

    g. ☐ Preliminary title report for the policy of title insurance, which report Second Party will cause escrow to hand First Party as soon as reasonably possible after acceptance.

    h. ☐ An estoppel certificate executed by each tenant affirming the terms of their occupancy, which certificates Second Party will hand First Party prior to seven days before closing. [ft Form 598]

    i. ☐ Criminal activity and security statement prepared by the Second Party and setting forth recent criminal activity on or about the Second Property relevant to the security of persons and their belongings on the property and any security arrangements undertaken or which should be undertaken in response.

    j. ☐ Submission of the exchange agreement, escrow instructions and any other documentation related to this transaction to the First Party's attorney or accountant within _____ days after acceptance for their further approval of this transaction as qualifying, in its entirety or partially, as an IRC §1031 tax exempt transaction reportable by the First Party.

    k. ☐ _____

6. PROPERTY CONDITIONS ON CLOSING:

Prior to closing, each party with regard to the property they are conveying, will comply with or furnish the other party the following items:

6.1 ☐ A structural pest control report and clearance.

6.2 ☐ A one-year property warranty policy.
    Insurer: _____
    Coverage: _____

6.3 A certificate of occupancy, or other clearance or retrofitting, required by local ordinance for the transfer of possession or title.

6.4 Smoke detector(s) and water heater bracing in compliance with the law.

6.5 Maintain the property in good condition until possession is delivered.

6.6 Fixtures and fittings attached to the property include but are not limited to: window shades, blinds, light fixtures, plumbing fixtures, curtain rods, wall-to-wall carpeting, draperies, hardware, antennas, air coolers and conditioners, trees, shrubs, mailboxes and other similar items.

6.7 New agreements and modifications of existing agreements to rent space or to service, alter or equip the property will not be entered into without the other party's prior written consent, which will not be unreasonably withheld.

6.8 _____
    _____ .

7. CLOSING CONDITIONS

7.1 This transaction to be escrowed with _____ .
    Parties to deliver instructions to Escrow as soon as reasonably possible after acceptance.

    a. ☐ Escrow holder is authorized and instructed to act on the provisions of this agreement as the mutual escrow instructions of the parties and to draft any additional instructions necessary to close this transaction. [ft Form 401]

    b. ☐ Escrow instructions, prepared and signed by the parties, are attached to be handed to Escrow on acceptance. [ft Form 401]

7.2 Escrow to be handed all instruments needed to close escrow ☐ on or before _____, 20_____, or ☐ within _____ days after acceptance. Parties to hand Escrow all documents required by the title insurer, lenders or other third parties to this transaction prior to seven days before the date scheduled for closing.

    a. Each party to pay its customary escrow charges. [ft Forms 310 and 311]

7.3 Title to be vested in Grantee or Assignee free of encumbrances other than convenants, conditions and restrictions, reservations and easements of record and liens as set forth herein.

7.4 Each Grantee's interest in title to all real estate conveyed to be insured by _____ under a ☐ CLTA or ☐ ALTA from policy of the title insurance.

    a. Endorsements: _____
    b. Title insurance premium to be paid by Grantor.

7.5 Taxes, assessments, insurance premiums, rents, interest and other expenses to be prorated to close of escrow, unless otherwise provided.

7.6 Any difference in the principal amounts remaining due on loans taken over or assumed as stated in this agreement and as disclosed by beneficiary's statements is to be adjusted into: ☐ cash, ☐ carryback note or ☐ market value.

7.7 Each party to assign to the other party all existing lease and rental agreements on the property they convey. [ft Form 595]

    a. Each party assigning leases and rental agreements to the other to notify each tenant of the change of ownership on or before close of escrow. [ft Form 554]

7.8 Bill of sale to be executed by Grantor for any personal property being transferred by Grantor.

    a. ☐ A UCC-3 request for the conditions of title to the personal property transferred by bill of sale to be obtained by escrow and approved by the party taking title.

7.9 Grantees to furnish a new fire insurance policy on the property acquired.

7.10 Possession of the property and keys/access codes to be delivered on the close of escrow.

7.11 If one party is unable to convey marketable title as agreed or if the improvements on the property are materially damaged prior to closing, the other party may terminate the agreement. The party unable to convey or owning the damaged property to pay all reasonable escrow cancellation charges. [ft Form 183]

8. Brokerage fees:

   8.1 First Party to pay $_____ on closing to _____.

   8.2 Second Party to pay $_____ on closing to_____.

   8.3 On wrongful prevention of the change of ownership's by either party, such party to then pay the brokerage fees.

   8.4 The brokerage fees due may be shared by the brokers.

   8.5 Brokers may report the transaction, pricing and terms to brokerage trade associations and listing services for dissemination and use by their participants.

9. _____

_____

_____

_____

_____

_____

_____

First
Party's Broker: _____

By: _____

Is the agent of: ☐ First Party exclusively.
                ☐ Both parties.

Second
Party's Broker: _____

By: _____

Is the agent of: ☐ Second Party exclusively.
                ☐ Both parties.

I agree to the terms stated above.

Date:_____, 20_____

First Party: _____

First Party: _____

Signature: _____

Signature: _____

Address: _____

_____

Phone:_____

Fax: _____

Email: _____

I agree to the terms stated above.

Date:_____, 20_____

Second Party:_____

Second Party:_____

Signature: _____

Signature: _____

Address: _____

_____

Phone:_____

Fax: _____

Email: _____

REJECTION OF EXCHANGE OFFER

The Second Party hereby rejects this offer in its entirety. No counteroffer will be forthcoming.

Date:_____, 20_____

Second Party's Name: _____

Second Party's Name: _____

Signature: _____

Signature: _____

FORM 171   01-06   ©2006 **first tuesday**, P.O. BOX 20069, RIVERSIDE, CA 92516 (800) 794-0494

tered into a purchase agreement to sell his property to a cash buyer will make a separate offer to purchase a replacement property by using a purchase agreement form to reinvest the proceeds from his sale.

Locating properties for exchange

Taxwise, a client making an offer to exchange *like-kind* real estate usually plans to complete a fully qualified §1031 reinvestment. Thus, he will acquire real estate with **greater debt** and **greater equity** than exists in the property he now owns, a *trade-up* arrangement for estate building, not a piecemeal liquidation of his asset for a partial §1031 exemption. [See Chapters 13 and 14]

When the exchange is a fully qualified §1031 reinvestment, all the profit in the property sold or exchanged is tax exempt.

Thus, the profit on the sale of the property is literally transferred, untaxed, to the replacement property. As a result, the entire cost basis in the property exchanged is always carried forward to the replacement property acquired in the exchange.

In the quest to locate suitable replacement properties for a client, the listing broker marketing the client's property needs to locate properties which are owned by a person who will consider acquiring the client's property. In essence, the broker attempts to arrange a transaction which will **match two owners** and their properties, a somewhat daunting task requiring a constant search for properties whose owners are willing to take other property in exchange.

To locate such an exchange-minded owner who is willing to consider owning the client's property, the listing broker is nearly always limited to those owners known to the broker to have acceptable replacement property or have listed their properties with other brokers. Hopefully, the other brokers have **counseled their clients** on an exchange of properties.

The most productive environment for locating owners of qualifying properties who have an interest in acquiring the client's property seems to exist at marketing sessions attended by many brokers and agents. At these meetings, they "pitch" their listings and advise attendees about the types of property their clients will accept in an exchange.

Multiple listing service (MLS) printouts, websites and large brokerage firms with income property sales sections also help in the process of locating qualifying properties. However, the agent considering an exchange usually needs to make a personal contact with the agent who represents the owner of suitable property to determine the likelihood of that owner entering into an exchange.

To get an initial response from other brokers and agents regarding the inclination of their owners to exchange, a preliminary inquiry about a **possible match up** of properties and owners can be made in the form of a written proposal. The proposal should precede any analysis or investigation into the property listed by the other broker, and include only its type, size and location to qualify it as a potential match for the client.

Prudently, an offer to exchange would not be prepared and submitted before getting a reading on the other owner's willingness to consider an exchange of properties, and more particularly, an exchange for a property of the type owned by the client.

To inquire of another broker or agent into the possibility of an exchange and at the same time document the inquiry for further reference, a **preliminary proposal form** is often prepared and personally handed or faxed to the other broker or agent. The proposal will note the type of properties involved, their equities and debt, and arrange for the exchange of information or a discussion between the agents before preparing an exchange agreement. [See Form 170 accompanying this chapter]

PRELIMINARY PROPOSAL
Mini-Form

DATE:_____, 20_____, at _____, California

TO: _____Profile#_____ _____ _____ Email: _____ Phone:_____Fax: _____ Cell: _____	**FROM:** _____Profile#_____ _____ _____ Email: _____ Phone:_____Fax: _____ Cell: _____

1. MY PROPERTY: _____
_____

Location: _____
_____
_____

1.1 Equity: $ _____

Loan 1:_____

_____

Loan 2:_____

2. YOUR PROPERTY: _____
_____

Location: _____
_____
_____

2.1 Equity $ _____

Loan 1:_____

_____

Loan 2:_____

_____

3. TERMS: _____
_____
_____
_____

4. REMARKS: _____
_____
_____

5. Agent Accord:

5.1 Data on the properties is attached.

5.2 Any additional property data requested will be promptly submitted.

5.3 This proposal is subject to further approval by my client, and client's inspection of the property and its operating data.

5.4 Terms to be detailed in further agreements or in escrow instructions.
   a. ☐ I see this as a 2-way transaction.   b. ☐ I see this as a multiple transaction.

6. Let's get together and talk:
   ☐ I'll contact you within _____days.   ☐ I'm in room _____.
   ☐ Please send me a back-up package.   ☐ Other_____

I respectfully submit this proposal for consideration by you and your client.

Submitting Agent's Signature: _____

Response: _____
_____
_____

Responding Agent's Signature _____ Date:_____, 20_____

The preliminary proposal is not an offer and does not contain contract wording. The clients are not involved in the proposal, only the brokers. Their effort is to locate properties to be submitted to their clients for exchange consideration. Only after the probability of actually entering into an exchange is established will an exchange agreement offer be prepared, signed by the client and submitted for acceptance.

Equity valuation adjustments

Once replacement property is located and its owner has indicated a willingness to consider an exchange of properties, the dollar amount of the market value of each property must be established. Once the market value of each property is established, the value of the equity can be set. **Valuation** is the single most important task in negotiating an agreement to exchange. [See Form 171 §§1.1, 1.3, 2.1 and 2.3]

Until a consensus exists between the owners about the value of the equity in each owner's property, negotiations tend not to go forward. Without an agreement on valuation, it follows that the amount of the **adjustment** for any difference between the equities in each property to the exchange cannot be set. Property disclosures and due diligence investigations tend to fall in place only when the values of the equities have been agreed to.

The broker begins negotiations to set the dollar amount of equity each owner has in his property by preparing an **exchange agreement offer**. The offer is based on the owner's and the broker's analysis of valuations, including:

- the **market value** (price) of each property to be exchanged [See Form 171 §1.3 and 2.3];

- the **loan amounts** encumbering each owner's property, whether or not they are to remain of record [See Form 171 §1.2 and 2.2]; and

- the **equity valuations** calculated as the market value of each property less the amount of loans of record.

Having stated the present value of the equity in each property (as viewed by the owner), adjustments need to be entered in the offer to cover the difference between the equity valuations in each property. [See Form 171 §§3.1a and 3.2a]

Since the equities in properties exchanged rarely are of the same dollar amount, adjustments will nearly always have to be negotiated. Thus, a contribution of **money** (cash or carryback promissory notes) or **other property**, collectively called *cash boot*, must be given by the owner of the property with the lesser amount of equity value, a consideration paid in a process called *adjusting* or *balancing the equities*.

Thus, the owner of the property with the larger amount of equity will receive one or more **cash items** as consideration for the adjustment, including:

- cash [See Form 171 §3.1b or 3.2b];

- carryback note [See Form 171 §3.1e or 3.2e]; or

- other property, either real or personal, with a dollar amount of value. [See Form 171 §3.1f or 3.2f]

Regarding the existence of financing which encumbers the properties being exchanged, negotiations may call for the loans to remain of record or be paid off and reconveyed. [See Form 171 §3.1c, 3.1d, 3.2c or 3.2d]

Refinancing of the replacement property may be necessary to generate cash funds for the payoff and reconveyance of the loans now encumbering the property. A contingency provision for new financing is needed if additional cash for the payoff of loans is required. [See Form 171 §3.1h or 3.2h]

Cultivating an exchange environment

Consider an agent who has a working knowledge of income property transactions in the region surrounding his office. The agent regularly attends marketing sessions and visits with brokers and agents whose clients have properties they would like to convert to cash or exchange for other properties.

An investor who is an acquaintance of the agent is known to the agent to be unhappy with the management aspect of a smaller residential rental property he owns. The investor would prefer to own a single-user property requiring little of his time to oversee maintenance and repairs.

Discussions the agent has with the investor about selling the units and locating a more suitable property to meet the investor's ownership objectives culminates in a listing of the property with the agent (on behalf of his broker).

A *reinvestment provision* is included in the listing calling for the location and acquisition of replacement property to provide the continuing investment in real estate required to qualify the sale for the Internal Revenue Code (IRC) §1031 exemption from any profit tax. The investor has owned the property for quite some time and his basis is low compared to the property's present market value.

Soon the agent locates an industrial property which is owned by a businessman whose company occupies the entire building. The property is listed with another broker who explains his client would be willing to lease back the property from the buyer rather than move to other premises. The businessman's broker knows his client's objective is to reduce his debt so he can enlarge the credit line for his business.

On inquiry as to whether the businessman would take residential income units (with a much smaller loan) in exchange for his property, the agent gets a positive response. It happens the businessman owns other residential properties and their management does not pose a problem for him.

Information on the properties is exchanged. The investor's units are priced at $600,000 with a debt of $200,000 and an equity valued at $400,000. The industrial building belonging to the businessman is listed at $1,200,000 subject to a loan of $700,000 with an equity of $500,000.

When data on the industrial property is reviewed with the investor as a probable replacement property under a net lease with the owner/occupant, the investor indicates it is just the situation he is looking for. He will be acquiring a property with a higher value to add to his investment portfolio and the demands on management will be minimal. The flow of rental income will cover payments on the loan and generate spendable income. The agent then conducts preliminary investigations into the property and the loan encumbering it.

The agent prepares an exchange offer. Besides the routine due diligence investigation into each property and typical contingencies and closing provisions, the agent needs to negotiate the **adjustment** for the $100,000 difference between the equities in the two properties and the **terms of a lease** for the businessman's continued occupancy of the industrial building.

Thus, the consideration the investor will offer to pay the price of $1,200,000 for the industrial property includes:

- the $400,000 equity in his residential units [See Form 171 §3.1a];

- an assumption of the $700,000 loan on the industrial building [See Form 171 §3.1d]; and

- execution of a $100,000 note in favor of the businessman, the adjustment necessary to balance the equities between the two properties exchanged. [See Form 171 §3.1e]

Thus, the total consideration offered by the investor to buy the industrial building is $1,200,000. [See Form 171 §3.1h]

Conversely, the consideration the investor wants from the businessman in exchange for the investor's residential units and the investor's execution of a carryback note in favor of the businessman includes:

- the $500,000 equity in the industrial property [See Form 171 §3.2a];

- an assumption of the $200,000 loan on the residential units; and

- a $100,000 **offset** by the investor's execution of a carryback note to be secured by the industrial property. [See Form 171 §3.2g]

Thus, the total consideration the businessman will pay for the residential units on acceptance of this offer is $600,000. [See Form 171 §3.2h]

The **leaseback arrangements** offered by the investor are based on the market value of the industrial property and rents paid for comparable properties. The terms of the lease are set out in an addendum attached to the exchange agreement offer.

The offer is submitted to the broker representing the businessman. In turn, a counteroffer is submitted to the investor based on all the terms of the exchange agreement, modified as follows:

- the carryback note provision is deleted; and

- the amount of $100,000 in cash is to be paid to adjust the equities.

Ultimately, escrow is opened based on an adjustment in the amount of $90,000; comprised of a $50,000 note and $40,000 in cash and a price reduction for the $10,000 difference. [See Form 171 §3.1b and 3.1e]

Analyzing the exchange agreement

The exchange agreement, **first tuesday** Form 171, is used to prepare and submit a property owner's offer to acquire other real estate in exchange for property he owns, neither property being a one-to-four unit residential property.

The exchange agreement offer, if accepted, becomes the binding written contract between each owner. Its terms must be complete and clear to prevent misunderstandings so the agreement can be judicially enforced.

Each section in Form 171 has a separate purpose and used for enforcement. The sections include:

1. *Identification*: The date of preparation for referencing the agreement, the names of the owners, the description of the properties to be exchanged and each property's fair market value, equity valuation and loan encumbrances are set forth in sections 1 and 2 to establish the facts on which the agreement is negotiated.

2. *Terms of exchange*: The total consideration each owner is to deliver to the other owner, such as the transfer of their equity and adjustments in the form of cash, carryback note, loan assumptions or value in additional property, and any new financing required to generate the cash needed to acquire the replacement property are set forth in section 3.

3. *Acceptance and performance*: Aspects of the formation of a contract, excuses for nonperformance and termination of the agreement are provided for in section 4, such as the time period for acceptance of the offer, the broker's control over enforcement of performance dates, the financing of the price as a closing contingency, procedures for cancellation of the agreement, cooperation to effect a §1031 transaction and limitations on monetary liability for breach of contract.

4. *Property conditions*: Each owner's confirmation of the physical condition of the property received as disclosed prior to acceptance is **confirmed** as set forth in sections 5 and 6 by each owner's delivery of information on their property for the other party's due diligence review and approval, such as rental income, expenses and tenant estoppels, natural and environmental hazards, physical conditions of improvements, title condition, security from crime, as well as providing certification of their property's condition on transfer, such as structural pest control, compliance with local occupancy ordinances and safety standards.

5. *Closing conditions*: The escrow holder, escrow instruction arrangements and the date of closing are established in section 7, as are title conditions, title insurance, hazard insurance, prorates and loan adjustments.

6. *Brokerage and agency*: The release of sales data on the transaction to trade associations is authorized, the brokerage fee is set and the delivery of the agency law disclosure to both parties is provided for as set forth in section 7, as well as the confirmation of the agency undertaken by the brokers and their agents on behalf of one or both parties to the agreement.

7. *Signatures*: Both parties bind each other to perform as agreed in the exchange agreement by signing and dating their signatures to establish the date of offer and acceptance.

Preparing the exchange agreement

The following instructions are for the preparation and use of the Exchange Agreement, **first tuesday** Form 171. Form 171 is designed as a checklist of practical provisions so a broker or his agent can prepare an offer for an owner to exchange properties located in California that do not include one-to-four unit residential property.

Each instruction corresponds to the provision in the form bearing the same number.

*Editor's note — **Check** and **enter** items throughout the agreement in each provision with boxes and blanks, unless the provision is not intended to be included as part of the final agreement, in which case it is left unchecked or blank.*

*To alter the wording of a provision or to delete or add a provision, use addendum **first tuesday** Form 250. On it, reference the section number in the exchange agreement to be altered or deleted. If altered, enter the copy that is to supersede the boilerplate provision referenced.*

Document identification:

Enter the date and name of the city where the offer is prepared. This date is used when referring to this exchange agreement.

Properties to be exchanged:

1. *First party and his property*: **Enter** as the first party the name of the owner who is initiating this offer to exchange properties.

   Enter the city, county and state in which the first property is located. **Enter** the legal description or common address of the property, or the assessor's parcel number (APN). If more than one like-kind property is being exchanged by the first party, include the description, financing and equity of the additional property in an addendum. [See **first tuesday** Form 250]

   1.1 *Equity valuations*: **Enter** the dollar amount of the equity in the first property, calculated as the property's fair market value minus the principal balance on the loans of record.

   1.2 *Existing loans*: **Enter** the total amount of the principal debt outstanding on the loans encumbering the first property.

a. *First trust deed*: **Enter** the amount of the unpaid principal, monthly principal and interest (PI) payment and the interest rate on the first trust deed loan encumbering the first property. **Check** the box to indicate whether the interest is adjustable (ARM). **Enter** the due date for any final balloon payment due on the loan. **Enter** any unique loan conditions such as impounds, alienation restraints, prepayment penalties, guarantees, etc.

b. *Second trust deed*: **Enter** the amount of the unpaid principal, monthly PI payments and the interest rate on the second trust deed loan encumbering the first property. **Check** the box to indicate whether the interest is adjustable (ARM). **Enter** the due date for any final balloon payment due on the loan. **Enter** any unique loan conditions such as impounds, alienation restraints, prepay penalties, guarantees, all-inclusive trust deed (AITD) provisions, etc.

1.3 *Market value*: **Enter** the total dollar amount of the first property's fair market value, i.e., the "price" the first party is to receive in exchange for his property.

Editor's note — The market value set for the first property determines the amount of title insurance, sales and transfer taxes and reassessment for property taxes, as well as fixes the price the first party is paying (and taxable profit) for any non-§1031 property he may be receiving in exchange for his property.

1.4 *Personal property included*: **Enter** the description of any personal property or inventory the first party is to transfer as part of the total property value. If an itemized list is available, **attach** it as an addendum to the exchange agreement and **enter** the words "see attached inventory."

2. *Second party and his property*: **Enter** as the second party the name of the owner of the **replacement property** sought to be acquired in the exchange.

Enter the city, county and state in which the replacement property is located. **Enter** the legal description or common address of the replacement property, or the APN. If the first party is to acquire more than one like-kind property as a replacement in this exchange, include the description, financing and equity of the additional property in an addendum. [See Form 250]

2.1 *Equity valuation*: **Enter** the dollar amount of the equity in the replacement property, calculated as the property's fair market value minus the principal balance on the loans of record.

2.2 *Existing loans*: **Enter** the total amount of the principal debt outstanding on the loans encumbering the replacement property.

a. *First trust deed*: **Enter** the amount of the unpaid principal, monthly PI payments and the interest rate on the first trust deed loan encumbering the replacement property. **Check** the box to indicate whether the interest is adjustable (ARM). **Enter** the due date for any final balloon payment due on the loan. **Enter** any unique loan provisions such as impounds, alienation restraints, prepay penalties, guarantees, etc.

b. *Second trust deed*: **Enter** the amount of the unpaid principal, monthly PI payments and the interest rate on the second trust deed loan encumbering the replacement property. **Check** the box to indicate whether the interest is adjustable (ARM). **Enter** the due date for any final balloon payment due on the loan. **Enter** any unique loan provisions such as impounds, alienation restraints, prepay penalties, guarantees, AITD provisions, etc.

2.3 *Market value*: **Enter** the total dollar amount of the replacement property's fair market value, i.e., the "price" the first party is to pay in exchange for the replacement property.

Editor's note — The market value set for the replacement property determines the amount of title insurance, sales and transfer taxes and reassessment for property taxes, as well as fixes the price the second party is paying (and taxable profit) for any non-§1031 property the first party may be contributing in exchange for the replacement property.

2.4 *Personal property included*: **Enter** the description of any personal property or inventory the first party is to receive as part of the total replacement property value. If an itemized list is available, **attach** it to the exchange agreement and **enter** the words "see attached inventory."

3. **Terms of the exchange:**

3.1 *Acquisition of the replacement property*: **Details** the total consideration the first party will **deliver** to the second party to acquire the replacement property.

*Editor's note — The consideration given by the first party for the replacement property includes the **equity value** in the first property and **adjustments** in the form of cash, carryback note or additional property to reflect the difference*

between the lesser equity value in the first property than the equity value in the replacement property. Also, **financial** provisions for the first party's take-over or refinancing of the loans of record on the replacement property are included.

a. *Equity value in first property*: **Enter** the dollar amount of the equity value set at section 1.1.

b. *Cash adjustment*: **Enter** the dollar amount of any cash payment to be made by the first party to adjust for any difference due to a lesser amount of equity value in the first property than the equity value in the replacement property.

Editor's note — Only one of the parties will add cash, if at all, to adjust for the differences in equity amounts. Cash for loan payoffs is handled separately at sections 3.1c and 3.2c.

c. *Additional cash payment*: **Enter** the amount of the principal balance remaining due on the loans of record encumbering the replacement property as set at section 2.2 if the first party will not be taking over the loans of record on the replacement property (section 3.1d) and the second party is to pay off and reconvey these loans. Funding for this payoff will be provided by the first party refinancing or further encumbering the replacement property.

d. *Loan take-over*: **Check** the appropriate box to indicate whether the first party will take title to the replacement property subject to the loans of record or will assume the loans if the loans are to remain of record on the replacement property. **Enter** the amount of the principal balance remaining on the loans of record on the replacement property as set forth at section 2.2.

Editor's note — This boilerplate provision for loan takeover does not include the alternative of a **novation agreement** *between both parties and the lender that would terminate the second party's liability on the loan and, unlike an assumption, would shift all loan liability to the first party.*

e. *Promissory note adjustment*: **Enter** the dollar amount of any carryback note and trust deed the first party will execute in favor of the second party to adjust for differences in equity valuations due to a lesser equity value in the first property than in the replacement property. **Enter** as the terms for payment of the carryback note the amount of the monthly payment, the interest rate and the number of years after close of escrow to set the due date for a final balloon payment.

f. *Additional property as adjustment*: **Enter** the dollar amount of the equity in any additional property the first party is to contribute to this exchange to adjust for the difference in the larger equity he will receive in the replacement property. The equity in the additional property is calculated as the difference between its fair market value and any debt encumbering it. **Enter** the description of the additional property. **Enter** the amount of any debt.

g. *Offset for adjustments received*: **Enter** the dollar amount of any cash boot (money, carryback note

or other property) the first party is to receive as compensation for the difference between the greater value of the equity in the first property and the lesser equity value in the replacement property. This amount is the sum of any amounts entered in section 3.2b, e and f. The first party's receipt of an adjustment is subtracted to determine the total consideration the first party will pay to acquire the replacement property.

h. *Total consideration*: **Enter** the total dollar amount of all consideration to be paid by the first party to acquire the replacement property as the sum of the amounts entered in this section 3.1 at subsections a, b, c, d, e and f, less the amount entered at subsection g.

i. *New financing for replacement property*: **Check** the appropriate box to indicate whether any new financing to be originated by the first party on the replacement property will be a first or second trust deed loan. **Enter** the amount of the loan, the monthly payment and the interest rate limitations on the loan. **Check** the box to indicate whether the interest rate will be adjustable. If so, **enter** the index name controlling the ARM. **Enter** the number of years the loan is to run until it will be due on a final balloon payment.

3.2 *Disposition of the first property*: This section details the total consideration the first party will receive from the second party in exchange for the first property.

a. *Equity value in the replacement property*: **Enter** the dollar amount of the equity value set at section 2.1.

b. *Cash adjustment*: **Enter** the dollar amount of any cash payment to be made by the second party to adjust for any difference due to a lesser amount of equity value in the replacement property than the equity value in the first property.

c. *Additional cash payment*: **Enter** the amount of the principal balances remaining due on the loans of record encumbering the first property as set at section 1.2 if the second party will not be taking over the loans of record on the first property (section 3.2d) and the first party is to pay off and reconvey these loans. Funding for this payoff will be provided by the second party refinancing or further encumbering the first property.

d. *Loan takeover*: **Check** the appropriate box to indicate whether the second party will take title to the first property subject to the loans of record or will assume the loans if the loans are to remain of record on the first property. **Enter** the amount of the principal balance remaining on the loans of record on the first property as set forth at section 1.2.

e. *Promissory note adjustment*: **Enter** the dollar amount of any carryback note and trust deed the second party will execute in favor of the first party to adjust for the difference in equity valuations due to a lesser equity value in the replacement property than in the first property. **Enter** as the terms for payment of the carryback note the amount of the monthly payment, the interest rate and the number of years after close of escrow to set the due date for a final balloon payment.

f. *Additional property as adjustment*: **Enter** the dollar amount of the equity in any additional property the second party is to contribute to this exchange to adjust for the difference in the larger equity he will receive in the first property. The equity in the additional property is calculated as the difference between its fair market value and any debt encumbering it. **Enter** the description of the additional property. **Enter** the amount of any debt.

g. *Offset for adjustment received*: **Enter** the dollar amount of any cash boot (money, carryback note or other property) the second party is to receive as compensation for the difference between the greater value of the equity in the second property and the lesser equity value in the first property. This amount is the sum of any amounts entered in section 3.1b, e and f. The second party's receipt of adjustment is subtracted to determine the total consideration the second party will pay to acquire the first property.

h. *Total consideration*: **Enter** the total dollar amount of all consideration to be paid by the second party to acquire the first property as the sum of the amounts entered in this section 3.2 at subsections a, b, c, d, e and f, less the amount entered at subsection g.

i. *New financing for first property*: **Check** the appropriate box to indicate whether any new financing to be originated by the second party on the first property will be a first or second trust deed loan. **Enter** the amount of the loan, the monthly payment and the interest rate limitations on the loan. **Check** the box to indicate whether the interest rate will be adjustable. If so, **enter** the index name controlling the ARM. **Enter** the number of years the loan will run until it will be due on a final balloon payment.

3.3 *Carryback note conditions*: **Provides** for any carryback note and trust deed, executed to adjust for the equity differences between the properties, to include or be subject to the term and conditions of this section, in addition to the terms for payment of the note established by either section 3.1e or 3.2e.

a. *Financial disclosure statement*: **Check** the box to indicate a carryback disclosure statement is to be prepared and handed to the party executing the note, as is mandated in one-to-four unit residential transactions. If so, **attach** a completed carryback disclosure statement to the exchange agreement for signatures. [See **first tuesday** Form 300]

b. *Special provisions*: **Check** the appropriate box to indicate any special provisions to be included in the carryback note or trust deed. **Enter** the name of any other unlisted special provisions, such as impounds, discount options, extension clauses, guarantee arrangements or right of first refusal on a sale or hypothecation of the note.

c. *Notice of delinquency*: **Check** the box to indicate the party executing the note is also to execute a request for notice of delinquency and pay the cost of recording and serving it on senior lenders. [See **first tuesday** Form 412]

d. *Creditworthiness analysis*: **Check** the box to indicate the party executing the note is to provide the other party with a completed credit application. [See **first tuesday** Form 302]

e. *Approval of creditworthiness*: **Enter** the number of days in which the party carrying back the note may cancel the transaction based on his reasonable disapproval of the other party's creditworthiness. [See **first tuesday** Form 183]

f. *Subordination of trust deed*: **Authorizes** the party carrying back the note and trust deed to terminate the transaction should the terms arranged for the origination or assumption of loans, secured by trust deeds with priority on title and senior to the trust deed securing the carryback note, fall outside the parameters for amount, payments, interest rate and due dates agreed to in this agreement.

g. *UCC-1 for additional security*: **Requires** a security agreement and UCC-1 financing statements to be completed and the UCC-1 to be filed with the Secretary of State to *perfect* a security interest in any personal property being transferred by the party carrying back the note and trust deed.

4. **Acceptance and performance periods:**

4.1 *Authorized acceptance*: **Enter** the number of days in which the second party may accept this exchange offer and form a binding contract.

4.2 *Extension of performance dates*: **Authorizes** the brokers to extend performance dates up to one month to meet the objectives of this exchange agreement, time being a reasonable period of duration and not of the essence in the initially scheduled performance of this agreement.

4.3 *Loan contingency*: **Authorizes** the party taking title to a property to cancel the transaction at the time scheduled for closing if the new financing or loan assumption arrangements agreed to fail to occur.

4.4 *Cancellation procedures*: **Provides** for termination of the agreement when the right to cancel is triggered by other provisions in the agreement, such as contingency and performance provisions. The method for any cancellation of this exchange agreement is controlled by this provision.

4.5 *Exchange cooperation*: **Requires** the parties to cooperate with one another in an IRS §1031 transaction on further written notice by either party. **Provides** for the parties to assign their interests in this agreement. [See **first tuesday** Form 172 or 173]

4.6 *Liability limited on breach*: To limit the liability of either party due to their breach of this agreement, **enter** the dollar amount representing the maximum amount of money losses the other party may recover due to the breach.

Editor's note — Liability limitation provisions avoid the misleading and unenforceable forfeiture called for under liquidated damage clauses included in most purchase agreement forms provided by other publishers of forms.

5. **Due diligence contingencies:**

5.1 *Satisfaction or cancellation*: **Enter** the number of days in which the second party may terminate the exchange agreement after receipt of data on the first property that is unacceptable to the second party.

a. *Operating documentation*: **Check** the box to indicate the first party is to make his income and expense records and all supporting documentation available for inspection by the second party.

b. *Rental rolls*: **Check** the box to indicate the first party is to provide an itemized spreadsheet detailing all aspects of each tenancy in the property. [See **first tuesday** Form 380]

45

c. *Natural hazard disclosure (NHD) statement*: **Check** the box to indicate the first party is to prepare and provide the second party with an NHD statement disclosing the first party's knowledge about the hazards listed on the form. [See **first tuesday** Form 314]

d. *Physical condition of the property*: **Check** the box to indicate the first party is to prepare and provide the second party with a disclosure of the first party's knowledge about the physical conditions of the land and improvements which may have an adverse effect on the value of the first property.

e. *Personal property inventory*: **Check** the box to indicate the first party is to prepare an itemized list of the personal property he is to transfer with the first property.

f. *Buyer's inspection*: **Check** the box to authorize the second party to carry out an inspection of the first property, himself or by his agents or consultants, to confirm the property's value. **Enter** the number of days after acceptance in which the second party is to carry out the inspection.

g. *Title conditions*: **Check** the box to indicate the first party is to cause escrow to order out a preliminary title report for purposes of issuing a policy of title insurance on the first property and deliver the preliminary report to the second party as soon as possible.

h. *Tenant estoppel certificates*: **Check** the box to indicate the first party will prepare, mail and collect estoppel certificates from all his tenants to be delivered to the second party.

i. *Tenant personal security*: **Check** the box to indicate the first party will prepare a criminal activity and security statement disclosing his knowledge of crimes that affect the tenants' use and occupancy of the property, and the steps he has taken or should take to provide personal security for the tenants.

j. *Qualifying for §1031 exemption*: **Check** the box to indicate the closing of the transaction is subject to the further approval of the second party's tax advisors that the transaction qualifies for §1031 treatment.

k. *Additional disclosures or investigations*: **Enter** copy addressing any further information the second party wants in order to confirm expectations about the first property not covered in the boilerplate provisions of this form, such as investigations into zoning, use plans, permits or other governmental and private activities which may affect the property's value to the second party.

5.2 *Satisfaction or cancellation*: **Enter** the number of days in which the first party may terminate the exchange agreement after receipt of data on the replacement property that is unacceptable to the first party.

a. *Operating documentation*: **Check** the box to indicate the second party is to make his income and expense records and all supporting documentation available for inspection by the first party.

b.   *Rental rolls*: **Check** the box to indicate the second party is to provide an itemized spreadsheet detailing all aspects of each tenancy in the property. [See Form 380]

c.   *Natural hazard disclosure (NHD) statement*: **Check** the box to indicate the second party is to prepare and provide the first party with an NHD statement disclosing the second party's knowledge about the hazards listed on the form. [See Form 314]

d.   *Physical condition of the property*: **Check** the box to indicate the second party is to prepare and provide the first party with a disclosure of the second party's knowledge about the physical conditions of the land and improvements which may have an adverse effect on the value of the replacement property.

e.   *Personal property inventory*: **Check** the box to indicate the second party is to prepare an itemized list of the personal property he is to transfer with the replacement property.

f.   *Buyer's inspection*: **Check** the box to authorize the first party to carry out an inspection of the replacement property, himself or by his agents or consultants, to confirm the property's value. **Enter** the number of days after acceptance in which the first party is to carry out the inspection.

g.   *Title conditions*: **Check** the box to indicate the second party is to cause escrow to order out a preliminary title report for purposes of issuing a policy of title insurance on the replacement property and deliver the preliminary report to the first party as soon as possible.

h.   *Tenant estoppel certificates*: **Check** the box to indicate the second party will prepare, mail and collect estoppel certificates from all his tenants to be delivered to the first party.

i.   *Tenant personal security*: **Check** the box to indicate the second party will prepare a criminal activity and security statement disclosing his knowledge of crimes that affect the tenants' use and occupancy of his property, and the steps he has taken or should take to provide personal security for the tenants.

j.   *Qualifying for §1031 exemption*: **Check** the box to indicate the closing of the transaction is subject to the further approval of the first party's tax advisors that the transaction qualifies for §1031 treatment.

k.   *Additional disclosures or investigations*: **Enter** copy addressing any further information the first party wants in order to confirm expectations about the replacement property not covered in the boilerplate provisions of this form, such as investigations into zoning, use plans, permits or other governmental and private activities which may affect the property's value to the first party.

6.   Property conditions on closing: **Provides** for the first and second parties to deliver up their properties at closing in a condition commonly expected of all properties bought and sold in California. These items are not those generally necessary to be confirmed as part of a due diligence investigation by the party acquiring title.

6.1 *Structural pest control*: **Check** the box if each party is to provide a report and certified clearance by a structural pest control operator on the property he conveys.

6.2 *Improvement warranty policy*: **Check** the box if each party is to furnish an insurance policy on the property he conveys for emergency repairs to components of the structures which are improvements on the property. **Enter** the name of the insurer who is to issue the policy. **Enter** the type of coverage desired, such as air conditioning units, water heaters, etc.

6.3 *Local ordinance compliance*: **Provides** for each party to furnish a certificate of occupancy or other clearances required by local ordinances on the property he conveys.

6.4 *Safety law compliance*: **Provides** for each property to meet smoke detector placement and water heater bracing required by state law.

6.5 *Property maintenance*: **Requires** each party to maintain the present condition of his property until the close of escrow.

6.6 *Fixtures and fittings*: **Confirms** this exchange includes real estate fixtures and fittings as part of the property acquired.

6.7 *Further leasing and contracting*: **Requires** each party to submit for approval (consent) by the other party all new or modified tenancy arrangements, service contracts and improvement alterations or equipment installation contracts relating to the property he is conveying.

6.8 *Additional affirmative conditions*: **Enter** any other conditions on or about

the properties each party is expected to comply with prior to closing, such as obtaining permits, eliminating property defects, certification regarding components of the improvements on the properties, etc.

7. Closing conditions:

7.1 *Escrow closing agent*: **Enter** the name of the escrow company handling the closing.

a. *Escrow instructions*: **Check** the box to indicate the exchange agreement is to also serve as the mutual instructions to escrow from the parties. Typically, escrow companies will (or the broker will) prepare supplemental instructions needed to handle and close the transaction. [See **first tuesday** Form 401]

b. *Escrow instructions*: **Check** the box to indicate escrow instructions have been prepared and are attached to this purchase agreement. **Attach** the prepared escrow instructions to the purchase agreement and **obtain** the signatures of the parties. [See **first tuesday** Form 401]

7.2 *Closing date*: **Check** the appropriate box to indicate the manner for setting the date on which escrow is scheduled to close. Following the box checked, **enter** as appropriate the specific date for closing or the number of days anticipated as necessary for the parties to perform and close escrow. Note that prior to seven days before closing, the parties are to deliver all documents regarding the property they are conveying that are needed by third parties to perform their services by the date scheduled for closing.

a. *Escrow charges*: **Provides** for each party to pay their customary closing costs and charges, amounts any competent escrow officer can provide on inquiry. [See **first tuesday** Forms 310 and 311]

7.3 *Title conditions*: **Provides** for title to be vested in the name of the party acquiring the respective properties, or their assignees, subject to covenants, conditions and restrictions (CC&Rs) of record and mortgage liens agreed to in this exchange agreement.

Editor's note — *The inclusion of the preliminary title policy contingency at section 5.1g or 5.2g will control the CC&Rs to remain of record at closing, subject to exercise of the right to cancel the transaction if they are unacceptable to the party acquiring title.*

7.4 *Title insurance*: **Enter** the name of the title company which will provide a preliminary title report and issue the title insurance policy. **Check** the appropriate box to indicate the type of policy to be issued.

a. *Policy endorsements*: **Enter** any endorsements to be issued with the policy of title insurance.

b. *Insurance premium*: **Provides** for the owner of each property to pay the premium for the policy insuring his conveyance.

7.5 *Prorates and adjustments*: **Authorizes** prorations and adjustments on close of escrow for taxes, rents, interest, loan balances, service contracts and other property operating expenses, prepaid or accrued.

7.6 *Loan balance adjustments*: **Check** the appropriate box to indicate the financial adjustment desired for loan balance adjustments brought about by any difference between the principal bal-

ance as stated in the exchange agreement at sections 1.2 and 2.2 and the amount stated in beneficiary statements from the lender on the date escrow closes.

Editor's note — *Often the parties will treat the equities as fixed and not subject to adjustments for variances in the balances of loans taken over by the new owner. Thus, loan balances adjustments are made into the "market value" of the property encumbered. More typically, the loan balance adjustments are made into any carryback note created in the exchange. Thus, the equity in encumbered property is adjusted to reflect a greater or lesser loan balance on the beneficiary's statement than as stated in the exchange agreement. Adjustment into cash is seldom agreed to in exchanges.*

7.7 *Lease assignments*: **Provides** for all leases and rental agreements to be assigned to the new owner on closing. [See **first tuesday** Form 595]

a. *Change of ownership notice*: **Requires** each party assigning lease and rental agreements to notify each tenant of the change of ownership. The notice eliminates any further liability to the tenants of the party assigning the agreements. [See **first tuesday** Form 554]

7.8 *Personal property transferred*: **Provides** for a bill of sale to be executed on any personal property to be transferred with the property.

a. *UCC-3 clearance*: **Check** the box if escrow is to order a UCC-3 condition of title report from the Secretary of State on the personal property being transferred by a bill of sale for approval by the party taking ownership of the personal property.

7.9 *Fire insurance*: **Requires** the party taking title to provide a new policy of fire insurance.

7.10 *Possession*: **Provides** for possession of the property to be transferred to the party acquiring title on the close of escrow.

7.11 *Title failure and property destruction*: **Provides** for the cancellation of the exchange agreement by the party taking title if marketable title cannot be delivered or the property improvements suffer major damage.

8. **Brokerage fees:**

8.1 *Fees paid by first party*: **Enter** the dollar amount of fees to be paid by the first party to his broker. **Enter** the name of the first party's broker. If the fees are to be paid under a separate agreement, **enter** the words "per separate agreement" in lieu of the broker's name.

8.2 *Fees paid by second party*: **Enter** the dollar amount of fees to be paid by the second party to his broker. **Enter** the name of the second party's broker. If the fees are to be paid under a separate agreement, **enter** the words "per separate agreement" in lieu of the broker's name.

8.3 *Fees on default*: **Provides** for the defaulting party to pay all brokerage fees due to be paid the brokers under section 8.

8.4 *Fee-sharing arrangements*: **Authorizes** the brokers to share the fees due them.

8.5 *Transaction data disclosure*: **Authorizes** the brokers to release information on the price of the properties and terms of the exchange to trade organizations and multiple listing services.

8.6 *Agency Law Disclosure*: **Check** the box to indicate an Agency Law Disclosure addendum is attached to the exchange agreement. **Attach** a copy of the addendum for all parties to sign if the addendum is to made a part of the exchange agreement. The disclosure is mandated on one-to-four unit residential transactions for enforcement of fee provisions by the brokers. [See **first tuesday** Form 305]

Agency confirmation:

First party's broker: **Enter** the name of the broker who represents the owner of the first property making the offer to exchange. **Obtain** the signature of the broker or the agent acting on behalf of the first party's broker. **Check** the appropriate box to indicate the nature of the agency created with the parties by the conduct of the broker and his agent.

Second party's broker: **Enter** the name of the broker who represents the owner of the replacement property to whom this exchange agreement offer will be submitted for acceptance (or rejection). **Obtain** the signature of the broker or the agent acting on behalf of the second party's broker. **Check** the appropriate box to indicate the nature of the agency created with the parties by the conduct of the broker and his agent.

Signatures:

First party's signature: **Enter** the date the first party making the offer signs the exchange agreement. **Obtain** the signature of each of the persons who are the owners of the first property. **Enter** the first party's name, address, telephone and fax numbers, and email address. **Confirm** that the parties signing this exchange agreement also sign all the attachments requiring their signatures.

Second party's signature: **Enter** the date second party signs the exchange agreement offer. **Ob-**

tain the signature of each of the persons who are the owners of the replacement property. **Enter** the second party's name, address, telephone and fax numbers, and email address. **Confirm** that the parties signing this exchange agreement also sign all the attachments requiring their signatures.

Rejection of offer:

Should the offer contained in the exchange agreement be rejected by the second party instead of accepted, and the rejection will not result in a counteroffer, **enter** the date of the rejection and the names of the second party. **Obtain** the signatures of the second party.

Observations:

As the policy of the publisher, this exchange agreement **does not contain** clauses which tend to increase the risk of litigation or are generally felt to work against the best interests of the buyer, seller and broker. Excluded provisions include:

- an *attorney fee provision*, which tends to **promote litigation** and inhibit contracting;

- an *arbitration clause*, which, if included and initialed, absolutely **waives** the buyer's and seller's right to a fair and correct decision by trial and appeal; and

- a *time-essence clause*, since future performance (closing) dates are, at best, estimates by the broker and his agent of the time needed to close and are too often **improperly used** by sellers in rising markets to cancel the transaction before the buyer or broker can reasonably comply with the terms of the purchase agreement.

Chapter 4

The sales price

This chapter assists in the clarification of the many components of a sales price and its mathematics.

Different views, different aspects

Quite often, and properly so, brokers and listing agents **advise sellers** on the amount of net proceeds they can expect from the sales price. Agents do so by preparing and reviewing a seller's net sheet, based initially on the listing price. The preparation is repeated to analyze the price offered in each purchase agreement offer submitted.

The seller's net sheet is enough to estimate the dollar amount of the seller's **net equity** and the net proceeds likely to be received on a sale.

But what about the *profit* (or loss) which is also a component of the sales price? Taxwise, the data is important. A sale at a profit produces a tax liability, unless exempt or excluded. Sellers frequently believe the profit on which they will pay taxes is somehow related to the amount of net proceeds they will receive on the sale.

In other words, a belief commonly held by sellers is that their equity equals their profit, however, it does not. The differences become more distinguished when the seller has refinanced the property and increased the debt encumbering the property.

The **equity** in a property and the **profit** on a sale are derived from different data, respectively, the *debt* and the *basis*. On a sale, they are never the same amount.

Before breaking down the **sales price** into its components for various purposes, several economic fundamentals of real estate ownership must first be understood and differentiated:

- *capital investment* made to acquire and improve the property (cash contributions and funds from loans);

- *annual operating data* generated by rents and expenses of ongoing ownership; and

- *tax consequences* of buying, ownership operations and selling.

A property's sales price, also called *market value*, is the only term common to all economic analysis regarding the ownership of a home, business-use property or rental real estate, residential or nonresidential. However, homebuyers are not (yet) demanding much information disclosing a residence's operating data (and the state legislature has not yet required it). Also, homebuyers are less informed. Thus, they are less inquisitive about acquisition costs, operating expenses and income taxes than are buyers of business or investment real estate.

Capital aspects of the sales price

When marketing real estate for sale, the published sales price of a property can be quickly broken down into its **debt** and **equity**, as it should be, by any buyer interested in the property. It is the seller's equity a buyer is cashing out, no matter how the buyer might be financing his purchase.

The amount of debt encumbering a property is deducted from the sales price to determine the **seller's gross equity** in the property. However, debt never aids in the determination of the seller's profit on a sale. [See Figure 1 accompanying this chapter]

Also, a seller's present **capital interest** in a property is the total sum of the dollar amount of the property's current debt and equity or the property's current fair market value — its price. The capital interest is distinguished from the seller's previous **capital investment** in the property of cash and loan proceeds, originally used to purchase, improve or carry the property, that establishes his cost basis in the property.

Buyers seeking information about a property should be interested in the dollar amount of equity the seller has in the property. The buyer acts to "buy out" the seller's equity, the seller's *net worth* in the property, when the buyer purchases the property and generates net sales proceeds for the seller.

Any debt encumbering the property is either **assumed** by the buyer or **paid off** with funds from the buyer. Neither action ever puts money in the hands of the seller. Funds received by escrow for payoff of an existing loan are either advanced by the buyer or obtained from purchase-assist financing arranged by the buyer.

Further, the **market value** (the sales price for the property) bears no relationship to the seller's original capital investment in the property, whenever it was made. The sales price does not reflect a value based on a trend line of the *historic value* or *equilibrium value* of property, much less the seller's *book value* (which is the depreciated cost basis remaining from the original capital investment).

A related financial concern is **interest** paid on mortgage debt borrowed to provide capital to purchase investment property. Interest is a **cost of capital** and is incurred by owners who are not solvent enough to own "free and clear" property. Interest paid on the debt is not a capital investment expended to acquire or improve property. Further, as a cost of capital, interest is not an operating expense incurred for the care and maintenance of the property. Thus, interest is not included in a rental property's net operating income (NOI).

However, to determine a property's income or loss for annual tax reporting, interest, like depre-

ciation, is **deductible** from the property's NOI. While interest is not an operating expense incurred by the property, it is an allowable deduction for **undercapitalized owners** who must borrow to obtain capital to acquire property.

Operating data sets the sales price

A property's sales price is also viewed as the *capitalization* of the property's NOI based on a yield, an alternative to other methods of property valuation. The income and expense data comprising the NOI are the **fundamentals** upon which value, and thus the sales price, is established.

As a reference to value, the mathematical relationship between the sales price and NOI produces a **multiplier** (a ratio) and a **rate of return** (a percentage). These are used to calculate probable value and are reciprocals of one another. The same indicators are used in the stock market for a cursory analysis of share value, called "price-to-earnings ratios."

Rental properties produce income by way of rents paid by tenants. In exchange for receiving rent, landlords incur expenses to care for and maintain the physical condition and earning power of the properties. Collectively, the rents and expenses produce the NOI of a property, which in turn give the property a value — the sales price.

A rental property's operating expenses do not include interest payments or capital recovery through depreciation schedules. **Interest** is related (as a cost of capital) to the financing of the owner's capital investment which is needed to purchase or improve the property, not to operate the property (unless it produces a negative cash flow).

Depreciation is an orderly, tax-free recovery from rents of that portion of the owner's total capital investment allocated to improvements. Interest and depreciation deductions are unrelated to the operation of the property or the

Figure 1

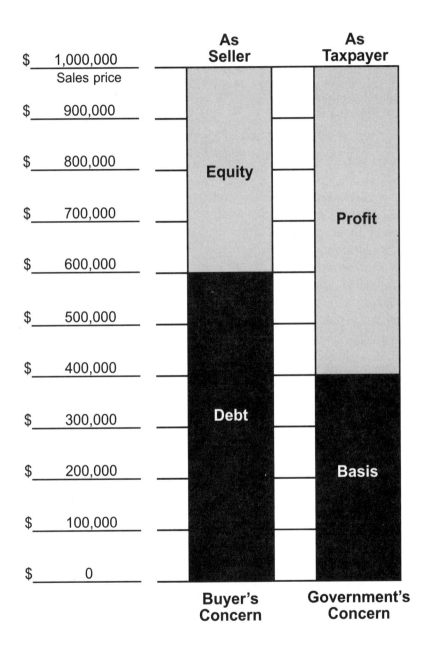

property's current sales price. Arguably, however, an above market interest rate on a locked-in loan which cannot be prepaid would depress the property's sales price.

Each parcel of income-producing property has a calculable *scheduled income*: the total rents collectible if the property is 100% occupied, without reduction for vacancy, turnover or uncollectible rents.

Also, the **sales price** of a residential or nonresidential rental is often roughly stated as a *gross multiplier* or *percentage of value* based on the scheduled income, called *rules-of-thumb*. As approaches to pricing, these determinations are preliminary and superficial.

Historically, the scheduled monthly rents for a residential rental, when viewed as a **percentage of value**, are said to represent about 1% of the sales price, an unsophisticated but initial indicator of value. This *monthly income indicator* is used to approximate a reasonable price for a property which enjoys reasonable income and expenses in a market based on minimal current and expected future inflation rates.

The asking price of income property is often tested for its reasonableness by the application of a **multiplier** to the scheduled annual rents or the NOI, another variable which helps predict a property's value. Historically, a gross multiplier of 7 or 8 (arguably higher at 10 to 12 during periods of excessive asset inflation) times annual rents is used on residential units as a quick glimpse into the reasonableness of the sales price.

However, an analysis of a sales price is more properly based on the NOI a rental property is expected to produce each year in the future. The NOI is the **annual return** a property produces based on collectible rental income minus operating expenses. Again, interest on the mortgage debt is of no concern to a buyer when evaluating property which is or will be financed by the buyer at interest rates no greater than the buyer's capitalization rate, his *rate of return*.

The annual **rate of return** sought by a buyer is applied to the NOI to produce a sales price the buyer will pay for the property — its value to a buyer before considerations for financing the price.

The annual rate of return expected from ownership of a property is called a *capitalization rate* or *yield*.

The **capitalization rate** applied to the NOI comprises an implicit, anticipated future inflation rate (CPI) of, for example, 2% annually, a recovery of the seller's investment of 3% annually, and a "real" (after inflation) *rate of return* for the buyer of 3% to 4% annually. During the early to mid-1990s, this aggregate capitalization rate was represented by a 9% to 10% annual yield (a gross multiplier of 11 or 10).

The large sums of equity (stock) market financing available to real estate investment trusts (REITs) and secondary mortgage pools in the late 1990s drove the annual expected yield for real estate income down to around 6.5% to 7% and lower into 2004 (a multiplier of 14 to 15 times NOI and higher into 2004). The excessive demand for assets and readily available and historically cheap mortgage financing pushed prices up, possibly in anticipation of strong future increases in rental income or a reduced risk of lost value due to cyclically collapsing real estate markets.

Tax components in the sales price

Taxwise, the **sales price** is broken down into *basis* and *profit* to determine the income tax consequences of a sale. The short formula for profit is: price minus basis equals profit.

However, a tax analysis of the price only reflects the **consequences of a sale**. Neither a seller's remaining basis nor the profit he may seek plays any role in setting the market price a buyer may be willing to pay for a property.

A seller's basis and profit, an element of state and federal tax reporting, are of no concern to a buyer. A buyer can never acquire a seller's basis, and a seller's basis does not in any way contribute to or help a buyer establish a property's value.

Also, a seller's remaining cost basis in a property never is equal to the amount remaining unpaid on the loans encumbering the property. Likewise, deducting basis from the sales price sets the seller's profit; basis never sets the equity acquired by the buyer because price minus debt equals equity.

When a buyer acquires property, a **cost basis**, also called *book value*, is established as a total of all the expenditures related to the purchase of the property and the improvements necessary to attract tenants, called "placing the property in service." During the period of ownership prior to resale, a property's cost basis is adjusted periodically due to depreciation (capital recovery), hazard losses and further improvements.

Taxwise, the cost basis remaining at the time of resale is deducted from the net sales price to determine whether a profit or loss has been realized by the seller.

A buyer's payment of the **purchase price** is his capital contribution. The price paid consists of any cash contributed to fund the price and transactional costs, the principal balance of existing trust deed loans assumed, net proceeds from new loans and the fair market value of the equity in other property (except §1031 like-kind real estate) used to purchase or improve the property acquired, collectively called *costs of acquisition*.

Editor's note — If the purchase price paid includes an equity from §1031 like-kind real estate, the basis in the property purchased will include the remaining cost basis in the property sold (not its sales price), adjusted for additional contributions or the withdrawal of money (cash boot) and differences in the amount of existing debt (mortgage boot) on the properties. [See Chapter 26]

Additional improvements do contribute to a property's value. Thus, the expenditures for the **cost of improvements** are added to the basis in the property. Conversely, expenditures for the upkeep, maintenance, repair and operations of the property are **operating expenses** deducted from rental income. While operating expenses add nothing to the cost basis in the property, they do maintain — and often increase — the property's value and sales price.

Net cash proceeds from **refinancing** or equity financing which are not used to purchase or improve property do not contribute to the cost basis (or affect the property's value). While any financing affects a property's equity, the assumption (take-over) of existing financing and the investment of funds from the proceeds of a purchase-assist or construction loan will make up part of the buyer's cost basis on acquisition.

The **depreciation allowance** is a tax-free annual return to an owner (from rents) of the percentage of his total capital contribution allocated to the improvements. Accordingly, the **cost basis**, being the total capital contribution, is reduced each year on the *deduction* of the annual depreciation allowance from the NOI, and establishes the property's current cost basis on the owner's books.

Assuming the property will receive future maintenance, none of the depreciation taken in anticipation of deterioration and obsolescence weighs in to set the sales price. Again, tax accounting and book value do not play a part in the calculation of a property's market value (sales price).

On resale of a property, the seller's initial tax concern is the amount of profit that exists in the sales price. The structuring of the terms for payment of the sales price or reinvestment determines whether the profit in the sales price will be taxed, and if so, when the seller will pay those taxes.

Chapter 5

Income tax categories

This chapter discusses the three income categories for segregating the income, profit and losses resulting from property ownership, and the rules for determining the tax consequences within each category.

The many types of income

A central concept, requisite to understanding the tax aspects of annually reporting real estate operations and sales, is the existence of **three income categories**, sometimes referred to as *income pots*. The category, or pot, into which a property falls controls the accounting and the reporting of the property's income, profits and losses, collectively called income by the Internal Revenue Service (IRS). [See Figure 1 accompanying this chapter]

When an owner of real estate, his accountant or broker prepares an estimate of the owner's annual income tax liability, the owner's total income, profits and losses from all sources are first classified as belonging in one of **three income categories**:

- professional trade or owner-operated business opportunities, called *trade or business income*, including any real estate owned and used in the production of the owner's trade or business income [Internal Revenue Code §469(c)(6)];

- rentals and non-owner-operated business opportunities, called *passive income* [IRC §469(c)(1)]; and

- investments, called *portfolio income*. [Revenue Regulations §1.469-2T(c)(3)]

The categories relate to the **type** and **use** of the real estate generating the income, profit or loss. The vesting employed by the individual owner or co-owners to hold title is not relevant, unless a C corporation, taxable trust or estate of a deceased holds title as the **owner** and **operator** of the property since they are taxed separately from their owners (shareholders or beneficiaries).

For example, the ownership of rentals (exceeding 30-day average occupancies) by a limited liability company (LLC) is not a trade or business of the LLC or its owners, called *members*. Each member of the LLC reports the income, profit or loss from the rental operation as passive category income since an LLC is treated as a partnership. Thus, as in any partnership, income is passed through to the members before it is taxed. [IRC §701]

Conversely, **property management services** rendered by an individual broker on behalf of owners of rentals constitute a trade or business category activity for the broker.

The three income categories are mutually exclusive of one another. Simply put, losses from one category cannot be used — *commingled* — to directly offset income or profit within another category. Each category is tallied separately to establish the end-of-year income, profit or loss within the category.

If a reportable end-of-year income or profit exists within any category, it is added to the owner's *adjusted gross income (AGI)*. However, if the end-of-year result is a reportable loss, only the amount of loss in the business category is fully subtracted without qualification from the AGI.

Each category has different internal accounting rules. For instance, the operating income or loss from each assessor-identified parcel of **rental (passive) category** property owned by the taxpayer is treated and accounted for separately

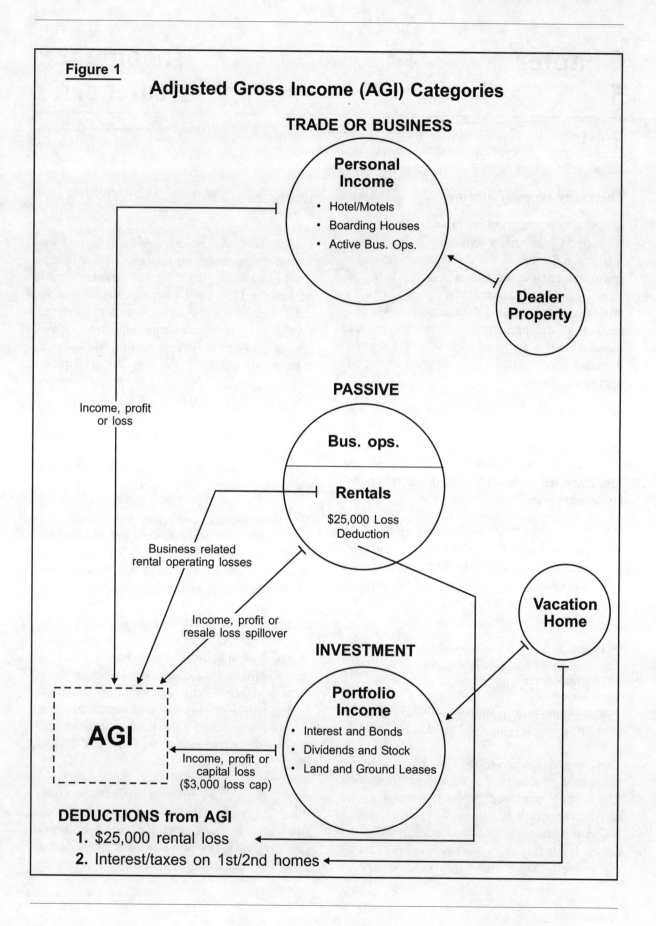

Figure 1

Adjusted Gross Income (AGI) Categories

TRADE OR BUSINESS

Personal Income
- Hotel/Motels
- Boarding Houses
- Active Bus. Ops.

Dealer Property

Income, profit or loss

PASSIVE

Bus. ops.

Rentals

$25,000 Loss Deduction

Business related rental operating losses

Income, profit or resale loss spillover

Vacation Home

INVESTMENT

Portfolio Income
- Interest and Bonds
- Dividends and Stock
- Land and Ground Leases

AGI

Income, profit or capital loss ($3,000 loss cap)

DEDUCTIONS from AGI
1. $25,000 rental loss
2. Interest/taxes on 1st/2nd homes

from that of every other parcel of rental property the taxpayer owns (unless in the same complex), called *tracking*. The tracking is necessary to maintain the integrity of suspended losses as available only for the offset of income or profit on the property which generated the loss. No such tracking requirement exists within the business income category or the portfolio income category.

Another accounting difference unique to the passive income category is the requirement that an annual operating loss on rentals be carried forward, called a *suspended loss*. Any rental operating loss which becomes suspended is only deductible in future years from income or profit reported on the properties that generated the loss.

Further, the rental operating loss cannot be used to offset income or profit in other categories, unless the owner qualifies for either:

- a real estate related business adjustment to his AGI; or

- the $25,000 rental loss deduction from his AGI.

In contrast, **portfolio investments**, such as land and management-free, triple-net and long-term leases, while not subject to the tracking of losses by parcel, gather together the annual income, profits and losses from all properties within the category. If an annual operating loss is incurred within the category, the loss is **carried forward** to offset income or profits in future years from any source within the portfolio category.

As for offsetting between the categories, the end-of-year income, profits and allowable losses are first totalled within each category. The totals from each of the categories are then brought together (subject to limitations on passive or portfolio losses) to establish the owner's AGI.

For the owner or broker to analyze and estimate the owner's annual income tax liability resulting from a sale or purchase of real estate, two major accounting components must first be estimated:

- the owner's AGI, derived from any net annual **operating income** and **sales profits** generated within each income category, less any loss from the trade or business category, loss on the sale of rentals, rental operating losses allowed for owners involved in real estate related businesses, and capital losses up to $3,000 from the portfolio category; and

- the owner's *taxable income*, the AGI less personal deductions, exemptions and any $25,000 rental property operating loss deduction.

Business category or owner's trade

Trade or **business** income and loss includes:

- earnings from the individual's trade or business and use of his real estate in the conduct of that trade or business, including ordinary income from the sale of parcels held as inventory by subdividers, builders and dealers [IRC §469(c)(6)(A)];

- income and losses from the individual's business opportunity (sole ownership, partnership, LLC or S corporation) and the real estate owned and used in the business, if the individual is a *material participant* in the management of the business [IRC §469(c)(1)]; and

- income and losses from the individual's owner-operated hotel, motel or inn operations (sole ownership, partnership, LLC or S corporation) with average occupancies of 30 days or less, if the individual is a *material participant* in management. [Rev. Regs. §1.469-1T(e)(3)(ii)(B)]

Rentals and passive category

An individual's real estate income property operations (excluding business category hotels, motels and inns), referred to by the IRS as *rental income*, are accounted for within the **passive income category** which includes:

- rents, expenses, interest, depreciation from annual operations and profit and losses from sales, of residential and non-residential *rental real estate* that has an average occupancy of more than 30 days; and

- income or losses from business opportunities owned or co-owned but not operated by the individual (no material participation in its management). [IRC §469(c)]

Income received from rental operations is often referred to as passive income. Ironically, for income property to be a rental, and thus reported within the passive income category, the owner must be committed to the *active management* of the property.

To be considered **active** in the management of a property, the landlord must have some legal responsibility to care for the property under his lease(s) or rental agreement(s). If the landlord has no responsibility for care and maintenance of the property, such as occurs in a long-term, triple-net lease agreement since the tenant cares for and maintains the property and structures, the income property is a portfolio category property, not a passive category rental property due to the lack of management requirements on the ownership.

An owner who rises to a higher level of activity in rental operations or in a real estate related profession, called a *material participant*, such as an owner/operator of rentals, a licensee providing real estate brokerage services or a real estate developer, qualifies to write off all rental operating losses for the year against income from all categories to reduce the owner's AGI, and thus his taxable income. [IRC §469(c)(7)]

Investments held for profit — portfolio category

Investment income, profits and losses taken by an individual, referred to as **portfolio income** by the IRS, include:

- interest earned on bonds, savings accounts and secured or unsecured notes (such as carryback trust deeds, interest on delayed §1031 reinvestment funds, and trust deed loans);

- annuities, dividends and royalties from personal property investments (stocks, bonds, commodities); and

- income, profits and losses from the ownership of land subject to ground leases, management-free, triple-net leased real estate and unimproved land held for profit on resale. [IRC §469(e)(1)(A)]

Chapter 6

Tiered tax rates for profits

This chapter sets forth the different tax rates for various amounts of ordinary income and gains, the definition of terms and the accounting procedures for reporting profits.

The batching and taxing of gains

As a professional tool in the hands of a broker and his agents, knowledge about income tax law is a valuable asset to be put to work when assisting clients in real estate transactions. Tax knowledge, dispensed as advice in an **opinion** given to a client by a broker or sales agent, becomes goodwill. In turn, the earning power of the goodwill generates further employment, i.e., more and superior listings, repeat clientele and the entrusted handling of larger dollar transactions.

Counseling a client on the tax aspects of a sale, reinvestment or exchange early on in an agency relationship typically induces an ongoing tax discussion. Of course, the objective of the discussion is to achieve the most favorable tax results available to the client without altering the underlying financial benefits and risks of a sale.

The earlier in the client relationship the tax discussion is held, the more likely the client is to consult with and ask questions of **other competent professionals** about his tax-related discussion with his broker. An early consultation with others allows the client to consider alternatives suggested by his broker, such as an installment sale or the purchase of replacement property in a §1031 reinvestment plan.

Encouraging a client to discuss the transaction with other advisors available to the client (or allowing the broker to do so before the client contacts them) actually results in their cooperation with the broker, unless the client has objectives not disclosed to the broker.

In situations involving other professional advisors, the broker still has a duty of care owed to his client to present the client with information the broker believes may impact the client or be contrary to the advice given to the client by others, such as the client's attorney. [**Brown** v. **Critchfield** (1980) 100 CA3d 858]

Through the collective efforts of all advisors, the transaction will be structured to meet the client's needs, including obtaining the best possible tax result under the circumstances.

A broker's influence over a client's decisions should be maintained, as it is important. The changing market conditions and the innuendos and nuances of real estate negotiations are usually better known to those brokers and agents who are regularly involved in real estate transactions than their clients. Also, alliances built by a broker with other professionals who are brought into a transaction by a client survive long after the transaction involving them is closed and mostly forgot.

Also, a broker's failure to recognize and coordinate activity in a transaction with other advisors of the client can produce disastrous results for the broker. A broker who **persuades** a client to rely on his advice over the contrary (and correct) advice of other professionals will be liable for any losses suffered by the client due to his (unsound) advice. [**In re Jogert, Inc.** (1991) 950 F2d 1498]

Worksheet estimates for the seller

The sale of every parcel of real estate, except dealer property, produces a profit for a seller if the price exceeds the seller's cost basis in the property. This profit formula, coupled with an understanding that the taking of a profit on the sale typically produces a tax liability owed to the federal (and state) tax collecting agency, is commonly known to all brokers and sales agents who represent sellers. This knowledge is probably also held by most sellers. Thus, a discussion entered into with a seller, initiated by the seller's broker or listing agent, will come as no surprise to the seller.

Before commencing a discussion about the tax aspects of a sale, a worksheet needs to be prepared. On it, the listing agent breaks down the profit taken on a sale into the different types of gains, called *batching*. Without first batching the gains, the seller's tax liability on closing a sale cannot be estimated. A secondary objective sought by a listing agent during a review of the profit tax liabilities estimated on the worksheet is a follow-up discussion on how to *exclude*, *exempt* or *defer* the profit or tax.

Thus, the seller who initially sought only to "cash out" his ownership of real estate might be converted to a §1031 reinvestment plan and acquire a replacement property. As an alternative, the seller might structure a sale as an installment sale to retain the earning power of his untaxed equity until the deferred tax on the profit is actually paid.

The worksheet conveniently suited for this introductory discussion about profit taxes is entitled the Individual Tax Analysis Form (INTAX). [See Form 351 accompanying this chapter]

The top half of the form is a mere review of the items of income, profit and loss which can be gathered to set the seller's taxable income or loss. However, the estimated taxable income for the year of the sale for a high income earner is not needed to batch the gains and estimate the profit tax on a sale.

A seller who is a **high income earner** is more likely to respond favorably to the agent's tax analysis than a low income earner. The agent's

INTAX analysis (of the profit only) should be made at the time the listing is taken (or shortly thereafter), and then again when a purchase agreement offer is reviewed for acceptance or a counteroffer. The discussion with the seller on each occasion should be limited to the amount of his profit on the sale, the batching of his different gains (in the profit) and the tax liability due on those gains.

The INTAX worksheet contains separate columns for calculating the standard income tax (SIT) and the alternative minimum income tax (AMT). The distinction between them is critical as it may well affect the seller's tax liability for his business, professional and investment income. However, the distinction has no influence on the profit taxes due on the sale of a capital asset. The taxation of gains (profit) on a sale are the same no matter the other income and deductions of a high income earner.

Thus, a listing broker's tax discussion of a capital asset is limited to the types of gains contained in the profit on the sale, and the tax due on those gains. [See Form 351 §§5.3 and 5.4]

It is unnecessary to use the INTAX to assist a buyer of real estate in the selection of property based on tax consequences. The Annual Property Operating Data (APOD) sheet provides the depreciation schedule for the only tax benefit available to a buyer during his ownership and operation of the property. [See **first tuesday** Form 352]

Further, the increase or decrease in the buyer's annual taxes brought about by his acquisition of a property is calculated on a Comparative Analysis Projection (CAP) Worksheet. [See **first tuesday** Form 353 §5.3]

When a seller enters into a §1031 reinvestment plan and acquires a replacement property of equal-or-greater debt and equal-or-greater equity than the property he sold, he has no profit which will be taxed. (Other formulas produce

Date:_____, 20_____

Client: _____

Prepared by: _____

This form and the Comparative Analysis Projection (CAP) (Form 353) are used in tandem to determine the federal tax impact on a proposed purchase or sale.

Items	Standard Income Tax (SIT)	Alternative Minimum Tax (AMT)
1. ADJUSTED GROSS INCOME (AGI)		
1.1 Salary/professional fees/wage . . . . (+) $_____		(+) $_____
1.2 Trade or Business income/loss. . . . . (+/-) $_____		(+/-) $_____
1.3 Sale of business property. . . . . (+/-) $_____		(+/-) $_____
1.4 Rental income/profit. . . . . (+) $_____		(+) $_____
1.5 Loss spillover of rental sales . . . . (-) $_____		(-) $_____
1.6 Business related rental operating loss . . . . (-) $_____		(-) $_____
1.7 Investment category income. . . . . (+) $_____		(+) $_____
1.8 Investment category capital losses (up to $3,000) (-) $_____		(-) $_____
1.9 Retirement, pension and annuity plans. . . . . . . (-) $_____		(-) $_____
1.10 ADJUSTED GROSS INCOME	$_____	$_____
2. REAL ESTATE RELATED DEDUCTIONS		
2.1 First/second home interest ($1,100,000 loan cap). (-) $_____		(-) $_____
2.2 Property taxes on residences . . . . (-) $_____		_____NONE_____
2.3 $25,000 rental loss deduction . . . . (-) $_____		(-) $_____
2.4 TOTAL REAL ESTATE RELATED DEDUCTIONS	(-) $_____	(-) $_____
3. OTHER DEDUCTIONS AND EXEMPTIONS		
3.1 Medical and dental. . . . . (-) $_____		(-) $_____
3.2 State income taxes. . . . . (-) $_____		_____NONE_____
3.3 Other deductions (charitable contributions, etc.) . . (-) $_____		(-) $_____
3.4 Personal exemption . . . . (-) $_____		_____NONE_____
3.5 AMT exemption . . . . _____NONE_____		(-) $_____
3.6 TOTAL OTHER DEDUCTIONS & EXEMPTIONS	(-) $_____	(-) $_____
4. TAXABLE INCOME	$_____	$_____
5. TAX BATCHING		
5.1 Net profits and short term losses . . . . $_____		$_____
5.2 Ordinary Income (Line 4 minus Line 5.1, but not less than zero). . . . $_____		$_____
(a) Tax: See Standard and AMT Tax Bracket Rates for line 5.2 . . $_____		$_____
5.3 Unrecaptured depreciation gain . . . . $_____		
(b) Tax: 15% in lowest bracket; 25% on balance . . . . $_____		$_____
5.4 Long-term capital gain. . . . . $_____		
(c) Tax: 5% in lowest bracket; 15% on balance . . . . $_____ (Lines 5.2, 5.3, and 5.4 are not to exceed Line 4)		$_____
6. INCOME TAX -- the **greater** amount of:(Line a,b,c)	$_____ or	(Line a,b,c) $_____

FORM 351　　　　10-00　　　　©2005 **first tuesday**, P.O. BOX 20069, RIVERSIDE, CA 92516 (800) 794-0494

the same no-tax result.) The avoidance of tax on the profit is demonstrated by the preparation of a Profit and Basis Recap Sheet. [See **first tuesday** Form 354; see Chapter 25]

However, the seller's §1031 reinvestment plan might entitle him only to a **partial §1031 exemption** due to the withdrawal of cash, receipt of a carryback note or a reduction in mortgage debt on the reinvestment. Here, the INTAX form section for batching the profit which will be taxed is most informative since it will help establish the amount of cash the seller will need to pay profit taxes on the sale in his partial §1031 transaction. [Internal Revenue Code §1031(b)]

The 25% and 15% profit tax ceilings

Typically, the sale of investment real estate or business-use real estate held for more than one year is at a price greater than the depreciated cost basis remaining in the property. Thus, the seller **takes a profit** on the sale.

The *gross profit* taken on a sale is the **difference between** the sales price and the seller's remaining cost basis in the property he sold (price minus basis equals profit). Deduct the **transactional costs** of the sale from the gross profit and the result you get is the *net profit*.

Net profit, like ordinary income, is taxed, unless *exempt* or *excluded* (or reduced by other losses, called an *offset*). [IRC §1001]

However, net profit is taxed as a **gain** and not as ordinary income. Several types of gain exist within the net profit on a sale, each gain having a different tax rate.

Before taxing the amount of profit taken on a sale of property, the amount is reduced by all short-term and long-term **capital losses** (current and carried forward) the seller has incurred due to other sales within the income category for the property sold. Thus, the net profit is established within each of the three income categories (business, passive and portfolio).

The net profits from each income category are then combined to set the owner's net profits for the year, called *net capital gains* by the IRS. It is the net capital gains that are batched by type of gain and taxed, unless first offset by losses incurred by the owner in his rental operations or business. [See IRS Form 1041 Schedule D, Part IV]

The tax rates applied to net profit taken on the sale of real estate depend on the type of gains the profit represents.

Net profits from real estate sales include gains, such as:

- *recaptured gain*, represented by the amount of excess *accelerated depreciation* (occasionally taken on acquisitions prior to mid-1986) over straight-line depreciation for the period, which is taxed at **ordinary income** rates ranging from 10% to 35%, a type of gain which will not exist on a sale after 2005;

- *unrecaptured gain*, represented by the total amount of *straight-line depreciation* deductions taken on the property sold (limited to the profit on a sale when the sales price is less than the price the seller paid for the property), which is taxed at the maximum rate of 25% [IRC §1(h)(1)(D); see Form 351 §5.3]; and

- *long-term gain*, also called *adjusted net capital gain* by the IRS, represented by the amount of profit remaining after subtracting all depreciation deductions (unrecaptured gain) from the net profit, which is taxed at the maximum rate of 15%. [IRC §1(h)(1)(C); see Form 351 §5.4]

Recaptured gain has no relevance today. For properties acquired in 1985 or early 1986, and then depreciated on an 18- or 19-year *accelerated cost recovery schedule (ACRS)*, only a very small portion of the profit on a sale in 2005 will be taxed at ordinary income rates, and none in 2006 and beyond. All other properties, no matter when acquired, will, as a result of today's cost recovery schedules, have no excess depreciation (over the straight-line amount) to declare. Thus, no portion of their profits will be taxed at ordinary income rates.

Unrecaptured gain is the deceptive title applied to the amount of all straight-line depreciation deductions taken on a property. Thus, on the sale of property, the portion of the net profit produced by the depreciation the seller deducted during the period of his ownership will be taxed at a maximum rate of 25% as unrecaptured gain.

For example, a seller of a rental property paid $1,000,000 for the property 10 years ago. His depreciation deductions taken during his ownership total $250,000, approximately 1/3 of the value of the improvements when he bought the property. He is now selling the property for $1,600,000, a profit of $850,000 over his remaining cost basis of $750,000. Also, his taxable income from other sources pushes him into the 28% ordinary income tax bracket. [See Form 351 §4]

The seller's profit of $850,000 is now broken down — *batched* — into:

- **unrecaptured gain**, consisting of the $250,000 in depreciation deductions, which is taxed at the 25% rate for a tax liability of $62,500 [See Form 351 §5.3]; and

- **long-term gain**, consisting of the remaining profit of $600,000, which is taxed at the 15% rate for a tax liability of $90,000.

The **long-term gain** is that portion of the net profit represented by the increase in the sales price received by the seller over the amount the seller paid to acquire the property (plus or minus new or destroyed improvements). If the long-term gain is not offset by losses incurred by the owner, the amount of the gain will be taxed at the maximum rate of 15%.

The reverse order of descending rates

Sometimes the net profits from a sale are greater than the seller's taxable income for the year of the sale due to excessive operating losses experienced by the seller on this or other properties (expenses exceeded income in rentals or the owner's business). If profits are greater than the taxable income, the profits taxed are limited to the amount of the taxable income. Thus, excess rental or business operating losses have **offset profits** on the sale.

However, profits are offset from taxation in the **reverse order of descending rates**. Thus, the result is that the lowest profit bracket of 15% (long-term gains) is the first to be offset by the owner's operating losses.

For example, consider the same facts as in the prior example, except that the seller suffered a $200,000 loss operating his rentals and his business (which motivated him to sell the property). Thus, his taxable income amounts to $650,000, less than the $850,000 profit taken on the sale. He will pay profit tax only on the $650,000 taxable income as follows:

- an **unrecaptured gain** of $250,000, taxed at the 25% rate; and

- a **long-term gain** of $400,000, consisting of only a portion of the remaining $600,000 balance of the profit, and taxed at the 15% rate for a tax liability of $60,000, not $90,000, the amount which would have been paid without the operating losses.

Thus, the seller receives a tax savings of $30,000 to subsidize 15% of the seller's $200,000 operating loss.

Other types of profit do exist. Profit on the sale of coins and art is called a *collectibles gain* and is taxed at a maximum rate of 28%, unless the collectibles sold are the subject of a §1031 reinvestment exemption. Profit taken on the sale of small business stock is called a *§1202 gain* and is also taxed at a maximum rate of 28%. [IRC §§1(h)(4); 1(h)(5); 1(h)(7)]

Netting gains and taxing priorities

The total amount of all income, profits and allowable losses from each income category is called *adjusted gross income (AGI)*. AGI, less any personal and rental loss deductions, becomes the seller's *taxable income*. [IRC §63(a)]

To determine the tax liability of the seller, the **taxable income** is broken down into two major components:

- *net profit* (net capital gain) [See Form 351 §5.1]; and

- *ordinary income*. [See Form 351 §5.2]

To accomplish this breakdown of the taxable income, the net profits within each income category are added together. The combined total is then entered as the **net profit component** of the taxable income. [See Form 351 §5.1]

The combined net profit is then subtracted from taxable income. The result is the amount which will be taxed as ordinary income. [See Form 351 §5.2]

Ordinary income is taxed at SIT rates ranging from 10% to a ceiling of 35%, or at AMT rates of 26% and 28%, whichever produces the greater amount of taxes. [See Figure 1]

Batching gains to set taxes

To calculate the tax on **net profits**, profits are broken down and *batched* into the types of gain which constitute the net profit. Then, profits are taxed by their type of gain in the **order of descending rates**, until no profit remains to be taxed:

- first, any *recaptured gain* (excess depreciation), taxed at ordinary income rates (10% to 35%);

- next, any *collectibles gain* and business stock gain, taxed at a 28% rate;

- next, any *unrecaptured gain* (straight-line depreciation), taxed at a 25% rate; and

- last, any *long-term gain* not offset by operating losses from rentals or business, taxed at a 15% rate. [See IRS Form 1041, Schedule D Part IV]

Earnings on the sale of **dealer property**, also called *inventory*, are reported as business income, not profits on the sale of assets. Dealer property is property held primarily for sale to customers of a business, not for investment or productive use in a business. [IRC §1231(b)]

§121 principal residence exclusion

Profits remaining on the sale of a **principal residence** which are not offset by the IRC §121 $250,000 per person *profit exclusion* are reported as a short- or long-term gain (held, respectively, less or more than one year).

For example, a homeowner and spouse paid $250,000 years ago for their principal residence which they are now offering for sale at $900,000. On the sale, they will take a profit of $650,000 since a principal residence is a capital asset. They qualify for a combined §121 exclusion from profit tax of $500,000. Thus, they must report a profit of $150,000.

The homeowners did not take any depreciation deductions on the residence as a home office or as a rental, in whole or in part. Thus, their cost basis remains unchanged as the price they originally paid for the residence.

Further, their taxable income exceeds the profit on the home and places them in the 28% ordinary income reporting bracket. Thus, the $150,000 in profit remaining (after deducting their combined $500,000 principal residence

Figure 1

2005 Tax Rate Schedule

Single		
If taxable income is over —	**But not over —**	**The tax is:**
$0	$7,300	10% of the amount over $0
$7,300	$29,700	$730 plus 15% of the amount over 7,300
$29,700	$71,950	$4,090.00 plus 25% of the amount over 29,700
$71,950	$150,150	$14,652.50 plus 28% of the amount over 71,950
$150,150	$326,450	$36,548.50 plus 33% of the amount over 150,150
$326,450	no limit	$94,727.50 plus 35% of the amount over 326,450

Married Filing Jointly or Qualifying Widow(er)		
If taxable income is over —	**But not over —**	**The tax is:**
$0	$14,600	10% of the amount over $0
$14,600	$59,400	$1,460.00 plus 15% of the amount over 14,600
$59,400	$119,950	$8,180 plus 25% of the amount over 59,400
$119,950	$182,800	$23,317.50 plus 28% of the amount over 119,950
$182,800	$326,450	$40,915.50 plus 33% of the amount over 182,800
$326,450	no limit	$88,320 plus 35% of the amount over 326,450

Married Filing Separately		
If taxable income is over —	**But not over —**	**The tax is:**
$0	$7,300	10% of the amount over $0
$7,300	$29,700	$730 plus 15% of the amount over 7,300
$29,700	$59,975	$4,090 plus 25% of the amount over 29,700
$59,975	$91,400	$11,658.75 plus 28% of the amount over 59,975
$91,400	$163,225	$20,457.75 plus 33% of the amount over 91,400
$163,225	no limit	$44,160.00 plus 35% of the amount over 163,225

profit exclusion) will be reported as a long-term capital gain and taxed at the 15% rate, a tax liability on the sale of the residence of $22,500. [See Form 351 §5.4]

However, no loss on the sale of the principal residence may be reported or used to offset investment or business category income or profits.

Installment sale profit reporting

Also, the profit allocated to any note carried back by a seller on an IRC §453 **installment sale** is reported each year as the principal payment is received. The profit allocated to the principal in the installment payments is also batched (by the type of gains taken on the sale) and reported as principal is received on the note. The first profits in the down payment and installments to be taxed (until they no longer exist) are the gains with the highest rate among the gains involved.

For example, real estate used to provide warehouse space for a seller's business is sold for the **net sales price** of $1,000,000. Terms include a $100,000 down payment, the buyer's assumption of a $400,000 mortgage and the execution of a $500,000 carryback note for the balance of the price. Depreciation deductions of $150,000 have been taken during his ownership, leaving an adjusted cost basis of $500,000 at the time of sale. Thus, the profit on the sale is $500,000 (price minus basis equals profit).

As a result, the installment sale's *contract ratio* of **profit-to-equity** ($500,000/$600,000) is 83.3%. Accordingly, the down payment of $100,000 is 83.3% profit ($83,333) and the carryback note of $500,000 is 83.3% profit ($416,666), both amounts making up the total profit on the sale.

Also, as the result of batching, $150,000 of the profits is *unrecaptured gain* (depreciation),

which will be reported first before reporting any long-term gain on the sale. Thus, profit taxes will be paid as cash is received from the down payment, and later as installments of principal are received.

Thus, the entire profit of $83,333 in the down payment will be reported as unrecaptured depreciation gain taxed at the 25% rate. The balance of the unrecaptured depreciation gain will be reported on 83.3% of the principal payments as these are received on the carryback note, until the unrecaptured gain has been fully reported. All remaining profit received in subsequent installments on the carryback note will be long-term gains taxed at 15% when received. [See Form 351 §§5.3 and 5.4]

The alternative minimum tax

The tax on ordinary income must be **calculated twice**, once under the SIT rates and again under the AMT rates.

Not so for profits.

Whichever SIT or AMT calculation sets the highest amount will be the tax paid on the ordinary income portion of the taxable income. [IRC §55(a); see Form 351 §§5.2(a) and 6]

The AMT rates on **ordinary AMT income** (taxable income less profits) are:

- 26% on amounts up to $175,000; and

- 28% on amounts over $175,000. [IRC §55(b)(1)(A)]

When reporting AMT, straight-line depreciation taken on a property is reported as **unrecaptured gain** and taxed at 25%, the same handling and rate as the ceiling rate for SIT treatment of unrecaptured gain.

Likewise, the 15% long-term gain rate ceiling applies to AMT reporting of long-term profits. [IRC §55(b)(3)(C)]

SECTION B

§1031
Fundamentals

Chapter 7

Like-kind §1031 property: real and personal

This chapter identifies the types of property which are §1031 like-kind property and distinguishes those that do not qualify as §1031 property in a real estate transaction.

Qualified to sell or buy under §1031

Properties owned either for **productive use** in a trade or business, or for rental or other **investment** purposes are referred to as either *like-kind property* or *qualified property* in a §1031 reinvestment plan. [Internal Revenue Code §1031(a)(1)]

The profit taken on the sale of real estate (or personal property) is exempt from income tax if both the real estate sold and the real estate purchased qualify as Internal Revenue Code (IRC) §1031 like-kind property in the hands of the owner seeking the profit tax exemption.

Property which does not qualify as §1031 property, called *unqualified property*, *unlike-kind property* or simply *other property*, includes:

- **dealer property**, such as inventory items and real estate bought for resale rather than for business use, (rental) operating income or for increase in value due to appreciation or inflation [IRC §1031(a)(2)(A)];

- **stock** (although it can be issued in exchange for real estate under a §351/§1032 tax-exempt exchange) [IRC §1031(a)(2)(B)];

- **bonds**, such as certificates of indebtedness or interest-bearing obligations issued by corporations or government entities [IRC §1031(a)(2)(B)];

- promissory **notes**, whether secured or unsecured, that are sold or purchased, such as carryback notes [IRC §1031(a)(2)(B)];

- other security devices or **evidences of indebtedness** that are similar to security devices, such as post-dated checks or assignments of payment rights held by trust deed lenders to evidence debt [IRC §1031(a)(2)(C)];

- **choses in action** (payment rights or rights to receive future payments), such as a seller's (assignable) interest under a purchase agreement [IRC §1031(a)(2)(F)];

- **beneficial interests** in a trust (other than a revocable inter vivos trust) [IRC §1031(a)(2)(E)];

- **foreign real estate** located outside the U.S. [IRC §1031(h)]; and

- **fractional interests** in co-ownerships conducted as tax partnerships (although an interest in a partnership can be *issued* by a partnership in exchange for its receipt of real estate as a §721 tax-exempt exchange). [IRC §1031(a)(2)(D); see Chapter 12]

Also, properties exchanged between **related persons** must be held for two years, called a *holding period*, by both persons before the profit made on the sale of the property exchanged is exempt and the property acquired is qualified as §1031 property for sale or further exchange. [IRC §1031(f)(1)]

If a resale of property exchanged between related persons occurs within two years, the property acquired is considered disposition property in the hands of the seller under the exchange and fails to be like-kind property. The exchange no longer qualifies for the §1031 exemption. [See Chapter 1]

Additionally, depreciable property used productively in a **trade** or **business** has a one-year holding period before it qualifies to be sold or exchanged as §1031 property. After one year of ownership, **business-use property** can then be sold or exchanged as §1031 property. [IRC §1231(b)]

Investment vs. trade or business property

Section 1031 (like-kind) property consists of two classifications of property:

- investment property, called *capital assets* [IRC §1221]; and

- trade or business property. [IRC §1231]

Thus, the principal residence of the taxpayer does not qualify as §1031 property (even though it is a capital asset) since it is not used in a business or held for investment purposes.

Investment property includes:

- rental properties, residential and nonresidential;

- vacation homes held for profit or resale [See Chapter 8]; and

- investment (portfolio) real estate. [IRC §1221]

The investment property does not include property held primarily for sale to customers of the owner's trade or business, called *dealer property*. Inventory and other **dealer property**, such as subdivided lots, land held as builder inventory or properties purchased at auction for the purpose of renovation and resale, are held for immediate sale in the ordinary course of the owner's trade or business. Dealer property does not qualify as property used in a trade or business even though it is owned by the trade or business. [IRC §1231(b)]

Like investment property, real estate used as the premises which houses the owner's trade or business or the operation of a hotel or motel is §1031 property.

Unlike investment property, trade or business property must be owned for a **one-year holding period** before it qualifies as like-kind property to be replaced in a §1031 reinvestment plan by acquiring trade or business property, rentals or investment property. [IRC §1231(b)(1)]

Similarly, rentals and investment property can be sold and then replaced by trade or business property, rentals or investment property in a §1031 reinvestment plan.

Small investors can exchange too

Many novice investors owning one-to-four unit properties and small businesses whose business occupies a building they own mistakenly believe §1031 benefits are available exclusively to wealthy investors who own large income projects. However, no investment or business-use property is too small (or too big) to qualify for §1031 tax-exempt treatment. The property's **dollar value** is irrelevant.

By planning his sales and acquisition, an investor can build his estate (personal net worth) and avoid the diminution of wealth wrought by profit taxes on the sale of unwanted property. The investor need only coordinate a §1031 reinvestment plan to sell, avoid receipt of the net sales proceeds and identify and acquire replacement property with the proceeds.

Also, a **leasehold interest** in real estate qualifies as §1031 property if the remaining term of the lease period exceeds 30 years, including options to extend or renew. [Revenue Regulations §1.1031(a)-1(c)]

No limitations are placed on size, value and location of the property involved in a §1031 reinvestment plan, as long as the properties are located within the United States. An owner can reside in California, sell Texas real estate and purchase Hawaiian replacement property.

A §1031 reinvestment plan can involve the sale of one or more parcels of undeveloped real estate and the purchase of one or more parcels of improved real estate, for use in a business or to be operated as rentals.

The reverse is also true, but until 2006, it may trigger ordinary income reporting for the *recapture* of excess accelerated depreciation taken on improved property purchased in 1985 or 1986.

Two or more investors may be brought together in a "syndicated" transaction, called a *consolidation exchange*. Each investor sells his solely owned like-kind property and consolidates the net sales proceeds with those of other investors, each acquiring a fractional interest in one replacement property which itself qualifies as §1031 property.

For example, a $30,000 equity in one parcel of real estate plus a $70,000 equity in another parcel of real estate can be sold and replaced with a single parcel of real estate with an equity of $100,000 or more.

However, the reverse is not always true. The sale or exchange by one investor of his **fractional co-ownership interest** in §1031 property that requires less than unanimous consent to sell or exchange, refinance or lease, such as occurs in the co-ownership of rental property under a limited liability investment (LLC), does not qualify the investor's separate interest as §1031 property for a reinvestment plan. [IRC §1031(a)(2)(D); see Chapter 12]

Section 1031 tax-free reinvestment of sales proceeds encourages estate building into bigger, more efficient and more suitable properties. The tax which would otherwise have been paid on the profit made from the property sold is retained, working for the investor.

Thus, an investor will have more after-tax dollars working for him if he sells his property and buys replacement property in a **§1031 reinvestment plan**. Conversely, he can cash out, report profits, pay capital gains taxes and then reinvest the greatly diminished after-tax funds.

Adaptation for §1031 treatment

Taxwise, an owner usually holds real estate for one of four purposes:

- **immediate resale** for business income, called *inventory, dealer property* or *disposition property*;

- **business use**, such as real estate in which the owner operates his trade or business;

- **investment** for rental income from operations or long-term profit on resale; or

- **personal use**, such as the owner's principal residence.

Property held for **immediate resale** to customers in the ordinary course of a real estate business, such as lots in a subdivision or new construction, is referred to as dealer property or inventory.

Dealer property is business inventory, not property used productively for the operation of the business or a capital asset such as a rental. Dealer property generates *ordinary income* on resale, not profits as occurs on the resale of a productive property held and occupied by the business for more than 12 months. Thus, the sale of dealer property is not entitled to §1031 tax-exempt benefits or capital gains tax treatment when sold. [IRC §§1031(a)(2)(A), 1231(b); see Chapter 9]

Property used in a business or held for investment, such as unimproved land, can later be reclassified as dealer property and can no longer qualify as §1031 property. This transformation can occur at any time during ownership.

The owner alters the tax status of his ownership by simply modifying his intent and conduct in his use of the property. For example, an owner shifts his goals from holding property for investment or business use purposes to retail sales purposes by initiating plans to subdivide land previously held for investment and then marketing the resulting parcels for sale.

Stock in trade (inventory/dealer property) is specifically excluded from qualifying for the §1031 profit reporting exemption since it is held and marketed to be sold in the *ordinary course of business*. Thus it generates ordinary income on its sale, not a profit. [IRC §1031(a)(2)(A)]

Residential and nonresidential rental properties, being capital assets called *rentals*, qualify as §1031 investment property.

Property held for investment

Capital assets make up the *investment* classification of §1031 property unless selectively excluded. Capital assets do not include:

- inventory (dealer property) [IRC §1221(a)(1)];

- §1231 property used to house a business (however, this does qualify as §1031 property under trade or business assets when held for more than one year) [IRC §1221(a)(2)];

- copyrighted material and literary, musical or artistic compositions held by the creator of the material or the person for whom it was produced [IRC §1221(a)(3)];

- accounts receivable, such as unpaid rent [IRC §1221(a)(4)]; and

- government debt obligations, such as treasury bills, notes and bonds. [IRC §1221(a)(5)]

Real estate, furnishings, stamps/coins, gems, paintings, antiques, precious metals, manuscripts and other valuables held for long-term appreciation qualify as **capital assets**, unless held or acquired for immediate resale as inventory in a trade or business.

For example, an owner has several individual residential rental properties held for investment and one residence held for his personal use.

The residences held for investment (rental) purposes can be sold and purchased in a §1031 reinvestment plan. However, an owner's personal residence does not qualify as §1031 property since it is not owned and operated as either a rental or to house his business.

Yet, a **personal residence** qualifies as a capital asset since it is not excluded from the definition of an IRC §1221 asset. Thus, profits upon sale of a personal residence which are not excluded from taxes under the $250,000 IRC §121 exclusion are reported as capital gains, not ordinary income (and any capital loss is disallowed since it is a personal loss).

A leasehold estate in property that has a remaining period of over 30 years on the lease term (including extension or renewal periods), fee or equitable ownership of residential and nonresidential rentals, vacation property and land held for long-term profit are investment properties. Thus, they qualify as §1031 properties.

Property used in a trade or business

Trade or business property includes real estate used primarily by the owner to house and operate his trade or business. Trade or business property is not strictly classified as a capital asset. For purposes of §1031 treatment, trade and business property is subject to a **different holding period**, after which it is "treated" as a capital asset for profit tax purposes.

To qualify as §1031 property on its sale or exchange, business property must first be held by the owner for **more than one year**. [IRC §1231(b)]

Examples of property used in a trade or business include land and its nonresidential improvements, parking lots, timberland, hotels, motels, inns and vacation rentals not personally used by the owner.

Property not considered trade or business property, even though owned by the business, includes:

- inventory property, such as lots or homes in a subdivision created by the owner [IRC §1231(b)(1)(A)];

- dealer property, bought to be immediately resold, or held to be improved and sold [IRC §1231(b)(1)(B)];

- copyrights [IRC §1231(b)(1)(C)];

- timber, coal or domestic iron ore [IRC §1231(b)(2)];

- livestock [IRC §1231(b)(3)]; and

- unharvested crops on land used for trade or business — unless the land is held for more than one year and the crop and the land are sold or exchanged at the same time and to the same person. [IRC §1231(b)(4)]

Disposition property: §1031 nullified

Replacement properties acquired in a §1031 reinvestment plan that are to be immediately resold in a cash-out sale or conveyed to another individual or taxable entity are called *disposition property* and do not qualify as §1031 property. The attributes of ownership regarding the use and operation of disposition property by the owner are the same as for dealer property.

When **replacement property** is acquired on the sale or exchange of other property and put to some dealer activity, such as promptly cashing out or subdividing, restoring, renovating, building or improving the property and then immediately reselling it in a **cash-out sale**, the disposition disqualifies the replacement property as §1031 property.

These properties acquired with the intent to cash out on a resale are tainted with the intention to manage them as *dealer property*, often by spending time and effort to prepare them (and upgrade them) for resale. Simply put, the properties are acquired to be upgraded and "flipped" for a profit in a cash-out sale as inventory of a trade or occupation. [**Little** v. **Commissioner of Internal Revenue** (9th Cir. 1997) 106 F3d 1445]

Property purchased by an individual to complete a reinvestment and is promptly conveyed or sold to a corporation under IRC §351 (in a tax-free exchange for the issuance of stock) is not classified as property acquired by the individual for productive use in a trade or business or for investment. It is disposition property. The owner immediately on acquisition conveyed it to an entity (the corporation) that is a separate taxpayer. [IRS Revenue Ruling 75-292]

Conversely, when an owner acquires replacement property and later deeds it to a partnership or LLC for the same percentage of ownership as the percentage he held in the replacement property, such as in a *syndicated exchange* or a *consolidation exchange*, the further conveyance is not a disposition of the property.

The further conveyance to a partnership or LLC does not alter the tax impact on the owner who previously or concurrently **acquired title** to property on his completion of a §1031 reinvestment. The income tax reporting by the owner after acquiring the property produces the same tax result whether he retains title or further deeds the property to a partnership or LLC. However, this is not so for further conveyances to a corporation on completion of a §1031 reinvestment. [**Magneson** v. **Commissioner** (1985) 753 F2d 1490]

Chapter 8

Vacation homes

This chapter analyzes a vacation home as §1031 like-kind property held for investment.

Held for investment and personal use

A **vacation home**, also known as a second home, is any dwelling unit, such as a house, apartment, condominium, mobile home, recreational vehicle or boat, personally used by the owner, co-owners, their families or friends as a residence other than as a principal residence.

As a second home, the real estate **taxes** and **interest**, accrued and paid on loans secured by the vacation home, are deductible. The deductions are allowed whether the property is rented to others or occupied solely by the owner, without concern for the length of occupancy by the owner or the tenants and transient occupants who pay rent for their stay on the property. [Internal Revenue Code §§163(h)(4)(A)(iii), 164, 280A(e)(2)]

However, the deduction of repair and maintenance expenses is limited if the home is rented. Also, depreciation deductions are not allowed when the property is rented if the owner, his family and friends personally use the vacation home beyond a threshold period of days.

Interest deductions for second homes

Two categories of **interest deductions** exist for all loans secured by the first or second home:

- interest on purchase or improvement loan balances up to a combined amount of $1,000,000, called *purchase-assist loans*; and

- interest on all other loan amounts up to $100,000, called *home equity loans*.

Due to the special home loan interest deduction rules, the owner may deduct the interest accrued and paid on those loan amounts which funded payment of the purchase price or costs of improvement. The loans must be secured by the owner's principal residence or second home. Without the home loan rule, the interest would not be deductible since the loans constitute a generally undeductible personal expense, not a business or investment expense. [IRC §163(h)]

Also, equity loans secured by the first or second residence are controlled by the home loan interest deduction rules, regardless of whether the loan's net proceeds are used for personal or investment/business purposes.

Interest paid on that portion of the total of the loan balances on the first and second homes which exceeds $1,100,000 is not deductible.

The deduction of interest paid on the first and second home loans reduces taxable income under both the standard income tax (SIT) and alternative minimum tax (AMT) reporting rules.

In contrast, the real estate property tax deduction on the first and second homes only reduces the owner's SIT, not his AMT.

Real estate property taxes paid on the vacation home may be deducted from SIT income in their entirety, without reduction for having rented the property for any period of time. [IRC §164]

Deductibility of expenses

Expenses the owner incurs in the repair and maintenance of the vacation home may or may not be partially deducted. **Deductibility of expenses** is based on whether:

1. The vacation home is **used exclusively** by the owner and his family or friends and is not rented, in which case the use is solely personal and the expenses for repair and maintenance cannot be written off as a deduction against any income. [IRC §280A(a)]

2. The vacation home is rented for periods totaling **14 days or less**, in which case no expenses can be written off (and no rental income is reported). [IRC §280A(g)]

3. The vacation home is rented for periods **exceeding a total of 14 days**, in which case the expenses incurred to operate the vacation home are partially deductible. Deductions are limited to a pro rata amount of the expenses, a percentage based on the number of days rented over the total number of days the vacation home was occupied for any purpose, including the personal use by the owner, co-owners, their families, friends, and all other occupants who did or did not pay rent for their stay. Days qualifying as repair and maintenance days are excluded from the formula. [IRC §280A(e); Revenue Regulations §1.280A-1(e)(6)]

A capital asset and portfolio property

A vacation home bought as a real estate investment and used exclusively for personal enjoyment or intermittently rented for any length of time is a *capital asset*. [IRC §1221]

A vacation home personally used for any period during the year is not a trade or business property even though guests renting the property are transient occupants with an average occupancy of 30 days or less. [IRC §§1231(b)(1), 280A(a)]

Depending on the days in an average rental occupancy period, a vacation home which is personally used by the owner and also rented to others is reported as either:

- a rental property in the passive income category; or

- an investment property in the portfolio income category.

To be a rental property, the vacation home income must come from occupancies which average more than 30 days. If the average occupancy is 30 days or less, the vacation home cannot be classified as a rental. Thus, it is not a passive income category property.

Most vacation homes are rented to transient occupants for periods of several days to a week or two, typically under a guest occupancy agreement. Accordingly, the average occupancy of a transient occupant is 30 days or less.

When a capital asset is held for investment, such as a personal use vacation home rented to transient occupants, its income and expenses are reported in the *portfolio income category*. Other assets held for investment and profit on resale as portfolio properties include undeveloped land, ground leases, triple net leases, trust deed (loan) notes, interest income, stocks, dividends and bonds.

Conversely, if the dwelling unit is a vacation rental which is **not** personally used as a second home by the owner, his family or friends, the nature of the business of renting to transient occupants (for an average occupancy of less than 30 days) would establish the vacation rental as a *trade or business property*. The income expenses, interest and depreciation for the **vacation rental property** would be treated the same as for a motel, inn or hotel operation and not as for a rental or investment property. Again, any personal use of the property would make the vacation rental a second home and a portfolio category investment.

Depreciation deductions based on use

The depreciation of a vacation home to recover the cost of the improvements is a deduction allowed to offset rental income from the property and income from other sources. However, depreciation may not be taken on a vacation home if the owner, co-owners, their families or friends occupy the vacation home during the year for periods of personal use totaling more than 14 days or 10% of the days the property is rented, whichever number of days is greater. [IRC §280A(d)(1)]

For example, a vacation home is rented to others during the year at a fair rental rate for a total of 140 days or less. The owner and others who pay less than fair rent, or no rent at all, occupy the property for no more than 14 days. Here, the owner may take the full amount of his scheduled depreciation deduction.

However, should the property be rented out for more than 140 days during the year, for example, 200 days, then the total number of days of personal use the owner may make of the vacation home without losing the right to depreciation deductions may exceed 14 days, limited to 10% of the days rented, being 20 days in this example. [IRC §§163(h)(4)(A)(i)(II), 280A(d)(1)]

Two straight-line **depreciation schedules** are mandated to be used for income tax reporting. The depreciation schedules for residential vacation properties are:

- 27.5 years straight-line depreciation for standard (regular) income tax reporting; and

- 40 years straight-line depreciation for alternative minimum income tax reporting.

The days of personal use affecting the deduction of expenses and depreciation do not include days during which the owner conducts a full-time schedule of repair and maintenance on the property. [IRC §280A(d)(2)]

For example, the owner and his family arrive on Saturday afternoon at their vacation home to stay until the following Saturday. The primary purpose for the stay is to relax and perform annual repairs and maintenance to prepare the property for the season. They do no maintenance work on Saturday. The owner and his wife relax the entire week, fishing, walking and visiting neighbors. They occasionally assist other family members in the maintenance work on the property.

Some members of the family work substantially full-time each day, except for the day of arrival and departure. They all leave on the following Saturday. Here, the purpose for the use of the vacation home is not personal. Thus, none of the days spent at the property are personal use days. [Revenue Regulations §1.280A-1(e)(7), Example 3]

For personal use days, when the occupation by the owner and his family is not for the purpose of maintenance, the day of arrival and day of departure are considered to be only one day if the total hours at the property during the two days does not exceed 24 hours. [Prop. Rev. Regs. §1.280A-1(f)]

A vacation home as §1031 property

Consider the owner of a vacation home who purchased the property for the personal use of his family and friends. The objective of the purchase was to own the property until it was no longer of use to him as his vacation home.

The owner is now working with a broker to buy another, more expensive vacation home in a different resort area of more interest to the family members. The owner informs the broker he is selling the vacation home and taking a large profit and he is unsure of the tax consequences.

Regarding the profit on his sale of other types of property, the owner is aware he can avoid profit taxes under:

- the Internal Revenue Code (IRC) §121 $250,000 profit exclusion for each owner or occupant should he sell his principal residence; and

- the IRC §1031 profit tax exemption for the sale of trade or business property, rentals and other properties held for investment, if sold as part of a reinvestment plan.

However, the owner is unaware of any tax avoidance for profits from the sale of a vacation home that he and his family have enjoyed as a personal residence and was rented infrequently. He asks his broker what the broker knows about the profit tax avoidance available on a vacation home.

The broker, aware of the tax status of vacation homes, points out that the use of a vacation home as a personal residence solely for family and friends to enjoy is not a factor in the property's tax status. Rather, the intention to hold the vacation home for eventual resale at a profit establishes the vacation home as an investment property in the *portfolio income category* and thus a like-kind §1031 property.

The owner had erroneously thought his personal use of the vacation home would disqualify the sale of the property for a §1031 tax-free reinvestment of the net proceeds from the sale.

Here, the vacation home was never intended to be a vacation residence to be retained in the family as property held in trust, such as a retreat estate made available for the personal use of succeeding generations. Thus, a vacation home used exclusively or primarily for personal use and held as an investment for eventual resale may be sold as part of a tax-exempt reinvestment plan to acquire a replacement vacation home or any other type of like-kind property. [IRC §1031(a); IRS Private Letter Ruling 8103117]

Chapter 9

Avoiding dealer status

This chapter contrasts ordinary income assets, such as dealer property and inventory, from capital assets and trade or business production assets which are §1031 like-kind property.

The owner's intended use of property

Real estate held by an owner primarily for **investment** and **profit** is classified as a *capital asset*. Capital assets include property actively operated as *rentals* (passive income category) or held as a management-free investment for income or profit (portfolio income category). Properties in both income categories are classified as *§1031 investment properties*. [Internal Revenue Code §1221(a)(1)]

Real estate used to house or facilitate the operation of an owner's **trade** or **business** and owned for more than one year is classified as a *trade or business asset*. For purposes of the §1031 profit tax exemption, real estate used as a trade or business asset is treated the same as a capital asset, the only distinctions between them being the business use of the property and a requisite one-year ownership of the property prior to sale or exchange.

Any crop on the business asset (such as on a farm) at the time the asset is sold is considered part of the business asset entitled to capital gains profit tax treatment, if both are acquired by the same buyer at the same time.

On the other hand, real estate held primarily as **inventory for sale** to customers in the ordinary course of an owner's trade or business is an *ordinary income asset*, more commonly called *dealer property*. [IRC §§64, 1231(b)(1)(A), 1231(b)(1)(B)]

An **ordinary income asset** typically includes inventories bought and actively sold in what could be construed as a business. Inventory includes properties such as developable or subdivisible land and lots sold in cash-out sales by a developer or properties acquired at foreclosure by an individual with the intent to liquidate them and acquire more foreclosure properties (even after operating them as rentals for 12 months). [**Little** v. **Commissioner of Internal Revenue** (9th Cir. 1997) 106 F3d 1445]

Owners of dealer property sold at a price exceeding its cost do not take a profit on its sale. Dealer property is inventory, a non-capital asset. On the sale of a parcel by a developer to a customer, the business has *ordinary income*, not profit. The denial of capital gains (profit) treatment on the sale of a parcel of real estate held as inventory for sale to customers is due to its classification as dealer property.

Likewise, dealer property is not afforded the **deferred reporting** of profit tax on installment sales under the standard income tax (SIT) and alternative minimum tax (AMT), since ordinary income is reported and taxed when received. With the exception of the deferral of ordinary income on the installment sale of farms, vacant residential lots and short-term time shares, ordinary income, be it cash or paper, is classified as dealer property. [IRC §453(l)]

Conversely, taxes on gains from a profit taken on the sale of a capital asset are deferred to future years when the price is paid in installments. [IRC §§453(b)(2)(A), 453(l)(1)]

Also, an Internal Revenue Code (IRC) §1031 tax-exempt reinvestment is only allowed when both the property sold and the replacement property purchased are real estate which qualify as held for productive use in a business or as investment property. Dealer property and other inventory items sold as merchandise in a trade or business are excluded from being classified as §1031 like-kind property. [IRC §1031(a)(2)(A)]

Usually, dealer property issues arise when a property is sold in a **cash-out transaction**, devoid of a continued investment in replacement real estate.

Dealer property vs. capital assets

Whether real estate is dealer property or a capital asset depends on the circumstances existing during the entire period of ownership of the property, from purchase to the ultimate resale.

Also, the ownership of property by an individual must be distinguished from the ownership of property by an *entity* (LLC, limited partnership or corporation), co-owned as a syndicated investment by **two or more individuals**. When the entity is the owner of a property, such as land held for investment, the intention and conduct of the entity during its ownership is tested against the factors used to determine dealer property.

The individuals who receive distributions of the entity's earnings are not the owners of the property. Thus, their personal dealer activities are unrelated to the entity's ownership of the land and are not in issue.

Ownership factors which distinguish dealer property from investment property include:

- the owner's intentions when acquiring the property (to either take steps to promptly cash out on its resale or hold it as a rental or an investment for resale at a profit);

- the owner's intentions manifested while owning and operating the property;

- duration of ownership before advertising or listing the property for sale;

- use of the property at the time of sale;

- the frequency, continuity and substance of the owner's sales of other properties;

- the extent of advertising for buyers, property listings for sale, other promotional sales activities and personal earnings from the sale of other similar properties by the owner;

- the time and effort devoted to the sale of the property by the owner;

- the extent of subdividing, construction of improvements, planning, zoning efforts, arranging for utilities, etc. for the property; and

- the nature and extent of the owner's regular business as related to the sale of the property. [**Matthews** v. **Commissioner of Internal Revenue** (6th Cir. 1963) 315 F2d 101]

No single factor is conclusive. Usually, the frequency and substantiality of the owner's sales play the most important role. Is he or is he not in the business of selling this type of real estate to customers paying cash?

For example, an owner sells several similar properties, single-family residences, in cash-out sales. He has held the properties for a relatively short period of time, two years. Here, the real estate is more likely to receive dealer status, as it resembles inventory, rather than be classified as property held for income or as an appreciable investment before a cash-out sale occurs. [**Suburban Realty Company** v. **United States** (5th Cir. 1980) 615 F2d 171]

For an owner's **cashed-out sales** activities, the greater the frequency of sales and the more the owner demonstrates he intends to buy, build (or renovate) and sell property for a quick cash profit, the more likely the real estate sold will be considered dealer property. [Little, *supra*]

Conversely, when an owner intends to buy, build and maintain a **continuing investment** in real estate for a period of years, the real estate is a *capital asset*. Its resale for cash after a few years of ownership qualifies the earnings on a sale to be reported as a profit, not income.

Again, the dealer property issue arises on a cash-out sale of the property, not when a §1031 reinvestment of the proceeds from a sale of real estate continues the owner's investment in like-kind property.

The purpose of acquiring property

An owner's **original motivation** for purchasing a property is one factor used to classify the property.

For example, a second trust deed lender bids on a secured real estate to prevent foreclosure by the first trust deed lender. The property consists of two or more parcels. He then disposes of the real estate by selling individual parcels since a piecemeal disposition is the best way to cash out his failed trust deed investment.

The private lender's primary purpose for the purchase and resale of the real estate is to protect his second trust deed investment and avoid holding real estate-owned properties.

Does the sell-off of the real estate in parcels mean the real estate was held as dealer property?

No! The lender's intention on acquisition of the property was to protect and preserve the security for his trust deed investment. The sell-off of the security was to raise cash to remain an investor in trust deed notes, not to acquire real estate for resale to consumers — a business occupation engaged in by the lender. [**Malat** v. **Riddell** (1966) 383 US 569]

Ownership intentions and operations

Use of the real estate during the period of ownership is likewise a significant indication of the property's status as inventory or a capital asset when it is sold.

For example, a builder buys a parcel of real estate and constructs an apartment complex on it. The property now produces income for the builder, who takes depreciation deductions.

After owning and operating the apartment, the builder sells the property and acquires a larger complex as a replacement property in a §1031 reinvestment plan.

Here, the real estate built and sold is a capital asset, not dealer property. The builder's purpose at both the time of purchase and throughout his period of ownership was to buy, build and operate the property as an income-producing investment.

On the sale, he **reinvested** the net sales proceeds in a like-kind property. He did not cash out and return his net sales proceeds to buying land, developing it and selling the completed project, which is the business of a developer and builder.

The fact that the builder constructs improvements on the property to alter or enlarge its use does not throw the property into the dealer category without more evidence, such as its liquidation for cash. Had the property been classified as dealer property due to repeated conduct of building, selling and reinvesting in land to again build, sell and reinvest in land, the §1031 reinvestment would have been disallowed for lack of like-kind status. [**Heller Trust** v. **Commissioner of Internal Revenue** (9th Cir. 1967) 382 F2d 675]

An owner who continuously buys, builds and sells properties after each attains the level of occupancy necessary to successfully market it and cash out, such as occurs with professional builders, the real estate is dealer property. The improved properties constitute inventory available for purchase by customers of the builder's trade or business. [**Bush** v. **Commissioner** TCM 1977-75]

Tract development of lots and construction of residential property for sale to the public are classic examples of dealer property situations. In contrast, an owner who holds real estate as rental or appreciable investment property, spending little effort or money to sell it compared to managing his ownership of it, has demonstrated by the time he cashes out and realizes a profit, that the property is held as a capital asset.

Dealer income is derived from the activities of a business, such as continuously acquiring properties in foreclosure, fixing them up or refinancing the debt and "flipping" them in a resale.

Here, the owner's earnings are mostly derived from preparing the property for resale by improvement activities. The property's value increased due to the owner's value-adding activities. The increased value was not due to inflation and appreciation on the property being held over three or more years by inflation and appreciation.

Acquired to resell and reinvest

An investor acquires ownership to a property at a price or with a cost basis significantly below its resale value. The property was acquired under one of several **purchase arrangements**, including:

- the exercise of an **option to purchase** or a right of first refusal the investor had acquired;

- the **liquidation** of his solely owned development corporation;

- a purchase agreement entered into with a **distressed seller**; or

- as **§1031 replacement property** for property the investor sold.

Before acquiring the property, the investor determines he will not retain ownership, but will sell the property as soon as possible. The inves-

tor lacks the ability (or desire) to finance his long-term ownership or to develop the property to its highest and best use. Thus, he will dispose of the property and take the profit resulting from his low cost basis. Simply put, he will acquire the property to make money by disposing of the property.

To accomplish a prompt resale, the investor lists the property for sale with the broker who originally assisted him in the purchase of the property. The listing is conditioned on locating suitable replacement property for a §1031 reinvestment in the event the property sells. Further, the listing requires any sale of the property negotiated by the broker to be contingent on the purchase of that replacement property.

Almost immediately, the broker locates a buyer willing to purchase the property on terms and provisions calling for the buyer's cooperation with the investor's reinvestment of the net sales proceeds and the investor's purchase of other property.

Within three months of acquiring the property, several properties acceptable to the investor for reinvestment of his net sales proceeds are located. The investor determines he will be able to purchase one or more of the properties. As a result, mutual **closing instructions** for escrow are prepared, calling for the investor's net sales proceeds to be made payable and delivered to either a purchase escrow he has opened to acquire a replacement property or a §1031 trustee established under a buyer's trust agreement to hold the funds until the purchase escrow for the replacement property can close. The contingency calling for the purchase of other property is **waived**. [See **first tuesday** Form 172-2; see Chapter 19]

Escrow is closed on the sale. The investor accomplished his goal by completing the prompt disposition of property he did not at any time intend to keep as a long-term investment, but merely intended to use **to make money** by taking a profit on its resale.

After closing the sale and within 180 days, the investor acquires the replacement property which he identified prior to expiration of the 45-day identification period.

The investor reports the transactions on his tax returns for the year of the sale as a reinvestment of his net sales proceeds from §1031 property "held for investment" by acquiring replacement property to be "held for investment," claiming the profit he realized on the sale was exempt from taxation under IRC §1031.

Does the sale of a property owned for a very short period of time and held with the intent from the moment of acquisition to sell it for a profit qualify the property as §1031 property and exempt the profit from being reported and taxed?

Yes! The investor owned and had possession of the property from the moment he closed escrow on its purchase. Further, and most importantly, he reinvested the sales proceeds in §1031 real estate without liquidating his real estate investment by **cashing out** on the sale.

Thus, he continued his investment in one property he owned and held, with the sole intent of making money by disposing of it and **reinvesting** the net proceeds from its sale in a property he acquired also for the purpose of making money as an investment. The sale was not part of a business conducted to sell property to customers.

§1031 lacks a holding period

To be §1031 properties, both the property sold and the property acquired must have been held:

- for investment; or

- for productive use in a trade or business.

No **holding period** requirement exists in a §1031 transaction that compels the property to **be held** indefinitely as an investment before deciding to sell it and reinvest in other §1031 property. To **hold property** requires the person selling and conveying it to merely **own and possess** the property.

Further, no holding period exists for the ownership of a property before the property sold qualifies as *investment property*.

The §1031 requirement that the property be owned *for investment purposes* is satisfied by:

- avoiding an actual or constructive receipt of the net sales proceeds (partial or fully), called a *liquidation of the investment* or a *cash-out sale*; and

- reinvesting the sequestered funds by the timely acquisition of identified replacement property.

The required continuation of an investment in real estate required to qualify for the §1031 profit tax exemption exists when ownership of a replacement property is acquired with the intent to make money, called *investment real estate*. [**Bolker** v. **Commissioner** (9th Cir. 1985) 760 F2d 1039]

Chapter 10

The purchase and control of replacement property

This chapter explains the full control an investor may assert over the purchase and improvement of replacement property acquired in a §1031 reinvestment plan.

Conduct connected to direct deeding

Taxwise, the sale of §1031 property is the first step an investor takes in a reinvestment plan designed to maintain a continuing capital investment in §1031 real estate, called an *exchange* or a *delayed exchange* by the Internal Revenue Service (IRS). The second step is the acquisition of ownership to replacement property.

Prior to an investor closing escrow on the sale of property, a *buyer's trustee*, also called a *§1031 trustee*, is chosen by the investor to hold the net proceeds from his sale. The funds held by the trustee will be placed in an interest-bearing **trust account**, available to fund the investor's purchase of replacement property and the cost of any construction to be completed prior to taking title. [See Chapter 18]

Neither the buyer of the investor's property nor the §1031 trustee have any obligation or need to research, locate, approve, take title to or construct the replacement property, unless they agree to do so. The trustee's sole task under the *general rules* for avoiding receipt of sales proceeds is to fund the investor's purchase and any construction of improvements on replacement property from the sales proceeds held in trust. [**Biggs** v. **Commissioner** (5th Cir. 1980) 632 F2d 1171]

Use of any type of purchase contract

An investor locates a replacement property and enters into a purchase agreement with a seller to buy the property.

The investor may enter into any type of contract in his own name, to purchase the replacement property he and his broker have located, including:

- a purchase option;

- a purchase agreement;

- a purchase escrow, with or without an underlying purchase agreement or option; or

- an exchange agreement.

Full involvement in the purchase

When purchasing the replacement property, the investor, now acting as a buyer, may perform any of the following acts:

1. Negotiate the price and terms for payment of the price, as well as all conditions and contingencies.

2. Make a good-faith deposit with the purchase offer, payable to escrow, using his own funds or funds held by the buyer's trustee.

3. Enter into the purchase agreement or option and sign escrow instructions as the named buyer.

4. Satisfy or waive conditions and contingencies with the investor directly handling his due diligence investigation.

5. Oversee and direct renovation or construction on the property prior to closing and assume liability for any funding such as the co-signing or guaranteeing of a construction loan. However, the investor may not undertake personal liability for the actual renovation or construction of improvements, nor may he take title to the property. Thus, he cannot sign on the trust deed securing the construction loan, but can enter

into the note as a co-signer obligating himself to pay the loan. [**Coastal Terminals, Inc.** v. **United States** (4th Cir. 1963) 320 F2d 333]

6. Originate refinancing or further financing or assume loans on the replacement property concurrent with taking title to the replacement property on completion of the §1031 transaction.

7. Advance at any time any additional funds or properties necessary to fund the closing of the purchase escrow on the replacement property.

8. Execute any carryback notes and trust deeds which finance the purchase of the replacement property.

9. Assign to an *interim owner* the investor's rights to purchase and take possession of the replacement property prior to the sale of the investor's property, a *reverse exchange*, and concurrently enter into a purchase agreement to acquire the property from the interim owner concurrent with the close of the sale on the property the investor is selling. [See Chapter 23]

10. Receive all the interest earned on the net sales proceeds held by the buyer's trustee, less trustee fees. Receipt of the interest is deferred until replacement property is acquired. [**Starker** v. **United States** (9th Cir. 1979) 602 F2d 1341; see Chapter 17]

§1031 provisions and documentation

To assure the investor has the ability to complete a §1031 reinvestment, it should be noted in the documentation for the investor's sales transaction that:

- the buyer has agreed to a mutual §1031 **cooperation clause** in the purchase agreement [See **first tuesday** Form 159 §10.6]; and

- supplemental **escrow closing instructions**, worded to prevent the investor's receipt of the net sales proceeds on closing, have been signed by the buyer. [See **first tuesday** Forms 172-2 and 173-2]

Taxwise, the two steps required in any §1031 reinvestment plan, one being the sale of the investor's property and the other the purchase of replacement property, are not isolated and separately analyzed to determine the tax result of any interim economic or legal consequences. All steps taken together are treated as **one complete transaction**. On completion of the reinvestment, the tax consequences are then calculated based on whether any net *mortgage boot* or *cash boot* was withdrawn from the investment in the property sold. [Starker, *supra*]

The only **restrictions** on how the §1031 reinvestment plan must be completed include:

- the investor may not **refinance** the property he is selling as part of or in contemplation of his §1031 reinvestment plan [See Chapter 24];

- the investor must avoid **actual and constructive receipt** of some, but not all of the net proceeds from the sale of his property [**Carlton** v. **United States** (5th Cir. 1967) 385 F2d 238];

- the investor's right to receive any **interest accruing** on the net sales proceeds held by the §1031 trustee must be enforceable only on or after acquisition of all replacement property [See Chapter 17];

- the replacement property must be **identified** within 45 days after close of escrow on the property sold [Internal Revenue Code §1031(a)(3)(A); see Chapter 15];

- **ownership** to the replacement property must be acquired within 180 days after close of escrow on the transfer of the property sold [IRC §1031(a)(3)(B); see Chapter 15]; and

- the owner cannot **own both properties** concurrently. [**Bezdjian** v. **Commissioner** (9th Cir. 1988) 845 F2d 217; see Chapter 23]

The receipt of excess proceeds from any refinancing or equity financing of the property the investor is selling, originated by the investor in preparation for its sale or exchange, or the investor's receipt of a portion of the net sales proceeds prior to acquiring the replacement property is *cash boot* which cannot later be offset on acquiring replacement property. [Revenue Regulations §1.1031(k)-1(f)]

Escrowing the replacement property

An investor opens a purchase escrow on a replacement property as the named buyer.

As the buyer, the investor approves or disapproves all of the **buyer's contingencies** in the purchase escrow. Contingencies include preliminary title reports, zoning, new loan commitments, leases and rental operating data, inventories, property inspections, termite reports or clearances, structural conditions and property inspections.

The investor, on fulfilling all other obligations of the purchase agreement and escrow for his acquisition of the replacement property, then instructs the §1031 trustee who holds his net sales proceeds to deposit the funds in escrow when escrow calls for a wire of funds.

However, the investor cannot first receive the net proceeds himself and then deposit them into the purchase escrow, a financial event called *actual or constructive receipt*. [Carlton, *supra*]

To avoid actual or constructive receipt of the net sales proceeds, the proceeds may be deposited to the investor's account in the escrow opened by the investor to purchase the replacement property. The funds come either directly from the sales escrow for the property the investor sold or from the §1031 trustee who holds the proceeds.

On deposit of the net sales proceeds to the **investor's account** in the purchase escrow for the replacement property, constructive receipt is again avoided since the funds cannot be released from escrow until the seller of the replacement property approves of their release or the escrow is closed.

The §1031 trustee funds the purchase price and the cost of any improvements for the replacement property with the impounded net sales proceeds he holds. These disbursements should be made through the purchase escrow for the replacement property in order to document their use in acquiring and improving the property.

If additional funds are required beyond the amount held by the trustee, the investor can advance them as part of the purchase price, again through the escrow opened for the purchase of the replacement property.

The investor will take title to the replacement property directly from the seller of the replacement property. It is unnecessary for the §1031 trustee or a facilitator under the *general rules* for avoidance of receipt to hold title or any interest in the replacement property at any time, unless the alternative *safe harbor rules* of sequential deeding are employed. [**Alderson** v. **Commissioner** (9th Cir. 1963) 317 F2d 790; IRS Revenue Ruling 90-34]

The policy of **title insurance** on the replacement property will always be in the name of the investor, as will the assumption of any loans.

The §1031 trustee will not take title to the property. Accordingly, a second escrow involving the trustee as vestee during the transition of title will not be necessary. Again, the trustee's only task is to fund the investor's purchase of the replacement property. The trustee has no need to act as a *strawman* to take title and further convey the replacement property to the investor.

Unused sales proceeds

Should the funds held by the trustee not be entirely disbursed on completion of the §1031 transaction, the trustee, after deducting his fee, may deliver the remaining impounded funds, as well as any **interest accrued,** directly to the investor.

However, the investor should instruct escrow to call for all funds held by the §1031 trustee to be sent to the purchase escrow for the replacement property and credited to the investor's account. Then, any excess funds remaining unused on the close of his purchase escrow go to the investor on a disbursement accounted for by escrow.

Receipt of the unused funds from the sales proceeds on acquiring the replacement property is reported as a cash item in the §1031 transaction. [Rev. Regs. §1.1031(k)-1(f)]

Interest received by the investor that has accrued on the sales proceeds held by the §1031 trustee is separately reported as the investor's portfolio or investment category income during the year the interest accrues. [Rev. Regs. §1.1031(k)-1(h)]

Chapter 11

An installment sale coupled with a §1031

This chapter demonstrates the opportunities presented by the tandem use of exempt and deferred profit reporting when arranging a carryback note on the sale of property in a partial §1031 reinvestment.

Profits: tax exempt and tax deferred

An investor owns and operates a large, income-producing parcel of real estate. Taxwise, the property is classified as both:

§1031 investment property, composed of the ownership of rental properties and portfolio assets, which, as **like-kind property**, qualifies the profit on its sale for exemption from taxes on reinvestment [Internal Revenue Code §1031]; and

- *rental property*, whose income, profit and losses are reported in the **passive income category**, different and separate from **portfolio category income** (triple-net leased properties, land, trust deed notes, stocks and bonds) and **business category income** (brokered property management services, motels and hotels).

The investor's property is encumbered by a loan. The loan balance is greater than the investor's depreciated cost basis in the property, a financial condition referred to as *mortgage-over-basis*. In this situation, taxes will adversely affect the net proceeds of a cash-out sale. Further, the greater the loan amount is in excess of the cost basis, the greater the portion of the net sales proceeds is needed to pay the profit tax.

Thus, the investor is left with less after-tax proceeds than had the basis been higher. This diminishing of net proceeds from a sale does not exist when the amount of the debt on the property sold is less than the remaining cost basis.

However, the adverse tax consequences of a mortgage-over-basis situation are alleviated by carryback financing and totally eliminated by a fully qualified §1031 reinvestment plan.

Here, the investor wants to sell the property and use the net proceeds to acquire interest-bearing investments. As an alternative, he will accept income-producing real estate that generates a net spendable income if it requires considerably less time and effort to manage than the property he now owns.

The investor does not need to withdraw cash from a sale. However, he does want to maintain a continuing flow of income that, unless replaced, will end on the sale of his property.

The avoidance of profit taxes on the sale is another goal the investor would like to meet.

The investor's real estate broker suggests the terms for a sale of the property in the current market could include a carryback note for the balance of the investor's equity after a cash down payment of approximately 20% of the price. The carryback note would in large part also satisfy the investor's cash flow needs.

The carryback note could be structured with monthly installments sufficient in amount to meet the investor's future monthly income requirements over a long period of time, ending on a due date for final payoff. The note would contain a prepayment penalty provision to fund the payment of profit taxes the investor would incur on any early payoff of the carryback note.

The mortgage-over-basis tax burdens

Taxwise, the economic function of the **mortgage-over-basis situation** in a sale where the investor withdraws equity capital by receiving cash or carrying a note in lieu of all cash, leaves the investor with less after-tax sales proceeds than had the cost basis been greater than the principal amount of the loan encumbering the property.

When loans exceed an investor's cost basis in the property, the **entire equity** in the property is profit. Further, and more financially critical, the portion of the **unpaid principal** on the loans encumbering the property is also *profit*. The portion of the principal loan amount that is not profit represents the investor's cost basis remaining in the property.

The broker in this example properly concludes, due to the mortgage-over-basis situation, that the profit on the sale will cause 100% of the principal in a regular note carried back by the investor to be reported as profit. The result is the same even if the installment sale is combined with the use of the cash proceeds to buy replacement property in a §1031 reinvestment plan. [See **first tuesday** Form 355 §2]

The investor is aware the carryback note qualifies for Internal Revenue Code (IRC) §453 installment sale reporting. The payment of taxes on profit allocated to the principal amount of the note will be *deferred* under §453.

The payment of taxes on the portion of the profit allocated to the note's principal is automatically deferred from the time of the sale to each year as the principal is paid on the note. [IRC §453]

Combining a carryback with a §1031

An investor correctly understands the sale of his property, including receipt of cash, a carryback note and debt relief, will not trigger profit reporting on the sale if:

- the net proceeds from the sale (cash and note) are used to purchase replacement real estate and the investor avoids actual or constructive receipt of the sales proceeds [See Chapter 20]; and

- the replacement property is (or will be) encumbered by debt equal-or-greater in amount than the loan on the property being sold. [Revenue Regulations §§1.1031(d)-2, 1.1031(k)-1(f)]

Can the investor receive the carryback note on the sale and then combine the installment sale reporting of the note with a §1031 exemption for the rest of his profit by using the cash down payment to purchase replacement property in a **tandem tax avoidance plan**?

Yes! When the investor's cash proceeds from the sale of his property are properly disbursed to acquire §1031 property and the carryback note is retained by the investor, installment sale reporting on that portion of the profit allocated to principal in the note is automatic, even though the sale is reported as a §1031 reinvestment of the cash down payment. [**Mitchell** v. **Commissioner** (1964) 42 TC 953]

When a carryback note is received by an investor on a sale in which the cash proceeds from the sale are used to acquire replacement property, the §1031 reinvestment plan is reported as a *partial §1031*. In the partial §1031 transaction, the note carried back and retained by the investor is considered *cash boot*.

Again, the receipt of cash items prior to acquiring a replacement property cannot be later offset. Thus, a portion of the profit on the sale becomes reportable and taxed on the **cash items** received — the carryback note. [IRC §1031(b)]

However, the combined §453 and partial §1031 reinvestment raises an accounting question which affects the structuring of the carryback note:

Should the carryback note be structured as an all-inclusive trust deed (AITD) note to avoid profit reporting on the principal of the loan that exceeds the property's cost basis in the mortgage-over-basis situation?

Often, property is refinanced during ownership or was acquired on a small down payment or in a §1031 reinvestment. As a result, the principal amount of the loans on the property becomes greater than the cost basis. When a mortgage-over-basis financial condition exists on a cash-out sale of property, part of the profit taken on the sale is attributable (allocated) to the principal amount of the debt relief and immediately taxed. While the debt relief can only be offset in a §1031 reinvestment, the debt relief can be entirely avoided in a cash-out sale with no §1031 reinvestment by retaining responsibility for periodic payments on the loans by use of an AITD.

No AITD with mortgage-over-basis §1031

When a property sold has a mortgage-over-basis situation and the net sales proceeds will **not** be reinvested in a §1031 replacement property, it is proper (and taxwise, always prudent) to use an AITD note to wrap the existing loans on the property. An AITD is used in lieu of a regular carryback note. [**Professional Equities, Inc.** v. **Commissioner** (1987) 89 TC 165]

The AITD note always **maximizes** the portion of the profit on the sale that is allocated to the principal amount of the carryback in a mortgage-over-basis situation. With an AITD note, no debt relief occurs due to the loan wrap-around arrangements made for the existing loan on the property. Responsibility for making the periodic payments on the loan remains with the investor when an AITD is used.

However, in a §1031 reinvestment plan, the AITD note becomes a **disadvantage** when a mortgage-over-basis situation exists. An AITD carryback reduces the amount of tax-exempt profit carried forward to the replacement property, the opposite result of what is desired in a §1031 reinvestment plan.

For example, a real estate investor agrees to sell property on terms that include:

- a cash down payment;

- the buyer's assumption of the existing loan; and

- a carryback note for the balance of his equity, called a *regular note*.

The principal balance of the loan encumbering the property is greater than the investor's remaining cost basis, a mortgage-over-basis situation, and no §1031 reinvestment is involved.

Here, the profit the investor will be reporting is larger than the investor's net equity in the property, the result of the mortgage-over-basis condition. Thus, the profit exceeds the net sales proceeds of cash and carryback note. The investor is then taxed on an amount greater than his actual net sales proceeds.

However, had the existing loan been wrapped by a carryback AITD note instead of allowing the buyer to assume it, the AITD note (for the balance of the purchase price minus the down payment) increases the dollar amount of the investor's net sales proceeds. The sales proceeds would then equal the entire sales price amount, not just the equity amount in the property. Thus, the sales proceeds (cash and AITD note) would be greater than the profit, and the profit taxable at the time the investor receives his cash proceeds would be hugely reduced.

As a result, the portion of the profit that is allocated to the principal in the AITD note is far larger than had a regular carryback note been used to structure the installment sale. With an AITD, the investor does not pay taxes in teh year of the sale on an amount of profit that exceeds the cash he actually receives. [See Figure 1 accompanying this chapter]

However, the tax results are quite different for an installment sale when it is coupled with a §1031 reinvestment plan. In a §1031 transaction, the entire amount of the cash down payment used to buy replacement real estate is treated as tax-exempt profit. Thus, the cash reinvested is deducted from the profit on the sale and any profit remaining is allocated to the principal in the carryback note to be taxed in future years.

It is important to note all of the profit that is not allocated to the principal in the carryback note is carried forward to the replacement property **untaxed**. With the use of a regular note, a smaller amount of profit will be taxed in deferred installment sale reporting than had an AITD note been used.

In contrast to the use of a regular note in a mortgage-over-basis situation in a §1031 reinvestment plan, an AITD note carried back by the seller **decreases** the amount of profit from the sale that is **exempt** from taxes under §1031. When the loans exceed the property's basis, the AITD increases the amount of taxable profit reported as part of the installment sale. Thus, the smaller the amount of the note, the smaller the amount of profit that can be allocated to it and taxed in a combined §1031 and §453 transaction.

Allocating profit to the carryback note

On any sale or exchange of real estate, the investor **takes a profit** when the sales price exceeds the investor's remaining cost basis in the property sold. When an installment sale is coupled with a §1031 reinvestment of the cash proceeds, the question becomes: How much of the profit taken on the sale must the investor report as a *recognized gain* that is taxed, and, if so, when does he report the recognized gain and pay taxes?

For example, in a **fully qualified** §1031 reinvestment plan, the basis in the property sold, along with the entire profit on a sale, is carried forward to the replacement real estate. However, in a **partial** §1031 reinvestment plan, only some of the profit is carried forward with the basis . Some capital is withdrawn by the investor on the sale in the form of *cash items*, such as a carryback note. On the withdrawal of capital, profit taken on the sale is allocated to the

principal amount withdrawn, and taxed. That is, any amount of profit remaining after deducting the amount of the down payment is taxed in an amount not to exceed the amount of the note. [IRC §1031(b)]

Capital is **withdrawn** in a §1031 reinvestment plan:

- in the form of cash or carryback note received on the sale of the property sold, or by the receipt of unqualified property in the exchange, called *cash items* or *cash boot*; or

- by assuming a lesser amount of debt on the purchase of the replacement property than the amount of the debts encumbering the property sold (and not otherwise offset by cash item contributions), called *net debt relief* or *mortgage boot*.

In an installment sale, for example, an investor receives a carryback note for a portion of his sales price. In a §1031 reinvestment, an investor uses a cash down payment to purchase replacement property.

When the cash down payment is reinvested to purchase replacement property, the allocation of profit from the sale to the principal amount of the carryback note is a three-step analysis:

1. Calculate the profit in the price received by the investor on the sale or exchange (net sales price minus basis equals profit). [See **first tuesday** Form 354 §3.13]

2. Deduct from the profit the cash down payment the investor used to purchase replacement property, sometimes called *§1031 money.*

3. Allocate a portion (or all) of the remaining profit to the principal in the carryback note, limited to the total principal in the note, to be taxed annually as principal is paid. [IRC §453(f)(6)(A); Rev. Regs. §15A.453-1(b)(2)(iii)]

Tax analysis on the property sold in a combined §453/§1031

Figure 1 — Basis exceeds mortgage

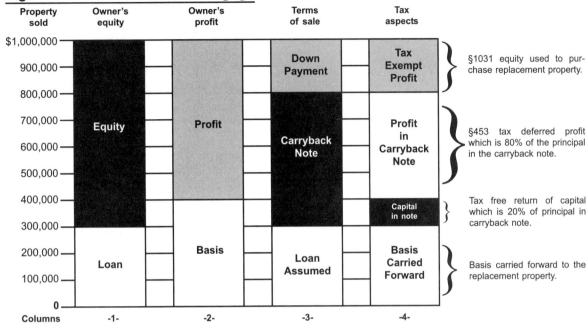

§1031 equity used to purchase replacement property.

§453 tax deferred profit which is 80% of the principal in the carryback note.

Tax free return of capital which is 20% of principal in carryback note.

Basis carried forward to the replacement property.

Figure 2 — Mortgage exceeds basis

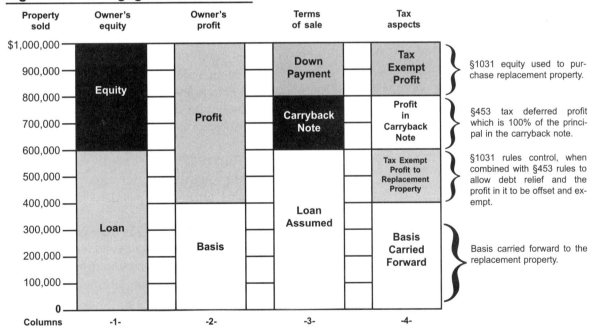

§1031 equity used to purchase replacement property.

§453 tax deferred profit which is 100% of the principal in the carryback note.

§1031 rules control, when combined with §453 rules to allow debt relief and the profit in it to be offset and exempt.

Basis carried forward to the replacement property.

Each column represents a separate set of facts, each column having the $1,000,000 sales price as its common factor. The tax exempt profit in Column 4 is tax exempt only if the loan assumed by the buyer in Column 3 (debt relief) is offset by the owner's assumption of equal or greater debt or the contribution of cash items to purchase the replacement property.

4. Any profit then remaining is implicitly carried forward with the basis to the §1031 replacement property as *tax exempt*. [See Figure 2 accompanying this chapter]

The profit allocated to the principal in the carryback note in step 3 will not be taxed at the time of the sale, but will be reported and taxed annually as principal is paid on the carryback note.

Calculating profit in a §453 and §1031 sale

To apply the rules for the allocation of profit to the carryback note, consider an investor who sells real estate for $1,000,000.

The investor's basis in the property sold is $400,000 and the existing encumbrance on the property is $300,000, a *basis-over-mortgage* situation.

The buyer will purchase the property on terms that include:

- a cash down payment of $200,000, which the investor will use to purchase replacement property;

- assumption of the existing $300,000 loan; and

- execution of a carryback note payable to the investor for $500,000.

The investor's profit on the sale is $600,000 ($1,000,000 price minus the $400,000 basis). The $200,000 cash down payment the investor uses (as §1031 money) to purchase replacement property is first deducted from the profit, leaving a $400,000 profit to be then allocated to the principal amount of the carryback note.

The entire $400,000 profit remaining is allocated to the principal in the carryback note since the profit remaining after deducting the amount of the down payment is less than the amount of the carryback note. Here, an AITD note would have produced the same §1031 tax

exemption results and will always do so in a *basis-over-mortgage* situation. (However, as reviewed earlier in this chapter, the §453 installment sales tax result on a cash-out sale that uses an AITD note will be quite different.)

Thus, 80% of each **principal payment** will be reported annually as profit received on the carryback note, calculated by dividing the $400,000 profit by the $500,000 carryback note. The other 20% of all principal payments represents a tax-free return of originally invested capital. [See Figure 1]

Now consider the same $1,000,000 property with its $400,000 basis. But unlike the prior example, it is encumbered with a larger loan amount of $600,000 — a *mortgage-over-basis* situation.

With a $1,000,000 selling price and a $200,000 cash down payment, the investor will carry back a note in the principal amount of $200,000 for the remaining balance of his $400,000 equity.

As in the prior example, the entire profit on the sale is $600,000. Again, the $200,000 cash down payment reinvested to purchase §1031 replacement property is deducted from the $600,000 profit, leaving a $400,000 profit to be next allocated to the principal in the carryback note.

However, unlike the prior example, the profit remaining after deducting the §1031 money is greater than the principal in the $200,000 carryback note due to the mortgage-over-basis situation. Thus, only $200,000 of the profit is the portion allocated to the principal in the note, the **allocation being limited** to the principal amount of the note.

Here, the $200,000 balance of the profit remaining after allocation to the carryback note will not be taxed, as it is implicitly carried forward with the cost basis to the replacement property.

Thus, 100% of the entire principal amount of the carryback note will be reported as profit and taxed annually as principal is paid on the note. [See Figure 2]

Had the carryback in this mortgage-over-basis example (but not in the prior basis-over-mortgage situation) been an $800,000 AITD note for the balance of the purchase price after the cash down payment, the amount of the principal in the AITD note would then exceed the profit remaining after first deducting the §1031 money from the profit. As a result, the entire $400,000 remaining profit would have been allocated to the principal in the carryback AITD note and taxed.

Chapter 12

Tax partners or independent co-owners

This chapter presents the arrangements co-owners of fractional interests in a real estate investment must undertake to qualify a fractional ownership interest as §1031 property.

§1031 fractional ownerships

For the profit taken on the sale or exchange of an interest in real estate to be exempt from taxes under Internal Revenue Code (IRC) §1031, the interest sold or exchanged must be an **ownership** which qualifies as *like-kind property*, commonly called §1031 property. The ownership acquired in the replacement real estate must also be §1031 property.

In any §1031 reinvestment plan, both "legs" of the plan, namely the property sold and the property acquired, must qualify as the investor's **ownership** of §1031 property. Section 1031 property is property held either for **investment** or **productive use** in a business. [Internal Revenue Code §1031]

Consider the sale or acquisition of a **fractional ownership interest** in income-producing real estate co-owned by two or more investors for investment under each of the following four scenarios:

1. An investor joins with one or more other investors, all of whom **contribute cash** to jointly acquire income-producing real estate.

2. An investor sells his ownership interest in §1031 property producing **§1031 money** which he **reinvests** either by, 1) joining with one or more other investors to pool funds and acquire income-producing real estate, or, 2) buying a fractional interest from a co-owner in a property presently owned by a group of investors.

3. An investor **sells his fractional ownership** interest in income-producing real estate, while the other co-owners remain in ownership of the property, and **reinvests** his net sales proceeds by acquiring the sole ownership of §1031 property.

4. An income-producing property co-owned by two or more investors is sold and one co-owner **withdraws** his share of the net sales proceeds and **reinvests** the funds independently of the other co-owners by acquiring sole ownership of like-kind property.

In each example, co-owners joined together to buy, own or sell a property held or to be held for investment. Also, the parcel of real estate bought or sold in each of these examples is itself managed and operated as §1031 property. Thus, the real estate **qualifies its group ownership** (the group) for a §1031 exemption on the sale of the entire parcel, regardless of whether the ownership of the real estate is a limited partnership (LP), limited liability company (LLC), common law tenants in common (TIC), tax partnership, corporation or sole ownership.

However, a fractional ownership interest sold or acquired by an investor does not qualify as §1031 property if the interest is a **co-ownership interest** in an entity, such as an LP, LLC, corporation or other co-ownership arrangement calling for the alienation of the property or fractional interest by less than unanimous consent. It is the entity which owns the real estate. An investor's reinvestment plan does not qualify for the §1031 exemption when the plan includes the sale or purchase of a fractional ownership interest in an entity. [See Scenarios 2, 3 and 4, *ante*]

Taxwise, a co-owner vested as a tenant-in-common with a group of co-owners is considered a *tax partner* in the co-ownership of §1031 property if he has **agreed to restraints** on his common law rights as a tenant-in-common to freely manage his interest in the property, independent of control by other co-owners and as he sees fit.

Once classified as a **tax partner** for income tax reporting, the tenant-in-common investor is considered a co-owner of an interest in a *tax partnership*, not a co-owner holding an ownership interest in the real estate. As a result, the tax partnership is treated for tax purposes only as the sole owner of the §1031 property, since the tenants in common are now partners who only own the partnership.

When a tenant-in-common co-owner, by agreement or by definition, is a *tax partner* with others in each of the four scenarios given above, then none of the profit taken on the sales leg in each scenario qualifies as exempt from taxes. Both the sales and purchase legs of a §1031 plan must manifest the attributes of an ownership interest directly in the real estate, not the investor's mere ownership of an interest in a partnership. A partnership operates independently of each tenant-in-common to **control the ownership rights** of all co-owners.

A tax partnership vs. a California partnership

The **coordinated conduct** of co-owners in the exercise of *ownership rights* to operate the investment real estate they co-own is viewed differently under federal income tax law than under California partnership law.

Basically, if co-owners **share** the income, profit and losses generated by a joint investment in real estate operating under an unincorporated ownership arrangement, California partnership law, which broadly defines a partnership, classifies the profit-sharing group as a partnership. Thus, California imposes *agency obligations* on each co-owner to act in concert for the mutual benefit of the group from the moment of first discussions about a syndicated investment. Thus, anarchy within the group of co-owners is legally avoided as public policy.

Conversely, federal tax law places emphasis on TIC law to establish co-owner rights. Tenant-in-common ownership does not rise to tax partner status unless the co-owners are operating as a declared partnership, LLC or cooperating TICs.

To avoid tax partnership status, each co-owner vested as a tenant-in-common must have the unrestricted common law right to independently *alienate* his fractional interest without the prior consent of other co-owners. Further, each co-owner must have the unrestricted right to independently block any *alienation* of the entire property co-owned by the group.

Alienation of the entire property refers to its sale, further encumbrance or a lease for a period exceeding one year.

Taxwise, the ownership of a TIC interest which retains its common law right of alienation in real estate is viewed as being the ownership of a fractional interest in the real estate itself. Thus, the tenant-in-common is not the owner of an interest in a partnership that actually owns the property.

Further, TIC co-ownership arrangements may provide for **cooperation among the co-owners** in the ongoing management and operation of the property. Operating the property by *centralizing management* does not violate the requirement of unanimous approval for alienation of property owned by common law TICS. Thus, the alienation rights inherent in ownership are distinguished from the day-to-day operations of the property.

An understanding of the distinctions between federal tax law, which defines §1031 property investments as excluding fractional interests held by *tax partners*, and California's partnership law, which controls joint ventures and profit sharing ownerships, is helpful to all individuals involved in investment groups, such as:

- **syndicators** structuring the ownership for acquisition of property by an investment group they are forming;

- **investors** acquiring or withdrawing a fractional interest from a syndicated real estate investment; and

- **brokers** (or other advisors) representing a person who is buying into or withdrawing from a real estate syndicated investment.

Knowing the parameters for activities that establish a partner under California partnership law versus activities that establish a tax partnership for federal income tax reporting avoids unintended and unexpected results under either set of laws, or worse, the loss of a transaction because of insufficient knowledge to explain the distinctions to clients, their advisors and others.

Accordingly, this chapter contains an analysis and application of the overlapping partnership laws controlling the syndication of real estate investments (state law) and the exemption of profits from taxes (federal law) on a sale or purchase with §1031 money of a fractional interest in a syndicated investment.

We cooperate in California

A group of investors acquire income-producing property located in California. Title is taken as **tenants in common**, naming each investor and stating his percentage or fractional share of *undivided ownership* in the property. The property is occupied by tenants under short-term leases and periodic rental agreements which provide for the landlord to care for and maintain the premises.

The co-owners orally agree:

- to divide annual operating income (or losses) and resale profits pro rata based on their percentage of ownership;

- to hire the broker who organized the group to manage the property with authority to locate tenants, enter into short-term lease and rental agreements, collect rents, contract for the repair, maintenance, utilities and security to be provided by the landlord under the lease agreements, pay operating expenses and mortgage payments, and distribute spendable income to the co-owners quarterly;

- to grant each other a right of first refusal on a resale of their fractional TIC interest; and

- to grant the syndicator the option to purchase the property at its fair market value.

Are the co-owners conducting themselves as partners under California partnership law despite the tenancy in common vesting placing each co-owner on title?

Yes! Co-owners of California real estate vested as tenants in common, when engaged in the business of jointly operating the property on terms calling for them to **share income and profits**, are conducting themselves as partners. Thus, they are considered agents of one another, charged as a fiduciary with the duty **to cooperate in the ownership** of the property. [Calif. Corporations Code §§16202(a), 16202(c)(3)]

A tenancy in common vesting does not control the **possessory rights** of the co-owners when the co-ownership in fact constitutes a state law partnership. For example, a partner may use or possess partnership property only on behalf of the partnership, while a tenant-in-common (at common law) may use, possess or lease the property himself. [Corp C §16401(g)]

Further, tenants in common who conduct themselves as *joint operators* of a property, such as occurs with a rental property, are not co-owners of the real estate. They are partners who co-own their partnership. Thus, the partnership owns the property without concern for the type of vesting the group of investors has chosen. As a partner, the vested co-owner holds no right to a possessory interest in the property which he can independently possess or separately transfer by leasing the property to a tenant without concern for the other co-owners.

The only *transferable interest* the tenant-in-common owns is his **fractional interest in the partnership**. The partnership interest entitles him to share profits and receive distributions. Thus, the co-owner's fractional interest, vested as a tenant-in-common, is no more than a **personal property** share of ownership in a California partnership. [Corp C §16502]

Trustees for one another by law

Although title to the income-producing property held by the co-owners for profit is vested in the names of all the co-owners, each co-owner actually **holds title as a trustee** on behalf of all the tenants in common, collectively called a *partnership*. [Calif. Civil Code §682; Corp C §16404(b)(1)]

As co-owners and operators of a rental property, they have formed a partnership, holding title in the most troublesome of all California co-ownership vestings: tenants in common, a TIC.

Thus, the conveyance of a co-owner's TIC interest to another person conveys nothing more than the co-owner's interest in the partnership's *equitable ownership* of the property. The partnership's title to the property is **held in trust**, in the name of each co-owner for the benefit of all co-owners.

The defining acts of partners

Prior to California's 1949 enactment creating *tenancies in partnership*, tenants in common who owned rental property that required centralized management did not constitute a partnership. No *agency relationship* existed between tenants in common before 1949 to protect the common interests of the co-owners to share profits. The federal tax law defining TIC interests remains the same today. [**Johnston** v. **Kitchin** (1928) 203 C 766]

Since 1949, a California partnership exists when two or more co-owners join together to carry on a business for income and profit in California. A California business includes every trade, occupation or profession. [Corp C §16101(1)]

While landlording is not a trade or business category activity for federal income tax purposes (as the property is a passive rental operation or a portfolio asset), landlording by a syndicated group is an occupation under California partnership law. A co-ownership is a California partnership if the co-owners are involved in **sharing earnings and profits** from rental operations, refinancing and resale of the property they own. [Corp C §§16202(a), 16202(c)(3)]

Also, the receipt of income (from operations) and profits (from a sale) by co-owners from their joint investment is considered evidence of a California partnership, unless the earnings are received by a co-owner in payment:

- of an installment note, including one given in consideration for the sale of goodwill or property;

- for wages or rent due the co-owner;

- on an annuity to a surviving spouse, representative or a deceased co-owner; or

- as interest on a loan. [Corp C §16202(c)(3)]

The tenancy-in-common partnership

With a tenancy-in-common vesting, the sharing of income and profits earned by each co-owner's **separate use** of the property — such as occurs with the extraction of minerals from the property by each co-owner for their own separate use — does not in itself create a California partnership. It takes more than the sharing of use and possession by co-owners to constitute conduct on the level of a partnership. [Corp C §16202(c)(1)]

It is the interaction and **coordinated conduct** of the co-owners while directly or indirectly managing or operating the investment that determines whether a state law partnership relationship exists between them. Once the conduct of co-owners in a coordinated ongoing operation of the property constitutes a **joint and mutually beneficial activity**, an agency relationship exists between the co-owners.

With the agency relationship comes *fiduciary duties* owed to partners which obligates each prospective or actual co-owner to **act in the best interest** of the group, not to act independently on the investment opportunity before them. [Corp C §16404; **Leff** v. **Gunter** (1983) 33 C3d 508]

Thus, co-owners of rental property who are vested as tenants in common and who **act collectively** to manage the property or authorize a property manager to operate the property on their behalf, hold ownership to the real estate under what has been best entitled a *tenancy in partnership*, each co-owner being a tenant in partnership with all other co-owners.

By the *sharing of income* among co-owners who are vested as tenants in common, a **tenancy in common partnership** is established, subjecting each co-owner to the rights and obligations of a partner, such as:

- the duty to hold title to the real estate as a trustee for the benefit of the partnership [Corp C §16404(a)(1)];

- the right of each co-owner to use and possess the real estate — but only for group purposes [Corp C §16401(g)];

- the right to use and possess the real estate is nontransferable unless all co-owners **collectively transfer** the partnership's right to possession of the property [Corp C §§16203, 16501]; and

- the property co-owned by the group is not subject to *attachment or execution* on a judgment against an individual co-owner, only on claims against the partnership. [Corp C §§16201, 16501]

Even when co-owners do not characterize their mutual working relationship in a profit-sharing investment as a partnership, they are still obligated to act on behalf of the group as though they were partners in a partnership. [Corp C §16202(a)]

Under state law tenant-in-common co-owners hold no interest in the real estate they co-own which they can legally transfer, voluntarily or involuntarily, independent of the rights of the resulting California partnership. [Corp C §16502]

However, federal tax law for determining tax partner status of TICs excludes the results of state laws to the contrary. [Revenue Procedure 2002-22]

A tax partner's profits disqualified

The penalty for a tenant-in-common co-owner who is federally classified as a *tax partner* in the ownership of either the property sold or the property acquired in a §1031 reinvestment plan is the loss of the entire §1031 tax exemption for profit taken on the property sold.

Thus, just what arrangements or activities a co-owner, other co-owners, a property manager, syndicator or lender agree to between themselves which would make a co-owner a tax partner is or may become of great concern to investors in syndicated real estate investments programs.

When a co-owner of investment real estate is classified by the IRC as a **partner**, the real estate is considered to be owned by a *tax partnership*. Classified as a partner, the co-owner's ownership interest is that of a share in a partnership that **does not qualify** as §1031 property.

To avoid tax partner status, a co-owner in a real estate investment does not want to be financially coupled with a co-owner or manager who provides the tenants with services which are **unrelated to the operation** of the property.

Thus, an investor with after-tax cash he has accumulated, or §1031 money to reinvest, who makes a *capital contribution* to a group being formed to jointly own and operate an income-producing parcel of real estate must be assured no co-owner is sharing in any income from tenants other than rent. Co-owners who occasionally provide tenants with business or professional services for a fee separate from rent, or share in the income received by others providing services to tenants which go beyond the **customary services** required under a lease, establish tax partner status.

Co-owners or partners

Tax partner status is of no concern to an investor, unless and until the investor:

- withdraws from a group to separately invest on his own; or

- desires to exchange his sole ownership in real estate (or the cash from its sale) for a fractional ownership in a replacement property.

To get a mental grip on the **federal distinction** between a co-owner's non-partner status and tax partner status in the co-ownership of an investment in real estate, it is instructive to know the purposes behind the different income categories established to report and account for income, profits and losses from the ownership and sale of real estate. [See Chapter 5]

Three income categories have been established for reporting income. The source or nature of the income, profit or loss determines the income category in which the income, profit or loss will be reported, such as:

- *trade or business income category*, which includes real estate occupied and used in the business owned and operated by the person who owns or co-owns the real estate, including residential housing with an average occupancy of less than 30 days, such as motels, hotels, vacation rentals and other transient housing and boarding facilities that provide occupants with services unrelated to the care and maintenance of the property;

- *passive income category*, which includes residential and nonresidential rental properties with an average occupancy of 30 days or more, but with a tenancy less than a triple net (master or ground) lease, providing the resident with, by the lease or rental agreements, the repair, maintenance, security, utilities and management typically included in exchange for rent under lease and rental agreements or as required by state law; and

- *portfolio income category*, which includes income-producing real estate subject to long-term lease agreements which shift the responsibility for the care, maintenance, repair and operation of the property and the payment of expenses of ownership such as property taxes, assessments and insurance premiums to the tenant (as in a master lease, ground lease or other type of management-free triple-net lease), and includes other like-type flows of management-free income such as bonds, stocks, interest on loans (trust deed investments) and vacant, unimproved real estate held for profit on a resale (not as dealer property). [See Chapter 5]

Thus, income-producing real estate *held for investment* and leased to tenants is classified as either:

- rental (passive income) property requiring **management services** related to the tenancies; or

- portfolio income property requiring very little or no **tenant-related services** to be provided by management.

Land held for investment requiring no management services, except for the annual payment of taxes, assessments, insurance premiums and the like, is classified as portfolio property. However, land held for development, subdivision and resale by the owner or a co-owner is trade or business category inventory.

Stated another way, rental (passive income) property and portfolio income property are not business property. On the other hand, a motel or hotel is a business property since services unrelated to rental property operations are provided.

And as a further distinction, the co-ownership arrangements relating to the management of rental or portfolio properties consists of services customarily provided for tenants by a landlord, directly or through an agent. The **landlord's services** provided for tenants are not business-related services, such as maid services, food, laundry pickup and delivery and towels and linens, which are provided to more transient occupants of trade or business category property, such as hotels, motels, transient housing or vacation rentals.

Thus, negotiations with prospective tenants to lease units or space within the property, limited to providing customary landlord services, such as the collection of rent, evictions, repairs and maintenance of the property, utilities, security and other real estate-related services typically included in the rent, is not a business. Obviously, the property is not a business income category asset which provides **business-related service**, as an operator of a hotel, motel, boarding house or vacation rental property does.

Without being coupled to a business service, the capital contribution of a co-owner and landlord services the co-owner provides in the form of rental property operations for the care and operation of the property as a rental or portfolio asset, does not make the co-owner a tax partner. None of the co-owners are involved rendering *additional services* to the tenants through a business, enterprise or joint venture in which one or more of the co-owners share profits or losses in trade or business services offered to tenants.

A property manager and his authority

Co-owners can join together to own and operate income-producing property and will not be considered tax partners when they hire a broker (who may be a co-owner) as an independent property manager. The manager may be given all the authority he needs to do all acts necessary to provide for tenants under standard leasing arrangements.

However, the manager may not be given the authority to enter into long-term leases, sell or encumber the property. These are the rights of *alienation* held by each co-owner which must remain unrestrained and require unanimous approval by all co-owners to be exercised.

The authority co-owners may give a property manager without becoming tax partners is extensive, and includes the authority to:

- act on behalf of the co-owners to negotiate and enter into leases and rental agreements with prospective or current tenants;

- collect deposits, rents and other amounts due from tenants and deposit them into a common bank account maintained for (but not in the name of) the co-owners;

- contract for all services customarily provided to tenants under similar circumstances as part of the rent, including normal repair and maintenance of the property, utilities, garbage/trash pickup, a resident manager and security;

- pay from rents (and additional funding by co-owners made necessary due to insufficient rental income) the charges for all services the manager contracts for as authorized, including the payment of property taxes, assessments, insurance premiums, mortgage payments and management fees;

- disburse to the co-owners no less than quarterly their share of spendable income; and

- prepare annual statements for each co-owner setting forth his share of income, expenses, interest and depreciation. [IRS Revenue Ruling 75-374]

Thus, co-owners are merely limited to the classic relationship between a property manager and an owner of income-producing property. No co-owner, directly or indirectly through another person, will carry on or share profits in a trade or business which will provide additional services to the tenants beyond those customarily provided under common leasing arrangements in exchange for rent.

However, each co-owner will be considered a tax partner who is carrying on a trade or business, financial operation or venture in a tax partnership if he is:

- any co-owner renders the additional **business-related service** to tenants; or

- the property manager renders the additional business services and one or more co-owners **share in the income** the manager receives for providing the business-related service to the tenant.

Thus, the **tax partnership** includes the person rendering the business-related services whose income for those services provided is shared with one or more of the co-owners of the real estate. It does not matter that the person rendering the services (such as the property manager) may have no claim to the spendable income from the rental operation, proceeds from a refinance or net proceeds from its resale.

The property manager hired by the co-owners may not be a tenant and must be on a short-term management agreement not to exceed one year. The management agreement may only be extended or renewed for a period not to exceed one year by a unanimous vote of the co-owners (or by a failure to vote). The property manager's pay must be comparable to fees paid brokers in the area for managing similar properties and providing similar management services.

While the manager may not be a tenant, a long-term lease, pre-existing or unanimously agreed to by all the co-owners, could provide for a **lessee** to care for, operate and incur at his expense all the typical services (sub)tenants may need to occupy the premises, including the right to sublet the property, an arrangement called a *master lease*.

Also, the property manager may be granted an option to purchase the property. However, the price to be paid for the property on exercise of the option must be set as the **fair market value** of the property at the time of purchase.

The devolution of TIC control

Some flexibility exists regarding the annual unanimous consent of the tenant-in-common co-owners to the renewal of property management agreements and the extent of authority which may be granted to management to enter into long-term leases of portions of the property. [IRS Private Letter Ruling 2005-13010]

Each long-term lease must be unanimously approved by all tenant-in-common co-owners to qualify each individually owned fractional ownership interest as §1031 property. This unanimous approval may be satisfied by an **annual unanimous approval** of a set of leasing guidelines for management. Management would then follow the guidelines in the exercise of the leasing authority given management in the property management agreement.

Thus, the authority given in the leasing guidelines is viewed as a method by which each tenant-in-common co-owner retains direct control over his right to disapprove a proposed lease. The parameters set in the guidelines place a limit on management's flexibility in the discretionary leasing of the property.

The Internal Revenue Service example for leasing guidelines include the typical standards any landlord sets for qualifying prospective tenants and structuring the terms and conditions of lease provisions. Guidelines for leasing include the tenant's and landlord's obligation to care for and maintain the property, selection of the type of tenants, tenant creditworthiness, a range of rent amounts to charge tenants, the term of the lease and the content of lease provisions.

Interestingly, the syndicator managing the property is allowed, as outlined in the IRS letter ruling, to bar any tenant-in-common co- owner from altering the guidelines during the year following their approval since the unilateral change would be less than unanimous approval. Until the next annual approval of leasing guidelines occurs, each tenant-in-common co-owner agrees not to alter the guidelines by exercising his ownership rights to lease the property, himself or through a competitive leasing agent, on conflicting, and possibly more advantageous, long-term arrangements. [PLR 2005-13010]

Also, while the requirement for unanimous annual approval of the property management agreement is an anarchic condition detrimental to current management, apparently automatic one-year approval by **mere silence** at the time of the annual renewal of the management agreement is deemed a sufficient exercise of a tenant-in-common co-owner's right to approve or disapprove annual contracts with management.

For example, a TIC operating agreement entered into by all tenant-in-common co-owners calls for **automatic annual renewal** of the property management agreement. Should all tenant-in-common co-owners **fail to object** to any provisions submitted by the management

team in a *notice of renewal* of the management agreement, management has been approved for another year — by silence. Thus, a tenant-in-common co-owner exercises his right to control his interest in the property by objecting. However, if he does object he will be penalized.

The conduct of management permitted in the letter ruling gives co-owners who agree with management the right to buy out the objecting co-owner's interest. If not bought out, the objecting co-owner is limited to hiring his own property manager. However, for doing so, he will alone bear the cost of his manager. Further, his manager will only be an advisor to the current management, unable to exercise any objection he or his employing co-owner may have. Could management have it any better? You bet they can!

As a final detriment for objections to the current management's unaltered or continued involvement, a co-owner's objection triggers an option for a buy out of the objecting co-owner's TIC interest (without a corresponding option to buy out his non-objecting co-owners' interests if they do not purchase his interest). The option price to be paid for the objecting co-owner's TIC interest is his fractional portion of the property's fair market value (set by an appraiser chosen by a majority vote of tenant-in-common co-owners). The buy out provision places a co-owner at risk of a loss on his investment if he should object to the renewal.

Normally, a co-owner objecting to management has a reasonable basis for doing so, namely that management procedures and policies are deteriorating the future worth of the property and new management to take corrective action to preserve and build up equity in the property.

Hence, the property's present fair market value at the time of a co-owner's objection, especially in syndicated property which attracted §1031 monies, is an amount less than the price paid by the group to acquire the property (usually from the syndicator or a related entity) since poor management has deteriorated its worth.

Accordingly, if the non-objecting tenant-in-common co-owners exercise their option to purchase the objecting tenant-in-common co-owner's co-ownership interest, they will most likely be able to pay an amount less than the price paid by the objecting co-owner for his fractional interest in the property.

Resale by an individual tenant-in-common as §1031 property

Consider a syndicator who seeks to bring together several property owners and cash investors to form a group to co-own an income-producing property located by the syndicator. They will take title as **tenants in common**, each for their fractional share of undivided ownership, based on the pro rata value of their contribution to the purchase price.

The entire property is or will be leased to a single tenant. The tenant will be either a single user of the property or a master tenant with the right to sublet portions of the premises. Either way, the lease is a triple-net lease which imposes no responsibility on the co-owners for maintenance of the property or the supplying of any tenant services.

The co-ownership agreement places no restrictions on each co-owner's ability to sell or encumber their individual TIC interest. Also, **no voting** is established to sell, release or encumber the whole of the property. Thus, any *alienation* of the entire ownership of the real estate requires **unanimous approval** of all the co-owners — the essence of the conduct required to avoid the status of a tax partnership.

Based on these co-ownership arrangements, the syndicator requests of the IRS an **advance ruling** stating the arrangements for the TIC investment do not establish the investors as tax partners or members in an entity. On receipt of the IRC ruling, the fractional interest of a co-owner vested as a tenant-in-common can be acquired or sold as like-kind property.

Thus, an investor's acquisition of a fractional interest in a TIC investment group (with §1031 monies) which is the subject of an IRS advance ruling that the group is not a tax partnership allows the profits an investor realizes on the sale of his property to qualify for the §1031 profit tax exemption by buying replacement property. [Rev. Proc. 2002-22]

To receive an **advance ruling**, the syndicator of a TIC co-ownership arrangement must, as a minimum, present extensive documentation to the IRS. In particular, the syndicator must demonstrate the following conditions exist:

1. Title will be vested in the name of all co-owners as tenants in common as to their fractional or percentage ownership based on their proportionate contribution to the purchase of the property.

2. The co-owners will share in the income, profit and losses based on their percentage ownership.

3. No more than 35 participants will be co-owners, husband and wife are considered as one.

4. The co-owners will not file a joint partnership return, will not operate the property under a common business name, and the co-ownership agreement will not classify the co-owners as shareholders, members or partners.

5. The co-ownership agreement may provide for a right of first refusal to anyone (co-owner, manager, syndicator or lessee) to acquire a co-owner's fractional interest should the co-owner decide to sue for a partition and sale of the property. The fractional interest will be sold at a price set as the fair market value of the property at the time the right to purchase is exercised.

6. Any sale, encumbrance, lease, management or release agreement may only be entered into by unanimous approval of all co-owners (and no one related to the investment may hold a co-owner's power of attorney to act on his behalf).

7. Each co-owner may sell, encumber or lease his fractional ownership interest in the real estate without any prior restraints or approvals needed to permit the transfer, and should a transfer occur, a right of first refusal may exist in favor of any co-owner, the syndicator or the tenant to purchase the fractional interest transferred (based on the current market value of the entire property).

8. Any advances made by any other co-owner, the syndicator or manager to cover a co-owner's failure to meet a call for additional funds must be recourse and due within 31 days.

9. A co-owner may grant an option to purchase his interest to anyone. The price to be paid is the co-owner's fractional share of the whole property's fair market value on the date the option is exercised, however, no guaranteed buy out (put option) can be held by a co-owner to sell to anyone involved in the investment or the property.

10. A property manager may be hired for a period of no more than one year, renewable by unanimous agreement of the co-owners. He may be anyone except a lessee of the property, may collect rents, pay expenses incurred for the services to be provided to tenants as part of the rent, make distributions to co-owners from one bank account, prepare annual profit and loss statements for each co-owner's proportionate share of income, expenses, interest and depreciation, place insurance, negotiate leases to be executed only by unanimous approval of the co-owners and receive a fee in an amount comparable to fees received by competitive brokers, but the fee cannot be based on a percentage of distribution to co-owners.

11. No lender providing funds for the investment program may be a related person to the co-owners, the syndicator, manager or lessee.

12. The syndicator may not sell any co-owner an interest in the property for less than the fractional interest's proportionate share of the whole property's fair market value (and services rendered by the syndicator to form the group), and no promotional fee or contribution by a co-owner may be contingent on the financial success of the investment program. [Rev. Proc. 2002-22]

However, in spite of all these threshold arrangements to obtain a ruling, the IRS provides **no rules or guidelines** for the syndicator's actual formation of a group of co-owners outside the confines of a ruling. Further, the IRS provides **no guidance** for their audit on a co-owner's sale or exchange of a fractional co-ownership interest. The IRS only provides a procedure for requesting an advance ruling by a syndicator based on a very limited set of facts.

As a legal complication, an investment program designed to qualify for an advance ruling from the IRS and sold to investors in California most likely creates a risk of loss for the co-owners which is controlled by *California's securities law* and the *Subdivided Lands Act (SLA)*. Ironically, both laws require more protection for investors than is required by the IRS for the TIC to qualify for an advance ruling regarding the non-partner status of a fractional co-ownership interest sold or acquired in a §1031 reinvestment plan.

Equity sharing co-ownership investment

Now consider an **equity sharing** transaction, called a *shared equity financing agreement* by the IRS. The real estate, a single family residence, will be co-owned by two individuals, generally on the basis of 50:50 proportionate contributions of the cash required for a down payment, closing costs and reserves.

One or both of the co-owners will qualify for a purchase-assist loan or an assumption of the existing loan to pay the balance remaining due on the purchase price.

One co-owner will occupy the property as his principal residence; the other will hold his ownership interest for investment, called a *mixed use property*. Often the investor is a parent of the resident co-owner. [IRC §280A(d)(3)]

The resident co-owner's motivation is to own a home. However, he does not have sufficient cash reserves for the down payment needed to make up the difference between the maximum loan available and the price demanded by the seller. The investor co-owner's motivation is to simply invest in appreciable real estate which will require no management on his part and is likely to turn a profit (on a sale) after three to five years of ownership.

The economic glue holding the two co-owners together is an **option to purchase** which the investor grants to the resident co-owner so he can acquire sole ownership of his residence in the future. The price under the option to purchase the ownership held by the investor co-owner is one-half of the net equity in the property based on the **fair market value** of the property when the option is exercised or the **capital contribution** of the investor, whichever amount is greater.

The price to be paid on exercise of the option to purchase is not pre-set. If it is, the amount of return the investor would receive for his investment would be set, as though he had made a loan. Normal closing costs of a sale and the remaining principal balance due on the loan encumbering the property are first deducted from the property's fair market value before the price is set.

A co-owner's **equity sharing agreement** is entered into calling for these conditions:

1. The resident co-owner will occupy the entire property as a single user under a **triple-net lease** for a term of five years. The rent amount is set at the fair market value for the use and occupancy of the property. The rent is variable (to cover rising costs, interest, etc.), and in an amount sufficient to cover mortgage payments, property taxes, assessments and insurance premiums.

2. The resident co-owner will pay for all other expenses incurred to repair and maintain the property to protect and conserve its value, as well as for services the resident co-owner may require to occupy the property as his residence.

3. The lease will not prohibit the resident co-owner from **subletting or assigning** his interest in the lease.

4. No restrictions will be placed on each co-owner's right to individually transfer his undivided fractional ownership interest in the property by sale, encumbrance or long-term lease, called the *right of alienation*. However, each co-owner holds a right of first refusal to buy the other co-owner's interest should the other co-owner actually exercise his right to alienate his undivided interest. The price paid on exercise of the option is the co-owner's proportionate share of the property's fair market value at the time of exercise of the first refusal right, less normal closing costs for a sale.

5. The property in its entirety can be sold, encumbered or leased for a long term only with the unanimous approval of the co-owners (both agreeing on the initial five-year lease to the resident co-owner).

6. Any income, profit or loss on the operations, sale, further encumbrance or leasing of the property will be shared based on each co-owner's contribution to capital.

7. The co-ownership will file no partnership returns, nor issue K-1 schedules. The investor co-owner will report his proportionate share of the annual income and expenses on his Schedule E and the resident co-owner will report his proportionate share of those expenses which are deductible by the owner of a principal residence.

8. The investor co-owner will be designated as the property manager (or a real estate broker is employed as the property manager) to collect rent from the resident co-owner under the lease, maintain a bank account in his name (not a trade name or common name) for deposit of income and payment of expenses (property taxes, insurance premiums, homeowners' association charges and mortgage payments), and to disburse, at least quarterly, to the co-owners in proportion to their share of ownership, the spendable income remaining after paying operating and ownership expenses.

9. The investor co-owner will grant an option to purchase (call option) to the resident co-owner, exercisable at anytime during the fourth and fifth year of co-ownership by paying the amount of one half of the net equity in the property after deducting the loan balance remaining and customary seller closing costs from the fair market value of the property on the date of exercise, but the amount will not be less than the original capital investment of the investor co-owner in the property.

Should the resident co-owner exercise the option he holds to purchase the property, will the investor co-owner be able to qualify any profit on the sale of his one-half fractional ownership interest in the property for the §1031 profit tax exemption?

Before a quick answer can be given, one more co-ownership fact must be known: How did the co-owners vest title to the real estate?

If the co-owners vest title to the real estate in their individual names as tenants in common, each as to their individual fractional interest the answer is yes. As a tenant-in-common co-owner, the investor's ownership of a fractional interest in the real estate, not a partner's interest in a *tax partnership*, will qualify any profit taken on the sale of his interest for the §1031 exemption.

Here, the capital interest of the co-owners in the property, represented by a fractional share of participation in income, expenses and loan payments, was managed solely to **protect and conserve** the property held for investment. The services rendered to the tenant to meet those objections were established by the lease in exchange for rent. No source of income existed which was related to a **business service** provided to the tenant for an additional charge.

Further, each co-owner was vested as a tenant-in-common and retained their fundamental ownership rights of alienation. As tenants-in-common, the co-owners were unrestrained by the requirement that co-owners must consent to the sale, encumbrance or long-term lease or partition of their individual undivided fractional interest in the property.

Also, unanimous approval was required of the co-owners to sell, encumber or enter into a long-term lease of the entire property. The granting of options to purchase and rights of first refusal do not place a restraint on a co-owner's right to sell or encumber his fractional interest. However, should a co-owner decide to do so, the right of first refusal is triggered and may be exercised by the other co-owners to buy out the interest acquired, — at a price representing the co-owner's pro rata share of the property's fair market value on the date of exercise.

However, a **tax partnership** exists if restrictions on alienation rights held by each co-owner call for prior consent to a transfer by a co-owner, or an agreement exists for a co-owner to share in the profits of a business-related service provided to a tenant. Thus, the co-ownership would be a tax partnership which is then considered the owner of the property, even if the co-owners vest the title in their names as tenants in common.

For co-owners who are tax partners, the §1031 exemption is available to the entire group of co-owners on the sale of the entire property and the joint reinvestment of the net sales proceeds in replacement property. The same analysis applies to investors organized as a partnership or an LLC.

Qualifying fractional interests as §1031

When the resident co-owner in an equity sharing plan exercises his purchase option to buy out the investor co-owner (or on the investor's resale of his fractional interest to others), the investor co-owner must avoid partner status if he is to qualify the profit on the sale of his fractional ownership interest for the §1031 exemption.

Three viable exit strategies exist, the selection of one being the investor's decision, including:

- an IRC §761-(a) **election** by the co-owners to be treated as non-partner co-owners of separate interests in the real estate, not as co-owners of the partnership they previously established [IRC §1031(a)];

- a **distribution** by the vested partnership, LLC or DBA ("doing business as") to the co-owner, by granting the co-owner a fractional interest in title to the real estate, vested and with the rights of a common law tenant-in-common, for the co-owner's proportionate share of the ownership in the partnership or LLC; and

- a reliance on the co-owner's prior **Schedule E tax reporting** as an individual owner of an interest in real estate and on the stated purpose in the partnership/LLC operating agreement that the entity holds title for the co-owners, and does not own or operate the real estate.

The dilemma of an entity

An LLC or LP entity is typically used in **real estate syndications** to structure the co-ownership by investors of real estate. The use of an entity is both a practical and prudent title holding arrangement.

For example, California's property tax laws cause a **reassessment** of the property vested in an LLC or LP only when more than 50% of the ownership of the partnership is assigned to others by the original members of the LLC/LP.

Conversely, when title for the same co-owners is vested as tenants in common, each co-owner who conveys his TIC interests to others (including other co-owners), triggers reassessment of the fractional portion he conveyed. Thus, property taxes rise on each conveyance of a fractional interest, not just the 100% reassessment when a change of more than 50% of the original ownership in an LLC/LP eventually occurs.

Also, a **voluntary conveyance** or encumbrance by a co-owner of his interest in the property (as required to be allowed without restraint to receive federal non-partner status) may not concern other co-owners. However, a judgment lien imposed by a creditor on a vested co-owner's interest in title and a foreclosure by way of a judicial sale of the interest becomes an **involuntary conveyance** of the co-owner's interest to another person.

The creditor foreclosing or another party will acquire the debtor's co-ownership interest in the property. On acquisition as the highest bidder, they will in all likelihood file for the partition and eventual sale of the entire property, i.e., a forced sale by a creditor which an LLC/LP vesting avoids.

Another issue for vested co-owners is the release of their names to tenants as required on acquisition or change of management unless they appoint an agent for service of process. An LLC/LP vesting avoids the **public release** of their names since the co-owners are secreted behind a title holding entity they have formed — the LLC/LP vesting — to either own or simply hold title for the co-owners.

Most important of all, the co-owner is *shielded from liability* for any uninsured obligation he may incur as an owner of the property.

Thus, LLC/LP vestings are preferable for those co-owners not concerned about managing their profit tax avoidance when they invest or withdraw their investment from the group.

Acquiring a fractional interest

Consider an investor who sells his ownership interest in §1031 real estate. The investor is either the sole owner of the property or the owner of a fractional interest in property co-owned by a group. The investor has located a replacement property with an equity far greater than the net proceeds from his sale.

The seller of the replacement property is unwilling to sell on terms consisting of a purchase-money note for the balance due the seller after a down payment. Further, the investor is unwilling (or unable) to commit additional cash funds himself.

However, the investor has solicited another investor who will join with him as a co-owner and contribute the additional funds needed to cash out the seller's equity and purchase the property.

A purchase agreement is entered into to acquire the property. On closing, the two investors take title to the property as tenants in common, each as to an undivided fraction of the title in proportion to their contribution of cash toward the purchase.

They enter into a co-ownership agreement to spell out the arrangements they have agreed to between themselves regarding:

- the **management and operation** of the ongoing rental of the property; and

- the management of their **ownership interest** in the property to sell, encumber or lease (long-term) their interests or the entire property.

The co-ownership agreement addresses their **arrangements for management** of the entire property, as well as each individual's management of their fractional ownership interest, as follows:

1. Title will be vested as a TIC.

2. The property will be managed by one of the investors (or a broker) as the property manager for a one-year period with authority to locate tenants, enter into and enforce short-term leases and rental agreements in his own name, provide normal and customary tenant services, repair and maintenance of the property and maintain a bank account in the manager's name for deposits or receipts from the tenants and disbursements for expenses, mortgage payments and distributions to the co-owners.

3. The co-owners will share income, profits and losses in proportion to their fractional ownership share in the property.

4. Each co-owner will maintain separate tax reporting for their share of operating data, cost basis in their ownership interest and depreciation deductions, and will report their income and losses on their Schedule E with no partnership return to be filed.

5. Any sale, encumbrance, long-term lease or property management contract for the property will be unanimously approved by the co-owners.

6. The right of each co-owner to sell, encumber or partition their fractional ownership interest in the property will be unrestrained by any approval or consent by the other co-owner.

An **option to purchase** either another co-owner's fractional interest or the whole property may be granted to a co-owner or the syndicator who packaged the investment program.

Also, a **right of first refusal** may be granted to co-owners (or the syndicator) to be exercised on another co-owner's decision to sell, encumber or partition his fractional interest in the property.

The price paid on the exercise of the purchase rights is a pro rata amount of the fair market value of the entire property based on the co-owner's fractional ownership interest in the property.

Does the co-ownership agreement establish a *tax partnership* which would disqualify the sale of a co-owner's TIC interest from use of the §1031 profit tax exemption?

No! Neither co-owner is entering into a business relationship with any tenant by providing services unrelated to the rent paid for the property, nor are they sharing income received by a third party who is operating a business providing tenants with services unrelated to operating the rental, such as laundry, food, maid service or towels and linens.

Further, as tenant-in-common co-owners, they **unanimously approve** the hiring of a property manager who has authorization to carry out only those managerial steps necessary to operate the rental property, including customary landlord services and the repair and maintenance necessary to protect the property's improvements and conserve the property's value.

Thus, the co-owner has not relinquished his common law right of a tenant-in-common to act independently of the other co-owner to sell, encumber, enter into long-term leases and partition the property. No trade name, no joint operating (bank) account and no partnership agreement have been used or entered into to coordinate any sale, further encumbrance or long-term lease of the property.

The only "pooling" by the co-owners is the capital investment and its income, operating expenses and mortgage obligations of the ongoing ownership. Each co-owner has retained the ultimate property right to unilaterally withdraw from the investment by sale, encumbrance or partition without the consent of the other co-owner.

An alternative available for the vesting of a co-owner's interest is the use of a wholly owned, one-man LP or LLC for the **vesting** of his fractional interest. Title to his interest would be held in the name of his LP/LLC as a tenant-in-common with all other co-owners. Such a vesting for his undivided fractional interest would be considered by the IRS as title held by a *disregarded entity*. [Revenue Regulations §301.7701-3]

As a **disregarded entity**, an individual co-owner's use of his solely-owned LLC for the vesting of his fractional share of ownership would have absolutely no tax impact on the *non-partner status* of the co-owner's undivided interest.

If title to the entire property is vested in an entity such as an LP or LLC, the co-owners' arrangements must be limited so the entity is merely **holding title** for each individual co-owner, as tenants in common. Further, the entity and the co-owners will not file a partnership return (as 10 or less are already excused from doing so). The operating agreement for the LP/LLC needs to establish the entity holding title has no ownership interest in the property, and is acting solely as a trustee holding title for the co-owners. [Rev. Rul. 79-77]

A vesting change to benefit a partner

A multiple-unit, income-producing real estate project is owned and operated by an investment group as an unincorporated association structured as an LP or LLC.

A broker operates the property as the property manager, locating tenants, entering into leases, contracting for routine repairs and maintenance, depositing all rents into his trust account, disbursing funds for payment of operating expenses, mortgage payments and distributing spendable income to the co-owners.

The investment group (10 or less) does not file an IRS 1065 return and a K-1 information statement on annual operating income, expenses, interest and depreciation is not handed to the co-owners, since these filings are not required. [Rev. Proc. 84-35]

Each co-owner separately reports his fractional share of each year's rental operations on Schedule E of his return based on information provided him by the property manager.

One of the co-owners is selling his fractional interest to another co-owner or an outside party.

The price or value the co-owner receives for his fractional interest exceeds his adjusted cost basis remaining in this investment. Thus, the co-owner will take a profit on the sale or exchange, which for tax purposes must be reported, unless *exempt* or *excluded*. [IRC §1001]

While the co-owner desires to get out of the investment, he does not want to report the profit and pay taxes. He needs all the net proceeds from the sale, undiminished by taxes, to invest in his personal trade or business.

The co-owner locates other property which he will acquire for his own account and use as the premises which houses his business.

The property the co-owner wants to buy will be used in the co-owner's *trade or business* (or rented to his corporate business). Thus, the property he will acquire qualifies as §1031 property since it will be *held for productive use* in his trade or business. [IRC §1231]

Editor's note — If the property acquired is rented to the co-owner's corporate business, it will then be a rental classified as §1031 investment property, not §1031 business property. [IRC §1221]

To structure the sale of his fractional co-ownership interest in the investment group as the first leg of a §1031 reinvestment plan, the LLC/LP will convey to the co-owner by grant deed an undivided interest in the real estate equal to the co-owner's percentage share in the partnership.

Thus, a **liquidation** of the co-owner's interest in the partnership occurs as a *distribution in kind* of the partnership asset — conveyance of his pro rata share in title, a non-taxable event. As a result of the conveyance, the partnership becomes a TIC with the prior partner who now holds title to a fractional interest in the real estate as a tenant-in-common. As a tenant-in-common, the co-owner by TIC agreement is given all the rights to alienate his TIC interest, unrestrained, while agreeing to the centralized management of the property's maintenance and customary tenant-related services for a short period of time (not more than one year).

Now, as owner of a TIC interest in real estate and no longer a partner in the partnership, the co-owner sells (or exchanges) and conveys by grant deed his newly acquired TIC interest to a third party. The cash receipts of the sale are used to acquire the real estate he has located as the replacement property to complete his §1031 reinvestment plan.

Has the co-owner held ownership to the TIC interest for a sufficient length of time and for the right reasons to qualify the TIC ownership for the §1031 profit tax exemption?

Yes! The co-owner acquired ownership of the TIC interest with **no intention of liquidating** his investment in real estate by "cashing out." Thus, the co-owner held the TIC interest, unrestrained by the need for prior consent from the co-owners on his sale of his interest. The co-owner's only intent is to make money by remaining **continuously invested** in real estate.

The duration of his ownership in any one particular property, such as his ownership of the TIC interest, is not of concern. It is that the ownership must be held either for productive use in a trade or business or for investment. Since it was so held, the continuation of his investment after a sale by acquiring an ownership interest in replacement property (no matter it be for a long or short period of time) demonstrated the intent required to **remain unliquidated** in real estate investments. [**Bolker** v. **Commissioner** (9th Cir. 1985) 760 F2d 1039]

Editor's note — For property used in a trade or business to qualify as §1031 property, ownership must be retained for a period of one year. [IRC §1231]

The §1031 "no holding" period

The duration of a real estate investment needed to qualify for the §1031 exemption is not the duration of ownership of any one particular property. The investment duration (from one property to the next) required to qualify a property as **held for investment** is similar to the concept of "tacking" ownerships to qualify for holding periods required under other laws.

To avoid possible duration of ownership questions, the distribution of an asset to a partner to establish his TIC ownership of an interest in real estate should occur in the year prior to the year he sells the TIC interest and purchases replacement property.

However, the **duration** of the ownership of a particular parcel of real estate which is part of a §1031 reinvestment plan does not determine whether that property is §1031 property. The test for §1031 is whether the ownership, even though temporary, is **reinvested** in like-kind replacement property, i.e., the owner did not cash out.

A co-owner's intent when acquiring ownership of a TIC interest as a non-taxable distribution by an LP or LLC, is to **make money** by owning it as part of the process of reinvesting in replacement real estate on its sale or exchange.

However, the LP or LLC which distributed the fractional interest by grant deed cannot in a related transaction (or series of transactions) become the owner once again of the fractional interest, at least not concurrently. A co-partner can buy the TIC interest and take title to it in his name and hold it as a TIC interest. However, the partnership cannot, in a related or interconnected series of transactions, reacquire the fractional interest distributed to the partner.

If the partnership does reacquire the co-partner's TIC interest distributed by the partnership for a cash payment made by the partnership, the entire series of related transactions is **collapsed**. Then, the co-partner who withdrew from the partnership is considered to have personally received the cash, not the TIC interest, as a liquidation of his partnership interest since the partnership **paid to re-bundle** the ownership of the whole property in the name of the partnership. [**Crenshaw** v. **United States** (5th Cir. 1971) 450 F2d 472]

The §1031 by a twist of Schedule E

A lack of understanding seems to exist among taxpayers, CPAs and drafters of IRS forms regarding the consequences of IRC partnership classification for fractional ownership interests, 1065/K-1 co-ownership reporting forms, the exemption from filing by partnerships comprising 10 or less members and Schedule E filing by co-owners.

Thus, an **unintended application** of the §1031 exemption from profit tax reporting permits the profit taken on the sale of a fractional interest in a group investment which would otherwise be classified as a *tax partnership* to go unreported.

For example, when co-owners in an investment group file their individual returns, they report the operating data for rental properties on Schedule E, attached to their annual 1040 return. The partnership does not file a return nor provide K-1 reports.

Schedule E lists the co-owners' proportionate share of income, expenses, interest and depreciation separately. No reference is made (unless volunteered) to the aggregate data generated by the combined ownership of the real estate described in Schedule E.

The property data itemized by the individual co-owner on his Schedule E are but an **undisclosed fraction** of the income, expenses and deductions of the property identified on the co-owner's Schedule E. So far, so good during the ownership of the property.

But on the sale of the ownership interest in real estate listed in Schedule E, the IRS does not know (without an audit or a gratuitous disclosure) whether the interest sold is:

- an ownership **interest in a tax partnership** and thus excluded from tax-free treatment [IRC §1031(a)(2)(D)]; or

- a TIC ownership **interest in the asset** itself which, if unrestrained in its alienation rights, qualifies as §1031 property.

Thus, Schedule E fails to request information from the taxpayer on whether:

- the property ownership is connected by arrangement to additional tenant services paid for separate from rent; or

- the interest listed is a fractional interest.

Likewise, the IRS §1031 disclosure form does not inquire into whether the interest sold or exchanged:

- is a fractional interest in property;

- a fractional ownership interest in a partnership which owns the property; or

- a sole ownership interest in the property. [See IRS Form 8824]

Thus, a co-owner's annual reporting of his fractional interest on Schedule E (or F or C), and the sale and replacement of the interest on a §1031 disclosure form, does not trigger automatic audit or disallowance by the IRS. As a result, the exemption from profit taxes declared by the taxpayer is cleared, without a question about the possible tax partner status of the owner whose fractional interest is sold or acquired.

Editor's note — A school of thought holds the view that these deficiencies in the IRS forms produce the result intended by a more friendly and lenient IRS. However, this might not be the case. [Rev. Proc. 2002-22]

Co-owner's guidelines for non-partner tax status

The following is a briefly stated outline of the parameters of the conduct permitted by tenant-in-common co-owners, their manager, lenders and providers of services that will allow each tenant-in-common co-owner to treat his vested TIC interest in the property as §1031 property and, on a sale and reinvestment, qualify its profit as exempt from taxes.

1. The *co-owned property* must be §1031 like-kind property in the hands of each co-owner, not a partnership, as either:

    1.1 *Investment property* is property in which tenant services provided by the co-owners are limited to those services customarily rendered to tenants under standard leasing arrangements. Income derived from investment property includes:

a. *Passive income* derived from rental property, residential or non-residential, actively managed with rental agreements and short-term leases. [IRC §1221]

b. *Portfolio income* derived from master or ground leases and unimproved land. [IRC §1231]

1.2 *Trade or business property* is real estate held for productive use in a business owned by co-owners who are treated as a tax partnership. The co-owners share the profits of the business, not a rental property.

2. A *tenants in common vesting* cannot be held in the name of more than 35 co-owners, each co-owner being an individual or a disregarded entity solely owned by an individual, such as an inter vivos trust, LP or LLC used by an investor to hold his TIC interest.

   2.1 *Partnership (LP or LLC) vesting* is established as an entity holding title for the tenant-in-common co-owners as its stated purpose in the partnership or operating agreement. [**Commissioner** v. **Bollinger** (1985) 485 US 340]

3. A *co-owner's right of alienation* is defined as each co-owner's unilateral control over his TIC interest, including:

   3.1 *Alienation or partition*: No restrictions are permitted on each co-owner's decision to sell, encumber or long-term lease, such as:

      a. Prior approval or consent by others to alienate a co-owner's fractional interest in the property is not allowed.

   b. Unanimous approval of all co-owners is required to alienate the whole property.

   c. The right of first refusal held by the other co-owners on any one co-owner's alienation or partition action is permitted at fair market value.

   d. A purchase (call) option on the sale of a co-owner's interest can be granted to anyone at fair market value or cost. [Rev. Proc. 79-77]

   e. A guaranteed buy out (put option) for a co-owner to sell is not permitted.

   3.2 *Loans*: Lenders may not participate in the property's operating income, equity increase or resale proceeds.

   3.3 *Subordinated interests*: All co-owners must share income, profit or loss in proportion to their contribution to capital and on a parity basis.

4. *Property protection and conservation*:

   4.1 The care and maintenance of the property by the property manager is limited to minor or non-structural repairs and maintenance. [Rev. Proc. 79-77]

      a. Structural repairs, maintenance or construction of improvements require unanimous approval of the co-owners.

   4.2 Tenant services customarily provided under lease and rental agreements can be provided by the property manager as part of the tenant's rent.

      a. Tenant improvements to ready the property for long-term tenants require unanimous approval of the co-owners.

4.3 Additional trade or business related services provided to the tenants by the property manager for an additional charge is permitted, so long as there is no sharing of that income with the co-owners.

5. *Property management operations*:

5.1 Co-owners may not operate under any trade name or DBA or refer to themselves as partners, shareholders or members of a group.

5.2 Co-owners may not maintain a joint bank account.

5.3 Co-owners may unanimously approve one co-owner as the property manager or hire a broker as the property manager, but a lessee cannot be the property manager.

   a. The term of the property manager's employment cannot exceed one year and any renewal or extension requires unanimous approval by the co-owners.

   b. The property manager may be authorized to locate tenants, enter into short-term lease and rental agreements and enforce the agreements in his name by eviction and collection of rent.

   c. The property manager's fee to be comparable to fees paid managers of similar properties and cannot be based on net income or distributions to co-owners, or be subordinated to distribution to co-owners.

5.4 The property manager may, in the manager's name, but not in a common name for the co-owners:

   a. Enter into service contracts to provide customary tenant services normally required by lease and rental agreements and undertake repairs and maintenance necessary to protect and conserve the property.

   b. Maintain a bank account for the deposit of rents, disbursements for expenses, payment of mortgages and distribution to co-owners of net spendable income.

   c. Place insurance.

   d. Hire a resident agent or manager.

   e. Prepare profit and loss operating statements reflecting each co-owner's proportionate share of income, expenses and interest.

6. *Tax returns and filings with the IRS*:

6.1 No partnership return may be filed.

6.2 Each co-owner must report their share of income, expenses, interest and depreciation on their Schedule E attached to their IRS Form 1041.

6.3 On a change of vesting from a partnership or LLC to a TIC and termination of reporting as a partnership, co-owners must file for an IRC §761 election out of partnership treatment for a distribution in kind to conduct themselves as common law tenant-in- common co-owners as required of §1031 rules.

SECTION C

Reinvestment Scenarios

Chapter 13

Estate building: equal-or-greater debt and equity

This chapter analyzes the profit reporting impact of commonly negotiated variations in price trade-up situations.

Variations of the price trade-up

An investor wants to increase the total dollar value of his real estate holdings, a venture called *estate building*. He will accomplish his goal by increasing his mortgage funded investment with income-producing real estate.

To acquire greater-valued property, the investor will use the large equity in a property he has owned for several years and no longer wants. The investor will sell the property and, with the net sales proceeds, purchase replacement properties in a **diversification** effort. Also, he will take on mortgage debt three or four times greater in amount than the loan now encumbering the property he will sell.

The entire amount of net proceeds the investor will receive from the sale will be reinvested in replacement properties.

Here, the investor can convert his equity in one property, by sale or exchange, into one or more other properties and report none of the profit on the sale of his property.

However, to **exempt all profit** on the sale of his property from taxes, the investor must:

- take on the responsibility for *equal-or-greater* debt and receive an *equal-or-greater* equity in replacement properties than the debt and equity on the property he will sell;

- avoid originating *equity financing* or *refinancing* on the property he is selling [See Chapter 24];

- avoid *actual and constructive receipt* of the sales proceeds from the sale of his property [See Chapters 18 and 21]; and

- comply with the 45-day *identification* restriction and the 180-day *acquisition* limitation rules for acquiring the replacement properties. [See Chapter 15]

In this scenario, no diminution of the owner's wealth will occur by taxation of profits on the sale. Thus, capital gains tax rates are uninvolved in the sale of his real estate. The investor is reinvesting in other real estate, implicitly carrying his profit forward to the replacement properties in a continuation of his investment in real estate.

The owner can either:

- "sell now and buy now" in a *concurrent closing* of the §1031 reinvestment; or

- "sell now and buy later" in a *delayed closing* of his §1031 reinvestment. [Internal Revenue Code §1031(a)(3)]

The objectives of the following examples of price trade-up situations include:

- exposing the reader to the **tax consequences** experienced by investors under various arrangements normally negotiated when selling, exchanging or purchasing property in a §1031 reinvestment plan; and

- presenting **alternative arrangements**, the terms of which provide different, and possibly more favorable, overall tax results.

FACTS OF EXAMPLE 1 — PRICE TRADE-UP

A. Remaining Cost Basis: $300,000

B. §1031 Transaction: Greater debt assumed and greater equity acquired.

Items:	Property sold and contributions made:	Property acquired and adjustments received:
1. Market price: 2. Existing debt:	$600,000 $200,000	$1200,000 $700,000
3. Existing equity: 4. Adjustments: Type:	$400,000 $100,000 Purchase-money note	$500,000 $0 _____

C. Observations:

Trade-up into greater debt.

Trade-up into a larger equity.

Investor executes a note to adjust for the larger equity he acquires.

The primary purpose for a price trade-up situation is the avoidance of the taxation of profits on a sale by locating and acquiring replacement properties to continue the investment in real estate.

Trade-up Example No. 1

To **fully qualify** the profit taken in a trade-up situation for the §1031 exemption, the amounts of the loan and the equity in the replacement property generally need to be equal to or greater than the respective amounts of loan and equity on the property sold. Thus, the **debt relief** from the property sold is fully offset. Also, the net proceeds from the equity in the property sold are fully reinvested in replacement properties and any withdrawals made are offset by the execution of a carryback note by the investor.

For example, an investor owns like-kind property valued at $600,000 which he has agreed to sell. The property has an existing debt of $200,000 and an equity of $400,000. The investor's remaining cost basis in the property is $300,000.

The like-kind replacement property selected for acquisition is priced at $1,200,000. It has an existing loan of $700,000 and a resulting equity of $500,000. The investor will use his $400,000 equity in the property he is selling (or exchanging) as a down payment to purchase the replacement property.

The investor will assume the existing loan of $700,000 and **execute a $100,000 note** to pay the balance remaining to be paid on the purchase price. The creation of the carryback note is referred to, for §1031 purposes, as "adjusting the differences" or "balancing the equities" between the properties. [See Figure 1(a) accompanying this chapter]

On the sale, the entire $300,000 basis is automatically carried forward to the replacement property he will buy. Implicitly, his $300,000 profit will also be carried forward to the replacement property if the combined "sell and buy" transactions fully meet the §1031 debt and equity offset tests. [See Figure 1(b) accompanying this chapter]

Here, the investor's entire profit on the sale will go unreported as *exempt*, since:

- the loan amount to be assumed by the investor on the replacement property will **exceed** the loan amount on the property he has sold [See Figure 1(b) §1.3]; and

- the entire net equity in the property he sold (the sales proceeds) will be **reinvested** in the replacement property.

Is the $100,000 carryback note created by the investor as part of the consideration he paid to purchase the replacement property reported and taxed as profit?

No! The note evidences debt owed by the investor which he created as a **promise to pay** part of the price of the replacement property in a credit sale. The investor's purchase of property on credit is not a taxable event. Further, the execution of the purchase-money note constitutes an additional capital investment to which the investor has committed himself. [See Figure 1(b) §1.11]

As capital invested, the amount of the purchase-money note is added to the basis in the replacement property, as though the amount of the note had now been paid in cash. [See Figure 1(b) §5.2(e)]

The investor receives a $500,000 equity in the replacement property in exchange for his $400,000 cash equity in the property sold or exchanged and the execution of the $100,000 purchase-money note.

To analyze the basis resulting from this example, the investor's broker will use a §1031 Profit and Basis Recap Sheet. The **adjustments** in the basis carried forward from the property sold include:

- the amount of any **increase in debt** due to the investor's assumption of a loan on the replacement property exceeding the amount of the loan which encumbered the property he sold; and

- the amount of the **carryback note** the investor executed to pay for the difference between the equity acquired in the replacement property and the cash sales proceeds from the property he sold. [See Figure 1(b) §§5.1 and 5.2]

Variations on the basic trade-up facts

Consistent with the first example, each of the following §1031 reinvestment plan examples retains the same price for both the property sold or exchanged and the replacement property — a price of $600,000 and $1,200,000 respectively — and thus the same $600,000 **price trade-up**. Also retained in the examples is the $300,000 remaining cost basis and $300,000 profit taken on the property sold.

The variations in each example from the first example are given to demonstrate the tax consequences resulting from various different terms commonly negotiated by buyers and sellers.

The facts varying from Example No. 1 include:

Example No. 2:

- **Cash** is withdrawn by the investor (from the impounded sales proceeds) on the purchase of the replacement property and the down payment is reduced. The **carryback note** executed to pay part of the purchase price for the replacement property is increased to cover the amount of cash withdrawn.

Figure 1(b)

§1031 PROFIT AND BASIS RECAP SHEET

Date _____, 20_____ Prepared by: _____

OWNER'S NAME: __Example Number 1_____

PROPERTY SOLD/EXCHANGED: _____

COMMENTS: _____
_____

REPLACEMENT PROPERTY: _____

COMMENTS: _____
_____

1. NET DEBT RELIEF AND CASH ITEMS

Net existing debt:

1.1   Balance of debt(s) owner is **relieved** of on
      all property sold/exchanged . . . . + $ __200,000__

1.2   Balance of debt(s) owner **assumed** on
      §1031 property acquired . . . . – $ __700,000__

1.3   **Total net existing debt:** Enter the sum of 1.1 & 1.2 as either:

      (a) **Net debt relief** (amount by which 1.1 exceeds 1.2) . . . . + $ ____0____

      (b) **Net debt assumed** (amount by which 1.2 exceeds 1.1) . . . . – $ __500,000__

Cash items received on close of the property sold:

1.4   Amount of cash **received** on sale (excluding prorations) . . . . . . $ _____

1.5   Amount of carryback note **received** on sale . . . . $ _____

1.6   Equity value in unqualified property **received** on sale . . . . $ _____

1.7   **Total of cash items received on closing the property sold:**
      (The sum of 1.4, 1.5 & 1.6) . . . . + $ ____0____

**Net cash items received or transferred on close of the
replacement property:**

1.8   Amount of cash items **received** with replacement property
      (excluding prorations) . . . . + $ _____

1.9   Amount of cash owner **contributed** (excluding prorations) . . . . . . $ _____

1.10 Transactional costs **disbursed** at any time on either property
      (excluding prorations and loan payoffs) . . . . $ _____

1.11 Amount of purchase-money notes **owner executed** in
      part payment for the replacement property . . . . $ __100,000__

1.12 Equity value of any unqualified property owner **exchanged** . . . . . $ _____

1.13 Subtotal of cash items owner **transferred** (1.9 through 1.12) . . . . – $ __100,000__

1.14 **Total net cash items:** Enter the sum of 1.8 & 1.13 as either:

      (a) **Net cash items owner received:**
           (amount by which 1.8 exceeds 1.13) . . . . + $ ____0____

      (b) **Net cash items owner transferred:**
           (amount by which 1.13 exceeds 1.8) . . . . – $ __100,000__

Netting all debt relief and cash items:

1.15 Enter net debt **relief** from 1.3(a) . . . . + $ _____

1.16 Enter net cash items

      (a) owner **received** from 1.14(a) . . . . + $ _____

      (b) owner **transferred** from 1.14(b) . . . . – $ __100,000__

1.17 Net debt relief and cash items, (1.15 & 1.16, but not less than zero) . . . . + $ ____0____

1.18 Cash items received on sale from 1.7 . . . . + $ ____0____

1.19 **TOTAL net money and other properties owner received:**
      (The sum of 1.17 and 1.18) . . . . + $ ____0____

2. PROFIT/LOSS ON TRANSFER OF UNQUALIFIED PROPERTY

2.1   Market value of unqualified property owner transferred. . . . . . . + $ _____

2.2   Remaining cost basis in unqualified property owner
      transferred . . . . – $ _____

2.3   **Total profit/loss on unqualified property owner transferred:** . . . . (+ or –) $ ____0____

— — — — — — — — — — — — — — — PAGE ONE OF TWO — FORM 354 — — — — — — — — — — — — — — — — — —

128

Figure 1(b) cont.

3. PROFIT REALIZED ON THE §1031 PROPERTY SOLD OR EXCHANGED (before applying the §1031 exemption)

Consideration owner received:

3.1 Debt relief: Enter amount from 1.1 . . . . $ __200,000__

3.2 Market value of §1031 placement property owner acquired . . . . . $ __1,200,000__

3.3 Total cash items received from property sold:
Enter amount from 1.7 . . . . $ _____

3.4 Total cash items received with replacement property:
Enter amount from 1.8 . . . . $ _____

3.5 Total consideration owner received (3.1 through 3.4) . . . . + $ __1,400,000__

Consideration owner transferred:

3.6 Debt owner assumed: Enter amount from 1.2 . . . . $ __700,000__

3.7 Enter remaining cost basis in all §1031 properties
owner transferred . . . . $ __300,000__

3.8 Cash owner contributed: Enter amount from 1.9 . . . . $ _____

3.9 Transactional costs disbursed: Enter amount from 1.10 . . . . $ _____

3.10 Purchase notes owner executed: Enter amount from 1.11 . . . . . . $ __100,000__

3.11 Remaining cost basis in unqualified property owner transferred:
Enter amount from 2.2 . . . . $ _____

3.12 Total consideration owner transferred (3.6 through 3.11) . . . . − $ __1,100,000__

3.13 **Total profits realized in §1031 property sold or exchanged:**
(3.5 less 3.12) . . . . (+)or −) $ __300,000__

4. REPORTABLE PROFIT/LOSS ON THE §1031 TRANSACTION

4.1 Total net debt relief and cash items owner receives:
Enter amount from 1.19, but not less than zero . . . . + $ __0__

    (a) Carryback basis allocation: Amount by which 3.7
        exceeds 1.1, but not more than the amount at 1.5. . . . . − $ __0__

4.2 Total profit/loss on unqualified property owner transferred:
Enter amount from 2.3 . . . . (+ or −) $ __0__

4.3 Subtotal: The amount of equity withdrawn:
(the sum of 4.1, (a) and 4.2) . . . . (+ or −) $ __0__

4.4 Total profits realized in §1031 property sold/exchanged:
Enter amount from 3.13 (But not less than zero) . . . . $ __300,000__

4.5 **Total reportable profit/loss:** (Enter lesser of 4.3 or 4.4) . . . . (+ or −) $ __0__

5. BASIS OF ALL PROPERTY(IES) RECEIVED

5.1 Debt relief. Enter amounts from:

    (a) 1.3(a) Net debt relief. . . . . − $ _____

    (b) 1.3(b) Net debt assumed . . . . + $ __500,000__

5.2 Cash items. Enter amounts from:

    (a) 1.7   Cash items received on the sale . . . . − $ _____

    (b) 1.8   Cash items received on purchase . . . . − $ _____

    (c) 1.9   Cash contributed . . . . + $ _____

    (d) 1.10   Transactional cost disbursed . . . . + $ _____

    (e) 1.11   Purchase-money notes executed . . . . + $ __100,000__

5.3 Remaining cost basis in all property transferred.
Enter amounts from:

    (a) 3.7   . . . . + $ __300,000__

    (b) 3.11   . . . . + $ _____

5.4 Reportable profit/loss. Enter amount from 4.5 . . . . (+ or −) $ _____

5.5 **Basis of Replacement Property(ies) and cash items:**
(The sum of 5.1 through 5.4) . . . . $ __900,000__
(See Form 354.5 for priority allocation to cash items, multiple
replacement properties and between land and improvements.)

Example No. 3:

- **Other property** is exchanged by the investor in lieu of executing a purchase-money note in part payment for the purchase of the replacement property.

Example No. 4:

- In an actual exchange of properties, the replacement property has a **lesser equity** which is adjusted for by the investor carrying back a note on the property sold.

As a rule in a price trade-up situation, no profit will be taxed unless an **equity trade-down** occurs by acquiring replacement property with a smaller equity than the equity in the property sold or exchanged. In order to adjust for the imbalance brought about by the acquisition of a smaller equity in a price trade-down situation, the investor **withdraws cash** (or receives other cash items) in lieu of using the cash to reduce the principal on the loan he assumes. A reduction would bring the equity in the replacement property in line with the equity in the property sold.

Further, the investor can reduce the principal on the loan assumed on his purchase of the replacement property if escrow applies the remainder of the investor's sales proceeds to the principal on the loan and thus eliminating the investor's receipt of cash. [See Example No. 4]

Trade-up Example No. 2

The facts of Example No. 2 differ from Example No. 1 as follows:

- the investor sells his property for cash and pays off the $200,000 existing loan on his property through escrow by using some of the cash proceeds from the sale;

- the investor purchases the replacement property on terms calling for a cash down payment which is $100,000 less than the net sales proceeds from the property he sold;

- the investor pays the balance due on his purchase of the replacement property by executing a $200,000 purchase-money note secured by a trust deed on the replacement property; and

- the investor receives $100,000 in cash from his impounded net sales proceeds when he acquires ownership of the replacement property. [See Figure 2(a) accompanying this chapter]

Question No. 1: Will the investor report profit on the portion of the cash price received for the property sold and used by the investor to pay off the loan encumbering the property?

No! The cash received by the investor on the sale of his property was **deposited into escrow** by the buyer. On closing, funds accruing to the account of the investor from the buyer's deposit were disbursed by escrow to pay off the loan encumbering the property the investor sold. Thus, the funds were not free to be received by the investor and are not reported as profit.

A §1031 transaction requires the investor to have had *actual or constructive receipt* of his sales proceeds before any taxable profit is reported. The investor received debt relief, not cash, no different than had his buyer assumed the loan. [See Figure 2(b) §1.1 accompanying this chapter]

The key to qualifying the profit for the §1031 exemption is the fact that the investor avoids actual or constructive receipt of cash when it is deposited in escrow by someone else and then disbursed by escrow to pay off the investor's loan to meet the conditions for escrow to close.

Here, the investor is unable to **unilaterally remove** the cash from escrow, on demand, at any time. Thus, he avoids constructive receipt. Escrow had instructions to pay off the investor's loan on closing from funds accruing to the account of the investor in order for escrow to deliver clear title to the buyer. [**Barker** v. **Commissioner** (1980) 74 TC 555]

Figure 2(a)

FACTS OF EXAMPLE 2 — PRICE TRADE-UP

A. Remaining Cost Basis: $300,000

B. §1031 Transaction: Greater debt assumed and greater equity acquired.

Items:	Property sold and adjustments made:	Replacement property and adjustments received:
1. Market price: 2. Existing debt:	$600,000 $200,000	$1,200,000 $700,000
3. Existing equity: 4. Adjustments: Type:	$400,000 $200,000 Purchase-money note	$500,000 $100,000 Cash

C. Observations:

Investor receives cash of $100,000 on completion.

The investor's property is refinanced by the buyer to generate cash that the investor uses to pay off his loans.

The investor executes a note to adjust equities and offset cash received by the investor on acquisition of the replacement property.

Question No. 2: Can the investor withdraw cash on completion of the §1031 reinvestment and avoid reporting any profits?

Yes! The $100,000 cash withdrawn is not reportable as profit since:

- the cash is **received on** or **after** ownership of the replacement property is acquired; and

- the cash received is **offset** by the investor's execution of a carryback note to the seller of the replacement property in an amount equal to or greater than the amount of cash the investor received. [See Figure 2(b) §§1.8 and 1.11]

The $200,000 carryback note was created both as a $100,000 payment on the purchase price for the replacement property and as evidence of a repayment of the $100,000 in cash received. [**Feldman** v. **Commissioner** (1930) 18 BTA 1222; IRS Revenue Ruling 72-456; IRC §1031(b)]

As a result, the investor's equity of $400,000 in the property he sold for cash has been replaced with a $500,000 equity in the property he purchased based on $300,000 in cash and $200,000 in carryback financing he negotiated.

The same tax result would have occurred had the investor **further encumbered** the replacement property on his acquisition with an equity loan,

Figure 2(b)

§1031 PROFIT AND BASIS RECAP SHEET

Date _____, 20_____ Prepared by: _____

OWNER'S NAME: _Example Number 2_____

PROPERTY SOLD/EXCHANGED: _____

COMMENTS: _____
_____

REPLACEMENT PROPERTY: _____

COMMENTS: _____
_____

1. NET DEBT RELIEF AND CASH ITEMS

Net existing debt:

1.1 Balance of debt(s) owner is **relieved** of on
     all property sold/exchanged . . . . + $ __200,000__

1.2 Balance of debt(s) owner **assumed** on
     §1031 property acquired . . . . − $ __700,000__

1.3 **Total net existing debt:** Enter the sum of 1.1 & 1.2 as either:

   (a) **Net debt relief** (amount by which 1.1 exceeds 1.2) . . . . + $ __0__

   (b) **Net debt assumed** (amount by which 1.2 exceeds 1.1) . . . . − $ __500,000__

Cash items received on close of the property sold:

1.4 Amount of cash **received** on sale (excluding prorations) . . . . $ _____

1.5 Amount of carryback note **received** on sale . . . . $ _____

1.6 Equity value in unqualified property **received** on sale . . . . $ _____

1.7 **Total of cash items received on closing the property sold:**
     (The sum of 1.4, 1.5 & 1.6) . . . . + $ __0__

Net cash items received or transferred on close of the replacement property:

1.8 Amount of cash items **received** with replacement property
     (excluding prorations) . . . . + $ __100,000__

1.9 Amount of cash owner **contributed** (excluding prorations) . . . . . . $ _____

1.10 Transactional costs **disbursed** at any time on either property
     (excluding prorations and loan payoffs) . . . . $ _____

1.11 Amount of purchase-money notes **owner executed** in
     part payment for the replacement property . . . . $ __200,000__

1.12 Equity value of any unqualified property owner **exchanged** . . . . . $ _____

1.13 Subtotal of cash items owner **transferred** (1.9 through 1.12) . . . . − $ __200,000__

1.14 **Total net cash items:** Enter the sum of 1.8 & 1.13 as either:

   (a) **Net cash items owner received:**
     (amount by which 1.8 exceeds 1.13) . . . . + $ _____

   (b) **Net cash items owner transferred:**
     (amount by which 1.13 exceeds 1.8) . . . . − $ __100,000__

Netting all debt relief and cash items:

1.15 Enter net debt **relief** from 1.3(a) . . . . + $ _____

1.16 Enter net cash items

   (a) owner **received** from 1.14(a) . . . . + $ _____

   (b) owner **transferred** from 1.14(b) . . . . − $ __100,000__

1.17 Net debt relief and cash items, (1.15 & 1.16, but not less than zero) . . . . + $ __0__

1.18 Cash items received on sale from 1.7 . . . . + $ __0__

1.19 **TOTAL net money and other properties owner received:**
     (The sum of 1.17 and 1.18) . . . . + $ __0__

2. PROFIT/LOSS ON TRANSFER OF UNQUALIFIED PROPERTY

2.1 Market value of unqualified property owner transferred. . . . . . . + $ _____

2.2 Remaining cost basis in unqualified property owner
     transferred . . . . − $ _____

2.3 **Total profit/loss on unqualified property owner transferred:** . . . . (+ or −) $ __0__

— — — — — — — — — — — — — PAGE ONE OF TWO — FORM 354 — — — — — — — — — — — — — — — — —

Figure 2(b) cont. — — — — — — — — PAGE TWO OF TWO — FORM 354 — — — — — — — — — — — — — —

3. PROFIT REALIZED ON THE §1031 PROPERTY SOLD OR EXCHANGED
(before applying the §1031 exemption)
Consideration owner received:

3.1 Debt relief: Enter amount from 1.1 . . . . $ **200,000**

3.2 Market value of §1031 placement property owner acquired . . . . . $ **1,200,000**

3.3 Total cash items received from property sold:
Enter amount from 1.7 . . . . $ _____

3.4 Total cash items received with replacement property:
Enter amount from 1.8 . . . . $ **100,000**

3.5 Total consideration owner received (3.1 through 3.4) . . . . + $ **1,500,000**

Consideration owner transferred:

3.6 Debt owner assumed: Enter amount from 1.2 . . . . $ **700,000**

3.7 Enter remaining cost basis in all §1031 properties
owner transferred . . . . $ **300,000**

3.8 Cash owner contributed: Enter amount from 1.9 . . . . $ _____

3.9 Transactional costs disbursed: Enter amount from 1.10 . . . . $ _____

3.10 Purchase notes owner executed: Enter amount from 1.11 . . . . . . $ **200,000**

3.11 Remaining cost basis in unqualified property owner transferred:
Enter amount from 2.2 . . . . $ _____

3.12 Total consideration owner transferred (3.6 through 3.11) . . . . – $ **1,200,000**

3.13 **Total profits realized in §1031 property sold or exchanged:**
(3.5 less 3.12) . . . . (+ or –) $ **300,000**

4. REPORTABLE PROFIT/LOSS ON THE §1031 TRANSACTION

4.1 Total net debt relief and cash items owner receives:
Enter amount from 1.19, but not less than zero . . . . + $ **0**

(a) Carryback basis allocation: Amount by which 3.7
exceeds 1.1, but not more than the amount at 1.5 . . . . – $ **0**

4.2 Total profit/loss on unqualified property owner transferred:
Enter amount from 2.3 . . . . (+ or –) $ **0**

4.3 Subtotal: The amount of equity withdrawn:
(the sum of 4.1, (a) and 4.2) . . . . (+ or –) $ **0**

4.4 Total profits realized in §1031 property sold/exchanged:
Enter amount from 3.13 (But not less than zero) . . . . $ **300,000**

4.5 **Total reportable profit/loss: (Enter lesser of 4.3 or 4.4)** . . . . (+ or –) $ **0**

5. BASIS OF ALL PROPERTY(IES) RECEIVED

5.1 Debt relief. Enter amounts from:

(a) 1.3(a) Net debt relief . . . . – $ **0**

(b) 1.3(b) Net debt assumed . . . . + $ **500,000**

5.2 Cash items. Enter amounts from:

(a) 1.7   Cash items received on the sale . . . . – $ _____

(b) 1.8   Cash items received on purchase . . . . – $ **100,000**

(c) 1.9   Cash contributed . . . . + $ _____

(d) 1.10 Transactional cost disbursed . . . . + $ _____

(e) 1.11 Purchase-money notes executed . . . . + $ **200,000**

5.3 Remaining cost basis in all property transferred.
Enter amounts from:

(a) 3.7 . . . . + $ **300,000**

(b) 3.11 . . . . + $ _____

5.4 Reportable profit/loss. Enter amount from 4.5 . . . . (+ or –) $ **0**

5.5 **Basis of Replacement Property(ies) and cash items:**
(The sum of 5.1 through 5.4) . . . . $ **900,000**
(See Form 354.5 for priority allocation to cash items, multiple
replacement properties and between land and improvements.)

FACTS OF EXAMPLE 3 — PRICE TRADE-UP

A. Remaining Cost Basis: $300,000; Boot has a basis of $75,000

B. §1031 Transaction: Greater debt assumed and greater equity acquired.

Items:	Property sold and adjustments made:	Replacement property and adjustments received:
1. Market price: 2. Existing debt:	$600,000 $200,000	$1,200,000 $700,000
3. Existing equity: 4. Adjustments: Type:	$400,000 $100,000 Boat	$500,000 $0 _____

C. Observations:

Investor transfers non-qualifying property — a boat.

Investor takes a profit of $25,000 on the sale/exchange of the boat.

The boat is unencumbered.

---

generating the $100,000 from a third-party lender instead of through the carryback note on the replacement property and the withdrawal of $100,000. The cash withdrawn had as its source the net proceeds held by the §1031 trustee from the sale of the investor's property.

Here, the trustee disburses the remaining funds from the sale to either:

- the escrow handling the investor's purchase of the replacement property, who will, in turn, release the funds to the investor on closing, which is the preferable handling; or

- the investor directly on or after the close of escrow on his purchase of the replacement property.

Trade-up Example No. 3

The facts of Example No. 3 differ from the first example as follows:

- the investor exchanges an unencumbered boat he owns for an agreed-to price of $100,000 to adjust for the larger equity in the replacement property he will acquire in exchange for his real estate; and

- the boat has a remaining cost basis of $75,000 (and thus a $25,000 profit). [See Figure 3(a) accompanying this chapter]

The $75,000 basis in the boat conveyed or exchanged by the investor is carried forward to the replacement property as is the $300,000 remaining cost basis in the property he sold or exchanged. The boat's basis becomes part of the cost basis for the replacement property. [See Figure 3(b) §5.3(b) accompanying this chapter]

Figure 3(b)

§1031 PROFIT AND BASIS RECAP SHEET

Date _____, 20_____ Prepared by: _____

OWNER'S NAME: _Example Number 3_____

PROPERTY SOLD/EXCHANGED: _____

COMMENTS: _____

_____

REPLACEMENT PROPERTY: _____

COMMENTS: _____

_____

1. NET DEBT RELIEF AND CASH ITEMS

Net existing debt:

1.1   Balance of debt(s) owner is **relieved** of on all property sold/exchanged . . . . + $ __200,000__

1.2   Balance of debt(s) owner **assumed** on §1031 property acquired . . . . − $ __700,000__

1.3   **Total net existing debt:** Enter the sum of 1.1 & 1.2 as either:

     (a) **Net debt relief** (amount by which 1.1 exceeds 1.2). . . . . + $ __0__

     (b) **Net debt assumed** (amount by which 1.2 exceeds 1.1) . . . . − $ __500,000__

Cash items received on close of the property sold:

1.4   Amount of cash **received** on sale (excluding prorations). . . . . . . $ _____

1.5   Amount of carryback note **received** on sale . . . . $ _____

1.6   Equity value in unqualified property **received** on sale . . . . $ _____

1.7   **Total of cash items received on closing the property sold:** (The sum of 1.4, 1.5 & 1.6). . . . . + $ __0__

Net cash items received or transferred on close of the replacement property:

1.8   Amount of cash items **received** with replacement property (excluding prorations). . . . . + $ _____

1.9   Amount of cash owner **contributed** (excluding prorations) . . . . . . $ _____

1.10   Transactional costs **disbursed** at any time on either property (excluding prorations and loan payoffs) . . . . $ _____

1.11   Amount of purchase-money notes **owner executed** in part payment for the replacement property . . . . $ _____

1.12   Equity value of any unqualified property owner **exchanged** . . . . . $ __100,000__

1.13   Subtotal of cash items owner **transferred** (1.9 through 1.12) . . . . − $ __100,000__

1.14   **Total net cash items:** Enter the sum of 1.8 & 1.13 as either:

     (a) **Net cash items owner received:** (amount by which 1.8 exceeds 1.13) . . . . + $ _____

     (b) **Net cash items owner transferred:** (amount by which 1.13 exceeds 1.8) . . . . − $ __100,000__

Netting all debt relief and cash items:

1.15   Enter net debt **relief** from 1.3(a) . . . . + $ _____

1.16   Enter net cash items

     (a) owner **received** from 1.14(a). . . . . + $ _____

     (b) owner **transferred** from 1.14(b). − $ __100,000__

1.17   Net debt relief and cash items, (1.15 & 1.16, but not less than zero) . . . . + $ __0__

1.18   Cash items received on sale from 1.7 . . . . + $ __0__

1.19   **TOTAL net money and other properties owner received:** (The sum of 1.17 and 1.18) . . . . + $ __0__

2. PROFIT/LOSS ON TRANSFER OF UNQUALIFIED PROPERTY

2.1   Market value of unqualified property owner transferred. . . . . . . + $ __100,000__

2.2   Remaining cost basis in unqualified property owner transferred . . . . − $ __75,000__

2.3   **Total profit/loss on unqualified property owner transferred:**. . . . . (+)or −) $ __25,000__

— — — — — — — — — — — — — — — PAGE ONE OF TWO — FORM 354 — — — — — — — — — — — — — — — — — —

135

Figure 3(b) cont.

3. PROFIT REALIZED ON THE §1031 PROPERTY SOLD OR EXCHANGED
   (before applying the §1031 exemption)
   Consideration owner received:

   3.1 Debt relief: Enter amount from 1.1 .... $ __200,000__
   3.2 Market value of §1031 placement property owner acquired ..... $ __1,200,000__
   3.3 Total cash items received from property sold:
        Enter amount from 1.7 .... $_____
   3.4 Total cash items received with replacement property:
        Enter amount from 1.8 .... $_____
   3.5 Total consideration owner received (3.1 through 3.4) .... + $ __1,400,000__

   Consideration owner transferred:

   3.6 Debt owner assumed: Enter amount from 1.2 .... $ __700,000__
   3.7 Enter remaining cost basis in all §1031 properties
        owner transferred .... $ __300,000__
   3.8 Cash owner contributed: Enter amount from 1.9 .... $_____
   3.9 Transactional costs disbursed: Enter amount from 1.10 .... $_____
   3.10 Purchase notes owner executed: Enter amount from 1.11 ...... $_____
   3.11 Remaining cost basis in unqualified property owner transferred:
        Enter amount from 2.2 .... $ __75,000__
   3.12 Total consideration owner transferred (3.6 through 3.11) .... – $ __1,075,000__
   3.13 **Total profits realized in §1031 property sold or exchanged:**
        (3.5 less 3.12) .... (+)or –) $ __325,000__

4. REPORTABLE PROFIT/LOSS ON THE §1031 TRANSACTION

   4.1 Total net debt relief and cash items owner receives:
        Enter amount from 1.19, but not less than zero .... + $ ____0____
        (a) Carryback basis allocation: Amount by which 3.7
            exceeds 1.1, but not more than the amount at 1.5........ – $_____
   4.2 Total profit/loss on unqualified property owner transferred:
        Enter amount from 2.3 .... (+)or –) $ __25,000__
   4.3 Subtotal: The amount of equity withdrawn:
        (the sum of 4.1, (a) and 4.2) .... (+)or –) $ __25,000__
   4.4 Total profits realized in §1031 property sold/exchanged:
        Enter amount from 3.13 (But not less than zero) .... $ __325,000__
   4.5 **Total reportable profit/loss:** (Enter lesser of 4.3 or 4.4) .... (+)or –) $ __25,000__

5. BASIS OF ALL PROPERTY(IES) RECEIVED

   5.1 Debt relief. Enter amounts from:
        (a) 1.3(a) Net debt relief .... – $_____
        (b) 1.3(b) Net debt assumed .... + $ __500,000__
   5.2 Cash items. Enter amounts from:
        (a) 1.7   Cash items received on the sale .... – $_____
        (b) 1.8   Cash items received on purchase .... – $_____
        (c) 1.9   Cash contributed .... + $_____
        (d) 1.10 Transactional cost disbursed .... + $_____
        (e) 1.11 Purchase-money notes executed .... + $_____
   5.3 Remaining cost basis in all property transferred.
        Enter amounts from:
        (a) 3.7 .... + $ __300,000__
        (b) 3.11 .... + $ __75,000__
   5.4 Reportable profit/loss. Enter amount from 4.5 .... (+)or –) $ __25,000__
   5.5 **Basis of Replacement Property(ies) and cash items:**
        (The sum of 5.1 through 5.4) .... $ __900,000__
        (See Form 354.5 for priority allocation to cash items, multiple
        replacement properties and between land and improvements.)

FORM 354   02-05   ©2006 **first tuesday**, P.O. BOX 20069, RIVERSIDE, CA 92516 (800) 794-0494

Is the $25,000 profit in the boat reported, and if so, is it also added to the basis in the replacement property the boat helped purchase?

Yes, the amount of the profit is both **taxed** and **added to the basis** for the replacement property since the value of the boat contributed to the purchase of the replacement property. The boat is *unqualified property*, not §1031 property whose profit is exempt from tax.

In exchange for the boat, the investor received a $100,000 credit toward the price he agreed to pay for the replacement property. Of the $100,000 credit on the price he received for the boat, $75,000 is a **return of invested capital** since the basis in the boat is $75,000, and $25,000 is profit, a **return on the investment** which is reported and taxed separately from the §1031 transaction. The profit is then added to the replacement property's cost basis along with the boat§s $75,000 basis. [See Figure 3(b) §§2.3, 4.2 and 5.4]

However, the purchase or exchange agreement entered into by the investor to acquire the replacement property **sets a price** for the boat which is greater than its basis. Thus, a taxable profit was built into the negotiated price. [See Figure 3(b) §2]

Consider an alternative pricing arrangement for the exchange value of the boat. The boat could remain **unpriced**, or priced at $75,000, the remaining cost basis. If the boat is unpriced in an exchange, the replacement property will also be unpriced in the exchange agreement. If not unpriced, set a reduced price at the amount of the boat's basis to eliminate any profit on the sale or exchange of the boat. [See Chapter 14, Example No. 5]

An *unpriced exchange* leaves open the exact price of both the unqualified property contributed and the like-kind property received in exchange. The investor will report the profit in the unpriced boat only if the boat's cash value exceeds the remaining basis — the benefit of hindsight at tax reporting time.

Trade-up Example No. 4

The facts of Example No. 4 differ from the first example as follows:

- the loan encumbering the replacement property is increased to $900,000;

- the equity in the replacement property is now a lesser amount than the equity in the investor's property, an *equity trade-down situation* unless corrected by a loan reduction on acquisition; and

- the investor carries back a note in the amount of $100,000 secured by a trust deed on the property he sold. [See Figures 4(a) and 4(b) §1.5 accompanying this chapter]

Question No. 1: Must the investor report any part of his profit on the sale of his property at the time he receives a carryback note?

No, and for two reasons. Any **profit** allocated to the carryback note is automatically reported on the tax-deferred installment sales method. Further, the **basis** in the property the investor sold exceeds the amount of the loan by an amount equal to or greater than the carryback note.

Thus, as part of a §1031 reinvestment plan, the principal amount of the carryback note receives a **priority allocation** of the basis for the amount of the excess basis-over-debt, up to the amount of the note. [See Figure 4(b) §4.1(a)]

Here, the excess basis covers the entire amount of the carryback note and provides the investor with a return of a portion of his original capital investment in the property sold, in the amount of the note. Thus, the note contains no profit to be reported whenever installments of principal are received. [See Chapters 11 and 26]

Conversely, had the debt on the property sold exceeded the basis remaining in the property

FACTS OF EXAMPLE 4 — PRICE TRADE-UP

A. **Remaining Cost Basis:** $300,000

B. **§1031 Transaction:** Greater debt assumed and less equity acquired.

Items:	Property sold and adjustments made:	Replacement property and adjustments received:
1. Market price:	$600,000	$1,200,000
2. Existing debt:	$200,000	$900,000
3. Existing equity:	$400,000	$300,000
4. Adjustments:	$0	$100,000
Type:	_____	Note carried back

C. **Observations:**

An equity trade-down has been allowed to occur.

Taxpayer carries back a note to adjust for his larger equity.

Basis exceeds debt allowing priority allocation of $100,000 excess basis to the note. (No profit in the note to report.)

sold, a *mortgage-over-basis* situation, the entire amount of the carryback note retained by the investor on the sale would be reported as profit. No basis would exist in excess of the loan amount encumbering the property and thus would not be allocated to the carryback note to "shelter" the note (as a return of capital) from profit taxes. In Example No. 4, had the basis been less than $200,000, no amount of basis over mortgage would have existed for any priority allocation of basis. Thus, the entire amount of the note would have represented taxable profit. [See **first tuesday** Form 355 §2]

An investor may not want to generate a monthly cash flow by carrying a note and trust deed. When the installment payments are reportable as interest income and profit as install-ments are received. The investor selling property on an installment sale should consider impounding the carryback note and trust deed on the close of the sales escrow with a §1031 trustee for later exchange. Then, the investor can **exchange** the carryback paper for additional §1031 real estate after the close of his sales escrow. [See Chapter 20]

An alternative to the carryback note

Cash-heavy investors entering into a §1031 sale and reinvestment have an alternative. They may **lend money** to the buyer who is purchasing their property in lieu of carrying back a note in an installment sale.

The investor's funding of a loan creates a purchase-assist mortgage and increases the amount

Figure 4(b)

§1031 PROFIT AND BASIS RECAP SHEET

Date _____, 20_____ Prepared by: _____

OWNER'S NAME: _Example Number 4_ _____

PROPERTY SOLD/EXCHANGED: _____

COMMENTS: _____
_____

REPLACEMENT PROPERTY: _____

COMMENTS: _____
_____

1. NET DEBT RELIEF AND CASH ITEMS

Net existing debt:

1.1   Balance of debt(s) owner is **relieved** of on
all property sold/exchanged . . . . + $ __200,000__

1.2   Balance of debt(s) owner **assumed** on
§1031 property acquired . . . . − $ __900,000__

1.3   **Total net existing debt:** Enter the sum of 1.1 & 1.2 as either:

     (a)   **Net debt relief** (amount by which 1.1 exceeds 1.2). . . . . + $ _____

     (b)   **Net debt assumed** (amount by which 1.2 exceeds 1.1) . . . . − $ __700,000__

Cash items received on close of the property sold:

1.4   Amount of cash **received** on sale (excluding prorations). . . . . . . $ _____

1.5   Amount of carryback note **received** on sale . . . . $ __100,000__

1.6   Equity value in unqualified property **received** on sale . . . . $ _____

1.7   **Total of cash items received on closing the property sold:**
(The sum of 1.4, 1.5 & 1.6) . . . . + $ __100,000__

**Net cash items received or transferred on close of the
replacement property:**

1.8   Amount of cash items **received** with replacement property
(excluding prorations) . . . . + $ _____

1.9   Amount of cash owner **contributed** (excluding prorations) . . . . . . $ _____

1.10   Transactional costs **disbursed** at any time on either property
(excluding prorations and loan payoffs) . . . . $ _____

1.11   Amount of purchase-money notes **owner executed** in
part payment for the replacement property . . . . $ _____

1.12   Equity value of any unqualified property owner **exchanged** . . . . . $ _____

1.13   Subtotal of cash items owner **transferred** (1.9 through 1.12) . . . . − $ _____

1.14   **Total net cash items:** Enter the sum of 1.8 & 1.13 as either:

     (a)   **Net cash items owner received:**
(amount by which 1.8 exceeds 1.13) . . . . + $ _____

     (b)   **Net cash items owner transferred:**
(amount by which 1.13 exceeds 1.8) . . . . − $ _____

Netting all debt relief and cash items:

1.15   Enter net debt **relief** from 1.3(a) . . . . + $ _____

1.16   Enter net cash items

     (a)   owner **received** from 1.14(a) . . . . + $ _____

     (b)   owner **transferred** from 1.14(b) . . . . − $ _____

1.17   Net debt relief and cash items, (1.15 & 1.16, but not less than zero) . . . . + $ _____

1.18   Cash items received on sale from 1.7 . . . . + $ __100,000__

1.19   **TOTAL net money and other properties owner received:**
(The sum of 1.17 and 1.18) . . . . + $ __100,000__

2. PROFIT/LOSS ON TRANSFER OF UNQUALIFIED PROPERTY

2.1   Market value of unqualified property owner transferred. . . . . . . + $ _____

2.2   Remaining cost basis in unqualified property owner
transferred . . . . − $ _____

2.3   **Total profit/loss on unqualified property owner transferred:** . . . . (+ or −) $ __0__

— —
— —
PAGE ONE OF TWO — FORM 354

Figure 4(b) cont.

3. **PROFIT REALIZED ON THE §1031 PROPERTY SOLD OR EXCHANGED**
   (before applying the §1031 exemption)
   Consideration owner received:

   3.1 Debt relief: Enter amount from 1.1 .... $ __200,000__

   3.2 Market value of §1031 placement property owner acquired ..... $ __1,200,000__

   3.3 Total cash items received from property sold:
   Enter amount from 1.7 .... $ __100,000__

   3.4 Total cash items received with replacement property:
   Enter amount from 1.8 .... $ _____

   3.5 Total consideration owner received (3.1 through 3.4) .... + $ __1,500,000__

   Consideration owner transferred:

   3.6 Debt owner assumed: Enter amount from 1.2 .... $ __900,000__

   3.7 Enter remaining cost basis in all §1031 properties
   owner transferred .... $ __300,000__

   3.8 Cash owner contributed: Enter amount from 1.9 .... $ _____

   3.9 Transactional costs disbursed: Enter amount from 1.10 .... $ _____

   3.10 Purchase notes owner executed: Enter amount from 1.11 ..... $ _____

   3.11 Remaining cost basis in unqualified property owner transferred:
   Enter amount from 2.2 .... $ _____

   3.12 Total consideration owner transferred (3.6 through 3.11) .... − $ __1,200,000__

   3.13 **Total profits realized in §1031 property sold or exchanged:**
   (3.5 less 3.12)....................................... (+)or −) $ __300,000__

4. **REPORTABLE PROFIT/LOSS ON THE §1031 TRANSACTION**

   4.1 Total net debt relief and cash items owner receives:
   Enter amount from 1.19, but not less than zero .... + $ __100,000__

   (a) Carryback basis allocation: Amount by which 3.7
   exceeds 1.1, but not more than the amount at 1.5........ − $ __100,000__

   4.2 Total profit/loss on unqualified property owner transferred:
   Enter amount from 2.3 ....(+ or −) $ __0__

   4.3 Subtotal: The amount of equity withdrawn:
   (the sum of 4.1, (a) and 4.2).........................(+ or −) $ __0__

   4.4 Total profits realized in §1031 property sold/exchanged:
   Enter amount from 3.13 (But not less than zero) .... $ __300,000__

   4.5 **Total reportable profit/loss:** (Enter lesser of 4.3 or 4.4)...................(+ or −) $ __0__

5. **BASIS OF ALL PROPERTY(IES) RECEIVED**

   5.1 Debt relief. Enter amounts from:

   (a) 1.3(a) Net debt relief.............................. − $ _____

   (b) 1.3(b) Net debt assumed .... + $ __700,000__

   5.2 Cash items. Enter amounts from:

   (a) 1.7 Cash items received on the sale .... − $ __100,000__

   (b) 1.8 Cash items received on purchase .... − $ _____

   (c) 1.9 Cash contributed .... + $ _____

   (d) 1.10 Transactional cost disbursed................... + $ _____

   (e) 1.11 Purchase-money notes executed .... + $ _____

   5.3 Remaining cost basis in all property transferred.
   Enter amounts from:

   (a) 3.7 .... + $ __300,000__

   (b) 3.11 .... + $ _____

   5.4 Reportable profit/loss. Enter amount from 4.5..........(+ or −) $ __0__

   5.5 **Basis of Replacement Property(ies) and cash items:**
   (The sum of 5.1 through 5.4)...................................... $ __900,000__
   (See Form 354.5 for priority allocation to cash items, multiple
   replacement properties and between land and improvements.)

FORM 354   02-05   ©2006 **first tuesday**, P.O. BOX 20069, RIVERSIDE, CA 92516 (800) 794-0494

of cash the buyer now has to purchase the investor's property. The loan funds, of course, become part of the owner's net sales proceeds held by the buyer's §1031 trustee on closing the sales escrow.

Here, the net proceeds from the sale will be used to purchase the replacement property. Thus, the investor will avoid carrying a note and paying taxes on profit by lending his buyer the down payment.

*Editor's note — Under California mortgage law, the note received by the seller structured contractually as a loan, not a carryback, will not escape the anti-deficiency laws which would render the note nonrecourse. [**Ziegler v. Barnes** (1988) 200 CA3d 224]*

Chapter 14

An orderly liquidation: a trade-down in price

This chapter presents several examples of price "trade-down" situations that result in partial §1031 reinvestments.

The partial §1031 reinvestment

A property owner, planning his retirement, begins selling off his investments in unimproved real estate. Each is encumbered by a loan.

The sales proceeds will be reinvested in order to generate income.

The income the owner seeks could take the form of monthly installments on a note carried back on the sale or spendable income from reinvestment in relatively management-free, income-producing real estate with little or no amount of loans.

The price the owner (now an investor) would pay and the loan amount he would assume to purchase replacement real estate is less than the price and loan amounts on the properties he will be selling, the result of a *price trade-down*.

A **price trade-down** will always cause some or all of the *profit realized* on the sale of property to be reported and taxed, called a *recognized gain*.

The tax analysis starts with the rule that income, profits and losses on all sales and exchanges must be reported, unless *exempt* or *excluded* from reporting. [Internal Revenue Code §1001]

Some or all of the profit realized on the sale or exchange of like-kind property can be transferred **tax-free** into the value of replacement property. Thus, the profit realized on a sale can go unreported and untaxed under an exemption, such as Internal Revenue Code (IRC) §1031, called *nonrecognized gain* by the Internal Revenue Service (IRS). [IRC §1031]

However, the sale of §1031 property triggers the reporting of profits when any debt relief and cash items the investor receives on the sale are not or cannot be offset on the purchase of replacement property. [IRC §1031(b)]

Can the investor still exempt a portion of the profit on a sale or exchange of property from taxes even when some of the profit will be taxed due to the investor's receipt of debt relief, cash or carryback notes on the sale or exchange?

Yes! The **profits remaining** from the property sold after deducting the amount of net debt relief, cash items and unqualified property received by the investor on the sale are covered by the §1031 exemption if §1031 replacement property is acquired in a *partial §1031 transaction*. [Revenue Regulations §1.1031(b)-1(a)(1)]

Thus, on a price trade-down, the investor follows §1031 exemption rules while at the same time reporting the profits that are not exempt from taxes under IRC §1001.

This chapter covers five examples of partial §1031 reinvestment plans that:

- demonstrate the fundamental rules of offsets within and between **mortgage boot**, commonly called *debt relief*, and **cash boot**, commonly called *cash items* and *unqualified property*;

- distinguish between offsetting debt relief on the sale, which is allowed, and offsetting cash items received on the sale or before acquiring replacement property, which is not allowed; and

- discuss the prohibited offsetting of cash items received at any time by the assumption of a loan on the purchase of the replacement property.

Profit carried forward

The investor's basis in the property he sells or exchanges is deducted from its sales price to establish the investor's *total profits realized* on the sale. As always, price minus basis equals profit.

Editor's note — The entire basis in the §1031 property sold is carried forward to the replacement property in both a fully qualified and partial §1031 reinvestment as the first step toward establishing the new basis for the replacement property. [See Chapter 25]

The profit reported and taxed in any reinvestment plan, called *recognized gain* by the IRS, will never exceed the total profit on the sale or exchange of property, called *realized gain* by the IRS. [IRC §1001; see Figure 1(a) §3.13 accompanying this chapter]

The profit on the sale which is reported in a partial §1031 transaction is determined by the *money* or *other properties* involved, including debt relief and cash items received that are not or cannot be offset by the terms for purchase of the replacement property.

The exempt profit not reported in a §1031 reinvestment plan is implicitly transferred to the replacement property when the investor shifts his cost basis by carrying it forward from the property sold to the replacement property. However, no separate accounting is made for the transfer of the profit.

The basic trade-down: Example No. 1

The facts in Example No. 1 demonstrate a typical price trade-down situation, by a sale or exchange of the investor's property, with mixed §1001 (taxable) and §1031 (tax exempt) reporting results. [See Figure 1(a)]

The **equities** in both the property sold and the replacement property purchased by the investor are equal at $400,000. Thus, no cash item adjustments are necessary to balance the equities.

In Example No. 1, the investor is purchasing replacement property with an equity equal to the equity in the property he sold. However, the transaction is a trade-down from the property he sold in both price and loan amount. Instead of receiving the net proceeds from the sale of his property, the investor receives:

- **ownership** of the §1031 replacement property he agreed to buy under a purchase agreement; and

- **relief** from responsibility for the loan encumbering the property he sold, called *debt relief*. [See Figure 1(a)]

The amount of the trade-down in price is the entire amount of the **debt relief**. Here, the replacement property is not encumbered by an existing loan for the investor to assume, and he cannot offset the debt relief on the property he sold. [See Figure 1(b) §1.3 accompanying this chapter]

On completing his reinvestment, the investor is left with **net debt relief**, a withdrawal of capital investment. Here, the debt relief on the sale of his property is not offset by:

- taking over debt on the replacement property;

- adding cash or executing a carryback note to purchase the replacement property; or

- acquiring additional replacement property encumbered with a loan.

The fact that some profit will be reported on the sale does not disqualify the remaining profit on the sale from §1031 tax-free status. The result is a *partial §1031*. Profit up to the amount of the net debt relief (not offset on acquiring the replacement property) is reported on the investor's tax return for the year he sold or exchanged his property. [IRC §1031(b)]

Figure 1(a)

FACTS OF EXAMPLE 1 — PRICE TRADE-DOWN

A. Remaining Cost Basis: $300,000

B. §1031 Transaction: Less debt assumed and equal equity acquired.

Items:	Property sold and contributions for adjustments:	Property acquired and adjustments received:
1. Market price:	$600,000	$400,000
2. Existing debt:	$200,000	$0
3. Existing equity:	$400,000	$400,000
4. Adjustments: Type:	$0 _____	$0 _____

C. Observations:

Equities are equal — no cash item adjustments.

Net debt relief requires IRC §1001 profit reporting.

The investor's unreported profits from the fact situation in Figure 1(a) are calculated on the Recap Sheet in Figure 1(b) by taking the following steps:

1. Determine the net debt relief and net cash items received ($200,000). [See Figure 1(b) §1.19]

2. Determine the total profits realized in the property sold ($300,000). [See Figure 1(b) §3.13]

3. Determine the portion of the profits to be reported and recognized under §1001 — the lesser of the above items 1 (net debt relief) and 2 (total profits realized), $200,000. [See Figure 1(b) §4.5]

4. Determine "off form" the unreported profit exempt from taxes under §1031 ($100,000). [See Figure 1(b) §§3.13 and 1.19]

Variations on the facts

In each of the following scenarios, the prices of the property sold and the replacement property remain the same as in Example No. 1: $600,000 and $400,000, respectively. Thus, the *price trade-down* of $200,000 remains the same in each example.

However, the equities, debt, basis and time of receipt of cash items are altered from example to example to demonstrate the tax consequences resulting from various different terms commonly negotiated by buyers and sellers when a trade-down in price occurs.

The following four variations from the fact situation of Example No. 1 include:

- Example No. 2: **Basis is increased** in the property sold to an amount greater than the price of the replacement property.

Figure 1(b)

§1031 PROFIT AND BASIS RECAP SHEET

Date _____, 20_____ Prepared by: _____

OWNER'S NAME: _Example Number 1_____

PROPERTY SOLD/EXCHANGED: _____

COMMENTS: _____
_____

REPLACEMENT PROPERTY: _____

COMMENTS: _____
_____

1. NET DEBT RELIEF AND CASH ITEMS

Net existing debt:

1.1   Balance of debt(s) owner is **relieved** of on
all property sold/exchanged . . . . + $ __200,000__

1.2   Balance of debt(s) owner **assumed** on
§1031 property acquired . . . . – $ _____

1.3   **Total net existing debt:** Enter the sum of 1.1 & 1.2 as either:

    (a)   **Net debt relief** (amount by which 1.1 exceeds 1.2) . . . . + $ __200,000__

    (b)   **Net debt assumed** (amount by which 1.2 exceeds 1.1) . . . . – $ _____

Cash items received on close of the property sold:

1.4   Amount of cash **received** on sale (excluding prorations) . . . . . . $ _____

1.5   Amount of carryback note **received** on sale . . . . $ _____

1.6   Equity value in unqualified property **received** on sale . . . . $ _____

1.7   **Total of cash items received on closing the property sold:**
(The sum of 1.4, 1.5 & 1.6) . . . . + $ __0__

Net cash items received or transferred on close of the replacement property:

1.8   Amount of cash items **received** with replacement property
(excluding prorations) . . . . + $ _____

1.9   Amount of cash owner **contributed** (excluding prorations) . . . . . . $ _____

1.10   Transactional costs **disbursed** at any time on either property
(excluding prorations and loan payoffs) . . . . $ _____

1.11   Amount of purchase-money notes **owner executed** in
part payment for the replacement property . . . . $ _____

1.12   Equity value of any unqualified property owner **exchanged** . . . . . $ _____

1.13   Subtotal of cash items owner **transferred** (1.9 through 1.12) . . . . – $ _____

1.14   **Total net cash items:** Enter the sum of 1.8 & 1.13 as either:

    (a)   **Net cash items owner received:**
(amount by which 1.8 exceeds 1.13) . . . . + $ __0__

    (b)   **Net cash items owner transferred:**
(amount by which 1.13 exceeds 1.8) . . . . – $ __0__

Netting all debt relief and cash items:

1.15   Enter net debt **relief** from 1.3(a) . . . . + $ __200,000__

1.16   Enter net cash items

    (a)   owner **received** from 1.14(a) . . . . + $ _____

    (b)   owner **transferred** from 1.14(b) . . . . – $ _____

1.17   Net debt relief and cash items, (1.15 & 1.16, but not less than zero) . . . . + $ __200,000__

1.18   Cash items received on sale from 1.7 . . . . + $ _____

1.19   **TOTAL net money and other properties owner received:**
(The sum of 1.17 and 1.18) . . . . + $ __200,000__

2. PROFIT/LOSS ON TRANSFER OF UNQUALIFIED PROPERTY

2.1   Market value of unqualified property owner transferred. . . . . . . + $ _____

2.2   Remaining cost basis in unqualified property owner
transferred . . . . – $ _____

2.3   **Total profit/loss on unqualified property owner transferred:** . . . . (+ or –) $ __0__

— — — — — — — — — — — — — — — — *PAGE ONE OF TWO — FORM 354* — — — — — — — — — — — — — — — — — —

Figure 1(b) cont. — — — — — — — — *PAGE TWO OF TWO — FORM 354* — — — — — — — — — — — — — —

3. PROFIT REALIZED ON THE §1031 PROPERTY SOLD OR EXCHANGED
(before applying the §1031 exemption)
Consideration owner received:

3.1   Debt relief: Enter amount from 1.1 .... $ <u>200,000</u>

3.2   Market value of §1031 placement property owner acquired ..... $ <u>400,000</u>

3.3   Total cash items received from property sold:
Enter amount from 1.7 .... $ <u> </u>

3.4   Total cash items received with replacement property:
Enter amount from 1.8 .... $ <u> </u>

3.5   Total consideration owner received (3.1 through 3.4) .... + $ <u>600,000</u>

Consideration owner transferred:

3.6   Debt owner assumed: Enter amount from 1.2 .... $ <u> </u>

3.7   Enter remaining cost basis in all §1031 properties
owner transferred .... $ <u>300,000</u>

3.8   Cash owner contributed: Enter amount from 1.9 .... $ <u> </u>

3.9   Transactional costs disbursed: Enter amount from 1.10 .... $ <u> </u>

3.10   Purchase notes owner executed: Enter amount from 1.11 ...... $ <u> </u>

3.11   Remaining cost basis in unqualified property owner transferred:
Enter amount from 2.2 .... $ <u> </u>

3.12   Total consideration owner transferred (3.6 through 3.11) .... − $ <u>300,000</u>

3.13   **Total profits realized in §1031 property sold or exchanged:**
(3.5 less 3.12)... (+)or −) $ <u>300,000</u>

4. REPORTABLE PROFIT/LOSS ON THE §1031 TRANSACTION

4.1   Total net debt relief and cash items owner receives:
Enter amount from 1.19, but not less than zero .... + $ <u>200,000</u>

   (a)   Carryback basis allocation: Amount by which 3.7
exceeds 1.1, but not more than the amount at 1.5........ − $ <u>0</u>

4.2   Total profit/loss on unqualified property owner transferred:
Enter amount from 2.3............................. (+ or −) $ <u> </u>

4.3   Subtotal: The amount of equity withdrawn:
(the sum of 4.1, (a) and 4.2)................................. (+)or −) $ <u>200,000</u>

4.4   Total profits realized in §1031 property sold/exchanged:
Enter amount from 3.13 (But not less than zero) .... $ <u>300,000</u>

4.5   **Total reportable profit/loss:** (Enter lesser of 4.3 or 4.4).................... (+)or −) $ <u>200,000</u>

5. BASIS OF ALL PROPERTY(IES) RECEIVED

5.1   Debt relief. Enter amounts from:

   (a)   1.3(a)   Net debt relief.............................. − $ <u>200,000</u>

   (b)   1.3(b)   Net debt assumed .... + $ <u> </u>

5.2   Cash items. Enter amounts from:

   (a)   1.7   Cash items received on the sale .... − $ <u> </u>

   (b)   1.8   Cash items received on purchase .... − $ <u> </u>

   (c)   1.9   Cash contributed .... + $ <u> </u>

   (d)   1.10   Transactional cost disbursed................... + $ <u> </u>

   (e)   1.11   Purchase-money notes executed .... + $ <u> </u>

5.3   Remaining cost basis in all property transferred.
Enter amounts from:

   (a)   3.7   .... + $ <u>300,000</u>

   (b)   3.11   .... + $ <u> </u>

5.4   Reportable profit/loss. Enter amount from 4.5......... (+)or −) $ <u>200,000</u>

5.5   **Basis of Replacement Property(ies) and cash items:**
(The sum of 5.1 through 5.4)................................... $ <u>300,000</u>
(See Form 354.5 for priority allocation to cash items, multiple
replacement properties and between land and improvements.)

FACTS OF EXAMPLE 2 — PRICE TRADE-DOWN

A. Remaining Cost Basis: $500,000

B. §1031 Transaction: Less debt assumed and equal equity acquired.

Items:	Property sold and contributions for adjustments:	Property acquired and adjustments received:
1. Market price: 2. Existing debt:	$600,000 $200,000	$400,000 $0
3. Existing equity: 4. Adjustments: Type:	$400,000 $0 _____	$400,000 $0 _____

C. Observations:

The basis carried forward exceeds the value of the acquired property.

Net debt relief exceeds the profit on the sale.

No part of the profit on the sale qualifies for §1031 exemption.

- Example No. 3: The **loan is increased** on the property sold and a cash item in the form of a purchase-money note is executed by the investor to pay for the larger equity in the replacement property he is acquiring.

- Example No. 4: A **loan exists** on the replacement property and the investor executes a purchase-money note in part payment of the purchase price and receives **cash** back.

- Example No. 5: **Unqualified property** of an undetermined value is received by the investor to adjust for the equity in the property he sold or exchanged being smaller than the equity in the replacement property.

The investor's goal is to avoid reporting profits on the sale as an exempt transaction under §1031 rules. However, on any price trade-down, a portion or all of the profit will be reportable.

Trade-down Example No. 2

The facts in Example No. 2 differ from Example No. 1 as follows: the **remaining cost basis** in the property sold or exchanged by the investor is $500,000, not $300,000. Thus, the profit the investor will realize on a sale or exchange is $100,000 ($600,000 price minus $500,000 basis). [See Figure 2(a) accompanying this chapter]

Note that this example is not a §1031 transaction, even though the investor and brokers might have structured the documentation as an actual exchange of equities. No profit remains to be exempt from reporting under §1031 since the $200,000 net debt relief, which triggers

Figure 2(b)

§1031 PROFIT AND BASIS RECAP SHEET

Date _____, 20_____ Prepared by: _____

OWNER'S NAME: __Example Number 2_____

PROPERTY SOLD/EXCHANGED: _____

COMMENTS: _____
_____

REPLACEMENT PROPERTY: _____

COMMENTS: _____
_____

1. NET DEBT RELIEF AND CASH ITEMS

Net existing debt:

1.1 Balance of debt(s) owner is **relieved** of on
all property sold/exchanged . . . . + $__200,000__

1.2 Balance of debt(s) owner **assumed** on
§1031 property acquired . . . . − $_____

1.3 **Total net existing debt:** Enter the sum of 1.1 & 1.2 as either:

   (a) **Net debt relief** (amount by which 1.1 exceeds 1.2) . . . . + $__200,000__

   (b) **Net debt assumed** (amount by which 1.2 exceeds 1.1) . . . . − $_____

Cash items received on close of the property sold:

1.4 Amount of cash **received** on sale (excluding prorations) . . . . $_____

1.5 Amount of carryback note **received** on sale . . . . $_____

1.6 Equity value in unqualified property **received** on sale . . . . $_____

1.7 **Total of cash items received on closing the property sold:**
(The sum of 1.4, 1.5 & 1.6) . . . . + $_____0_____

Net cash items received or transferred on close of the replacement property:

1.8 Amount of cash items **received** with replacement property
(excluding prorations) . . . . + $_____

1.9 Amount of cash owner **contributed** (excluding prorations) . . . . . . $_____

1.10 Transactional costs **disbursed** at any time on either property
(excluding prorations and loan payoffs) . . . . $_____

1.11 Amount of purchase-money notes **owner executed** in
part payment for the replacement property . . . . $_____

1.12 Equity value of any unqualified property owner **exchanged** . . . . . $_____

1.13 Subtotal of cash items owner **transferred** (1.9 through 1.12) . . . . − $_____

1.14 **Total net cash items:** Enter the sum of 1.8 & 1.13 as either:

   (a) **Net cash items owner received:**
(amount by which 1.8 exceeds 1.13) . . . . + $_____0_____

   (b) **Net cash items owner transferred:**
(amount by which 1.13 exceeds 1.8) . . . . − $_____0_____

Netting all debt relief and cash items:

1.15 Enter net debt **relief** from 1.3(a) . . . . + $__200,000__

1.16 Enter net cash items

   (a) owner **received** from 1.14(a) . . . . + $_____

   (b) owner **transferred** from 1.14(b) . . . . − $_____

1.17 Net debt relief and cash items, (1.15 & 1.16, but not less than zero) . . . . + $__200,000__

1.18 Cash items received on sale from 1.7 . . . . + $_____0_____

1.19 **TOTAL net money and other properties owner received:**
(The sum of 1.17 and 1.18) . . . . + $__200,000__

2. PROFIT/LOSS ON TRANSFER OF UNQUALIFIED PROPERTY

2.1 Market value of unqualified property owner transferred. . . . . . . + $_____

2.2 Remaining cost basis in unqualified property owner
transferred . . . . − $_____

2.3 **Total profit/loss on unqualified property owner transferred:** . . . . (+ or −) $_____0_____

— — — — — — — — — — — — *PAGE ONE OF TWO — FORM 354* — — — — — — — — — — — — — — — —

Figure 2(b) cont.

3. PROFIT REALIZED ON THE §1031 PROPERTY SOLD OR EXCHANGED
   (before applying the §1031 exemption)
   Consideration owner received:

   3.1   Debt relief: Enter amount from 1.1 . . . . $ __200,000__

   3.2   Market value of §1031 placement property owner acquired . . . . . $ __400,000__

   3.3   Total cash items received from property sold:
         Enter amount from 1.7 . . . . $_____

   3.4   Total cash items received with replacement property:
         Enter amount from 1.8 . . . . $_____

   3.5   Total consideration owner received (3.1 through 3.4) . . . . + $ __600,000__

   Consideration owner transferred:

   3.6   Debt owner assumed: Enter amount from 1.2 . . . . $_____

   3.7   Enter remaining cost basis in all §1031 properties
         owner transferred . . . . $ __500,000__

   3.8   Cash owner contributed: Enter amount from 1.9 . . . . $_____

   3.9   Transactional costs disbursed: Enter amount from 1.10 . . . . $_____

   3.10 Purchase notes owner executed: Enter amount from 1.11 . . . . . . $_____

   3.11 Remaining cost basis in unqualified property owner transferred:
         Enter amount from 2.2 . . . . $_____

   3.12 Total consideration owner transferred (3.6 through 3.11) . . . . – $ __500,000__

   3.13 **Total profits realized in §1031 property sold or exchanged:**
         (3.5 less 3.12) . . . . (+ or –) $ __100,000__

4. REPORTABLE PROFIT/LOSS ON THE §1031 TRANSACTION

   4.1   Total net debt relief and cash items owner receives:
         Enter amount from 1.19, but not less than zero . . . . + $ __200,000__

         (a) Carryback basis allocation: Amount by which 3.7
              exceeds 1.1, but not more than the amount at 1.5 . . . . – $ __0__

   4.2   Total profit/loss on unqualified property owner transferred:
         Enter amount from 2.3 . . . . (+ or –) $ __0__

   4.3   Subtotal: The amount of equity withdrawn:
         (the sum of 4.1, (a) and 4.2) . . . . (+ or –) $ __200,000__

   4.4   Total profits realized in §1031 property sold/exchanged:
         Enter amount from 3.13 (But not less than zero) . . . . $ __100,000__

   4.5   **Total reportable profit/loss:** (Enter lesser of 4.3 or 4.4) . . . . (+ or –) $ __100,000__

5. BASIS OF ALL PROPERTY(IES) RECEIVED

   5.1   Debt relief. Enter amounts from:

         (a) 1.3(a) Net debt relief . . . . – $ __200,000__

         (b) 1.3(b) Net debt assumed . . . . + $_____

   5.2   Cash items. Enter amounts from:

         (a) 1.7   Cash items received on the sale . . . . – $_____

         (b) 1.8   Cash items received on purchase . . . . – $_____

         (c) 1.9   Cash contributed . . . . + $_____

         (d) 1.10 Transactional cost disbursed . . . . + $_____

         (e) 1.11 Purchase-money notes executed . . . . + $_____

   5.3   Remaining cost basis in all property transferred.
         Enter amounts from:

         (a) 3.7 . . . . + $ __500,000__

         (b) 3.11 . . . . + $ __0__

   5.4   Reportable profit/loss. Enter amount from 4.5 . . . . (+ or –) $ __100,000__

   5.5   **Basis of Replacement Property(ies) and cash items:**
         (The sum of 5.1 through 5.4) . . . . $ __400,000__
         (See Form 354.5 for priority allocation to cash items, multiple
         replacement properties and between land and improvements.)

profit reporting, **exceeds the total profits** of $100,000 on the sale. [See Figure 2(b) §§1.19 and 3.13 accompanying this chapter, *ante*]

The reportable profit cannot exceed the actual *profit realized* on the sale — the $100,000 profit that is the difference between the price received ($600,000) and the basis ($500,000). [See Figure 2(b) §3.13]

The difference between the basis in the property sold ($500,000) and the price of the replacement property ($400,000) is a **return of capital** ($100,000) — a withdrawal of capital invested represented by a portion of the $200,000 debt relief experienced by the investor on the sale. The investor owes a lesser amount in loans on the completion of the reinvestment.

When the total amount of the net debt relief, cash and any carryback note received by the investor on a sale exceeds the profit in the property sold, the excess is a *return of capital*, reflected as a reduction in his cost basis in the replacement property. [See Figure 2(b) §5.1]

The return of an investor's capital, whether by the annual deduction of depreciation, debt reduction or the proceeds on a sale, is always untaxed when received; it is neither income nor profit.

Trade-down Example No. 3

This example demonstrates the rule allowing **debt relief** on the investor's sale of property to be later offset by his execution of a carryback note secured by the replacement property. The carryback note represents payment for part of the purchase price the investor pays to buy the replacement property.

The facts in Example No. 3 differ from Example No. 1 as follows:

- the **loan** on the property sold is greater;

- the **equity** in the property sold or exchanged by the investor is less than the equity in the replacement property the investor is buying; and

- a **carryback note** is executed by the investor to adjust for his purchase of a replacement property with a larger equity than the amount of his net proceeds from the property he sold. [See Figure 3(a) accompanying this chapter, *ante*]

In Example No. 3, the investor experiences debt relief in the amount of $450,000 on the sale of his property. His buyer either provides funds to pay off the loan or becomes primarily responsible for payments on the loan.

Here, the $450,000 net debt relief exceeds the $300,000 profit on the sale. [See Figure 3(b) §§1.3 and 3.13 accompanying this chapter]

Unless the debt relief is offset by the terms for purchase of the replacement property, the entire profit on the sale ($300,000) will be reported.

Debt relief on the property sold or exchanged can be offset to avoid profit reporting in a §1031 transaction by:

- the investor taking over existing debt on the replacement property; or

- the investor adding cash, obtaining a purchase-assist loan or executing a purchase-money note in part payment of the purchase price of the replacement property.

However, in Example No. 3, no encumbrance exists on the replacement property to be assumed by the investor. Thus, the only offset available to the investor is the amount of the $250,000 note he executes to purchase the replacement property (or a purchase-assist loan). [See Figure 3(b) §1.11]

An AITD observation

The $250,000 note the investor executes directly offsets part of his $450,000 debt relief. Thus, the remaining $200,000 in net debt relief represents the return of capital on completion of the §1031 transaction. [See Figure 3(b) §1.17]

Since the investor's net receipts of $200,000 in the return capital are less than the total profits of $300,000, the investor reports only $200,000 of his profit. [See Figure 3(b) §4.5]

The investor in Example No. 3 should consider alternative financing arrangements, such as an all-inclusive trust deed (AITD) for $450,000 or more. With an AITD, the investor wraps and remains primarily responsible for the first trust deed of $450,000 on the property sold. Thus, the AITD eliminates any debt relief and shifts profit to the replacement property equal to the cash reinvested ($150,000).

Here, an AITD carried back on the property sold will favorably alter the §1031 profit reporting result. The profit remaining to be allocated to the principal of the AITD carryback note after first deducting the net equity reinvested ($150,000) from the profit ($300,000) is $150,000, not the $200,000 in reportable profit which occurs with debt relief.

Thus, the AITD shifts more profit to the replacement property and the reporting of the taxable profit allocated to the principal of the AITD ($150,000) can be *deferred* as an installment sale. [See Chapter 11]

Instead of incurring debt relief, which triggers profit reporting of $200,000 in the year of the sale, the investor can carry back an AITD note in an amount equal to or greater than the wrapped mortgage. Thus, the $150,000 profit in the carryback AITD is taxed and reported, not in the year the note is executed, but each year as principal is received on the AITD note. [IRC §453; **Professional Equities, Inc.** v. **Commissioner** (1987) 89 TC 165; see Chapter 11]

Figure 3(b)

§1031 PROFIT AND BASIS RECAP SHEET

Date _____, 20_____ Prepared by: _____

OWNER'S NAME: __Example Number 3_____

PROPERTY SOLD/EXCHANGED: _____

COMMENTS: _____
_____

REPLACEMENT PROPERTY: _____

COMMENTS: _____
_____

1. NET DEBT RELIEF AND CASH ITEMS

Net existing debt:

1.1	Balance of debt(s) owner is **relieved** of on all property sold/exchanged	+ $	450,000
1.2	Balance of debt(s) owner **assumed** on §1031 property acquired	– $	0
1.3	**Total net existing debt:** Enter the sum of 1.1 & 1.2 as either:		
	(a) **Net debt relief** (amount by which 1.1 exceeds 1.2)	+ $	450,000
	(b) **Net debt assumed** (amount by which 1.2 exceeds 1.1)	– $	

Cash items received on close of the property sold:

1.4	Amount of cash **received** on sale (excluding prorations)	$	
1.5	Amount of carryback note **received** on sale	$	
1.6	Equity value in unqualified property **received** on sale	$	
1.7	**Total of cash items received on closing the property sold:** (The sum of 1.4, 1.5 & 1.6)	+ $	0

Net cash items received or transferred on close of the replacement property:

1.8	Amount of cash items **received** with replacement property (excluding prorations)	+ $	
1.9	Amount of cash owner **contributed** (excluding prorations)	$	
1.10	Transactional costs **disbursed** at any time on either property (excluding prorations and loan payoffs)	$	
1.11	Amount of purchase-money notes **owner executed** in part payment for the replacement property	$	250,000
1.12	Equity value of any unqualified property owner **exchanged**	$	
1.13	Subtotal of cash items owner **transferred** (1.9 through 1.12)	– $	250,000
1.14	**Total net cash items:** Enter the sum of 1.8 & 1.13 as either:		
	(a) **Net cash items owner received:** (amount by which 1.8 exceeds 1.13)	+ $	0
	(b) **Net cash items owner transferred:** (amount by which 1.13 exceeds 1.8)	– $	250,000

Netting all debt relief and cash items:

1.15	Enter net debt **relief** from 1.3(a)	+ $	450,000
1.16	Enter net cash items		
	(a) owner **received** from 1.14(a)	+ $	
	(b) owner **transferred** from 1.14(b)	– $	250,000
1.17	Net debt relief and cash items, (1.15 & 1.16, but not less than zero)	+ $	200,000
1.18	Cash items received on sale from 1.7	+ $	0
1.19	**TOTAL net money and other properties owner received:** (The sum of 1.17 and 1.18)	+ $	200,000

2. PROFIT/LOSS ON TRANSFER OF UNQUALIFIED PROPERTY

2.1	Market value of unqualified property owner transferred.	+ $	
2.2	Remaining cost basis in unqualified property owner transferred	– $	
2.3	**Total profit/loss on unqualified property owner transferred:**	(+ or –) $	0

– – – – – – – – – – – – – – – – – *PAGE ONE OF TWO — FORM 354* –

Figure 3(b) cont.

3. PROFIT REALIZED ON THE §1031 PROPERTY SOLD OR EXCHANGED
(before applying the §1031 exemption)
Consideration owner received:

3.1 Debt relief: Enter amount from 1.1 . . . . $ __450,000__

3.2 Market value of §1031 placement property owner acquired . . . . . $ __400,000__

3.3 Total cash items received from property sold:
Enter amount from 1.7 . . . . $ _____

3.4 Total cash items received with replacement property:
Enter amount from 1.8 . . . . $ _____

3.5 Total consideration owner received (3.1 through 3.4) . . . . + $ __850,000__

Consideration owner transferred:

3.6 Debt owner assumed: Enter amount from 1.2 . . . . $ _____

3.7 Enter remaining cost basis in all §1031 properties
owner transferred . . . . $ __300,000__

3.8 Cash owner contributed: Enter amount from 1.9 . . . . $ _____

3.9 Transactional costs disbursed: Enter amount from 1.10 . . . . $ _____

3.10 Purchase notes owner executed: Enter amount from 1.11 . . . . . . $ __250,000__

3.11 Remaining cost basis in unqualified property owner transferred:
Enter amount from 2.2 . . . . $ _____

3.12 Total consideration owner transferred (3.6 through 3.11) . . . . − $ __550,000__

3.13 **Total profits realized in §1031 property sold or exchanged:**
(3.5 less 3.12) . . . . (+)or −) $ __300,000__

4. REPORTABLE PROFIT/LOSS ON THE §1031 TRANSACTION

4.1 Total net debt relief and cash items owner receives:
Enter amount from 1.19, but not less than zero . . . . + $ __200,000__

   (a) Carryback basis allocation: Amount by which 3.7
       exceeds 1.1, but not more than the amount at 1.5 . . . . − $ __0__

4.2 Total profit/loss on unqualified property owner transferred:
Enter amount from 2.3 . . . . (+ or −) $ __0__

4.3 Subtotal: The amount of equity withdrawn:
(the sum of 4.1, (a) and 4.2) . . . . (+)or −) $ __200,000__

4.4 Total profits realized in §1031 property sold/exchanged:
Enter amount from 3.13 (But not less than zero) . . . . $ __300,000__

4.5 **Total reportable profit/loss:** (Enter lesser of 4.3 or 4.4) . . . . (+)or −) $ __200,000__

5. BASIS OF ALL PROPERTY(IES) RECEIVED

5.1 Debt relief. Enter amounts from:

   (a) 1.3(a) Net debt relief . . . . − $ __450,000__

   (b) 1.3(b) Net debt assumed . . . . + $ _____

5.2 Cash items. Enter amounts from:

   (a) 1.7   Cash items received on the sale . . . . − $ _____

   (b) 1.8   Cash items received on purchase . . . . − $ _____

   (c) 1.9   Cash contributed . . . . + $ _____

   (d) 1.10 Transactional cost disbursed . . . . + $ _____

   (e) 1.11 Purchase-money notes executed . . . . + $ __250,000__

5.3 Remaining cost basis in all property transferred.
Enter amounts from:

   (a) 3.7 . . . . + $ __300,000__

   (b) 3.11 . . . . + $ _____

5.4 Reportable profit/loss. Enter amount from 4.5 . . . . (+)or −) $ __200,000__

5.5 **Basis of Replacement Property(ies) and cash items:**
(The sum of 5.1 through 5.4) . . . . $ __300,000__
(See Form 354.5 for priority allocation to cash items, multiple
replacement properties and between land and improvements.)

FACTS OF EXAMPLE 4 — PRICE TRADE-DOWN

A. Remaining Cost Basis: $300,000

B. §1031 Transaction: Less debt assumed and less equity acquired.

Items:	Property sold and contributions for adjustments:	Property acquired and adjustments received:
1. Market price:	$600,000	$400,000
2. Existing debt:	$200,000	$100,000
3. Existing equity:	$400,000	$300,000
4. Adjustments:	$100,000	$200,000
Type:	Note	Cash

C. Observations:

Net debt relief of $100,000 and equity trade down of $100,000 are reportable profits for a partial §1031 transaction.

The $100,000 note the investor executes to buy replacement property offsets $100,000 of the cash received.

To assure the AITD is properly structured to effectively defer the reporting of profit, the terms of the AITD note carried back by the investor must be greater than those of the loan it is wrapping. The carryback note needs an *independent economic function*, separate from its tax benefits, to justify its creation as necessary, for purposes other than just tax avoidance. A higher interest rate, earlier due date or a principal amount significantly greater than the wrapped loan will supply the economic justification for its use. Somehow, the terms of the AITD note must "override" the terms of the wrapped loan and provide a financial benefit in addition to the tax benefit.

Trade-down Example No. 4

The facts in Example No. 4 differ from Example No. 1 as follows:

- a $100,000 trust deed loan on the replacement property is assumed by the investor;

- a $100,000 purchase-money trust deed note is executed by the investor in part payment for his acquisition of the replacement property; and

- the investor receives $200,000 in cash when he acquires the replacement property. [See Figure 4(a) accompanying this chapter]

Example No. 4 demonstrates the profit reporting that results when the investor receives cash on acquiring ownership of the smaller equity in the replacement property and assumes less debt on the replacement property.

The $100,000 **purchase-money note** executed by the investor to purchase the replacement property is a *cash item* he contributes to the

Figure 4(b)

§1031 PROFIT AND BASIS RECAP SHEET

Date _____, 20_____ Prepared by: _____

OWNER'S NAME: __Example Number 4_____

PROPERTY SOLD/EXCHANGED: _____

COMMENTS: _____
_____

REPLACEMENT PROPERTY: _____

COMMENTS: _____
_____

1. NET DEBT RELIEF AND CASH ITEMS

Net existing debt:

1.1 Balance of debt(s) owner is **relieved** of on
all property sold/exchanged . . . . + $ __200,000__

1.2 Balance of debt(s) owner **assumed** on
§1031 property acquired . . . . – $ __100,000__

1.3 **Total net existing debt:** Enter the sum of 1.1 & 1.2 as either:

   (a) **Net debt relief** (amount by which 1.1 exceeds 1.2) . . . . + $ __100,000__

   (b) **Net debt assumed** (amount by which 1.2 exceeds 1.1) . . . . – $ _____

Cash items received on close of the property sold:

1.4 Amount of cash **received** on sale (excluding prorations). . . . . . . $_____

1.5 Amount of carryback note **received** on sale . . . . $_____

1.6 Equity value in unqualified property **received** on sale . . . . $_____

1.7 **Total of cash items received on closing the property sold:**
(The sum of 1.4, 1.5 & 1.6) . . . . + $ _____0_____

**Net cash items received or transferred on close of the
replacement property:**

1.8 Amount of cash items **received** with replacement property
(excluding prorations) . . . . + $ __200,000__

1.9 Amount of cash owner **contributed** (excluding prorations) . . . . . . $_____

1.10 Transactional costs **disbursed** at any time on either property
(excluding prorations and loan payoffs) . . . . $_____

1.11 Amount of purchase-money notes **owner executed** in
part payment for the replacement property. . . . . $ __100,000__

1.12 Equity value of any unqualified property owner **exchanged** . . . . . $_____

1.13 Subtotal of cash items owner **transferred** (1.9 through 1.12) . . . . – $ __100,000__

1.14 **Total net cash items:** Enter the sum of 1.8 & 1.13 as either:

   (a) **Net cash items owner received:**
(amount by which 1.8 exceeds 1.13) . . . . + $ __100,000__

   (b) **Net cash items owner transferred:**
(amount by which 1.13 exceeds 1.8) . . . . – $ _____0_____

Netting all debt relief and cash items:

1.15 Enter net debt **relief** from 1.3(a) . . . . + $ __100,000__

1.16 Enter net cash items

   (a) owner **received** from 1.14(a). . . . . + $ __100,000__

   (b) owner **transferred** from 1.14(b). . . . . – $ _____

1.17 Net debt relief and cash items, (1.15 & 1.16, but not less than zero) . . . . + $ __200,000__

1.18 Cash items received on sale from 1.7 . . . . + $ _____0_____

1.19 **TOTAL net money and other properties owner received:**
(The sum of 1.17 and 1.18) . . . . + $ __200,000__

2. PROFIT/LOSS ON TRANSFER OF UNQUALIFIED PROPERTY

2.1 Market value of unqualified property owner transferred. . . . . . . + $_____

2.2 Remaining cost basis in unqualified property owner
transferred . . . . – $_____

2.3 **Total profit/loss on unqualified property owner transferred:**. . . . . (+ or –) $ _____0_____

— PAGE ONE OF TWO — FORM 354 —

Figure 4(b) cont. _ _ _ _ _ _ _ _ _ _ _ — PAGE TWO OF TWO — FORM 354 — — — — — — — — — — — — — — — — — —

3. PROFIT REALIZED ON THE §1031 PROPERTY SOLD OR EXCHANGED
(before applying the §1031 exemption)
Consideration owner received:

3.1   Debt relief: Enter amount from 1.1 . . . . $___**200,000**___

3.2   Market value of §1031 placement property owner acquired . . . . . $___**400,000**___

3.3   Total cash items received from property sold:
Enter amount from 1.7 . . . . $_____

3.4   Total cash items received with replacement property:
Enter amount from 1.8 . . . . $___**200,000**___

3.5   Total consideration owner received (3.1 through 3.4) . . . . + $___**800,000**___

Consideration owner transferred:

3.6   Debt owner assumed: Enter amount from 1.2 . . . . $___**100,000**___

3.7   Enter remaining cost basis in all §1031 properties
owner transferred . . . . $___**300,000**___

3.8   Cash owner contributed: Enter amount from 1.9 . . . . $_____

3.9   Transactional costs disbursed: Enter amount from 1.10 . . . . $_____

3.10 Purchase notes owner executed: Enter amount from 1.11 . . . . . . $___**100,000**___

3.11 Remaining cost basis in unqualified property owner transferred:
Enter amount from 2.2 . . . . $_____

3.12 Total consideration owner transferred (3.6 through 3.11) . . . . − $___**500,000**___

3.13 **Total profits realized in §1031 property sold or exchanged:**
(3.5 less 3.12). . . . . (+)or −) $___**300,000**___

4. REPORTABLE PROFIT/LOSS ON THE §1031 TRANSACTION

4.1   Total net debt relief and cash items owner receives:
Enter amount from 1.19, but not less than zero . . . . + $___**200,000**___

    (a) Carryback basis allocation: Amount by which 3.7
        exceeds 1.1, but not more than the amount at 1.5. . . . . . . − $_____**0**_____

4.2   Total profit/loss on unqualified property owner transferred:
Enter amount from 2.3. . . . . (+ or −) $_____**0**_____

4.3   Subtotal: The amount of equity withdrawn:
(the sum of 4.1, (a) and 4.2). . . . . (+)or −) $___**200,000**___

4.4   Total profits realized in §1031 property sold/exchanged:
Enter amount from 3.13 (But not less than zero) . . . . $___**300,000**___

4.5   **Total reportable profit/loss:** (Enter lesser of 4.3 or 4.4). . . . . (+)or −) $___**200,000**___

5. BASIS OF ALL PROPERTY(IES) RECEIVED

5.1   Debt relief. Enter amounts from:

    (a) 1.3(a) Net debt relief. . . . . − $___**100,000**___

    (b) 1.3(b) Net debt assumed . . . . + $_____

5.2   Cash items. Enter amounts from:

    (a) 1.7   Cash items received on the sale . . . . − $_____

    (b) 1.8   Cash items received on purchase . . . . − $___**200,000**___

    (c) 1.9   Cash contributed . . . . + $_____

    (d) 1.10   Transactional cost disbursed. . . . . + $_____

    (e) 1.11   Purchase-money notes executed . . . . + $___**100,000**___

5.3   Remaining cost basis in all property transferred.
Enter amounts from:

    (a) 3.7   . . . . + $___**300,000**___

    (b) 3.11 . . . . + $_____

5.4   Reportable profit/loss. Enter amount from 4.5. . . . . (+)or −) $___**200,000**___

5.5   **Basis of Replacement Property(ies) and cash items:**
(The sum of 5.1 through 5.4). . . . . $___**300,000**___
(See Form 354.5 for priority allocation to cash items, multiple
replacement properties and between land and improvements.)

FORM 354   02-05   ©2006 **first tuesday**, P.O. BOX 20069, RIVERSIDE, CA 92516 (800) 794-0494

transaction. The note offsets $100,000 of the $200,000 in cash withdrawn from the net sales proceeds held by the §1031 trustee. [See Figure 4(b) §§1.8 and 1.11 accompanying this chapter]

The result is a withdrawal of $100,000 in net cash items on completion of the §1031 reinvestment. [See Figure 4(b) §1.14(a)]

Further, the $100,000 existing debt on the replacement property is less than the $200,000 debt encumbering the property sold. Thus, the investor also withdraws $100,000 in **net debt relief**. [See Figure 4(b) §1.15]

The net debt relief ($100,000) and receipt of net cash items ($100,000) totals a withdrawal of $200,000 in capital from the §1031 transaction. [See Figure 4(b) §§1.17 and 1.19]

Since the $200,000 in total capital withdrawals are less than the $300,000 profit the investor realized on the sale, only $200,000 of the profit is reported. [See Figure 4(b) §4.5]

Pulling out cash

In Example No. 4, the investor used the equity he acquired in the replacement property as collateral to borrow money concurrent with closing.

Often it is necessary for the investor to arrange financing to **generate cash** when acquiring a replacement property. However, a loan sometimes cannot be arranged or it may only be arranged at a high or variable rate with a short amortization schedule or due date.

As an alternative to originating a loan on a lender's terms, the investor on his purchase of the replacement property can execute a carryback note and set his own terms for repayment. The carryback note is for the amount of cash he wants to withdraw, also called a *purchase-money note*. The note is an alternative to using all the cash held in the §1031 trust as a down payment. On closing, the cash impounded with the §1031 trustee that is not used to purchase the replacement property will be released

to the investor, either directly by the §1031 trustee or, more preferably, indirectly through the purchase escrow for the replacement property.

The profit reporting consequences are the same whether:

- a lender makes the investor an equity loan secured by the replacement property he acquires; or

- the impounded cash held by the §1031 trustee is disbursed to the investor and offset by a purchase-money note executed by the investor to purchase the replacement property.

Trade-down Example No. 5

The facts in Example No. 5 differ from Example No. 1 as follows:

- **unqualified property** (a boat) is received by the investor as part payment for the property he exchanged; and

- the price of the property exchanged by the investor and the price of the boat he acquired in exchange are not agreed to in writing, but left **unpriced**, called an *unpriced exchange*. [See Figure 5(a) accompanying this chapter]

Since the exchange agreement does not set the value of the boat, the profit in the property exchanged, which includes the price paid for in part by the value of the boat received by the investor, cannot be determined until the value of the boat is set. [See Figure 5(b) §4 accompanying this chapter]

The value ultimately placed on the unpriced boat received by the investor depends on the investor's goal in avoiding profit reporting. [See Figure 5(b) §1.6]

The amount of value ultimately set for the boat, less any debt assumed on the boat, is reported

FACTS OF EXAMPLE 5 — PRICE TRADE-DOWN

A. **Remaining Cost Basis:** $300,000

B. **§1031 Transaction:** Less debt assumed and less equity acquired, including personal property.

Items:	Property sold and contributions for adjustments:	Property acquired and adjustments received:
1. Market price: 2. Existing debt:	$ — Unpriced $200,000	$400,000 $100,000
3. Existing equity: 4. Adjustments: Type:	Unknown $0 _____	$300,000 $ — Unpriced Boat

C. **Observations:**

Profit reported on the sale or exchange is based on the equity received in the unpriced boat (and net debt relief).

Priority allocation of basis to the price paid for the unqualified property (boat) is determined later.

as taxable profit taken by the investor on the property he exchanged. The lower the price of the boat, the lower the profit reported on the property he sold or exchanged. [See Chapter 25]

Determining the value of unpriced boot

The value of boot received in an **unpriced exchange** is reported as profit taken by the investor on the exchange of his property. Since the pricing is not set by agreement, the investor has the benefit of time until he files his tax return to analyze the value that will be given to the properties.

To set the price of unqualified property at the time of the exchange is premature and is usually detrimentally high.

The IRS looks to all documentation to set the value of the property the investor exchanged, including the price and equity valuation set in the listing with the broker, exchange agreements, purchase agreements, escrow instructions, hazard insurance policies, documentary transfer tax, title insurance amounts, schedule of escrow fees, etc.

When the purchase agreement or other document contains an agreement on the price of any item, any later reflection on what that price should have been will meet IRS resistance. To change values once they are agreed to in writing, even if mistakenly done or hugely optimistic, will give rise to a challenge on audit.

Also, values of unpriced boot can be set by independent appraisal. An independent appraisal should be obtained if great fluctuations in the value of the boot exist.

Figure 5(b)

§1031 PROFIT AND BASIS RECAP SHEET

Date _____, 20_____   Prepared by: _____

OWNER'S NAME: _Example Number 5_____

PROPERTY SOLD/EXCHANGED: _____

COMMENTS: _____

_____

REPLACEMENT PROPERTY: _____

COMMENTS: _____

_____

1. NET DEBT RELIEF AND CASH ITEMS

Net existing debt:

1.1   Balance of debt(s) owner is **relieved** of on
       all property sold/exchanged . . . . + $ _**200,000**_

1.2   Balance of debt(s) owner **assumed** on
       §1031 property acquired . . . . – $ _**100,000**_

1.3   **Total net existing debt:** Enter the sum of 1.1 & 1.2 as either:

    (a)   **Net debt relief** (amount by which 1.1 exceeds 1.2) . . . . + $ _**100,000**_

    (b)   **Net debt assumed** (amount by which 1.2 exceeds 1.1) . . . . – $ _**0**_

Cash items received on close of the property sold:

1.4   Amount of cash **received** on sale (excluding prorations) . . . . . . $ _____

1.5   Amount of carryback note **received** on sale . . . . $ _____

1.6   Equity value in unqualified property **received** on sale . . . . $ _**unknown**_

1.7   **Total of cash items received on closing the property sold:**
       (The sum of 1.4, 1.5 & 1.6) . . . . + $ _**unknown**_

**Net cash items received or transferred on close of the
replacement property:**

1.8   Amount of cash items **received** with replacement property
       (excluding prorations) . . . . + $ _____

1.9   Amount of cash owner **contributed** (excluding prorations) . . . . . . $ _____

1.10 Transactional costs **disbursed** at any time on either property
       (excluding prorations and loan payoffs) . . . . $ _____

1.11 Amount of purchase-money notes **owner executed** in
       part payment for the replacement property . . . . $ _____

1.12 Equity value of any unqualified property owner **exchanged** . . . . . $ _____

1.13 Subtotal of cash items owner **transferred** (1.9 through 1.12) . . . . – $ _____

1.14 **Total net cash items:** Enter the sum of 1.8 & 1.13 as either:

    (a)   **Net cash items owner received:**
       (amount by which 1.8 exceeds 1.13) . . . . + $ _**0**_

    (b)   **Net cash items owner transferred:**
       (amount by which 1.13 exceeds 1.8) . . . . – $ _**0**_

Netting all debt relief and cash items:

1.15 Enter net debt **relief** from 1.3(a) . . . . + $ _**100,000**_

1.16 Enter net cash items

    (a)   owner **received** from 1.14(a) . . . . + $ _____

    (b)   owner **transferred** from 1.14(b) . . . . – $ _____

1.17 Net debt relief and cash items, (1.15 & 1.16, but not less than zero) . . . . + $ _**100,000**_

1.18 Cash items received on sale from 1.7 . . . . + $ _**unknown**_

1.19 **TOTAL net money and other properties owner received:**
       (The sum of 1.17 and 1.18) . . . . + $ _**unknown**_

2. PROFIT/LOSS ON TRANSFER OF UNQUALIFIED PROPERTY

2.1   Market value of unqualified property owner transferred. . . . . . . + $ _____

2.2   Remaining cost basis in unqualified property owner
       transferred . . . . – $ _____

2.3   **Total profit/loss on unqualified property owner transferred:** . . . . (+ or –) $ _**0**_

— — — — — — — — — — — — — PAGE ONE OF TWO — FORM 354 — — — — — — — — — — — — — — — — —

Figure 5(b) cont.

3. PROFIT REALIZED ON THE §1031 PROPERTY SOLD OR EXCHANGED
(before applying the §1031 exemption)

Consideration owner received:

3.1 Debt relief: Enter amount from 1.1 .... $ __200,000__

3.2 Market value of §1031 placement property owner acquired ..... $ __400,000__

3.3 Total cash items received from property sold:
Enter amount from 1.7 .... $ __unknown__

3.4 Total cash items received with replacement property:
Enter amount from 1.8 .... $ _____

3.5 Total consideration owner received (3.1 through 3.4) .... + $ __unknown__

Consideration owner transferred:

3.6 Debt owner assumed: Enter amount from 1.2 .... $ __100,000__

3.7 Enter remaining cost basis in all §1031 properties
owner transferred .... $ __300,000__

3.8 Cash owner contributed: Enter amount from 1.9 .... $ _____

3.9 Transactional costs disbursed: Enter amount from 1.10 .... $ _____

3.10 Purchase notes owner executed: Enter amount from 1.11 ...... $ _____

3.11 Remaining cost basis in unqualified property owner transferred:
Enter amount from 2.2 .... $ _____

3.12 Total consideration owner transferred (3.6 through 3.11) .... – $ __400,000__

3.13 **Total profits realized in §1031 property sold or exchanged:**
(3.5 less 3.12) .... (+ or –) $ __unknown__

4. REPORTABLE PROFIT/LOSS ON THE §1031 TRANSACTION

4.1 Total net debt relief and cash items owner receives:
Enter amount from 1.19, but not less than zero .... + $ __unknown__

(a) Carryback basis allocation: Amount by which 3.7
exceeds 1.1, but not more than the amount at 1.5 .... – $ __0__

4.2 Total profit/loss on unqualified property owner transferred:
Enter amount from 2.3 .... (+ or –) $ __0__

4.3 Subtotal: The amount of equity withdrawn:
(the sum of 4.1, (a) and 4.2) .... (+ or –) $ __unknown__

4.4 Total profits realized in §1031 property sold/exchanged:
Enter amount from 3.13 (But not less than zero) .... $ __unknown__

4.5 **Total reportable profit/loss:** (Enter lesser of 4.3 or 4.4) .... (+ or –) $ __unknown__

5. BASIS OF ALL PROPERTY(IES) RECEIVED

5.1 Debt relief. Enter amounts from:

(a) 1.3(a) Net debt relief .... – $ __100,000__

(b) 1.3(b) Net debt assumed .... + $ _____

5.2 Cash items. Enter amounts from:

(a) 1.7 Cash items received on the sale .... – $ __unknown__

(b) 1.8 Cash items received on purchase .... – $ _____

(c) 1.9 Cash contributed .... + $ _____

(d) 1.10 Transactional cost disbursed .... + $ _____

(e) 1.11 Purchase-money notes executed .... + $ _____

5.3 Remaining cost basis in all property transferred.
Enter amounts from:

(a) 3.7 .... + $ __300,000__

(b) 3.11 .... + $ _____

5.4 Reportable profit/loss. Enter amount from 4.5 .... (+ or –) $ __unknown__

5.5 **Basis of Replacement Property(ies) and cash items:**
(The sum of 5.1 through 5.4) .... $ __unknown__
(See Form 354.5 for priority allocation to cash items, multiple
replacement properties and between land and improvements.)

FORM 354   02-05   ©2006 **first tuesday**, P.O. BOX 20069, RIVERSIDE, CA 92516 (800) 794-0494

The more volatile the value of the boot, the greater the justification to leave the transaction unpriced. Acquisitions of businesses (business opportunities and their leaseholds), stock, airplanes, personal residence, livestock, equipment, inventory, furnishings, collections, etc., are situations in which unpriced exchanges should be considered.

SECTION D

Delayed Closing

Chapter 15

A delay in the §1031 reinvestment

This chapter discuss the time limitations and related restrictions for the identification and acquisition of replacement property in a delayed reinvestment of §1031 monies.

Identification and acquisition periods

An owner has entered into a purchase agreement to sell §1031 property. The purchase agreement provides for a 90-day escrow period and contains provisions calling for:

- the buyer to cooperate with the funding of the owner's §1031 reinvestment plan; and

- the owner to locate replacement property as a condition for closing escrow.

A broker is coordinating the sale and purchase of property on behalf of the owner in an effort to maintain the owner's commitment to a **continuing investment** in §1031 property.

A replacement property is soon located and the owner enters into a purchase agreement with the sellers, a tenants in common (TIC) investment group. Closing of the purchase escrow on the replacement property is scheduled to occur concurrent with the date set for the close of the owner's sales escrow.

However, one of the tenant-in-common co-owners has died. His interest has not yet been cleared from title by a transfer into the names of his heirs or beneficiaries or the remaining tenant-in-common co-owners.

Until title to the replacement property can be conveyed and a title insurance policy can be issued for the conveyance of the entire fee simple, the owner does not wish to waive his contingency in his sales escrow to remove the condition that he must first locate a replacement property before closing the sales escrow.

As the deadline for closing the two escrows draws near, it becomes clear that the title to the replacement property cannot be cleared in time for the purchase escrow to close as scheduled. Thus, a **concurrent closing** of the sales escrow and the purchase escrow will not be possible. The owner considers waiving the contingency and closing escrow on his sale before the replacement property's escrow closes.

The **risk** taken by the owner when waiving the contingency and closing escrow on the property sold concerns the conveyance and issuance of title insurance for the replacement property. If title cannot be delivered within 180 days of closing his sales escrow, he will lose his §1031 exemption. However, the attorneys involved on behalf of the owner believe the delay in clearing title is merely temporary and no other foreseeable obstacles exist to the issuance of title insurance and transfer of title within the next several weeks.

The broker is now confronted with the owner's purchase of replacement property after he closes escrow on his sale. The owner has become involved in a **delayed §1031 reinvestment**. The owner will close escrow on the sale of one property and on a different and later date will acquire ownership of another property in an unrelated transaction. Thus, the owner is still engaged in two mutually exclusive transactions, a sale and a purchase, only now the closings will not be *concurrent* or allow for a mere transfer of funds from one escrow to another.

To qualify the owner's profit on his sale for the §1031 exemption even when the purchase escrow for the replacement property does not close concurrent with the owner's sales escrow, the broker advises the owner to consider taking the following steps:

- prepare closing instructions directing the sales escrow to hand the owner's net proceeds to a buyer's trustee, commonly called a *facilitator* [See Chapters 18 and 19];

- prepare closing instructions directing escrow to credit the owner in the closing settlement statement with *Exchange Valuation Credits (EVCs)* in lieu of a check from escrow for the net sales proceeds as originally agreed;

- select an entity or individual the owner knows and trusts to be appointed (by the buyer under a buyer's trust agreement) as the *trustee* to receive and hold in trust the net proceeds from the sale, and, on further instructions from the owner, to fund the owner's down payment and closing costs in the purchase escrow for the replacement property;

- *identify* within 45 days after closing the sales escrow the replacement property now in escrow **and** two alternative replacement properties that could be purchased should the purchase escrow for the replacement property fail to close within the 45-day period for any reason; and

- *close escrow* on the purchase of a replacement property within 180 days after the sales escrow closes.

The owner decides his risks regarding a failure to timely close the purchase escrow are sufficiently covered in order to justify waiving the contingency to purchase other property he closes his sale.

The 180-day **reinvestment period** includes the 45-day identification period. Both commence on the day escrow closes on the property sold.

Should the owner fail to meet either the identification or reinvestment deadline, the property acquired does not qualify as replacement property. Thus, the profit in the property sold would not be exempt from taxes under §1031. [Revenue Regulations §1.1031(k)-1(a)]

If two or more properties are sold by an investor and their net sales proceeds **consolidated** into one replacement property, the periods for identification and acquisition of the replacement property begin to run from the closing date of the first property sold. [Rev. Regs. §1.1031(k)-1(b)(2)(iii)]

Replacement property identification period

An investor in a delayed §1031 reinvestment must, in writing, identify the replacement property by midnight on the 45th day after the date the sales escrow closed on the property sold. [Rev. Regs. §1.1031(k)-1(b)(2)(i)]

For example, an investor intends to complete a §1031 reinvestment of his net sales proceeds. Escrow for the sale of the investor's property closes on November 16. The last day for the investor to identify replacement property is December 31 — 45 days after the date escrow closed on the sale, day one being November 17.

If ownership to any §1031 replacement property is acquired within the 45-day identification period, the replacement property acquired is **treated as identified** without further documentation on a §1031 property identification form. [Rev. Regs. §1.1031(k)-1(c)(1)]

Thus, an investor entirely avoids the identification process by closing the purchase escrow on all replacement properties within the 45-day identification period.

When ownership of any replacement property is acquired after the 45-day identification period, the investor must sign and deliver a written **§1031 property identification statement** within the 45-day period. The form must be delivered to either:

- the owner who is conveying (selling) the replacement property to the investor; or

- any entity or individual involved in the §1031 transaction, except the investor or those who are **disqualified**, not just related. [Rev. Regs. §1.1031(k)-1(c)(2); see Form 360 accompanying this chapter; see Chapter 1]

The identification statement may be delivered to the escrow agent or title company who were involved in the sale of the investor's property, even though the sales escrow has already closed.

Persons to be notified of the identification

Consider a real estate broker who lists investment real estate for sale. The sale of the listed property is intended by the seller to be the first leg of a §1031 reinvestment plan.

The broker has acted as the investor's agent in real estate transactions during the preceding year. All listings and sales handled by the broker on behalf of the investor have been §1031 sales and reinvestments.

Is a real estate broker who has represented the investor only in §1031 transactions, a person who is qualified to receive the identification statement?

Yes! A *disqualified person* for receipt of the identification notice includes only those real estate brokers, attorneys, employees, accountants and investment bankers who, within two years prior to the closing of escrow on the property sold, performed any professional services on behalf of the investor that were **not** part of a §1031 transaction. [Rev. Regs. §1.1031(k)-1(k)(2)(i); see Chapter 1]

Also, financial institutions, title insurance companies or escrow companies who perform no more than routine financial, title insurance, escrow or trust services for the investor are qualified to receive the identification statement. [Rev. Regs. §1.1031(k)-1(k)(2)(ii)]

Thus, the broker handling a §1031 transaction for the investor can properly receive the property identification statement only if the broker's representation of the investor was as a §1031 exchange broker during the two-year period prior to the transaction. [Rev. Regs. §1.1031(k)-1(k)(5), Example 1 (iii)]

Other **disqualified persons** not able to receive the identification notice include:

- close **family members**, including brothers and sisters (whole or half blood), spouse, ancestors and lineal descendants; and

- a corporation or partnership in which **more than 10%** of outstanding stock, capital interest or profit interest is owned by the investor or the investor's agents. [Rev. Regs. §1.1031(k)-1(k)(3)]

To avoid the issues of a *disqualified person*, the investor should deliver the identification form to the escrow office or title company who handled the closing on the property he sold, not the escrow or title company he intends to use for the property he is identifying (although he could properly do so). A cover letter would be appropriate advising them where to file the identification form.

The identification form should not be delivered to the buyer's §1031 trustee since, while the trustee may be an unrelated person, the trustee may well be the investor's personal attorney, CPA or investment banker, persons who are disqualified.

Location and quantity of properties

The written identification of the selected replacement properties must include the legal description and street address or assessor's number of each property identified. [Rev. Regs. §1.1031(k)-1(c)(3)]

More than one replacement property may be identified. However, the number of potential replacement properties chosen to be identified places different restrictions on which properties may or must be acquired, such as:

- when identifying three or fewer properties, **without limit on their value**, any one or more may be purchased;

- when identifying four or more properties and the **combined value** of all properties identified is not more than twice (200% of) the price received for the property sold, any one or more may be purchased; or

- when identifying four or more properties and the **combined value** of all properties exceeds 200% of the price received for the property sold, the investor is required to purchase 95% of the total value of all replacement properties identified to qualify for the §1031 profit tax exemption.

If the investor identifies four or more properties with a combined value exceeding the 200% value ceiling and then does not purchase 95% of the total value of all replacement properties identified, no properties will be treated as having been identified since identification and acquisition requirements were not met. [Rev. Regs. §1.1031(k)-1(c)(4)(ii)]

The rules **limiting** the identification of properties include any replacement properties to which ownership was actively acquired by the investor during the identification period.

For example, an investor acquires ownership of a replacement property within the 45-day identification period which is priced below the price the investor received for the real estate he sold. Thus, the debt and equity in the property acquired do not fully offset the debt and equity in the property sold.

To complete a fully qualified tax-free §1031 reinvestment, the investor will purchase an additional replacement property with the funds remaining from his sale.

Since a replacement property has already been purchased during the identification period, it is treated as one of the **properties identified** when the investor identifies more properties. Thus, the investor who has already acquired one property is limited to either:

- identifying two additional replacement properties (for a total of three) of **any combined fair market value** and purchase one, both or neither; or

- identifying three or more additional properties whose values (including the value of the replacement property already purchased) **do not collectively exceed 200%** of the price the investor received for the property sold and purchase one or more or neither of the newly-identified properties. [Rev. Regs. §1.1031(k)-1(c)(4)(iii)]

Should the investor have a replacement property in escrow during the 45-day period which is not scheduled to close until after the 45 days expires, that property is still included as one of the three properties identified.

The investor must carefully plan the number of potential replacement properties he identifies. The investor risks losing the entire tax benefits of the §1031 exemption if:

- more properties are identified than allowed; or

- he does not acquire enough of the identified properties should he fall under the 95% rule.

Improper identification alone will cause the entire profit from the sale to be reported and taxed as *recognized gain*, even if the investor timely acquires some of the identified property.

Identification in the case of construction

Replacement property controlled by an investor or businessman under a purchase agreement, option or escrow instructions that will be improved by construction prior to taking title qualifies as §1031 property.

§1031 PROPERTY IDENTIFICATION STATEMENT
For Delayed §1031 Transactions

DATE:_____, 20_____, at _____, California

FACTS:

This is an addendum to the following:

☐ Sales escrow instructions

☐ Other:_____

> **NOTE: This taxpayer statement, prepared and delivered as noted within 45 days after closing a sale forth the properties acquired and those investigated for later acquisition within 180 days after closing the sale. [IRC §1031(A)(3)]**

Dated:_____, at _____, California

Entered into by:

Seller/Taxpayer: _____

Buyer or Buyer's Trustee: _____

Regarding replacement of real estate described as: _____

_____

This addendum is intended to comply with Internal Revenue Code Section 1031(a)(3)(A) within 45 days after closing the sale by identifying property to be received to complete a §1031 reinvestment plan.

AGREEMENT:

One or more of the following properties will be purchased to complete the terms of the above-referenced document.

> **NOTE: If four or more properties are identified within the 45-day identification period, the fair market value of each property identified or previously received must be listed and comply with the 200% aggregate-value rule or the 95%-of-value acquisition rule. [Rev. Regs. §§1.1031(c)-3(c)(4)(i),(ii)]**

1. ($_____) _____
2. ($_____) _____
3. ($_____) _____

4. ($_____) _____
5. ($_____) _____
6. ($_____) _____
7. ($_____) _____

_____

_____

_____

_____

_____

Buyer or Sales Escrow Officer: **Receipt is hereby acknowledged.**	**Seller/Taxpayer** **I hereby submit the above.**
Date:_____, 20_____	Date:_____, 20_____
Name: _____	Name: _____
Signature: _____	Signature: _____
Signature: _____	Signature: _____
Address: _____	Address: _____
_____	_____
Phone:_____	Phone:_____

However, should the property identification include four or more properties intended to comply with a total value of less than 200% of the price of the property sold, the value used for the real estate and improvements is the property's estimated value as improved on the date the investor is to acquire ownership. [Rev. Regs. §1.1031(k)-1(e)(2)(ii)]

Further, the identification adequately describes the property if the statement includes a legal description or parcel number for the underlying real estate and makes a reference to existing plans and specifications for the improvements to be constructed on the identified parcel. [Rev. Regs. §1.1031(k)-1(e)(2)]

If substantial changes in construction are made that deviate from the inherent nature of the construction identified by the plans and specifications in the identification notice and those changes produce an entirely different structure than the one identified (an apartment versus a mini-storage facility), the replacement property acquired as improved with improperly identified construction will not be considered the acquisition of §1031 property. [Rev. Regs. §1.1031(k)-1(e)(3)(i)]

The 15% incidental personal property rule

Consider an investor who is acquiring an apartment building as replacement property in a §1031 reinvestment plan. The building contains furnishings, washing machines and other personal property that will be acquired as part of the price paid to purchase the apartment building.

The value of the personal property does not exceed 15% of the price paid for the real estate. Put another way, of the total purchase price paid for the apartment and furnishings, the furnishings cannot exceed 13% of the aggregate price paid for the rental operation, land and improvements.

Does the investor have to list the personal property as part of the replacement property on the 45-day §1031 property identification form?

No! Personal property used in the operations of the real estate is considered included in the legal description of the replacement property on the identification form, unless the market value of the personal property exceeds 15% of the **separate value** of the apartment building. [Rev. Regs. §1.1031(k)-1(c)(5)(ii), Example 2]

Personal property which is used in the operation and management of the real estate, called *incidental property* by the Internal Revenue Service (IRS), is treated as part of the real estate under the **15% of value rule**.

Taxwise, personal property is treated as part of the real estate when:

- standard real estate transactions, such as the sale of a hotel or motel, typically transfer the personal property with the real estate; and

- the value of personal property does not exceed 15% of the separate value of the real estate. [Rev. Regs. §1.1031(k)-1(c)(5)(i)]

Here, the value of the **personal property** acquired is not reported as *cash boot* received for the property sold or exchanged.

Revoking an identification statement

An investor locates a few suitable replacement properties. He prematurely prepares and sends the property identification form listing the properties to the §1031 trustee (who is not a disqualified relative or advisor for receipt of the identification).

Before the end of the 45-day identification period, the broker locates other potential replacement properties that are more suitable. The investor sends another, entirely new identification form to the §1031 trustee, listing three of the newly-located properties, no others.

The new identification form contains a written statement **revoking** the prior identification of replacement properties.

Does the investor need to comply with the 200% rule since six properties were identified?

No! The investor properly revoked the first identification of replacement properties by preparing a *written revocation* of the prior identification statement and **listing the newly-identified properties**. Further, it was hand delivered, mailed or faxed to the same person who received the initial property identification statement prior to the expiration of the 45-day identification period. Oral revocations and conduct (merely supplying an identification of more properties) do not revoke the prior identifications. [Rev. Regs. §1.1031(k)-1(c)(6)]

The identification of replacement property may be revoked and different properties identified at any time before the end of the 45-day identification period. Later attempts are ineffective.

Acquisition period for reinvestment

After identifying the replacement property, ownership of the replacement property must be acquired within the **180-day §1031 reinvestment period**, called the *exchange period* by the IRS. The period for closing the purchase escrow and acquiring the replacement property ends on the earlier of:

- 180 days after the date escrow closed on the sale of the investor's property;

- the date the taxpayer's return for the year of sale is actually filed; or

- the due date for filing the investor's tax return for the year of the sale, including any extensions for filing. [Rev. Regs. §1.1031(k)-1(b)(2)(ii)]

For example, an investor sells real estate as part of a §1031 reinvestment plan. Escrow closes on December 22. The investor's federal income tax return for the year in which the property was sold is due the following April 15.

The investor dutifully files his tax return by April 15 instead of filing an extension (and paying any taxes he may owe).

The investor acquires the replacement property after the return is filed, but still within the 180-day reinvestment period after the sales escrow on the property sold is closed. He then amends his return to include the reporting of the §1031 transaction.

The IRS claims the reinvestment does not qualify the profit from the sale for §1031 tax treatment. The investor failed to acquire the real estate prior to filing his tax return on the sale and thus failed to acquire real estate within the reinvestment period established by regulations.

The investor claims the reinvestment period ended on June 20, not April 15, since he was entitled to the automatic six-month extension given by the IRS to file his tax return, whether or not he filed a return on April 15.

Does the transaction qualify for the §1031 exemption?

No! The investor did not elect to extend his tax return filing date by six months in order to take advantage of the entire 180-day reinvestment period available to him. The investor closed out his tax year (and his §1031 reinvestment plan) by filing his return. He was unable to couple the sale of his property, which was reported on his tax return, with the transfer of its basis to the replacement property, which was not reported on his return, since he had not yet acquired the replacement property when he filed his return.

The investor should have extended the due date of his return by filing the automatic six-month extension, not his return. With an extension, the reinvestment period would have ended on midnight of June 20 (except in a leap year), 180 days after the sale of the investor's property and before the due date for filing his return. [**Christensen** v. **Commissioner** TCM 1996-254; Rev. Regs. §1.1031(k)-1(b)(3)]

Basic character of property acquired

After 45 days and within the 180-day reinvestment period for completion of a delayed §1031 reinvestment, the investor must acquire ownership to *substantially the same* property he previously identified. [Rev. Regs. §1.1031(k)-1(d)(1)(ii)]

For example, an investor identifies an unimproved parcel of real estate as replacement property. Before expiration of the reinvestment period, and before he becomes the owner of the replacement property, the investor has improvements constructed on the real estate in the form of a fence.

Here, the investor is considered to have received substantially the same property as the property he identified, even though he had some minor improvements made before acquisition. The fence does not change the **basic character** of the parcel of real estate he identified. [Rev. Regs. §1.1031(k)-1(d)(2), Example 2]

Now consider an investor who identifies 20 acres of unimproved real estate with a fair market value of $250,000. The investor ultimately purchases only 15 acres of the real estate for $187,500.

The property is considered substantially the same property as the property he identified. The portion of the unimproved property acquired does not differ from the **character of the real estate identified**. The investor purchased 75% of the property identified at a fair market value of 75% of the fair market value of the whole, unimproved real estate identified. [Rev. Regs. §1.1031(k)-1(d)(2), Example 4]

Now consider an investor who identifies real estate and the improvements that are to be constructed before he acquires ownership. However, the construction has only been partially completed when the investor acquires the real estate (and the 180 days is about to run out).

Here, the real estate with construction incomplete is substantially the same real estate as the property identified. The improvements, to the extent they exist, are the same improvements the investor identified, just not all of them. [Rev. Regs. §1.1031(k)-1(e)(3)(iii)]

However, the value of the further improvements that are constructed after the investor closes escrow and acquires ownership are not part of the price paid (or debt assumed) for §1031 purposes. Thus, the value of the portion of the construction not yet completed is **not** part of the debt or equity in the replacement property. The value of the remaining, incomplete portion of the improvements that was needed to avoid taxes on some of the profit taken on the property sold will be taxed. [Rev. Regs. §1.1031(k)-1(e)(5)(iii)]

120-day extensions for disaster relief

An investor has already implemented his §1031 reinvestment plan when a disaster occurs, affecting his ability to timely complete his reinvestment plans.

On or before the date the disaster struck, the investor had taken his first step in the §1031 reinvestment plan:

- by conveying the property he was selling to either a buyer (direct deeding) or a safe harbor intermediary (sequential deeding); or

- by taking title in the name of an intermediary as the *interim titleholder* under the safe harbor election and acquiring control of replacement property in a reverse exchange.

Editor's note — Warehousing under the general rules are not affected. [See Chapter 23]

The disaster may have been a tsunami, earthquake, wildfire, drought or flood, or been brought about by a terroristic or military action. The President of the United States must declare the area affected a *presidentially declared disaster area*.

The IRS will publish a *Notice* or *News Release* authorizing the extension of §1031 reinvestment deadlines and the extension of expired 45-day identification deadlines, the duration of the extension (called a *postponement* by the IRS) and the location of the disaster area.

For the investor to qualify for the 120-day disaster extension of §1031 deadlines published by the IRS, he or his §1031 reinvestment plan must be affected by one of the following situations:

1. The investor's principal residence or his place of business is **located within** the area covered by the IRS Notice or News Release.

2. The investor has difficulty meeting his §1031 deadlines **due to** the disaster for one of the following reasons:

    - either an identified replacement property or, in a reverse exchange under the safe harbor election, the property to be sold, is located within the disaster area;

    - the principal place of business of any individual or person connected to the §1031 transaction, such as an intermediary, buyer, seller, attorney, lender, escrow or title company, is located within the disaster area;

    - any individual or employer connected to the §1031 transaction, was killed, injured or missing as a result of the disaster;

    - a document prepared in connection with the §1031 transactions or a relevant title record was destroyed, damaged or lost as a result of the disaster;

- a lender decides not to fund a closing, permanently or temporarily, due to the disaster or a disaster-related unavailability of hazard insurance; or

- a title insurance company refuses to issue a policy due to the disaster.

The 120-day postponement for transactions affected by the disaster applies to two categories of **expiration deadlines**:

- those §1031 deadlines **expiring on or after** the disaster's occurrence; and

- those 45-day identification periods **expiring prior** to the disaster's occurrence.

Section 1031 reinvestment and sales deadlines that **expire on or after** the date of the disaster and qualify for the 120-day disaster extension include:

- the 45-day identification period expiration date for a delayed reinvestment following the pre-disaster sale of the investor's property; and

- the 180-day reinvestment period expiration date.

The 120-day disaster extension does not apply to the postponed due date for the investor's tax return for the year of the sale.

In a *reverse exchange* following the investor's pre-disaster acquisition of the replacement property (in the name of the interim titleholder under the safe harbor election) and before the identified property owned by the investor has been sold, if a disaster has occurred, the investor can apply the 120-day disaster extension to these deadlines:

- the five business day period expiration date for entry into an interim title-holding agreement with a qualified intermediary;

- the 45-day identification period expiration date for the property to be sold;

- the 180-day period expiration date for the sale of the property identified; and

- the 180-day combined time period expiration date for the qualified intermediary to release the replacement property and property to be sold he has held.

Now consider a 45-day *identification period* which **expired before** the disaster occurred. One or more of the properties identified was *substantially damaged* by the disaster. The property damaged is in need of reconstruction or repair, or another property needs to be substituted for it in a new notice of property identification.

Here, the 120-day disaster extension of the expiration date for the identification period is allowed so other properties can now be identified by a cancellation of the original notice of property identification (which listed the substantially damaged property) and a new identification notice can be prepared and delivered to the appropriate person prior to expiration of the additional 120 days. [Revenue Procedure 2004-13 as modified by IRS Notice 2005-3]

Chapter 16

Direct deeding and avoiding receipt

This chapter debunks the myth that a formal exchange is a requisite in §1031 conveyancing and presents the general rule for direct deeding and the impounding of sales proceeds.

Preferable to sequential deeding

A property must have an equity over and above the loan encumbering it to be able to exchange it for other property. When an **equity** does exist in a property and allows an investor to demand something of value, a sale of the property will **cash out** the investor.

On entering into a sale of a property an investor's wish to avoid a tax on the profit from the sale establishes the foundation for a §1031 exchange. However, taxpayer arrangements and Internal Revenue Service (IRS) obstructions in a §1031 exchange have long entertained the courts.

Until the 1990s, the IRS demonstrated an aversion to an investor's conversion of a **cash-out sale** into a §1031 exchange. The IRS often disqualified a §1031 profit tax exemption when a cash-out sale of property was first entered into by an investor. That the investor entered into a separate agreement to purchase a replacement property and that, on closing the two transactions, the investor received nothing but the replacement property, made no difference in analysis to the IRS. It was the means used by the investor, not the end result of the reinvestment, that caused problems with the IRS.

The IRS stance was asserted repeatedly over decades in spite of a continuous flow of consistent judicial decisions to the contrary. The courts define a §1031 exchange as a sale of one property and the purchase of another by reinvestment, with the condition that the investor does not receive any cash from the sale prior to becoming the owner of a replacement property.

The position adhered to by the IRS was that an **economic exchange** must occur between two persons, each holding *true ownership* in the property sought by the other. The IRS felt no exchange could possibly occur if a buyer who acquired an investor's property only had cash to do so. The buyer acquiring the investor's property then would not be the *true owner* of the replacement property the investor eventually acquired with cash from the buyer.

Thus, to satisfy the IRS in the past, the buyer of the investor's property would had to have been burdened with all the benefits and obligations of ownership to the replacement property sought by the investor, in order for a direct exchange of property to occur. Ownership of a property entails possession, collection of rents, the obligation of operating expenses, loan payments, etc.

Passing title momentarily through the buyer, however, would not be acceptable to the IRS either. *Transitory title* carries with it no ownership. True ownership would still be with the seller of the replacement property who, for cash, passes it from himself to the investor who actually acquires the property. At no point in this transfer would the buyer ever hold true ownership. Thus, the IRS would have claimed the investor was merely using the cash from a sale as an **artifice** to acquire a replacement property by exchange. The IRS contended that a situation of this kind must be treated as a receipt of cash, which would disqualify most reinvestments in real estate.

The irony of the IRS persistence for the existence of a pure two-party exchange to qualify the investor's profit for a §1031 exemption was the accompanying rise within the real estate industry of support for the deed-for-a-deed barter approach. Escrows and those who hold themselves out as intermediaries were the most supportive. Further, all were accomplices in the exploitation of investors under the present IRS safe harbor rules as an alternative to the general rules for avoidance of receipt and the customary use of direct deeding between sellers and buyers of properties.

Yet, since 1980, the IRS has been remarkably lenient in its audits of §1031 exemptions taken by investors, as long as some effort was made to keep the cash sales proceeds out of the investor's personal bank account. IRS looked for, according to their audit manual in the early 1980s, a formal trust arrangement used to hold the funds during any delay between closing a sale and reinvestment.

The "exchange" without an exchange

"I'll trade this, which I own, for that, which you own." On an acceptance of this offer, a *bargain by barter* is created, an **exchange** in the plain meaning of the word "exchange". That said, rarely does an exchange of this kind exist today in real estate transactions, thanks primarily to the general stability of currencies and the ease of the transfer of monies as a *medium of exchange*.

The economic substance underlying the "this for that" exchange is that the *true ownership* in the property is actually held by each person who transfers to the other the beneficial rights to possess, sell, encumber or rent the property to be acquired in the exchange. Thus, an **actual exchange** is ownership for ownership.

Conversely, the person, such as an intermediary, who receives and momentarily holds a conveyance of *naked title*, namely **transitory title** (which does not include the transfer of any ownership rights in the property to possess, rent, encumber or sell in), receives nothing of legal consequence or economic substance. The legal function of the conveyance of mere transitory title of a property to someone is the creation of a *resulting trust* on that title. Title is held in trust for the true owner to possess, rent, encumber or sell the property. [**In re Sale Guaranty Corporation** (9th Cir. BAP 1998) 220 BR 660; **DeCleen** v. **Commissioner** (2000) 115 TC 457; see Chapters 18 and 21]

While an **exchange** in the world of economic arrangements is a two-party barter agreement, the **tax purpose** of a §1031 exemption requires the IRS to apply the exemption in light of the commercial realities of a sale and reinvestment in order to accomplish the congressional goal of transferring an equity in one property to an equity in another.

By necessity, cash is the primary, if not exclusive, incentive for buyers and sellers of property. Thus, the conduct of an investor in a §1031 exchange is in reality quite different from the two-party bartered exchange, although the end results for all involved are the same.

Consider, as we must, that a §1031 exchange represents a continuous commitment to an investment in the ownership of real estate. The component parts of the continuous investment include:

- the **sale of one property** by an investor; and

- the **purchase of replacement property** by the investor.

A break of 180 days in the continuity of the investment is permitted. During this reinvestment period, all or a portion of the **sales proceeds** must be held by a third party on behalf of the buyer. The funds are unavailable to the investor but available to be used by the investor solely for the purpose of reinvestment.

Any method or arrangement, no matter how simple or complex it may be, can be used to accomplish the objective of a sale of one property and the purchase of another in a §1031 reinvestment plan.

Delayed exchange schematic
The general rules for avoiding receipt

In the first step of a delayed §1031 reinvestment, the investor sells and **deeds his property** directly to a buyer. [See Figure 1, step 1]

Prior to closing, the **buyer cooperates** with the investor by establishing a trust and naming a §1031 trustee who will receive the net sales proceeds and prevent the investor's constructive receipt of those proceeds on closing. The cash proceeds and any notes carried back on the property sold by the investor are made payable by escrow to the §1031 trustee and delivered to the trustee on closing.

The **§1031 trustee**, under the trust agreement, impounds the cash funds in an interest-bearing trust account and collects installments on any carryback note. [See Figure 1, step 2]

Later, on the investor's instruction, the §1031 trustee disburses the money and assigns any carryback paper used by the investor to fund the purchase of acceptable replacement property located by the investor. [See Figure 1, step 3]

If a carryback note is created to pay part of the purchase price of the replacement property, the investor signs the note and trust deed and hands them to escrow. [See Figure 1, step 4]

To close out the §1031 Reinvestment plan, the replacement **property purchased is deeded** directly to the investor. [See Figure 1, step 5]

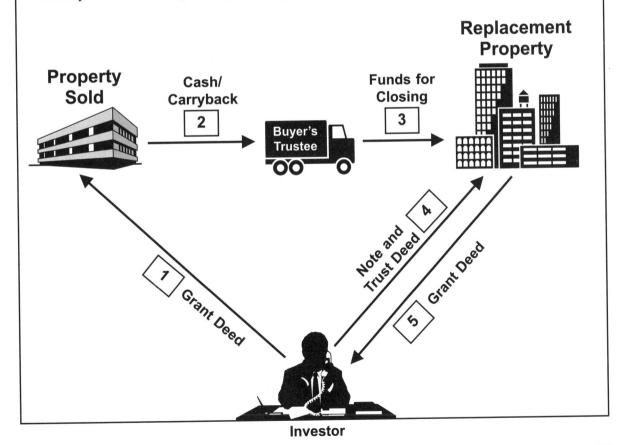

Thus, in a §1031 sale and reinvestment, only four parties need to be involved, albeit in entirely separate transactions on different properties, including:

- the **investor** with a property to be sold and a purchase to be made;

- the **buyer** of the investor's property;

- the **seller** of the replacement property the investor is acquiring; and

- the **depository** used to facilitate the transfer of funds between transactions and to avoid their receipt by the investor.

Arguably, as contended by the IRS until 1990, no exchange occurs under any plain meaning of the word "exchange" when a cash-out sale of one property is first negotiated and the funds from the sale are used to purchase other property, no matter how this is accomplished. However, this is precisely the economic substance of today's §1031 exchange, with the crucial addition of the depository necessary for the investor to avoid legal receipt of the sales proceeds he will reinvest.

The uncertain days of the pre-1980s are gone. Then, the common belief among brokers was that an **exchange** had to *look* like an exchange and *act* like an exchange, or it was not an exchange.

However, the actual exchange of properties in a §1031 exchange today, comprised of a sale of one property, impounded funds and the purchase of other property, is far from an "exchange".

Economics of the §1031 exemption

In the worlds of business and real estate operations, §1031 serves a singular purpose. The profit tax exemption is intended for those who **use** or **operate** real estate, such as businesses and landlords.

Should the businessman or landlord need to shift from one property to another to continue his line of business, be it a trade, a rental operation or ownership of unused land, the §1031 exemption allows him to do so without diminishing his working capital by regressive tax schemes.

If Internal Revenue Code (IRC) §1031 did not exist, the real estate owner confronted with the need to relocate his assets would be taxed. His wealth and ability to maintain the level of commercial or rental activity he engaged in before the exchange would be diminished. Thus, the general economy would suffer from a loss of assets from taxation, or, if no move was made because it would be taxed, the loss to the economy of more efficient and effective operating facilities or rental operations (residential or nonresidential). The result would be a failure of the economy to grow — a result of regressive taxation.

Also consider that §1031 applies to personal property, whether it is owned by a business operator, a rental landlord or a collector of personal property. Landlords and businessmen require a lot of equipment to operate. On trading equipment in when fully depreciated to acquire replacement fixtures, furniture, vehicles or furnishings to upgrade his operations, an owner will be taxed on the value of the items he traded in. Without §1031, he would have no relief from a diminished ability to operate due to the reduction in assets by the payment of taxes.

The intent of §1031 is to allow assets used in the business or real estate investment activities to be *exchanged* for replacement property without taxation so the owner can continue with his business or real estate investments unhindered by taxation.

For example, a farmer may need to relocate his operations to other, more suitable land due to encroaching residential or nonresidential development or zoning. Or he may need better quality land for higher production, a larger parcel for efficiency in the size of his operation, a shift in the location of crops to meet market demands, access to less expensive or greater quantities of water or just better weather conditions — all for the purpose of continuing his occupation.

Also, landlords are motivated to shift their current rental property, residential or nonresidential, due to numerous marketplace and personal reasons that are all related to the continuing use of real estate. The size or quality of improvements may need to be more manageable, or another geographic location is needed or desired by the landlord. Other reasons an investor shifts from one property to another could be socio-economic conditions in or about a rental property, land use changes rendering the property obsolescent as managed, or simply to build an equity by moving on up into a larger project to own and operate. These all qualify as §1031 exchanges.

In contrast, investors in the stock market do not have a profit exemption equivalent to the §1031 exchange. Congress deliberately intended they not get relief when selling shares and reinvesting in other shares. Stockholders, except venture capitalists and buyers of original issues, add nothing to the goods and services produced in this country. They buy and sell existing positions that are economically static.

Stockholders do not use the assets they own to provide goods and services, they do not participate in management of the business or real estate investment trusts (REITs) that originally issued the stock, nor do they operate the property involved. Stockholders buy and are inactive as they wait with the expectation that someone else will buy their position, hopefully at a higher price. [See Chapter 12]

It is the end result, not the means

The courtroom odyssey that eventually structured the streamlined §1031 reinvestment plans of today began in 1935 with the application of the principle of "substance over form" as the basis for applying the purposes of the tax code sections. The rule has since then been applied to determine whether a **sale** and **reinvestment** put together in a related series of contracts and conveyances was, in substance, a §1031 exchange.

For starters, to have an **ulterior tax motive** when entering into a transaction is a legal right held by taxpayers. If an investor can structure a transaction to avoid or at least decrease the amount of taxes he would pay on a sale of property and does so by any means permitted by law, he is entitled to do so. Thus, a series of transactions used by an investor in an attempt to qualify for a §1031 exemption is reviewed to determine whether the investor actually accomplished the activity intended by Congress to qualify for the §1031 exemption.

Setting aside the tax motives behind §1031 transactions, it is the actual end result of a series of transactions that sets the character of the reinvestment effort. Taxes are imposed based on the **economic substance** of the taxpayer's transactions, not whether an exchange between two parties actually occurred. [**Gregory** v. **Helvering** (1935) 293 US 465]

Further, the tax consequences of a sale of property are not determined by a review of the means employed by the investor to transfer legal title (except on a failure of the buyer to cooperate). Rather, the sale of one property and the purchase of another in a §1031 reinvestment plan are viewed as a whole. Each step prior to the completion of the related transactions, from the beginning of negotiations to the closing on the transfer of the replacement property, is relevant, sometimes called the *completed transaction theory*. [**Commissioner** v. **Court Holding Co.** (1945) 324 US 331]

In the midst of these judicial decisions on the substance of §1031 exchanges, the foundation was set for the judicial opinions that eventually simplified the character of a §1031 exchange as the sale and reinvestment we know today.

In the 1940s, consider a broker acting as a principal, who enters into an agreement with an investor to buy a property the investor no longer wants. In exchange for the property, the broker is to obtain a specifically identified replacement property the investor wishes to purchase.

First, the broker locates a cash buyer for the investor's property. The broker enters into a purchase agreement to sell the investor's property to the buyer for **cash**. The broker then negotiates with the seller of the specific replacement property to buy it for cash. They enter into a purchase agreement. Separate escrows are opened for each of the cash transactions in the name of the broker as the seller in one and as the buyer in the other.

No escrow is opened to handle the broker's agreement with the investor to acquire the investor's property in exchange for the replacement property.

The investor executes a deed to his property, conveying it **directly** to the cash buyer. The deed is placed in the sales escrow opened in the name of the broker as the seller of the investor's property. Escrow is instructed to record the investor's deed to the buyer once a deed to the replacement property can be recorded and insured in the investor's name.

The seller of the replacement property executes a deed conveying his property **directly** to the investor. The deed is placed in the purchase escrow opened by the broker as the buyer of the replacement property for cash.

At no time is the broker, or anyone else other than the investor, the common titleholder of both the properties, much less the true owner of both properties. Clearly, no exchange of titles occurs, nor, more importantly, does an exchange of ownership take place between just two parties.

The deeds conveyed title from the titleholders who owned the properties **directly** to the true

buyers of each property. No sequential deeding occurred to **mask** the cash sales by placing either:

- the buyer of the investor's property in the chain of title to the replacement property;

- the seller of the replacement property in the chain of title to the investor's property; or

- anyone else as a strawman in the chain of titles, called an *intermediary*.

Further, possession and rights of ownership were transferred directly from the investor to the cash buyer, and from the cashed-out seller of the replacement property to the investor. Does the exchange qualify for the §1031 exemption?

Yes! The broker, as the facilitator, bound himself to deliver properties he did not own and would never own. He merely contractually sandwiched himself between the sale of the investor's property and purchase of the replacement property, but not in the conveyancing. However, the result is still the same: the investor's reinvestment plan shifted his equity in one property into another property and qualified his profit for the §1031 exemption. [**W. D. Haden Co.** v. **Commissioner** (5th Cir. 1948) 165 F2d 588]

Thirty years later, an IRS ruling conceded one point in *Haden*. The buyer's cash, originally destined to pay for the investor's property, could, by amended escrow instructions, be used to purchase the replacement property and qualify for a §1031 exemption. Implicitly, the IRS, by their ruling, conceded that **ownership** of the replacement property does not need to be held first by the investor's cash buyer or any other third party.

Thus, another unnecessary step in the sale and reinvestment activities that qualify for the §1031 profit exemption was, by IRS ruling, eliminated by regulations to conform with

Haden. However, no mention of the direct deeding permitted by *Haden* case was included in the ruling. [Revenue Ruling 77-297; **Alderson** v. **Commissioner** (9th Cir. 1963) 317 F2d 790]

In the 1990s, nearly 40 years on from *Haden*, an IRS ruling finally conceded that title to the replacement property need not pass through the name of the buyer before the transaction may qualify as a §1031 exchange. The judicial decisions in all prior cases involving §1031 exchanges established the congressional intent that "the end result, not the means" eliminated any need for *sequential deeding*. [Rev. Rul. 90-34; **Biggs** v. **Commissioner** (5th Cir. 1980) 632 F2d 1171]

The artifice of concurrent closings

During the lapse of years between *Haden* and IRS acquiescence in revenue rulings and regulations, another unnecessary step previously insisted upon by the IRS was also eliminated in the process of selling one property and buying another in a §1031 exchange. It was a modification of the cash-out sales agreement.

Prior to the 1980s, the IRS had always insisted that amending escrow instructions to **re-rout and divert** the cash proceeds from the sale of an investor's property to buy replacement property in order for the investor to avoid **actual receipt**, was an artifice dressed up like an exchange. The modification of purchase agreements by amended escrow instructions made a sale and reinvestment look like an *actual exchange* and merely covered for what had actually occurred — a cash-out sale avoided only by redirecting the cash to the purchase of a replacement property. The IRS claimed this type of transaction did not qualify for the §1031 exemption.

Again, the courts had a simple answer: It was the end result that mattered, not the means by which the investor used escrow or other contracting devices to get the replacement property. As long as the investor did not actually or con-

structively receive all the sales proceeds before the replacement property was purchased, the transaction could qualify for the §1031 exemption. [**Barker** v. **Commissioner** (1980) 74 TC 555; Alderson and Biggs, *supra*]

After the IRS no longer required an exchange of ownership for ownership and there was no need to locate a cash buyer who would agree to use his cash to purchase the replacement property to concurrently exchange titles in sequential deeding, it was just a matter of time before the courts approved a delayed delivery of the replacement property to close out a §1031 reinvestment plan after closing the sale of property to a cash buyer. Judicial confirmation of the delayed closing of the reinvestment occurred in the 1970s, effectively ending the need for formal exchanges within the brokerage community and sequential deeding by escrows. [**Starker** v. **United States** (9th Cir. 1979) 602 F2d 1341]

In the 1980s, the IRS withdrew its opposition to cash-out sales and reinvestments, unless **escrow closing statements** confirmed the investor actually received the cash. However, the IRS did generate deferred exchange regulations that substantially complied with court decisions. In 1984, Congress embraced the cash sale and delayed reinvestment by enacting the 45-day and 180-day property identification and reinvestment codes.

The chaos of deeding remembered

Contractually convoluted movements of money and titles through multiple parties to sequentially pass the final deed to the investor is the subject of many §1031 court cases. In each case, the investor ultimately received replacement property, not the cash from his sale. In the judges' opinions, however, they disapproved of these convoluted approaches.

All of the delayed reinvestment transactions cases could have been handled in just three contracts:

1. A purchase agreement and escrow instructions for the sale of the investor's property, entered into by the investor and his buyer.

2. A purchase agreement and escrow instructions for the investor's purchase of the replacement property entered into by the investor and the seller of the replacement property.

3. An agreement between the buyer and a facilitator to, as the third party depository, receive and hold the cash from the sale, and then later disburse it for the investor's purchase of replacement property.

The use of unnecessary parties and sequential steps drove one judge to observe that the reinvestment plan being disputed, although it ultimately achieved the intended result, could have been accomplished with a fewer steps. [Biggs, *supra*]

In another case even more convoluted than *Biggs*, a creative escrow officer nearly lost track of the intended purpose of delivering the replacement property to the investor. The **sequential deeding** of all the properties involved through a strawman in a parade of title was seen by the court as unnecessary in determining the true character of the transaction for §1031 tax purposes.

The IRS had contended in this case that all the amendments, surplus documentation and transitory transfers of titles comprised an *artifice*, used by the investor to give the transaction the appearance of a true exchange, which it, in fact, was not. The IRS claimed the investor's actions placed him in receipt of the cash and constituted a taxable sale, not an exchange. In the end, however, the investor only received the replacement property, not the cash, thus qualifying the transaction for the §1031 exemption. [Barker, *supra*]

The distinction between a closed sale, which delivers cash to the investor, and a §1031 ex-change, which delivers the replacement property to the investor, is uniquely straight forward: A sale is evidenced by the receipt of cash for the property, but receipt of property for property does not constitute a sale.

Where the cash proceeds end up at the close of a sales escrow determines the tax results of a transaction. An investor who deposits the cash proceeds from a sale into a purchase escrow two days after his receipt of the proceeds, then closes it the following day does not avoid triggering taxation, even though the investor used all of his net proceeds to buy the replacement property.

The cash on close of escrow was freed of all restriction, and there were no contractual restraints on the investor to bar his use of the sales proceeds as he saw fit. The proceeds had to be taxed, and although the decision was harsh, the court was sympathetic but unyielding. The investor achieved exactly what Congress intended by shifting his equities to continue his trade or business on a bigger and grander scale than before, but he did not do so according to IRS rules and thus was taxed. [**Carlton** v. **United States** (5th Cir. 1967) 385 F2d 238]

A deed one step too soon

An investor can delay acquiring ownership to replacement property. However, he cannot reverse the process and delay the sale of his property without someone else temporarily taking title and ownership to it. An investor who acquires ownership of the replacement property in his name before he closes escrow on the property he is selling is not permitted in a §1031 reinvestment plan, because it is *concurrent ownership*.

The overlap of ownerships occurs when the investor advances funds to purchase the replacement property, and then takes title to it in his name prior to closing the sale of his property.

This situation arises when an investor is faced with losing the opportunity to acquire the replacement property and must prematurely close his purchase escrow.

Two procedures exist to avoid concurrent ownership. One, under the general rules, is an *interim ownership* held by an *unrelated person*. In this procedure, escrow instructions are modified by substituting the interim owner as the buyer of the replacement property in place of the investor, a transfer of rights called an *assignment*. The funds necessary for the interim owner to purchase the replacement property are borrowed from the investor.

Concurrently, the **interim owner** enters into a purchase agreement to resell the replacement property to the investor. The interim owner will deliver ownership to the replacement property when the investor closes escrow on the sale of his property, however long it may take. Here, the interim owner, for a period of unknown duration, is sandwiched into ownership of the replacement property. [See Chapter 23]

The other procedure to avoid concurrent ownership is a safe harbor process that vests mere title in an *interim titleholder* while placing the functional ownership of the replacement property into the hands of the investor. Each step in the process is controlled by IRS regulations and a 180-day period during which the investor's property must be sold or the opportunity to apply a future §1031 on the purchase of the replacement property is lost. [See Chapter 21]

The unwilling buyer alternative

The artifice of an exchange, while frowned on by the IRS in past §1031 cases, is a scheme now adopted by the IRS in their safe harbor regulations as an alternative to the general rules for avoiding the receipt of sales proceeds. The safe harbor regulations provide for sequential deeding of titles to all properties and the transfer of cash through a central intermediary to avoid receipt of the proceeds from a cash sale. An investor can elect to use the safe harbor in-

termediary to avoid receipt of his sales proceeds when he is confronted with a buyer who is **unwilling to cooperate** in the establishment of a §1031 trustee to hold the sales proceeds under the general rules for avoidance. [See Chapter 21]

The election to go with the safe harbor sequential deeding regulations is necessary when the buyer either:

- refuses to agree to the boilerplate, preprinted §1031 cooperation clause that is now standard copy in purchase agreement forms; or

- had agreed to cooperate and is now breaching the cooperation provision (and thus the purchase agreement).

Either way, the investor's only alternative, besides withdrawing from the purchase agreement with this buyer or worse, canceling the existing purchase agreement, is to resort to the safe harbor sequential deeding rules.

The IRS openly acknowledges an investor's use of the **general rules** for avoiding receipt of cash proceeds by calling for buyer cooperation in the establishment of a third-party depository. Each IRS example of an investor's election and use of the safe harbor intermediary is prefaced with the condition that the buyer is unwilling to participate in a §1031 reinvestment plan under the general rules for avoidance of receipt. [Revenue Regulations §§1.1031(k)-1(g)(8), Examples 3, 4 and 5, 1.1031(k)-1(j), Examples 2, 3 and 4]

A broker who negotiates the sale of property on behalf of an investor, believing the investor might reinvest the sales proceeds in replacement property, will include a §1031 cooperation clause in the buyer's offer to purchase. If the clause is not in the offer submitted by the buyer, the provision will be included in the counteroffer.

When the buyer cooperates, the investor reduces his risk of loss to just that carried by a §1031 trustee, selected from among the investor's friends and business acquaintances. Further, he reduces his costs of escrowing and managing the funds until needed for the purchase of his replacement property.

An intermediary holding the cash exposes the investor to an unnecessary risk of loss, comparable to the risk of delivering the funds by a motorbike or by the use of a tank, when electing, respectively, between the use of the safe harbor "non-trustee" intermediary procedures or the §1031 trustee under the general rules for avoiding receipt.

The §1031 exchange in future

The constant redefining and restructuring of §1031 reinvestments over the past 60 years, have reduced the events necessary to comprise a *§1031 exchange* to include just three steps:

- the sale of property;

- the avoidance of receipt of money; and

- the purchase of replacement property.

It is the avoidance of receipt step, concerning the handling of §1031 money, that remains as the last, unnecessary step. With time and more information, the requirement for avoidance of receipt will be seen as more than what Congress intended, especially when viewed against the backdrop of the 180-day period requirement for using the cash to complete the §1031 transaction.

IRC §1031 does not address actual or constructive receipt of sales proceeds during the 180-day reinvestment period. The code neither permits nor disallows a §1031 exemption if the investor were to get all of the sales proceeds, then personally deliver up the funds for the reinvestment within the 180-day delay period.

A decision by the IRS to lessen §1031 requirements by eliminating the actual or constructive receipt rule would reduce the chaos now faced by an investor or businessman who wants to acquire an economically more efficient property. The §1031 exchange in the future could do away with the following unnecessary steps:

1. The nonfunctional third-party position holding funds that could as easily be held by the investor to achieve the same tax accounting result.

2. The harsh, judicial results of an actual receipt of the cash sales proceeds and their reinvestment since the IRS objects to the end result due to the means used to obtain it.

3. The safe harbor rules of sequential deeding.

Prior planning for §1031 events

Prior to taking a listing on any property other than a seller's principal residence, the broker or agent soliciting the employment should know precisely what additional documentation and activities the seller will be confronted with, just in case the seller decides to buy replacement property to avoid profit taxes on the sale.

The following is a list identifying each party connected in some way to a §1031 reinvestment plan. For each party, an itemized list is included of the events they will be involved in.

The use of this information for §1031-related documentation and activities can only be applied to transactions in which the buyer promises to cooperate in the accommodation of the seller's §1031 reinvestment plan by the inclusion of the §1031 cooperation provision in a purchase agreement. If the buyer does not agree, or agrees and later refuses to cooperate in the documentation, then the only alternative for the seller is the safe harbor election to avoid receipt by the use of an intermediary.

Here, the list only includes the activities needed to comply with the **general rules** for avoiding receipt.

1. **The listing agent and his broker:**

    a. Conduct a tax analysis with the investor reviewing the benefits of a §1031 reinvestment plan.

    b. Know and discuss with the investor the documentation and activities imposed on each party involved in the sale and reinvestment.

    c. Maintain the investor's control over the sales proceeds, including personal knowledge about the person who receives the proceeds, how they are to be held and the risks of using a §1031 trustee selected by the investor as opposed to a safe harbor intermediary.

2. **The buyer of the listed property:**

    a. Include a §1031 cooperation clause in the purchase agreement by preprinted form or addendum.

    b. Enter into a Declaration of Trust agreement to establish a trust to hold the investor's sales proceeds, in order to complete the buyer's performance of his agreement to cooperate.

    c. Enter into closing instructions, authorizing escrow to deliver the investor's net sales proceeds to the trustee, and not the investor, on closing.

3. **The investor selling his property:**

    a. Include a §1031 cooperation clause in the purchase agreement or the investor's counteroffer to reduce paperwork and the risk of loss by use of a trustee.

    b. Select a person (other than a relative or controlled entity) to act as trustee (and an alternate as a successor) to hold the net sales proceeds, someone known to the investor as reliable and trustworthy.

    c. Confirm the buyer enters into a Declaration of Trust agreement appointing and authorizing the trustee to use the net sales proceeds on the seller's instructions and solely for the purpose of purchasing replacement property.

    d. Enter into amended escrow instructions redirecting the net sales proceeds to the trustee selected by the investor.

    e. Deed the property directly to the cash buyer.

    f. Instruct the trustee to fund the purchase for the replacement property on a call for funds from escrow.

4. **The §1031 trustee:**

    a. Enter into the Declaration of Trust agreement with the buyer.

    b. Receive delivery of the net sales proceeds on the close of the sales escrow and deposit them in an insured savings account in the name of the trustee.

    c. Withdraw the funds, payable to escrow or by a wire, for the purchase of the replacement property on instructions from the investor and a call from escrow for the funds.

5. **The seller of the replacement property:**

    a. No involvement in the §1031 reinvestment plan, other than closing escrow and deeding the replacement property directly to the investor.

6. **Escrow for the sale of the listed property:**

   a. Use standard sales escrow instructions.

   b. Prepare amended closing instructions calling for escrow to disburse the cash net sales proceeds to the trustee named in the instructions, not to the investor.

   c. Convey the property by deed directly from the investor to the buyer.

   d. Disburse the net sales proceeds to the trustee, not the investor.

   e. Prepare the closing statement (settlement sheet) to state the investor's receipt of consideration for the sale is Exchange Valuation Credits (EVCs) in

an amount equal to the cash proceeds (and any carryback note) disbursed to the trustee.

7. **Escrow for the purchase of the replacement property:**

   a. Use standard purchase escrow instructions.

   b. Call for the closing funds from the §1031 trustee, and, on a third-party receipt by escrow, credit the funds to the account of the investor in escrow.

   c. Convey the replacement property by deed directly from the seller to the investor.

Chapter 17

Interest earned on §1031 monies

This chapter clarifies the seller's right to receive the interest earned on impounded §1031 funds.

Disqualification on early receipt

A seller of §1031 property has agreed to purchase replacement property on which improvements are under construction. The improvements will be completed in four or five months, at which time the seller will acquire title.

The seller is concerned about generating disposable income during the period after his sale closes, before he takes ownership and possession of the replacement property. During the delay, the entire amount of net sales proceeds will remain on deposit with a §1031 trustee.

The real estate being sold has a large equity and generates a significant flow of spendable income. This income is the seller's primary monthly source of disposable income.

After the sale, the seller will not have sufficient income until he acquires ownership of the replacement real estate. The seller does not want to receive money from the net proceeds of the sale to carry him over until the replacement property is acquired. If he did, he would incur a 25% profit tax for unrecaptured gains (prior depreciation deductions) on the amount of money received from the sale.

However, the cash funds deposited with the §1031 trustee will **earn interest** in a savings account or certificate with a federally insured depository, such as a bank. The owner is entitled to all the earned interest by agreement, less reasonable §1031 trustee's fees for holding the funds.

Can the seller receive the interest **as it accrues** on the net proceeds, prior to acquiring ownership of the replacement property?

No! While the seller is entitled to the interest earned on the funds held by the trustee, the interest cannot be disbursed to the seller until he receives all parcels of replacement property. If the interest is prematurely disbursed prior to taking ownership of all the replacement property the investor is to receive in his plan, the entire §1031 exemption will be denied. [Revenue Regulations §§1.1031(k)-1(g)(5), 1.1031(k)-1(g)(6)(iii)(A); see **first tuesday** Form 173-4 §3.2(c)]

Typically, the interest earned is included as funds held by the §1031 trustee, called the *corpus* or *trust estate*. On or after the date the last parcel of replacement property is acquired, the interest may be either disbursed to the seller by the §1031 trustee or disbursed by escrow from funds deposited into escrow for the purchase of the replacement property.

Thus, the periodic income needs and expectations of a seller in a delayed §1031 reinvestment may not be satisfied by prematurely receiving interest, an economic benefit of his net sales proceeds that he must wait to receive until the completion of his §1031 reinvestment plan.

Reporting interest income

Receipt of interest by the seller, paid by the depository holding the net proceeds from the sale, requires the seller to report the interest as **income**, separate from his §1031 reinvestment plan. Thus, the seller will pay taxes on the interest for the year in which the interest is credited to the trust account, regardless of whether the interest is ultimately disbursed to the seller in cash or used to purchase the replacement property.

However, the interest is not cash boot received from the sale of §1031 property since interest is not generated by the property. Instead, interest earned on the net proceeds and received by the seller is reported separate from the §1031 transaction as portfolio/investment income, even if the interest income is used to buy like-kind property. [Rev. Regs. §1.1031(k)-1(h)(2)]

Growth factors as disguised interest

Now consider a seller of timberland who intends to buy replacement property in a delayed §1031 reinvestment. A buyer is located, a purchase agreement and escrow instructions are entered into and, on closing, the timberland is conveyed to the buyer.

During the interim period after closing the sale and until suitable replacement property is acquired, an annual *growth factor* accrues in the form of cash in an amount equal to 6% of the sales proceeds held by the §1031 trustee.

The growth factor is added to the net sales proceeds held by the §1031 trustee and is applied toward the down payment on the purchase of the replacement property. The seller reports the growth factor as part of his net proceeds and profit from the sale of his timberland.

On audit, the Internal Revenue Service (IRS) recharacterizes the growth factor as reportable interest income, taxable as *ordinary income*.

The seller claims the growth factor should be treated as profit, a capital gain exempt from taxation, and not as interest income since the growth factor compensated the seller for the appreciation in value he would have enjoyed on the property he sold due to timber growth during the interim period had he not sold the property.

Here, the earnings labeled as a growth factor is interest and taxed as **investment category** income, not profit. The growth factor was not re-lated to appreciation or inflation in the value of real estate since the seller no longer owned the property. Thus, the 6% earnings simply compensated the seller for the delay in his receipt and use of his net sales proceeds. Any compensation for the interim delay is treated as interest, regardless of the label placed on the annual yield the seller receives. [**Starker** v. **United States** (9th Cir. 1979) 602 F2d 1341]

Limits on the beneficial use of proceeds

One source of funds for the seller during the period of delay between closing escrow on the property sold and acquiring the replacement property would be to borrow funds from a bank to cover the seller's living expenses. The source of funds for repayment of the loan would be the interest the seller receives on taking ownership of a replacement property.

The seller must demonstrate to the lender he is entitled under the trust agreement to receive the interest that will be the source of repayment. However, his right to collect the interest may not be **assigned** or **pledged** to the lender as security for the loan. If the impounded funds are assigned, pledged or hypothecated in any way, the seller will lose his entire §1031 exemption. In that instance, the seller is considered to have **constructively received** the entire amount of the sales proceeds. [Rev. Regs. §§1.1031(k)-1(f), 1.1031(k)-1(g)(6)]

Once assured that interest income is building up in the trust account and will be disbursed to the seller on acquiring a replacement property (or upon the end of the 180-day reinvestment period), a lender will likely make the seller a personal loan based on the seller's promise:

- to use the interest funds as the primary source of repayment; and

- not to sell or collateralize the right to receive the interest.

While it is impermissible conduct in a §1031 transaction to give the lender a lien on the trust funds to secure repayment of a loan taken out by the seller, a common inducement offered to a bank as *compensation balances* to make a loan, is to call for the bank to be the depository holding the trust account funds. No lien or offset rights of any type would then exist for the bank.

Chapter 18

A §1031 trustee for the delayed reinvestment

This chapter discusses the use of a trust established by a buyer and a §1031 trustee selected by an investor to hold sales proceeds under the general rules for avoidance of receipt.

Controlling the disbursement of funds

The sole purpose for negotiating a contingency calling for the purchase of replacement property before the close of escrow, an extension of the escrow closing date or a §1031 cooperation provision in a sales agreement is to avoid **actual or constructive receipt** of the net sales proceeds the owner will be reinvesting in replacement property. [Revenue Regulations §1.1031(k)-1(a)]

If the replacement property is located before the sales escrow is ready to close, a §1031 trustee will not be needed if the escrow the owner opened for the purchase of the replacement property is ready to receive funds, a transaction called a *concurrent closing*.

With concurrent closings, mutual closing instructions are prepared calling for disbursement of the net sales proceeds to the purchase escrow for the replacement property. The owner's funds will be received in the purchase escrow for the account of the owner.

However, concurrent closings are not always possible. The closing date for a sales escrow may have arrived but a replacement property has not yet been located, or if it has been located, the purchase escrow is not ready to be funded and closed. Here, the sales escrow will be instructed to deposit the owner's sales proceeds with a *§1031 trustee* under a trust created by the buyer of the owner's property to accommodate the owner's delay in completing the reinvestment. [See **first tuesday** Form 172-4]

Further, escrow will be instructed to credit the owner with *Exchange Valuation Credits (EVCs)* on the closing statement in lieu of a "check herewith" for the sales proceeds. [See **first tuesday** Form 172-2 §3]

After closing the sales escrow, the buyer of the owner's property is no longer involved in any aspect of the owner's acquisition of the replacement property. The buyer's duty to cooperate will be carried out by the §1031 trustee and completed when the trustee funds the closing of the replacement property escrow.

The owner's control over the **disbursement** of the funds held by the §1031 trustee is limited to directing the trustee to fund the owner's purchase of a replacement property. [See **first tuesday** Form 172-3]

Facilitators acting as the §1031 trustee

Consider an owner who locates a buyer who will not agree to a contingency provision that allows the owner to cancel the sale if he does not locate a suitable replacement property or to extend the closing date until the owner locates suitable replacement property.

However, the buyer will agree to cooperate with the owner to complete a delayed §1031 reinvestment. The buyer determines the cooperation provision, escrow instructions and the trust agreement will in no way interfere with his purchase of the owner's property or expose the buyer to additional risks.

The buyer enters into a purchase agreement containing a §1031 cooperation clause, and a sales escrow is opened.

The owner advises escrow the sale will be the *first leg* of a delayed §1031 reinvestment plan. Thus, closing instructions will need to be prepared to accommodate the transfer of his sales proceeds to the trustee.

The escrow officer informs the owner about the escrow company's affiliated "Deferred Exchange Corporation." It acts as a facilitator in delayed acquisitions of replacement property to ensure that receipt of the sales proceeds by the seller is avoided.

The escrow officer explains the sale, the impounding of funds and the purchase of the replacement property should all be handled out of the same escrow office to assure compliance with §1031 rules for avoiding the receipt of the sales proceeds.

Must the owner use an affiliate of the escrow company to avoid constructive receipt of the net sales proceeds?

No, but he may! The owner is free to select who will be appointed as the §1031 trustee to hold and manage the net sales proceeds until they are reinvested. The owner may use any escrow company he chooses to escrow his purchase of the replacement property.

The owner, businesses controlled by the owner or any person considered to be **related to the owner** cannot be appointed the §1031 trustee. [Internal Revenue Code §§267(b), 707(b); see Chapter 1]

The owner's attorney, accountant or broker can be the trustee, as long as the trust is established by the buyer, not the owner. Thus, the trustee will not be holding the funds as an agent of the owner, but as a trustee appointed by the buyer. [Rev. Regs. §§1.1031(k)-1(f)(2), 1.1031(k)-1(g)(4)(iii), 1.1031(k)-1(k)(2)]

The risk with unregulated facilitators

Exchange corporations claiming to be facilitators often present themselves as "§1031 specialists" with expert analysis and creative handling.

However, these corporations are separate from the **licensed activity** of the escrow company that might recommend their use. Facilitator corporations do not fall under the governmental administrative requirements imposed on escrow companies, banks, thrifts, title companies or licensees. Licensees who operate an affiliated "facilitator business" do not act in the capacity of a licensed real estate or escrow agent.

For example, licensed escrow agents must belong to the state Escrow Agents' Fidelity Corporation (EAFC). [Calif. Financial Code §17301]

The EAFC has established a fund to indemnify its corporate members (independent escrow companies) against losses of trust funds deposited into escrow due to misappropriation or embezzlement by company officers or employees.

However, the fund insures EAFC members only when they are acting as escrow agents.

The facilitator business is not considered by the EAFC to be part of an escrow transaction. Despite the public appearance that the facilitator is "affiliated" with the escrow or a brokerage office, these affiliated facilitators are unregulated. In fact, facilitators commingle the §1031 funds in their general accounts, unless they act under an agreement that establishes a trust for their holding of the funds as a trustee.

The prudent owner will use a regulated, bonded or insured entity, such as a title company, bank, thrift or individual known to him to be trustworthy, to perform the duties of **holding** the funds in trust as a §1031 trustee and **delivering** them upon demand. Otherwise, the owner risks losing his funds to a dishonest or incompetent individual or organization.

Any bankruptcy petition filed by or involuntarily imposed on the §1031 trustee will not jeopardize the availability of the trust funds under the §1031 trust agreement. [**In re Sale Guaranty Corporation** (9th Cir. BAP 1998) 220 BR 660]

Chapter 19

A cash sale and a §1031 reinvestment

This chapter discusses an investor's handling of the net proceeds from a cash sale of his property to avoid their receipt when they will be used to purchase replacement property.

Re-routing the sales proceeds

An investor owns and manages several rental properties, both residential and nonresidential, and has done so for years. One of his properties has become more difficult to manage in recent years due to unabated neighborhood obsolescence, tenant demands for additional security, static rental income, an increase in operating costs and an increase in the amount of time and effort the investor spends managing the property.

These ongoing distractions and uncertainties about the property's future as an investment, as well as a recent rise in real estate prices, cause the investor to list the property for sale with a broker. The broker locates a buyer who submits a purchase agreement offer. The investor promptly accepts the offer, agreeing to sell the property.

The buyer of the property completes his due diligence investigation and locates a lender who will fund a purchase-assist loan. All contingencies have been eliminated and the lender and the buyer will soon fund the close of escrow.

Prior to locating the buyer, the listing broker broached the subject of the investor's tax consequences on a sale.

However, because of the investor's intense desire to dispose of his property, his priorities were set on marketing the property and locating a buyer, not on an analysis of the tax effects of a cash-out sale of the property. Further, the investor already has a general understanding that a reinvestment of his cash sales proceeds to acquire other real estate could be structured to totally avoid taxes on his profits from the sale. However, the investor's state of mind had not allowed him to be receptive to the idea of acquiring more real estate.

Now, with escrow about to close, the investor's broker is concerned the investor will later regret his receipt of the cash proceeds on closing and may change his mind and decide to reinvest his cash in another, more suitable property. If so, the investor must initiate a plan as an alternative to paying taxes on his profits and do so **prior to closing**.

Accordingly, the broker approaches the investor with a plan to consider. The plan provides the investor with the **option** to reinvest his cash proceeds in other property, exercisable after the close of escrow. The investor will be able to later acquire other property and avoid the payment of profit taxes on the sale by identifying a replacement property at any time within 45 days after the close of his sales escrow.

Two-step move into exemption

The discussion between the broker and the investor sets the stage for the investor to later use the tax exemption available for the profit he will realize on the sale. By entering into a delayed §1031 reinvestment plan before the close of his sales escrow, the investor may decide to acquire replacement property, an option he can exercise by identifying property within 45 days after closing.

The investor's **first step** in the reinvestment plan is to re-route escrow's disbursement of his net sales proceeds to a §1031 trustee. The consent of the buyer will be needed, as agreed to by the broker's inclusion of a **§1031 cooperation provision** in the purchase agreement negotiated with the buyer. The buyer will establish a trust prior to the close of escrow to receive the investor's net sales proceeds on closing. The funds will be received and held by a trustee, selected by the investor and appointed by the buyer, under a Declaration of Trust entered into by the buyer and the trustee. [See Form 172-4 accompanying this chapter]

The investor's **second step** is the location, identification and acquisition of a replacement property. The property must have sufficient value, debt and equity to qualify the entire profit the investor realizes on his sale for the §1031 tax exemption.

The investor will have 45 days after closing the sale, called the *identification period*, in which to decide whether he will:

- take the cash in lieu of purchasing replacement property and pay his profit taxes; or

- acquire replacement property, either by locating, entering into a purchase agreement and **acquiring ownership** of a replacement property, or by **identifying** no more than three suitable properties of any value, one or more of which he may purchase.

The broker and the investor review the benefits the investor will experience by reinvesting in real estate, such as having 25% to 30% more after-tax dollars to invest than would otherwise be available to the investor for investment in bonds, preferred stock or other interest-bearing instruments.

The investor agrees that he should act under the §1031 cooperation provision in the purchase agreement. Escrow instructions will be prepared as dictated by the broker to redirect the sales proceeds to a §1031 trustee on closing. [See Form 172-2 accompanying this chapter]

The investor concludes his worst case scenario would be a later election not to reinvest in real estate, and instead receive his funds at the end of the 45-day period after the close of his sales escrow for failure to identify replacement property.

The delayed reinvestment

A fully qualified §1031 reinvestment plan can be initiated after a cash-out sale has been agreed to, but before it has closed. Also, the replacement property can be located before escrow closes on the sale, called a *delayed exchange*. [**Starker** v. **United States** (9th Cir. 1979) 602 F2d 1341; see Chapter 15]

Any profit on the sale will be **exempt** from taxes as part of a delayed §1031 reinvestment if the investor:

- avoids **actual and constructive receipt** of the proceeds from the sale of his property [Revenue Regulations §1.1031(k)-1(f)]; and

- timely **identifies** and acquires like-kind replacement property which has equal or greater debt and equal or greater equity than the debt and equity in the property sold. [Rev. Regs. §1.1031(k)-1(b)(2); Internal Revenue Code §1031(a)]

Editor's note — If the investor employs the broker to locate replacement property, the broker who assists in a §1031 transaction will receive an additional fee for his efforts — one for the property sold and another for the purchase of the replacement property. A buyer's listing agreement is appropriate to document the employment and necessary to enforce collection. [See **first tuesday** *Forms 102 and 103]*

Time constraints are placed on the investor to successfully process a delayed completion of the §1031 reinvestment plan initiated prior to closing the sales escrow. [See Chapter 15]

After the sale closes, the investor has:

- 45 days to identify a replacement property; and

- 180 days, inclusive of the 45 days, or until the date required to file a tax return (including extensions) to acquire ownership of the replacement property, whichever date occurs first. [IRC §1031(a)(3)]

The buyer cooperates as agreed

A listing broker begins the §1031 reinvestment process at the time the investor enters into a purchase agreement to sell the listed property. The purchase agreement entered into will include a cooperation provision calling for the buyer to accommodate the investor's need to re-route the sales escrow's disbursement of the proceeds to a trustee for funding the purchase of a replacement property. The investor needs the cooperation provision to comply with the general rules for avoiding receipt of the net sales proceeds.

Before closing the sales escrow and to avoid receipt of the net sales proceeds, the investor decides to reinvest the proceeds in replacement property and exercises the right granted to him by the §1031 cooperation provision included in the purchase agreement.

Two documents are prepared and handed to the buyer to sign and return in order to complete the buyer's promise for an accommodation under the cooperation provision, including:

- *supplemental closing instructions* calling for escrow to disburse the net sales proceeds on closing to the trustee identified in the instructions and not to the investor as called for in the original instructions [See Form 172-2]; and

- a *declaration of trust* by which the buyer establishes a trust and appoints the trustee selected by the investor to hold the net sales proceeds until further instructed by the investor to disburse the money to the purchase escrow handling the investor's acquisition of a replacement property. [See Form 172-4]

The inclusion of the **cooperation provision** in the purchase agreement eliminates any need for the investor to later resort to the more risky election to use the *safe harbor rules* to avoid receipt of his sales proceeds, unless the buyer refuses to cooperate as agreed. [See Chapter 21]

Prior to preparing escrow instructions and the trust agreement, the investor must select the person who will be appointed by the buyer as the §1031 trustee. The §1031 trustee will hold the net sales proceeds as governed by the trust agreement. Any person may be selected by the investor to be the §1031 trustee, except for a family member and any business entity controlled by the investor, called *related persons*. [IRC §267(b); Rev. Regs. §1.1031(k)-1(k); see Chapter 1]

The cooperation needed from the buyer is limited solely to establishing a facilitator — a §1031 trustee or "buyer's trustee." Thus, the buyer fulfills his promise to cooperate in the disbursement of funds for the purchase of replacement property that is yet to be acquired by the investor.

After the sales escrow closes, the buyer no longer participates in the investor's §1031 reinvestment. The trustee carries on in place of the buyer, holding the funds and disbursing them to fund the investor's purchase of a replacement property.

§1031 instructions for escrow

Prior to closing the sales escrow, the broker will dictate supplemental escrow closing instructions that will be submitted to the investor, buyer and §1031 trustee for their signatures. [See Form 172-2]

The supplemental escrow instructions in no way alter the buyer's rights and obligations under the purchase agreement or original escrow instructions.

DECLARATION OF TRUST

DATE: _____, 20_____, at _____, California

BETWEEN TRUSTOR and BENEFICIARY _____(Buyer)

and TRUSTEE: _____

The trust created is entitled: "The _____Trust."

This trust is to perform Trustor's obligations under the terms of a §1031 provision in a purchase agreement

dated _____, 20_____, or escrow instruction No._____ with _____,

between _____ (Buyer),

and_____ (Seller)

Trustor hereby transfers and delivers to Trustee all of the property described hereunder to constitute, together with any other property that may become subject to this Declaration, the Trust Estate of an express trust to be held, administered and distributed by the Trustee as provided herein.

1. Trust Estate:

1.1 The Trust Estate shall consist of cash in the amount of $_____, caused to be delivered to the Trustee by Trustor.

2. Responsibility for Costs:

2.1 Trustee's fee for establishing the Trust and its management fee thereafter of $_____ per month shall be payable out of funds received and held by Trustee.

2.2 In the event the Trustee becomes involved in any litigation arising out of this Trust or the transaction between Trustor and Seller, reasonable attorneys fees incurred by the Trustee are recoverable from the Trust Estate.

3. Powers of the Trustee:

3.1 General Powers of the Trustee. In addition to all other powers and discretions granted to or vested in the Trustee by law or by this Declaration, the Trustee shall have power with respect to the Trust Estate, or any part of the Trust Estate, to:

a. Retain in the Trust any property received by it.

b. Fund the purchase of §1031 replacement property to perform Trustor's obligations under the §1031 addendum.

3.2 Special Powers of the Trustee.

a. Trustee is instructed and directed to use the Trust Estate to fund Seller's acquisition of §1031 replacement property(ies) selected by Seller. Seller's selection and request for funding shall be in writing directed to the Trustee.

b. Any remaining money in the Trust Estate after payment of expenses and funding of Seller's acquisition of replacement property(ies) to be delivered to Seller in complete and full performance of Trustor's obligations under the §1031 provision between Trustor and Seller.

c. During the existence of the Trust, and prior to the funding by the Trust of the purchase of §1031 property, the Trustee shall have the authority, in his sole discretion, to invest prudently in the name of the trust, any sums constituting part or all of the Trust Estate into federally insured passbook savings accounts or certificates of deposit or other like quality interest earning investments.

4. Termination of the Trust:

4.1 When the Trust Estate is disbursed by the Trustee to fund acquisition of §1031 property, the Trust shall terminate. On termination, the Trustee shall deliver to Seller any remaining assets and money held in the Trust Estate.

5. Income of the Trust:

5.1 The Trustee shall pay or apply all of the Trust Estate, including any interest earned thereon, toward the performance of powers of the Trustee.

6. Trust is Irrevocable:

6.1 This Trust is irrevocable pursuant to California Probate Code §15400 and may not be amended or modified in any way.

------------------ *PAGE ONE OF TWO — FORM 172-4* ------------------

7. Spendthrift Provisions:

7.1 No Beneficiary of this Trust shall have any right, power or authority to alienate, encumber or hypothecate his or her interest in the principal or income of this Trust in any manner, nor shall such interest of any Beneficiary be subject to claims of his or her creditors or liable to attachment, execution or other process of law.

8. Successor Trustee:

8.1 Should the Original Trustee become unable or unwilling to act as Trustee, then _____ shall become Trustee of this Trust, shall succeed to all title of the Trustee to the Trust Estate and to all powers, rights, discretion, obligations, and immunities of the Trustee under this Declaration.

9. Law for Construction of the Trust:

9.1 The Trust provided for in this Declaration will be governed by the laws of the State of California.

EXECUTED ON _____, at _____, California

Trustor:_____ Trustee:_____

Trustor:_____ Trustee:_____

FORM 172-4   10-00   ©2005 **first tuesday**, P.O. BOX 20069, RIVERSIDE, CA 92516 (800) 794-0494

The mutual supplemental escrow instructions direct the escrow officer to disburse funds that accrue to the account of the investor to the §1031 trustee on close of escrow, except for prorations and any portion of the net sales proceeds withdrawn by the investor.

The supplemental closing instructions authorize the sales escrow to:

- disburse the investor's net sales proceeds, less any withdrawals made by the seller, by issuing a check on the close of escrow made payable to the §1031 trustee for the amount of the investor's net proceeds; and

- issue a closing statement to the investor noting the investor received Exchange Valuation Credits (EVCs) in lieu of a "check herewith," in an amount equal to the amount of the cash proceeds disbursed by escrow to the §1031 trustee. [See Form 172-2]

The EVCs represent the amount of funds held by the §1031 trustee that are available for use in the investor's purchase of replacement property.

Even though disbursement of the net sales proceeds is, as a condition of closing escrow, diverted away from the investor to the §1031 trustee, the investor retains *full control* over the funds for their use as a down payment on the purchase price of replacement property.

Does the investor avoid constructive receipt of the net sales proceeds while retaining control over the use of the monies to fund the purchase of replacement property?

Yes! Actual and constructive receipt are avoided under the **general rules** established by the courts for handling the sales proceeds. Escrow instructions bar the investor from legal entitlement at any time prior to closing and to any funds held by escrow. The investor is only able to receive funds from escrow prior to closing if agreed to by the buyer. Thus, access by the investor is restricted by contract. The moment escrow closes, escrow no longer holds the funds. Thus, no funds exist for the investor to demand and receive, a result of the supplemental escrow instructions and escrow law. [Calif. Financial Code §17421]

The §1031 trustee appointed by the buyer will hold the funds from the moment of closing until the funds are called for by the purchase escrow. In turn, the trustee's instructions do not permit the disbursement of funds to the investor until after the trust has funded the purchase of a replacement property. Thus, the escrow instructions authorizing the transfer of the investor's funds from the sales escrow to the §1031 trustee limit use of the funds to the purchase of replacement property. These steps ensure the investor has avoided actual and constructive receipt of the sales proceeds. [Rev. Regs. §§1.1031(k)-1(f)(2), 1.1031(k)-1(f)(3)]

As originally agreed, the property sold by the investor is conveyed directly to the buyer by grant deed. At all times, control over title and funds is retained by the investor. He fully avoids the additional risk of loss created by a conveyance of title to a safe harbor intermediary and the lack of protection for funds provided by trust provisions.

§1031 trustee's limited role

The **trust** created by the buyer is solely for completing the transfer of the net sales proceeds from the investor's sales escrow to the purchase escrow handling the acquisition of replacement property. During the entire sale and reinvestment process, the investor does not have the legal right at any time to **demand** and **receive** the sales proceeds.

The trust is created when the buyer, acting as the *trustor*, appoints a trustee and funds the trust. The funding is governed by the supplemental escrow instructions entered into by the buyer, the §1031 trustee and the investor. Under the instructions, escrow closes when it can deliver to the trustee the remaining sales proceeds after all the investor's obligations of the sale are accounted for and deducted from the purchase price the buyer paid for the property.

On the closing of the sales escrow and the concurrent receipt by the trustee of the investor's net sales proceeds, the buyer is no longer obligated to assist in the investor's §1031 reinvestment. The §1031 trustee will, on behalf of the buyer, complete the §1031 cooperation by holding the funds and delivering them to the purchase escrow for the replacement property the investor is acquiring.

Thus, the buyer is also named as the *beneficiary* of the trust (as well as the trustor). The buyer's **continuing obligation** to cooperate by funding the acquisition of the replacement property is to be performed by the trustee. The investor is not a party to the trust agreement even though the trustee, as agreed to in the trust agreement, funds the purchase escrow for the replacement property as directed by the investor.

The trust agreement limits the §1031 trustee's **activities** in the §1031 reinvestment plan to:

- **depositing** the net proceeds of the sale in an interest-bearing trust account; and

- **disbursing** the net sales proceeds to fund the purchase of replacement property on instructions from the investor.

Investor's receipt of accrued interest

The §1031 trustee is instructed, by the terms of the trust agreement, to hold the trust funds on deposit in a government-insured, interest-bearing account.

The interest earned and credited to the account first bears the costs of maintaining the savings account and payment of any trustee's fee. Interest remaining after payment of the trustee's costs and fees belongs to the investor. The investor may, but need not, apply the excess interest toward the purchase of the replacement property. [See Chapter 17]

The investor is entitled to the interest earned on the funds impounded with the trustee since interest is the economic product of the investor's net sales proceeds while they are held in trust.

SUPPLEMENTAL ESCROW INSTRUCTIONS
§1031 Reinvestment In Lieu of a Cash-Out Sale

Date:_____, 20_____

To: _____

_____

_____

Attention_____

Re: Escrow No. _____

For use to comply with the general rules for avoidance of actual or constructive receipt of sales proceeds. IRS Regs. §1.1031 (k)-1(a)

Seller:_____

Buyer:_____

§1031 Trustee: _____

1. All prior instructions in this escrow and underlying agreements between the parties are amended as follows:

    1.1 Seller shall at no time receive cash or paper as consideration for the conveyance of the subject property, except the sum of $_____ cash through escrow.

    1.2 You are authorized to close this escrow when you cause or confirm that the Trustee holds for Buyer the sum of $_____ under the Trust entitled:

    _____

    1.3 You are to prepare Seller's closing statement showing the agreed-to charges and credits to include "Exchange Valuation Credits" due Seller in the amount of $_____, in lieu of the net proceeds originally provided for in your instructions.

2. The following are conditions with which escrow need not be concerned:

    2.1 Seller intends the sale to qualify as an Internal Revenue Code §1031 transaction, exempt from profit reporting. The ultimate tax status of the sale provides no consideration for the agreement between the parties, and failure to qualify under Internal Revenue Code §1031 provides no grounds for rescission.

    2.2 Buyer and §1031 Trustee, concurrent with the signing of these instructions, shall execute a trust agreement creating a trust to receive and hold as the trust estate the proceeds of this sale.

Dated:_____, 20_____

Seller:_____

Seller:_____

Dated:_____, 20_____

Buyer:_____

Buyer:_____

Dated:_____, 20_____

§1031 Trustee:_____

By: _____

FORM 172-2   06-05   ©2005 **first tuesday**, P.O. BOX 20069, RIVERSIDE, CA 92516 (800) 794-0494

The interest income will be reported as *portfolio* earnings of the investor. Interest is not part of the net sales proceeds, but merely taxable earnings generated by the net proceeds. [Starker, *supra*]

However, the interest cannot be disbursed to the investor before he acquires ownership of all the replacement property he receives in his reinvestment plan. If it is prematurely disbursed, the investor loses the entire §1031 exemption. [Rev. Regs. §§1.1031(k)-1(g)(5), 1.1031(k)-1(g)(6)(iii)(A)]

Funding the purchase of replacement property

The final stage of a delayed §1031 reinvestment plan is begun when the investor's enters into a purchase agreement to acquire replacement property. On the opening of escrow for the purchase, the investor instructs the §1031 trustee to forward funds to the purchase escrow on a **call for funds** from escrow. The call will occur at the time escrow is prepared to close. [See Form 172-3 accompanying this chapter]

If no further property is to be acquired by the investor to close out the reinvestment plan, then escrow's call for funds should be for the full amount held by the trustee. This transfer of funds removes the trustee from any further disbursement or any withholding of funds for the Franchise Tax Board (FTB) on a disbursement to other than a purchase escrow. [Calif. Revenue and Taxation Code §18662(e)(3)(D)]

On the purchase escrow's receipt of funds from the trustee, the funds will be credited to the account of the investor as the purchaser. The investor will take title to the replacement property by a direct grant deed conveyance from the owner of the property purchased directly to the investor. Thus the reinvestment plan is completed.

Any funds unused by escrow to pay the investor's down payment and transactional costs will be disbursed to the investor. Funds disbursed to the investor on or after acquiring the replacement property will be taxed as profit unless they are offset by the amount of any purchase-assist loan or carryback note executed by the investor to purchase the replacement property. [See Chapter 13, Example 2]

Thus, the investor has maintained control over an unbroken chain of events that allowed him to avoid actual and constructive receipt of the sales proceeds and to acquire the replacement property. The investor was not at any time entitled to **demand** and **receive** funds from either the sales escrow, the trustee or the purchase escrow until an acquisition of replacement property was complete.

Funds deposited by the trustee in the escrow for the investor's purchase of the replacement property were not available for the investor to receive until closing. On closing, only the funds remaining after the purchase of the replacement property are disbursed to the investor. Thus, the investor had no legal right to demand and receive any funds from escrow prior to closing. [Fin C §17421]

Chapter 20

Converting an installment sale to a §1031

This chapter presents the procedures and documents for converting an installment sale into the first leg of a fully tax-exempt §1031 reinvestment plan.

Exchanging the carryback note

Taxwise, **cash items** received by a seller of real estate in a §1031 transaction, called *cash boot* (in contrast to *mortgage boot*), include:

- **cash**;

- **notes** and **trust deeds** carried back on a credit sale of real estate; and

- **unqualified property**, which includes personal property, real estate held for immediate resale (also called *dealer property*) and the taxpayer's principal residence.

On the sale of §1031 real estate, the seller can avoid reporting any profit, called *gains* by the Internal Revenue Service (IRS), if the **cash items** received by the seller on the sale of the property:

- are not actually or constructively received by the seller; and

- are used to timely purchase like-kind replacement property that has sufficient debt (or the seller can contribute additional cash items) to offset the debt relief on the sale. [Internal Revenue Code §1031]

Thus, a seller who agrees to carry back a note and trust deed on the sale of his real estate can now avoid taxes on any profit that would have been allocated to the principal of the carryback note, by exchanging the note for §1031 replacement property. [See **first tuesday** Form 355 §2; see Chapter 26]

Section §1031 property includes real estate held for:

- **productive use** in a trade or business, such as a farm, office building or industrial space; or

- **investment**, such as income-producing property, a vacation home or vacant land. [Revenue Regulations §1.1031(a)-1(a)]

Anticipating reinvestment of the note

Consider a seller of real estate held as investment property, who interviews a broker to list the property for sale.

The broker advises the seller he should consider carrying back a note if he is serious about getting the price he wants for his property under current market conditions.

The seller agrees to carry back paper, employing the broker on an exclusive listing agreement, on the condition that the broker:

- locate a buyer with a significant down payment; and

- use any note and trust deed the seller may carry back as a down payment toward the purchase of replacement property.

The seller also enters into a separate **buyer's listing** agreement to further employ the broker exclusively to locate replacement real estate, conditioned on the sale of his listed property and completion of a §1031 tax-free transaction. [See **first tuesday** Form 103]

The broker later obtains a purchase offer that includes:

- an adequate cash down payment;

- a carryback note to be executed by the buyer and secured by a trust deed on the real estate;

- a contingency provision calling for the seller to further sell or exchange the carryback note to acquire replacement property; and

- a provision stating the buyer will cooperate to assist the seller in completing a §1031 reinvestment plan. [See **first tuesday** Form 150 §10.6]

The cooperation needed from the buyer for the seller to complete his §1031 reinvestment plan is typically limited to establishing a §1031 trust and authorizing and instructing escrow to make the cash and carryback note payable to a person selected by the seller to be the §1031 trustee.

The **person selected** by the seller to receive the cash and carryback paper may be either:

- a §1031 trustee, called a *buyer's trustee*, *accommodator* or *facilitator*, of a trust established by the buyer to hold the cash and note for use in the purchase of replacement property that is yet to be identified or acquired by the seller; or

- the owner of the replacement property when the replacement property has been located and contracted for by the seller before the close of the sales escrow.

The seller accepts the offer and escrow is opened.

However, when the time arrives for the sales escrow to close, the purchase of a replacement property has not yet been negotiated.

To avoid any delay in the close of the sales escrow, escrow closing instructions are prepared for the buyer and seller to sign.

The mutual escrow instructions will direct the buyer to perform as promised and cooperate with the seller to avoid the seller's receipt of the net proceeds from the sale.

The **mutual escrow instructions** state:

- the §1031 trustee will be selected by the seller and appointed by the buyer;

- the net sales proceeds from the buyer's cash down payment will be disbursed by escrow to the §1031 trustee;

- the carryback note and trust deed will be made payable to the §1031 trustee, not the seller; and

- the seller's closing statement will reflect the receipt of *Exchange Valuation Credits (EVCs)* instead of the cash and carryback note. [See Form 173-2 accompanying this chapter]

As a result of this closing arrangement, the seller avoids actual and constructive receipt of the net sales proceeds. Thus, the first step in a typical §1031 reinvestment plan under the **general rules** for avoidance of receipt has been successfully completed. [Rev. Regs. §1.1031(k)-1(f)(2)]

Use of a carryback in a reinvestment

A carryback trust deed note can be marketed — used in lieu of cash to purchase other real estate — if the yield on the carryback note and the loan-to-value (LTV) ratio for the trust deed meet current market demands. If not, a discount may be in order.

Also, as with the cash, a carryback note and trust deed can be made payable to a §1031 trustee. The trustee takes delivery on close of a sales escrow directly from the buyer through escrow, **not** by an assignment from the seller. Thus, the seller avoids actual or constructive receipt of a *cash item*, the carryback paper. [**Mitchell** v. **Commissioner** (1964) 42 TC 953]

SUPPLEMENTAL ESCROW INSTRUCTIONS
§1031 Reinvestment In Lieu of a Cash-Out Sale
(part cash, part paper)

Date:_____, 20_____

To: _____

_____

_____

Attention_____

Re: Escrow No. _____

For use to comply with the general rules for avoidance of actual or constructive receipt of sales proceeds. IRS Regs. §1.1031 (k)-1(a)

Seller:_____

Buyer:_____

§1031 Trustee: _____

1. All prior instructions in this escrow and underlying agreements between the parties are amended as follows:

   1.1 Seller shall at no time receive cash or paper as consideration for the conveyance of the subject property, except the sum of $_____ cash through escrow.

   1.2 You are authorized to close this escrow when you cause or confirm that the §1031 Trustee named below, as Trustee for the Trust entitled: The_____Trust, holds the following:

   a. Cash sum of $_____ and

   b. a promissory note in the face amount of $_____ executed by the Buyer in favor of the Trustee and secured by a deed of trust on the subject property.

   1.3 You are to prepare Seller's closing statement showing the agreed-to charges and credits to include "Exchange Valuation Credits" due Seller in the amount of $_____, in lieu of the disbursements of items originally provided for in your instructions.

   1.4 You are instructed to draft the promissory note and trust deed, which your present instructions call for the Buyer to execute, to reflect the payee of the note and beneficiary of the trust deed to be:

   "_____, Trustee,

   for The _____Trust."

   Address:_____

   You are instructed to deliver these documents or cause them to be delivered to the trustee on the close of escrow.

2. The following are conditions with which escrow need not be concerned:

   2.1 Seller intends the sale to qualify as an Internal Revenue Code §1031 transaction, exempt from profit reporting. The ultimate tax status of the sale provides no consideration for the agreement between the parties, and failure to qualify under Internal Revenue Code §1031 provides no grounds for recission.

   2.2 Buyer and §1031 trustee, concurrent with the signing of these instructions, shall execute a declaration of trust creating a trust to receive and hold as the trust estate the amounts and items delivered to the trustee by escrow on the close of this escrow.

Dated:_____, 20_____

Seller:_____

Seller:_____

Dated:_____, 20_____

Buyer:_____

Buyer:_____

Dated:_____, 20_____

§1031 Trustee:_____

By: _____

The carryback note held by the §1031 trustee is later used by the seller to purchase the replacement property, no differently than had the note been held by the seller.

For example, the seller's various uses of the cash and carryback note impounded with a §1031 trustee include:

- use of both the cash and carryback note as a down payment on the purchase of one or more replacement properties; or

- disbursement of the cash to purchase one replacement property and assignment of the note to purchase another replacement property.

Trustee's duties as noteholder

Until a seller closes escrow on the replacement property, a §1031 trustee will:

- hold the carryback note;

- collect installments;

- enforce collection of the note by foreclosure, if necessary;

- borrow funds collaterally secured by the trust deed note if requested by the seller to provide additional cash to purchase replacement property; and

- assign the carryback note and trust deed for cash or as a down payment to purchase replacement property on instructions from the seller. [See Form 173-3 accompanying this chapter]

The trustee should use the seller's tax identification number or social security number on any interest-bearing accounts the trustee opens to hold the impounded funds.

The seller is entitled to the economic benefit of the interest, which will be reported as portfolio/investment category income. [Rev. Regs. §1.1031(k)-1(h); see Chapter 17]

Editor's note — Even though the trust deed note was made payable to the §1031 trustee to meet the seller's contractually required tax objectives, the note was:

- *secured only by the property sold;*

- *signed by the buyer; and*

- *delivered as part payment of the price paid for real estate by the buyer.*

*Thus, the note is **purchase money paper**, subject to California anti-deficiency laws which prohibit recourse to the buyer, an example of the application of the axiom, substance over form. [**Ziegler** v. **Barnes** (1988) 200 CA3d 224].*

§1031 mutual escrow instructions

To close escrow on a replacement property, a seller instructs the §1031 trustee to disburse the cash and assign the trust deed note to fund the acquisition of replacement property. [See Form 173-3]

The escrow instructions signed by both the seller and the buyer state:

- the seller's intention to complete a qualified §1031 reinvestment; and

- the buyer's agreement to create a trust to hold the proceeds from the sale.

The role played by escrow under the §1031 closing instructions for the property sold includes:

- preparing the note and trust deed to be executed by the buyer in favor of and payable to the §1031 trustee, who is also the beneficiary on the trust deed;

INSTRUCTION TO TRUSTEE TO FUND ACQUISITION

Trustee: _____

Name of Trust: _____

1. You are hereby advised of my selection and intended acquisition of the following described real estate:

_____

_____

2. Further, you are hereby requested, on a demand by escrow on you for funds, to disburse cash from the Trust Estate, for credit toward the purchase price to be paid for the property, in the amount of $_____

payable to (Escrow Company): _____

Address:_____

Escrow #: _____

3. Also, you are requested to assign the note and trust deed you hold to _____

_____

and deliver to escrow the note, trust deed and assignment as requested by escrow.

Dated:_____, 20_____

Seller:_____

(As Named in Declaration of Trust)

- disbursing the cash net proceeds and delivering the note and trust deed to the §1031 trustee, not the seller; and

- noting in the seller's closing statement the seller's receipt of EVCs equal to and in lieu of the amount of the cash and carryback note handed to the trustee.

Moving the note, with a guarantee

An owner of replacement property a seller wants to acquire might not be willing to accept a carryback note as part payment of a property's purchase price.

Consider a seller who, on the sale of his property, instructs escrow to make the cash down payment, carryback note and trust deed payable to the §1031 trustee and to hand them to the trustee on closing.

The seller locates a replacement property and submits an offer to purchase the property, using the carryback note as part of the down payment.

The seller's offer is rejected by a counteroffer seeking all cash.

Here, the trustee could be instructed to **sell the note** and trust deed to another person (not the seller) for cash that could, in turn, be used to purchase the replacement property.

Alternatively, the seller could **personally guarantee** the carryback note if the guarantee would make the note more marketable for sale or for purchasing replacement property. The seller's guarantee could be secured by a performance trust deed on the replacement property he will be purchasing. [See **first tuesday** Forms 439 and 451]

DECLARATION OF TRUST

DATE: _____, 20_____, at _____, California

BETWEEN TRUSTOR and BENEFICIARY _____(Buyer)

and TRUSTEE:_____

The trust created is entitled: "The _____Trust."

This trust is to perform Trustor's obligations under the terms of a §1031 provision in a purchase agreement

dated _____, 20_____, or escrow instruction No._____ with _____,

between _____ (Trustor),

and_____ (Seller)

Trustor hereby transfers and delivers to Trustee all of the property described hereunder to constitute, together with any other property that may become subject to this Declaration, the Trust Estate of an express trust to be held, administered and distributed by the Trustee as provided herein.

1. Trust Estate:

1.1 The Trust Estate shall consist of cash in the amount of $_____, caused to be delivered to the Trustee by Trustor, and a promissory note in the face amount of $_____ executed by Trustor in favor of Trustee and secured by a Deed of Trust on property concurrently conveyed to Trustor by Seller.

2. Responsibility for Costs:

2.1 Trustee's fee for establishing the Trust and its management fee thereafter of $_____ per month shall be payable out of funds received and held by Trustee.

2.2 In the event the Trustee becomes involved in any litigation arising out of this Trust or the transaction between Trustor and Seller, reasonable attorneys fees incurred by the Trustee are recoverable from the Trust Estate.

3. Powers of the Trustee:

3.1 General Powers of the Trustee. In addition to all other powers and discretions granted to or vested in the Trustee by law or by this Declaration, the Trustee shall have power with respect to the Trust Estate, or any part of the Trust Estate, to:

    a. Retain in the Trust any property received by it.

    b. Convey, exchange or deliver any property received by it as instructed.

    c. Hypothecate or sell the trust deed note as may be arranged by Seller and use the proceeds as Trust Estate funds.

    d. Fund the purchase of §1031 replacement property to perform Trustor's obligations under the §1031 addendum.

3.2 Special Powers of the Trustee.

    a. Trustee is instructed and directed to use the Trust Estate to fund Seller's acquisition of §1031 replacement property(ies) selected by Seller. Seller's selection and request for funding shall be in writing directed to the Trustee.

    b. Any remaining money in the Trust Estate after payment of expenses and funding of Seller's acquisition of replacement property(ies) to be delivered to Seller in complete and full performance of Trustor's obligations under the §1031 provision between Trustor and Seller.

    c. During the existence of the Trust, and prior to the funding by the Trust of the purchase of §1031 property, the Trustee shall have the authority, in his sole discretion, to invest prudently in the name of the trust, any sums constituting part or all of the Trust Estate into federally insured passbook savings accounts or certificates of deposit or other like quality interest earning investments.

4. Termination of the Trust:

4.1 When the Trust Estate is disbursed by the Trustee to fund acquisition of §1031 property, the Trust shall terminate. On termination, the Trustee shall deliver to Seller any remaining assets and money held in the Trust Estate.

— — — — — — — — — — — — — — — — — — *PAGE ONE OF TWO — FORM 173-4* —

5. Income of the Trust:

5.1   The Trustee shall pay or apply all of the Trust Estate, including any interest earned thereon, toward the performance of powers of the Trustee.

6. Trust is Irrevocable:

6.1   This Trust is irrevocable pursuant to California Probate Code §15400 and may not be amended or modified in any way.

7. Spendthrift Provisions:

7.1   No Beneficiary of this Trust shall have any right, power or authority to alienate, encumber or hypothecate his or her interest in the principal or income of this Trust in any manner, nor shall such interest of any Beneficiary be subject to claims of his or her creditors or liable to attachment, execution or other process of law.

8. Successor Trustee:

8.1   Should the Original Trustee become unable or unwilling to act as Trustee, then _____ shall become Trustee of this Trust, shall succeed to all title of the Trustee to the Trust Estate and to all powers, rights, discretion, obligations, and immunities of the Trustee under this Declaration.

9. Law for Construction of the Trust:

9.1   The Trust provided for in this Declaration will be governed by the laws of the State of California.

EXECUTED ON _____, at _____, California

Trustor:_____   Trustee:_____

Trustor:_____   Trustee:_____

FORM 173-4   10-00   ©2005 **first tuesday**, P.O. BOX 20069, RIVERSIDE, CA 92516 (800) 794-0494

Documenting the transaction

For a seller to close the sales step of a §1031 transaction and receive the buyer's full assistance under the §1031 cooperation clause agreed to in the purchase agreement, the following three documents are required:

- a **trust agreement** establishing a trust created by the buyer to hold the net proceeds from the sale, authorizing the trustee to collect on the carryback note until the note is sold or assigned to purchase replacement property [See Form 173-4 accompanying this chapter];

- supplemental **escrow instructions** and provisions for establishing and funding the §1031 trust and closing the sale as part of a §1031 reinvestment plan [Form 173-2]; and

- **funding instructions** to the trustee from the seller authorizing disbursement of the cash and assignment of the trust deed note to fund the acquisition of replacement property. [Form 173-3]

SECTION E

Unique
Situations

Chapter 21

§1031 safe harbor rules

This chapter discusses the safe harbor rules for a delayed exchange and the complications and risks added by electing to include a qualified intermediary in a §1031 reinvestment plan.

The alternative for lack of cooperation

The initial concern when agreeing to sell or buy property in a §1031 reinvestment plan is the inclusion of a §1031 cooperation provision in the purchase agreements. With the buyer's cooperation, the unnecessary steps, expenses and risks inherent in the alternative safe harbor election for avoidance of actual and constructive receipt of the net sales proceeds can be prevented throughout the 180-day reinvestment period after a sale is closed.

The **cooperation provision** commits the buyer of the investor's property to enter into escrow and trust instructions necessary to divert the investor's net sales proceeds on close of the sales escrow to a §1031 trustee. The cooperation is needed to implement the **general rules** for avoidance of receipt when the investor is not yet ready to concurrently close his purchase escrow for acquisition of replacement property with the close of his sales escrow. [See **first tuesday** Form 150 §10.6]

The sole purpose of the interim diversion of the net sales proceeds to a trustee (or safe harbor intermediary) is to assist the investor to avoid, as he must to qualify for the tax exemption, the *actual and constructive receipt* of the funds during the delay following the close of a sale and before the close of a purchase of replacement property.

On closing of the sales escrow under the general rules for avoidance, escrow will forward the investor's net sales proceeds to either:

- the §1031 trustee, who will receive and hold them; or

- the purchase escrow opened by the investor to acquire the replacement property if it is ready to close.

The property sold will be conveyed by grant deed **directly** from the investor to the buyer. Thus, the safe harbor requirements of several additional contracting, assignments, transitory sequential deeding and escrowing activities are avoided.

The §1031 trustee's handling of the sales proceeds is limited by the trust agreement to:

- holding the net sales proceeds in an interest-bearing trust account; and

- disbursing the funds on the investor's instructions to a purchase escrow opened by the investor to acquire replacement property.

The abundance of outside advice

A broker has located a buyer for his investor's property. The property is not the investor's residence or dealer property. The buyer has submitted an offer and with oral negotiations and a formal counteroffer, has entered into a purchase agreement. It contains a buyer cooperation clause needed to accommodate a §1031 reinvestment of the investor's net sales proceeds.

The broker meets with the escrow company agreed to in the purchase agreement, one selected by the buyer. Standard escrow instructions are dictated for the sale of the investment property. The escrow officer is not initially advised of the investor's intention to use a buyer's trustee to receive the net sales proceeds on closing.

After all parties to the escrow have signed and returned the sales instructions, the broker gives escrow the closing instructions for the diversion of the sales proceeds to the trustee appointed by the buyer to hold the funds until the investor can close escrow on property he is buying.

The escrow officer tells the broker that he is handling the §1031 exchange improperly and the escrow company has a subsidiary that is *qualified* to act as an intermediary with all the documentation needed for the investor to properly engage in a §1031 exchange approved by the Internal Revenue Service (IRS).

The broker makes notes as the escrow officer explains the steps the investor is to follow to qualify his exchange. An *exchange agreement* must be entered into by the investor and the *qualified intermediary* calling for the following undertakings:

1. The investor is to assign to the intermediary all of his rights to sell his property under the purchase agreement and escrow instructions to the intermediary.

2. The investor is to deed the property he is selling to the intermediary.

3. The intermediary is to close the sales escrow as the seller, further deed the property to the buyer and receive the net sales proceeds, which will be placed in an escrow opened up between the investor and the intermediary to hold the funds for the purchase of the replacement property, called a *qualified escrow.*

4. The investor is to assign to the intermediary all of his purchase rights under the purchase agreement and escrow instructions he has entered into to acquire his replacement property.

5. The intermediary is to close the purchase escrow for the replacement property as the buyer, fund the purchase price from the es-crow set up to hold the investor's net sales proceeds and take title by deed from the seller of the replacement property.

6. The intermediary is to deed the replacement property to the investor.

7. The intermediary is to hand the investor any funds not needed to close escrow on the purchase of the replacement property.

The broker meets with his investor and explains the arrangements the escrow officer insists he undertake to qualify the §1031 reinvestment plan for the profit tax exemption.

Editor's note — The word "qualified" is used by the IRS to denote the person, be it an escrow, intermediary, trust arrangement, individual or entity, who is "not a disqualified person" under the safe harbor rules. No one, not even the IRS, qualifies a person in a §1031 safe harbor arrangement. Disqualified persons are different from unrelated persons who can act as the §1031 trustee under the general rules of buyer cooperation and direct deeding. Thus, the investor's attorney, who is disqualified as an intermediary and cannot receive the 45-day property identification notice, is also an unrelated person who can be the buyer's trustee to hold the sales proceeds. [See Chapter 1]

The broker believes the escrow officer is attempting to exploit the alternative IRS safe harbor rules solely for the escrow's advantage to gain more employment. The broker encourages the investor to consult with his accountant to determine which handling, either **direct deeding** between the buyer and seller or **sequential deeding** through an intermediary, is preferred. The broker believes the expenses and risks of double deeding can and should be avoided as unnecessary in a §1031 transaction.

The investor's accountant explains the safe harbor rules present an **alternative method** for avoiding the investor's actual and constructive receipt of his sales proceeds in a §1031 reinvestment plan. The sole purpose of the safe harbor rules is to provide an alternative to the general rules for avoiding receipt of the net sales proceeds and for the direct deeding of titles when the buyer fails to cooperate.

An investor can choose to follow the alternative safe harbor rules as one of several ways to avoid actual or constructive receipt of the sales proceeds. The safe harbor rules are but a few ways the investor can qualify the profit on his sale for the §1031 exemption.

The accountant further explains the safe harbor rules are designed to provide a method to qualify an exchange for a §1031 exemption when the buyer of an investor's property has not agreed, or if he has agreed, declines cooperate in the §1031 reinvestment plan.

Further, the safe harbor guidelines call for the investor's unnecessary and risky loss of control. Implementing the rules involves conveying all properties through a third party strawman, both when deeding out the property sold and when taking title to the replacement property. The accountant explains this practice is not mandatory as suggested by the escrow officer, but merely an alternative to the general rules for avoiding receipt and direct deeding.

The safe harbor rules are a "last ditch" alternative when **cooperation** from the buyer and the use of the §1031 trustee are denied by the buyer. Otherwise, the safe harbor rules can be entirely ignored when conveying property in a §1031 reinvestment plan. [Revenue Regulations §1.1031(k)-1(f)(2)]

After consulting with his accountant and broker, the investor decides to stay with the direct deeding arrangement and select his attorney as the buyer's trustee. There will not be any double deeding, double escrow, assignment of contracts, additional fees, risk of loss of title or money with the attorney handling the sales proceeds.

As in any purchase, the investor may acquire title directly from the seller of the replacement property. He can also deed the property he sold directly to his buyer.

The investor only needs to sell and buy §1031 property, avoid receipt of the net sales proceeds and timely identify and acquire replacement property. Title never has to pass through a strawman in spite of the claims of those who hold themselves out as intermediaries, accommodators or facilitators. [Revenue Ruling 90-34; **W. D. Haden Co.** v. **Commissioner** (5th Cir. 1948) 165 F2d 588]

The safe harbor trap

Escrow operators must share blame for perpetuating the concept of sequential, indirect deeding. The same operators advocate the use of a third party depository, typically an escrow, to act as a conduit for reinvestment funds even when both the sale escrow and purchase escrow are to close concurrently in a §1031 reinvestment plan.

Escrow companies often insist an investor cannot complete a §1031 transaction in a conventional manner by direct deeding between sellers and buyers. They insist title must pass through a strawman intermediary with an escrow opened solely to handle the funds. This misplaced emphasis, exploited by escrows and intermediaries (and some attorneys), finds its origins in the fully avoidable IRS regulations of *safe harbor rules*.

By definition, safe harbor rules need never be followed.

However, an investor who elects to follow the safe harbor rules must do so in full, absolute compliance and without variation or he will not qualify for the §1031 profit reporting exemption. [Rev. Regs. §1.1031(k)-1(g)(1)]

Only the safe harbor rules call for the use of a *qualified intermediary*. Persons who, prior to the issuance of the safe harbor rules, held themselves out as accommodators or facilitators to hold money and title for others, now cloak themselves in the title of "qualified intermediary" in order to secure more employment. [Rev. Regs. §1.1031(k)-1(g)(4)]

An investor never needs to deed his property to a stranger who is not the actual buyer when the he cooperates in implementing a §1031 reinvestment. The only situation where an investor would have to acquire title to replacement properties via a stranger to the transaction, is in the use of an *unrelated person,* known personally to the investor, to hold title as an *interim owner* in a reverse §1031 transaction. [**Biggs** v. **Commissioner** (5th Cir. 1980) 632 F2d 1171; see Chapter 23]

A strawman is not required to take title as a transitory owner in any §1031 transaction, unless alternative safe harbor rules suggested by escrows and intermediaries are implemented.

In a §1031 transaction, it is the *constructive receipt* of sales proceeds that must be avoided, not direct deeding. [Rev. Regs. §1.1031(k)-1(f)]

Intermediaries often claim the interest accruing on the sales proceeds they hold in trust cannot be earned or received by the investor without losing the §1031 capital gains exemption. This claim is also wrong.

An investor may earn all the interest that accrues on the net sales proceeds during the delay in closing out a reinvestment plan, even when following the safe harbor rules. The investor does not lose the §1031 exemption by earning and receiving the accrued interest unless the interest is disbursed to the investor **prior to acquiring** all of the replacement properties. [**Starker** v. **United States** (9th Cir. 1979) 602 F2d 1341; Rev. Regs. §§1.1031(k)-1(g)(5), 1.1031(k)-1(g)(6)(iii)(A)]

The risk of lost ownership

If investors considering a §1031 reinvestment are not dissuaded from enlisting the services of a qualified intermediary because of excessive fees, perhaps the risk of losing funds or property will dissuade them.

Facilitators, by any title, including title companies, are not required to be licensed, insured or bonded while acting as the trustee holding title or funds. The investor risks losing property and funds to incompetent or dishonest facilitators and intermediaries. Federally insured banks and thrifts acting as §1031 trustees provide the least risk of loss.

For example, an intermediary takes title to real estate an investor has not yet sold, claiming his services are necessary to properly facilitate a §1031 reinvestment plan. The intermediary holds title to the investor's property under a title-holding agreement until the property is sold. The investor is not given a trust deed lien on his property to secure the performance of his title-holding arrangement with the intermediary and to minimize the risk of losing his asset. [See **first tuesday** Form 451]

However, the investor retains possession and full ownership control over the property, even though naked title has been transferred to the intermediary by deed. It is the investor who lists the property for sale, rents to tenants, incurs expenses and otherwise treats the property as his, except for holding title.

Later, the intermediary is no longer able to meet funding commitments to close §1031 transactions. He files a Chapter 7 bankruptcy petition.

The investor's real estate becomes entangled with the bankruptcy estate since title is now held by the bankruptcy trustee of the bankrupt intermediary.

The bankruptcy trustee, as successor to the intermediary, attempts to eliminate the unrecorded interest of the investor in the real estate.

The investor claims the property is not part of the intermediary's estate, but was held in a *resulting trust* by the intermediary for the sole purpose of completing a §1031 reinvestment for the investor.

The bankruptcy trustee claims the property vested in the intermediary is held for the benefit of the bankruptcy estate since no trust agreement or security device was recorded.

Here, the bankruptcy trustee cannot avoid the **trust which results** on the title. The conduct of the investor and the intermediary, not their agreements, established a *resulting trust* in which title is held for the investor, since:

- the investor retained possession of the property after the transfer of title to the intermediary; and

- the intermediary's business included the holding of title and cash to complete §1031 transactions.

The bankruptcy trustee had notice of the investor's unrecorded ownership interest in the property since the investor was in possession of the property. Thus, the bankruptcy trustee is unable to eliminate the investor's ownership interest in the real estate. [**In re Sale Guaranty Corporation** (9th Cir. BAP 1998) 220 BR 660]

Editor's note — But for the safe harbor rules, the title would not have been deeded to the intermediary. Title would have been retained by the investor until the closing of his sales escrow. Litigation and risk of loss would have been avoided had the owner retained title and deeded it directly to his buyer.

The risk of lost funds

Now consider an investor who sells property. The sales proceeds are transferred to a facilitator so the investor can avoid constructive receipt of the funds until the §1031 reinvestment can be completed.

By an agreement with the investor (not the buyer), the facilitator will hold the sales proceeds until the investor locates a suitable replacement property and calls for the funds.

The sales proceeds received by the facilitator are deposited into the facilitator's **general account**, not a trust account since no trust agreement exists placing a duty on the facilitator to treat the funds as trust assets.

The facilitator files a Chapter 7 bankruptcy petition for lack of funds to meet demands to close §1031 reinvestment plans.

The bankruptcy trustee appointed by the court attempts to seize all the facilitator's funds, which include (what remains of) the investor's sales proceeds.

The investor claims the sales proceeds are held in a *resulting trust* by the facilitator, since the proceeds were handed to the facilitator to hold with the intent to fund the purchase of replacement property for completion of a §1031 reinvestment by the investor.

The bankruptcy trustee claims the sales proceeds are part of the bankruptcy estate since no trust agreement existed to protect the cash assets.

Here, the nature of the facilitator's business — to facilitate §1031 transactions — and his relationship with the investor in holding the funds, established a *resulting trust* for the funds, even though the investor and the facilitator never agreed to a trust.

Thus, the bankruptcy trustee is unable to reach the funds since they were actually held in trust for the investor. [In re Sale Guaranty Corporation, *supra*]

Editor's note — The §1031 trust should have been established by a written trust agreement entered into by the buyer of the property and the trustee selected by the investor. However, funds in a seller-established trust are held for the seller, which results in constructive receipt and loss of the §1031 exemption unless they comply with the safe harbor rules.

Further, the Sale Guaranty *court properly declined to comment on whether the transaction qualified for the §1031 exemption or was a tax evasion scheme.*

A proper trust for funds

The risk of losing property title or funds to an intermediary or facilitator can be avoided. On the sale of property in a §1031 reinvestment plan, the investor chooses the person who will be the §1031 trustee charged with holding the proceeds from the sale of property.

Persons an investor should consider using as the §1031 trustee include:

- a federally-insured depository, such as a bank or thrift; or

- a trustworthy individual known to the investor as a long-time acquaintance, who is not a family member or a controlled business entity of the investor. [IRC §267(b); Rev. Regs. §1.1031(k)-1(k); see Chapter 1]

A trust agreement, signed by the buyer of the investor's property under a §1031 cooperation provision in the purchase agreement, appoints and authorizes the §1031 trustee to accept and hold the sales proceeds in a separate, interest-bearing trust account. [See **first tuesday** Form 172-4]

The §1031 trustee will be later instructed by the investor to disburse the proceeds to fund his purchase of replacement property. [See **first tuesday** Form 172-3]

Thus, the investor avoids constructive receipt of the sales proceeds and ensures the funds are protected against creditors of the facilitator.

Despite the excessive fees and the risk of losing all their funds in improperly structured schemes, many uninformed or misinformed investors still use intermediaries and follow the safe harbor rules.

Investors still continue to double deed their property and relinquish their accrued interest to *qualified intermediaries* in the mistaken belief that they must do so to qualify their reinvestment for the §1031 exemption.

To qualify for a *concurrent* §1031 reinvestment, the investor merely needs to avoid the constructive receipt of sales proceeds. To qualify for a *delayed* §1031 reinvestment, the investor must:

- identify replacement properties through the closed sales escrow within 45 days of closing his sale;

- acquire the replacement property within 180 days of closing his sale, or before filing a tax return for the year of the sale [IRC §1031(a)]; and

- withdraw any accrued interest on the funds on or after closing the §1031 transaction. [Rev. Regs. §1.1031(k)-1(f)]

The method of conveyancing in a §1031 reinvestment plan does not determine whether the reinvestment qualifies for the §1031 exemption, unless the investor elects to follow the alternative safe harbor rules from the onset. [W. D. Haden Co., *supra*]

Chapter 22

Withholding profit tax and the §1031

This chapter describes the federal and state tax withholding requirements for a sale of real estate by a nonresidential foreigner and the exemptions available for sales in a §1031 reinvestment plan.

Qualifying an exempt §1031 sale

On the sale of real estate by a nonresident foreigner, a duty is imposed on the buyer to instruct escrow to **withhold** and **forward** 10% of the purchase price paid to the Internal Revenue Service (IRS), unless the transaction is *exempt*. [Internal Revenue Code §1445]

Further, when the real estate purchased is located in California, an additional duty is imposed on the buyer to instruct escrow to **withhold** and **forward** 3.33% ($3\frac{1}{3}$) of the price paid for the real estate to the Franchise Tax Board (FTB), unless the transaction is *exempt*. [Calif. Revenue and Taxation Code §18662; see FTB Forms 593 and 593-B accompanying this chapter]

The sole purpose for the federal withholding scheme is to collect a profit tax at the close of escrow on *all non-resident foreigners* who sell a parcel of real estate other than a residence sold for less than $300,000, which the buyer promises to occupy. A nonresident foreigner's §1031 reinvestment plan requires IRS written approval to avoid withholding.

For the California withholding scheme, the sole purpose is to tax *every individual* who sells business or investment property at a profit, unless the sale is exempt as part of a §1031 reinvestment plan (or other exemption).

The state and federal withholding schemes are completely separate from one another. Each requires **separate** withholding forms to be filed, and different withholding exemptions apply.

California withholding exemptions

A buyer is exempt and not required to withhold 3.33% of the sales price he pays for the property, if:

- the sales price is less than $100,000;

- the property is acquired at a nonjudicial (trustee's) or judicial foreclosure sale;

- the property is acquired by a deed in lieu of foreclosure;

- the seller is a bank acting as a trustee other than as a trustee of a trust deed; or

- escrow fails to provide a written notification of the withholding requirements to the buyer. [Rev & T C §18662(e)(3)]

The buyer is also exempt from California withholding requirements if the buyer receives the seller's written **real estate withholding certificate**, declaring under penalty of perjury that:

- the property sold is or was last used as the **seller's principal residence**, the price being of no concern;

- the property sold was the **decedent's principal residence**;

- the sale is part of the **seller's §1031 reinvestment plan**;

- the property has been **involuntarily converted**, (by destruction, seizure, condemnation, etc.) and the seller intends to acquire similar property to qualify for nonrecognition of gain under Internal Revenue Code (IRC) §1033;

- the property was sold at a **taxable loss** for the seller — a price less than the seller's remaining cost basis, a declaration that further requires the seller to prepare and execute a computation of his estimated gain or loss on the sale;

- the seller is a **Limited Liability Company (LLC)** or a **tax partnership**, but not a common law tenant-in-common co-ownership; or

- the seller is a corporation that maintains and staffs a permanent place of business in California. [Rev & T C §18662(e)(3)(D); see FTB Forms 593-C and 593-L accompanying this chapter]

If the replacement property in a §1031 reinvestment plan is not identified within the 45-day identification period or if identified, not acquired within the 180-day acquisition period, the profit on the sale fails to qualify for §1031 treatment. Here, the buyer (or buyer's trustee) must notify the FTB in writing within 10 days of the transaction's failure to qualify under §1031 rules and forward to the FTB the withholding amount. [Rev & T C §18662(e)(3)(D)(ii)(III)]

Installment sales require separate handling to avoid California withholding on the amount of the carryback note. Two steps are involved and both must be completed:

1. The seller makes his declaration on FTB Form 593-C indicating he has an exempt installment sale. [See FTB Form 593-C, Part III §12]

2. The buyer agrees to withhold on each principal payment by his signed declaration on the FTB form real estate withholding installment sales agreement. [See FTB Form 593-I, Part IV accompanying this chapter]

If the buyer agrees, a seller will only be able to require the buyer to withhold as each installment is paid, not in a lump sum of 3.33% of the total purchase price on close of escrow. The listing agent in a carryback sale needs to **include a provision** in either the purchase agreement or a counteroffer calling for the buyer to comply with FTB deferred withholding on installment sales.

Conflicting exemptions for nonresident foreigners

It is possible for a transaction to be exempt from California withholding requirements, but still subject to the federal withholding requirements, or vice versa.

For example, both the state and federal rules provide the buyer with an exemption based on the price paid. The California price paid exemption covers properties purchased at a price "less than $100,000," without concern for the type of property it is or the buyer's use of the property.

Conversely, the federal rules provide for a "$300,000 or less" exemption used solely by nonresident foreigners. However, the price-paid exemption applies only to the purchase of a residence the buyer intends to occupy. Thus, if the seller is a non-resident foreigner and the price paid for the property is between $100,000 and $300,000, California rules require withholding, but the federal rules exempt the purchase when the buyer occupies the property.

For all sales in California priced at $100,000 or more, California requires withholding unless the seller provides the exemption. For another example of the California and federal contrasts, a California property which is sold by a non-resident foreigner for "less than $100,000," is exempt in California. However, no exemption applies federally unless the buyer occupies the property as his residence.

The federal withholding scheme

Federal tax laws require a buyer of real estate to withhold on all purchases from a nonresident foreign seller unless the seller fills out, signs and hands the buyer a **residency declaration form** stating the seller's qualifications for a federal exemption.

Typically, the real estate broker preparing a purchase agreement will prepare and include a federal residency declaration for the seller and the buyer to sign as one of the addenda to the purchase agreement.

If the seller is a **United States citizen** or a **resident foreigner**, the sale is exempt from withholding 10% for the IRS. No federal withholding is required unless a non-resident foreigner is the seller.

For the sale to qualify for the federal residency exemption, the seller must supply the buyer with a **declaration** stating he is either a U.S. citizen or a resident foreigner. [See Form 301 accompanying this chapter]

Brokers are under a duty, imposed by federal law, to notify the buyer of any falsities in the seller's declaration regarding citizenship or alien residency status, falsities known to the broker that would require withholding.

Failure to advise the buyer of a known, false declaration imposes a liability on the broker for taxes unpaid on the sale by the nonresident foreign seller. The broker's liability to the IRS is limited to the amount of the broker's compensation on the sale. [IRC §1445(d)]

The buyer must retain the seller's declaration with his tax return for five years. [Revenue Regulations §1.1445-2(b)(3)]

Resident foreign sellers and the IRS

A foreign seller is considered a U.S. resident and the **sale is exempt** from federal withholding if:

- the foreign seller was present in the U.S. at least 31 days during the calendar year of the sale; and

- the number of days present in the U.S. in the current calendar year, plus one-third of the days present in the preceding year, plus one-sixth of the days present in the preceding two years, equals or exceeds 183 days. [IRC §7701(b)(3)(A)]

The foreign seller may **not** count as residency days, those days spent in the U.S. during which the seller:

- was present due to a medical condition that arose while visiting the U.S.;

- was a foreign government-related individual;

- was a teacher, trainee or student; or

- was a professional athlete temporarily in the U.S. to compete in a charitable event. [IRC §§7701(b)(3)(D)(ii); 7701(b)(5)(A)]

Should the foreign seller not meet the residency requirement for federal tax purposes, the sale is still exempt from federal withholding by the buyer if the property is:

- purchased for a price of $300,000 or less; and

- used as a residence by the buyer. [Rev. Regs. §1.1445-2(d)(1)]

The property is considered used as a residence if the buyer or a family member **plans to reside** on the property for at least 50% of the total number of days the property is occupied by anyone, including tenants, during each of the two 12-month periods following closing. The number of days the property is vacant (unused by anyone) is not taken into account in determining the number of days the property is used. [Rev. Regs. §1.1445-2(d)(1)]

The buyer makes his declaration for the use of the property as his residence in the **residency declaration** signed by both the buyer and the seller. No form or other documentation is to be filed with the IRS for the buyer to use the $300,000 residence exemption to avoid withholding.

However, the buyer or a family member might not **actually reside** on the property for the minimum 50% of all days the property is occupied. Because escrow was not instructed to withhold on the nonresident foreign seller, the buyer is liable to the IRS for the taxes on the sale should the foreign seller fail to pay taxes on his profit. [Rev. Regs. §1.1445-2(d)(1)]

Withholding for IRS in the §1031

Consider a **nonresident foreigner** who enters into an agreement with a broker to list a parcel of California real estate for sale.

The nonresident foreign seller will complete a §1031 reinvestment plan by purchasing replacement property in the United States.

When the broker lists the property for sale, the seller is handed a federal residency declaration to fill out and sign.

Because of the seller's nonresident foreign residency status, 10% of the sales price will be withheld on the sale of the real estate, unless the federal tax is *waived* by the IRS.

However, the non-resident seller intends to complete a tax-exempt §1031 reinvestment.

Does the fact that the nonresident foreign seller intends to complete a §1031 reinvestment change the federal withholding requirements?

Yes! Under federal tax law, the nonresident foreign seller can reduce or eliminate the amount required to be withheld in his §1031 reinvestment plan by requesting and receiving a **withholding certificate** from the IRS.

Further, if the price paid for the non-resident foreigner's real estate was below $300,000 and the buyer planned to reside in the property as his personal or family residence, the buyer need not comply with federal withholding requirements.

If a withholding certificate is not sought from the IRS and the seller is a non-resident foreigner subject to the federal withholding requirements, the buyer must withhold 10% of the purchase price and forward it to the IRS by the 20th day after closing escrow on the sale. [Rev. Regs. §1.1445-1(c)]

The withheld amounts are handled by escrow and filed with the IRS Center in Philadelphia, Pennsylvania. [See IRS Forms 8288 and 8288-A]

Under California withholding requirements, the sale will be exempt since the seller can prepare an FTB real estate withholding certificate form and declare that he will use the net sales proceeds in a §1031 reinvestment plan. [See FTB Form 593-C Part III, §§10 and 11]

The federal withholding certificate

A withholding certificate issued by the IRS to a non-resident foreign seller prior to his close of escrow notifies the buyer whether or not any withholding is required.

Either the buyer or the nonresident foreign seller may submit the application to the IRS for issuance of a withholding certificate. As a result of negotiations, the purchase agreement between the parties may contain a provision requiring the buyer to submit the application as a condition for closing the sale.

The IRS will act on an application for a withholding certificate no later than the 90th day after receipt of an application containing all information necessary for the IRS to make a decision. [Rev. Regs. §1.1445-3(a); Treasury Decision 9082]

FEDERAL RESIDENCY DECLARATIONS
IRC §1445 — Citizen Status

DATE:_____, 20_____, at _____, California

Items left blank or unchecked are not applicable.

FACTS:

> **NOTE:** If the declarations differ for individual Sellers, then each Seller must fill out a separate form.

1. This declaration complies with Section 1445 of the United States Internal Revenue Code regarding the Seller's status as a citizen or resident of the United States or otherwise, and is for reliance by the broker and any buyer.

    1.1 Seller:_____

        U.S. Tax Identification Number (or Social Security Number):

        Seller:_____

    1.2 U.S. Tax Identification Number (or Social Security Number):_____

2. Regarding the proposed sale of real estate described as: _____
_____

SELLER'S DECLARATION:

3. Seller hereby declares:

    3.1 ☐ I am a citizen of the United States of America;

    3.2 ☐ I am a resident alien of the United States of America; my resident status is established by the following:

        a. ☐ I have been declared a permanent legal resident of the United States by the U.S. Immigration and Naturalization Service. Resident Alien registration number: _____, or;

        b. ☐ I have resided at least 31 days in the United States during the current calendar year, and my days of residence in the United States over the last three years are as follows:

            Current calendar year . . . . _____ X 1   = _____

            Last calendar year . . . . _____ X 0.334 = _____

            Second preceding year . . . . _____ X 0.167 = _____

                              TOTAL DAYS _____

        Since the total days equals or exceeds 183 days, I meet the substantial presence test of Internal Revenue Code §7701(b)(3).

> **Exclusions:**
> Residency does not include days during which the seller:
> - remained in the U.S. due to a medical condition which arose while he was visiting;
> - was in transit between two points outside the U.S.;
> - worked for an agency of a foreign government;
> - was a teacher or trainee, or was a student; or participated as a professional athlete in a charitable event.

4. ☐ I am neither a United States citizen nor a resident alien as defined in item 3, above; and

    4.1 Unless I obtain a "qualifying statement" [IRC §1445(b)(4)], or other special permission from the Internal Revenue Service, I authorize the Buyer of the above-referenced real estate to deduct and withhold 10% of the sales price for the federal government. I further authorize escrow holder to deduct these amounts from funds due me at close of escrow, and to deposit it as a tax deposit in an authorized commercial bank.

5. I consent to the reliance on this declaration of the brokers, agents, escrow-holder, and Buyer in any transaction regarding this real estate.

6. Note: This transaction is exempt from IRC §1445 withholding if the sales price is $300,000 or less and the Buyer will use the real estate as his residence.

BUYER'S ACKNOWLEDGMENT:

7. I have read and received a copy of this Seller's Residency Declaration.

8. ☐ I hereby declare I will use the real estate as my residence. If the final sales price is $300,000 or less, I consent to reliance on this declaration by brokers, agents, escrow holder and the nonresident alien Seller.

I declare under penalty of perjury that the foregoing is true and correct.	I declare under penalty of perjury that the foregoing is true and correct.
Date:_____, 20_____	Date:_____, 20_____
Seller:_____	Buyer: _____
Date:_____, 20_____	Date:_____, 20_____
Seller:_____	Buyer: _____

FORM 301   06-05   ©2006 **first tuesday**, P.O. BOX 20069, RIVERSIDE, CA 92516 (800) 794-0494

Requesting an IRS withholding certificate

If the nonresident foreign seller submits the application for the **withholding certificate** to the IRS on or before the date the sales escrow closes, the seller must notify the buyer of the application.

The notice to the buyer must include:

- the seller's name, address and taxpayer identification number;

- a description of the property on which the withholding certificate is sought; and

- the date on which the application was submitted. [Rev. Regs. §1.1445-1(c)(2)(i)(B)]

However, even though an application for a withholding certificate is submitted to the IRS, if a withholding certificate is not received from the IRS prior to closing the buyer must still withhold the 10% required by federal law.

On receipt of the IRS withholding certificate, the amount to be withheld need not be reported and paid to the IRS until the 20th day following the IRS's **final decision** on the withholding certificate, which could be as long as 90 days after closing, depending on when the application was filed. [Rev. Regs. §1.1445-1(c)(2)(i)]

A final decision is considered made when the withholding certificate or notification denying the request is delivered by mail from the IRS.

The amount the IRS requires to be withheld may be less than the 10% retained in escrow after closing and while awaiting receipt of the IRS withholding certificate. Prior to closing, the nonresident foreign seller must ensure escrow has mutual instructions to transfer the amount remaining to the §1031 trustee established in the delayed reinvestment plan.

Any funds withheld and paid to the IRS or FTB in a §1031 transaction will be considered cash boot received by the nonresident seller.

Calculating the maximum tax on a sale

To establish the reason for the claimed exemption, the maximum federal tax that may be imposed on the property must be calculated. The nonresident foreign seller lists the tax as the maximum amount he could be required to pay on the sale of the real estate.

Profit on the individual's sale of real estate is subject to the capital gains tax rates of 15% and 25%. [See Chapter 6]

For an individual, the purchase price minus the property's adjusted basis is multiplied by 15% to calculate the maximum tax. [Rev. Regs. §1.1445-3(c)(2)]

For foreign corporations, the maximum tax is usually calculated multiplying the profit with the corporate capital gains tax rate.

The amount of the maximum tax is then adjusted for the following:

- the effect of IRC §1031 on the transaction;

- any reportable losses on the seller's previous disposition of other real estate interests during the taxable year;

- any amount that is treated as ordinary income on the sale, due to the recapture of excess depreciation (a type of gain that expires in 2005); and

- any other amounts that will increase or decrease the amount of tax. [Rev. Regs. §1.1445-3(c)(2)]

Also, any unpaid federal tax liability of the nonresident foreign seller must be included in the maximum tax amount. This unpaid amount of taxes may be disregarded if either:

- the amount is satisfied by a payment accompanying the application for a withholding certificate; or

- an agreement for the payment of the tax is entered into with the IRS. [Rev. Regs. §1.1445-3(c)(3)]

Further, if no previous tax liability exists for the nonresident foreign seller, evidence that the seller has no tax liability must be submitted with the application. The seller may show that he has had no previous tax liability by using any one of the following documents:

- a document showing the seller acquired the real estate prior to January 1, 1995;

- a copy of IRS Form 8288 which was filed by the seller and proof of payment of the amount due;

- a copy of the withholding certificate the seller received on acquisition of the property, plus a copy of Form 8288 and proof of any payment of the amount required to be withheld;

- a copy of the resident foreigner declaration of the person from whom the seller purchased the real estate;

- evidence the seller purchased the real estate being sold for $300,000 or less and the property was the seller's personal residence;

- evidence the previous owner of the property paid his taxes;

- a notice of nonrecognition provided to the seller by the previous owner of the real estate; or

- a statement, signed by the seller under penalty of perjury, on why the seller believed no withholding was required when the property was purchased. [Rev. Regs. §1.1445-3(c)(3)(ii)]

YEAR

2006 Real Estate Withholding Remittance Statement

CALIFORNIA FORM
593

Withholding Agent (Payer/Sender) Check one: ☐ Escrow/Title Company   ☐ Accommodator/Intermediary   ☐ Buyer

Name

☐ FEIN ☐ California Corporation Number

Address (number and street)

Private Mailbox No. (PMB) | Social Security Number (SSN)

City, State, and ZIP Code

Daytime telephone no.
(   )

Contact Person's Name and Title (please type or print)

1 Month and year of transfer, exchange completion, exchange failure, or installment payment for attached Forms 593-B ... 1 _____ / 06

2 Number of Forms 593-B attached .... 2 _____

3 Total withholding due for attached Forms 593-B .... 3 $_____

4 Interest on previous late payment(s) which were due in 2006 .... 4 $_____

5 Total amount of this payment. Add line 3 and line 4 .... 5 $_____

Attach a check or money order for the full amount payable to "Franchise Tax Board." Write the payer's federal employer identification number (FEIN), California corporation number, or social security number, and "2006 Form 593" on the check or money order.

Mail payment, Form 593, and Forms 593-B to: **FRANCHISE TAX BOARD**
PO BOX 942867
SACRAMENTO CA 94267-0651

General Information

California Revenue and Taxation Code Section 18662 requires the buyer or other transferee to withhold 3¹/₃ percent of the total sales price on the disposition of California real estate unless the seller certifies an exemption of Form 593-C, Real Estate Withholding Certificate.

Purpose

Use this form to report and remit the total real estate withholding for the month and to pay any interest assessed on late withholding payments for 2006. This form is also a transmittal for Form 593-B, Real Estate Withholding Tax Statement.

Note: You have the option to send one payment and Form 593 with the related Forms 593-B for each escrow instead of sending one total payment for all escrows that closed during the month.

Do not use Form 593 to pay interest on late payments related to escrows that closed prior to 2004. Continue to use the Form 592-A, Nonresident Withholding Remittance Statement, prepared for you by the FTB, for interest related to sales that closed before 2004. If the interest due is for 2004, get the 2004 Form 593. If the interest due is for 2005, get the 2005 Form 593.

Common Errors

Incomplete Forms – To speed processing and avoid our contacts for information, please provide all information, including your tax identification number, requested on the form.

Payments – Do not include payments for more than one month with a single Form 593.

Address – Make sure to use our new mailing address listed on this form. We changed our address last year.

Correct Year/Form – Make sure to only use this form for transactions in 2006. If the transaction closed in a different year, or the installment payment being reported was not made in 2006, go to our Website at www.ftb.ca.gov to get the form for the correct year.

Who Must File

Any person who withheld on the sale or transfer of California real property during the calendar month must file Form 593 to report and remit the amount withheld. Generally, this will be the title company, escrow company, accommodator, or intermediary. Normally, the buyer will only complete this form when reporting the withholding on installment payments.

When and Where to File

File Form 593 and Form 593-B, and pay the amount of tax withheld within 20 days following the end of the month in which the transaction occurred.

Sales: For sales, this is the month escrow closed.

Installment Payments: For installment payments, this is the month of the installment payment.

For Privacy Act Notice, get form FTB 1131 (Individuals only).

59305103

Form 593 2005 **Page 1**

YEAR

CALIFORNIA FORM

2006 Real Estate Withholding Tax Statement

593-B

Attach to Form 593, Real Estate Withholding Remittance Statement

Copy A FOR FRANCHISE TAX BOARD

Withholding Agent (Payer/Sender) Check one: ☐ Escrow/Title Company ☐ Accommodator/Intermediary ☐ Buyer

| Name, Mailing Address, City, State, and ZIP Code | Private Mailbox No. | ☐ FEIN ☐ California Corporation Number |
| | | Social Security Number (SSN) |

Seller or Transferor (Complete one 593-B for each seller, unless husband and wife)

Name, Mailing Address, City, State, and ZIP Code	Private Mailbox No.	Social Security Number (SSN)
		Spouse's SSN (if jointly owned)
		☐ FEIN ☐ California Corporation Number

Escrow or Exchange Information

1 Escrow or Exchange Number	2 Date of Transfer, Exchange Completion, Exchange Failure, or Installment Payment	3 Total Sales Price $	4 Ownership Percentage _____ . _____ %

5 Address (or parcel number and county) of the California real property transferred	6 Amount Subject to Withholding $ _____ Check One: ☐ Total Sales Price x Ownership % ☐ Installment Payment ☐ Boot ☐ Failed Exchange (Total Sales Price x Ownership %)	7 Amount Withheld From This Seller $ _____ (.0333 x Amount Subject to Withholding)

Preparer: Name and Title (please type or print)

Telephone Number ( )

Purpose

Use this form to report real estate withholding on sales closing in 2006, on installment payments made in 2006, or on exchanges which were completed or failed in 2006.

Use a separate Form 593-B to report the amount withheld from each seller. If the sellers are married and they plan to file a joint return, include both spouses on the same Form 593-B.

Common Errors

Year of Form - The year (upper left corner) of Form 593-B must be the same as the year in Box 2. See the instructions for Box 2. If you do not have Form 593-B with the correct year, go to our Website at **www.ftb.ca.gov** to get the correct form.

Related Form 593 - Forms 593-B must be sent to the Franchise Tax Board with Form 593, Real Estate Withholding Remittance Statement.

Incomplete Information - Be sure to complete all information.

Identification Numbers - Check to see that the withholding agent's and seller's tax identification numbers are correct and listed in the same order as the names. If both a husband and wife are listed, make sure their SSNs are listed in the same order as their names.

Trusts and Trustees - It is important to report the correct name and tax identification number when title is held in the name of a trust. If the

seller is a trust, see the instructions under "Seller or Transferor".

Examples - Examples for completing Form 593-B in various situations are on the Franchise Tax Board (FTB) Website at **www.ftb.ca.gov**. Look for "Withholding," "Sale of California Real Estate," and then "Form 593-B."

Who Must File

Any person who withheld on the sale or transfer of California real property during the calendar month must file Forms 593 and 593-B to report and remit the amount withheld. Generally, this will be the title company, escrow company, intermediary, or accommodator. Normally, the buyer will only complete these forms when reporting the withholding on installment payments.

When and Where to File

File **Copy A** of Form 593-B with Form 593 and pay the amount of tax withheld within 20 days following the end of the month in which the transaction occurred.

Attach **Copy A** of Form 593-B to the back of Form 593 and mail with payment to:

FRANCHISE TAX BOARD
PO BOX 942867
SACRAMENTO CA 94267-0651

Distribute the other copies as follows:

- **Copies B & C** – Send to sellers within 20 days following the end of the month in which the transaction occurred.
- **Copy D** – Retained by withholding agent.

Penalties

If the withholding agent does not furnish complete and correct copies of Form 593-B to the seller by the due date, the penalty is $50 per Form 593-B. If the failure is due to an intentional disregard of the requirement, the penalty is the greater of $100 or ten percent of the required withholding.

If the withholding agent does not furnish complete and correct copies of Form 593-B to FTB by the due date but does file them within 30 days of the due date, the penalty is $15 per Form 593-B. If Form 593-B is filed more than 30 days after the due date, the penalty is $50 per Form 593-B. If the failure is due to an intentional disregard of the requirement, the penalty is the greater of $100 or ten percent of the required withholding.

Amending Form 593-B

To amend Form 593-B:

- Complete a new Form 593-B with the correct information.
- Write "Amended" at the top of the revised form.

YEAR

2006 Real Estate Withholding Certificate

CALIFORNIA FORM

593-C

Part I – Seller's Information

Return this form to your escrow company.

Name (including spouse, if jointly owned - see instructions - type or print)

SSN, FEIN or CA Corporation no.

Address (number and street)

Private Mailbox no.

Spouse's SSN (if jointly owned)

City | State | ZIP Code

Note: If you do not furnish your tax ID number, this certificate is void and withholding is required.

Property address (if no street address, provide parcel number and county)

Ownership Percentage

. %

Read the following and check the appropriate boxes. (See line-by-line notes in the instructions.)

Part II – Certifications which fully exempt the sale from withholding:

	YES	NO
1. Does the property qualify as the seller's (or decedent's, if being sold by the decedent's estate) <u>principal residence</u> within the meaning of Internal Revenue Code (IRC) Section 121?	☐	☐
2. Did the seller (or decedent, if being sold by the decedent's estate) last use the property as the seller's (decedent's) principal residence within the meaning of IRC Section 121 without regard to the two-year time period?	☐	☐
3. Will the seller have a <u>loss</u> or <u>zero gain</u> for California income tax purposes on this sale? (To check "YES," you must complete Form 593-L, *Real Estate Withholding — Computation of Estimated Gain or Loss*, **and** have a loss or zero gain on line 16.)	☐	☐
4. Is the property being compulsorily or <u>involuntarily converted</u> and does the seller intend to acquire property that is similar or related in service or use to qualify for nonrecognition of gain for California income tax purposes under IRC Section 1033?	☐	☐
5. Will the transfer qualify for <u>nonrecognition</u> treatment under IRC Section 351 (transfer to a corporation controlled by the transferor) or IRC Section 721 (contribution to a partnership in exchange for a partnership interest)?	☐	☐
6. Is the seller a corporation (or an LLC classified as a corporation for federal and California income tax purposes) that is either qualified through the California Secretary of State or has a permanent place of Business in California?	☐	☐
7. Is the seller a partnership (or an LLC that is classified as a partnership for federal and California income tax purposes and is not a disregarded single member LLC) with recorded title to the property in the name of the partnership or LLC? (If yes, the partnership or LLC must withhold on nonresident partners or members as required.)	☐	☐
8. Is the seller a tax-exempt entity under either California or federal law?	☐	☐
9. Is the seller an insurance company, individual retirement account, qualified pension/profit sharing plan, or charitable remainder trust?	☐	☐

Part III – Certifications that may partially or fully exempt the sale from withholding:

Escrow Officer: See instructions for amounts to withhold.

10. Will the transfer qualify as a <u>simultaneous like-kind exchange</u> within the meaning of IRC Section 1031?	☐	☐
11. Will the transfer qualify as a <u>deferred like-kind exchange</u> within the meaning of IRC Section 1031?	☐	☐
12. Will the transfer of this property be an <u>installment sale</u> that you will report as such for California tax purposes **and** has the <u>buyer</u> agreed to withhold on each principal payment instead of withholding the full amount at the time of transfer?	☐	☐

Part IV – Seller's Signature

Under penalties of perjury, I hereby certify that the information provided above is, to the best of my knowledge, true and correct. If conditions change, I will promptly inform the withholding agent. I understand that completing this form does **not** exempt me from filing a California income or franchise tax return to report this sale.

Seller's Name and Title _____ Seller's Signature _____ Date _____

Spouse's Name _____ Spouse's Signature _____ Date _____

Seller: If you checked "YES" to **any** question in Part II, you are exempt from real estate withholding.

If you checked "YES" to **any** question in Part III, you may qualify for a partial or complete withholding exemption.

If you checked "NO" to **all** of the questions in Part II and Part III, the withholding will be 3 1/3 percent of the total sales price.

If you are withheld upon, the withholding agent should give you two copies of Form 593-B, *Real Estate Withholding Tax Statement*. Attach one copy to the lower front of your California income tax return and keep the other copy for your records.

Real Estate Withholding —
Computation of Estimated Gain or Loss

CALIFORNIA FORM
593-L

(You are required to complete this form only if you think you may certify a loss on Form 593-C.)

Property address (if no street address, provide parcel number and county)

1 **Selling price** .... 1 _____

2 Selling expenses **(optional)** .... 2 _____

3 **Amount You Will Realize.** Subtract line 2 from line 1 .... 3 _____

4 Enter the price you paid to purchase the property (If you acquired the property
  other than by purchase, see page 8, Table 1 to determine your basis.) .... 4 _____

5 Seller-paid points .... 5 _____

6 Depreciation .... 6 _____

7 Other decreases to basis .... 7 _____

8 Total decreases to basis. Add line 5 through line 7 .... 8 _____

9 Subtract line 8 from line 4 .... 9 _____

10 Cost of additions and improvements **(optional)** .... 10 _____

11 Other increases to basis **(optional)** .... 11 _____

12 Total increases to basis. Add line 10 and line 11 .... 12 _____

13 **Adjusted basis.** Add line 9 and line 12 .... 13 _____

14 Enter any suspended passive activity losses from <u>this</u> property **(optional)** .... 14 _____

15 Add line 13 and line 14 .... 15 _____

16 If line 3 is **less than** line 15, subtract line 3 from line 15. If line 3 is **equal to** line 15, enter zero. You have
   a **loss** or zero gain for withholding purposes. Skip line 17. Complete the Seller's Signature area below and
   check the "YES" box on Form 593-C, line 3 .... 16 _____

17 If line 3 is **more than** line 15, subtract line 15 from line 3. You have a **gain** for withhold purposes. You must check the
   "NO" box on Form 593-C, line 3. Escrow will withhold $3^1/_3$ percent of the total sales price .... 17 _____

Seller's Signature

Under penalties of perjury, I hereby certify that the information provided above is, to the best of my knowledge, true and correct in that any estimated loss calculated is no greater than the loss that I will recognize on my California tax return for this tax year. If conditions change, I will promptly inform the withholding agent. I understand that completing this form does **not** exempt me from filing a California income tax return to report this sale.

Seller's name (type or print) _____

Seller's signature _____ Date: _____

Spouse's name (if jointly owned) _____

Spouse's signature (if jointly owned) _____ Date: _____

For Privacy Act Notice, get form FTB 1131 (Individuals only).   593L05103   Form 593-L C2 2005

YEAR

2006

Real Estate Withholding Installment Sale Agreement

(This form can **only** be completed by the buyer. This is not a remittance document.)

CALIFORNIA FORM

593-I

Part I – Buyer's Information

Return this form to your escrow company.

Name (include spouse, if jointly purchased – see instructions – type or print)	Social security number (SSN)
	Spouse's SSN (if jointly purchased)
Address (number and street)	Private Mailbox no.	☐ CA Corporation number ☐ FEIN
City	State	ZIP Code	Daytime telephone number ( )	**Note:** If you do not furnish your tax ID number, this agreement is void.
Property address (if no street address, provide parcel number and county)	Ownership percentage . %

Part II – Seller's Information

Name (include spouse, if jointly owned – see instructions – type or print)	Social security number (SSN)
	Spouse's SSN (if jointly owned)
Mailing address (street)	Private Mailbox no.	☐ CA Corporation no. ☐ FEIN
City	State	ZIP Code	**Note:** If you do not furnish the seller's tax ID number, this agreement is void.

Part III – Installment Agreement

Attach a copy of the signed promissory note (showing the installment payment requirement) to this form.

Part IV – Buyer's Agreement to Withhold (Be sure to read the "Buyer" information below before you sign.)

Under penalties of perjury, I hereby agree to withhold on <u>each</u> **principal** payment for the above shown California real property to the above seller at the rate of 3¹/₃ percent of each principal payment. I will complete Form 593, Real Estate Withholding Remittance Statement, and Form 593-B, Real Estate Withholding Tax Statement, for each principal payment and send one copy of each to the Franchise Tax Board with the withholding payment and give two copies of Form 593-B to the seller. I will send each withholding payment by the 20th day of the month following the month of the installment payment. If the terms of the installment sale, promissory note, or payment schedule change, I will promptly inform the Franchise Tax Board. I understand that completing and signing this form will subject me to withholding penalties if I do not withhold on each principal payment and do not send the withholding, with Forms 593 and 593-B, to the Franchise Tax Board by the due date or I do not send two copies of Form 593-B to the seller by the due date.

Buyer's name (if the buyer is not an individual, buyer's agent's name and title) (type or print) _____

Buyer's signature _____ Date: _____

Buyer's spouse's name (if on title) _____

Buyer's spouse's signature (if applicable) _____ Date: _____

Buyer: **If you sign this agreement,** make a copy of this form. Make sure you copy the back so you will have the instructions for withholding on subsequent payments. Give the original, with a copy of the promissory note, to your escrow officer. Your escrow officer will withhold on the down payment. You must withhold on **all** subsequent principal payments (including payoff or balloon payments). Do not complete this form unless you are willing to withhold 3¹/₃ percent, complete Forms 593 and 593-B, **and** mail the forms and payment to the Franchise Tax Board for **each** principal payment.

Note: This agreement is between the buyer and the Franchise Tax Board. Neither the seller nor the buyer may modify the terms of the agreement.

If you choose not to sign this agreement, instruct your escrow officer to withhold the full 3¹/₃ percent of the total sales price. You will not be required to withhold on subsequent installment payments.

Escrow Officer: If this is an installment sale and the buyer has agreed to withhold on each principal payment instead of withholding on the full amount at the time of transfer, withhold only on the down payment in escrow. Make a copy of this form for your records. Attach the original Form 593-I and a copy of the promissory note to Form 593-B and send to Franchise Tax Board with Form 593 and the withholding payment.

For Privacy Act Notice, get form FTB 1131. 593I05103 Form 593-I C2 2005

Chapter 23

The reverse exchange

This chapter discusses the proper procedures for controlling, financing and acquiring replacement property in a §1031 warehousing transaction.

Warehousing the replacement property

An investor owns real estate he no longer wants. His desire is to shift his investment in the property he owns to another property that offers him a better investment opportunity. His market timing to purchase a property is right, but not so for a sale.

At the moment, the investor is confronted with a buyer's market in which real estate prices are soft and competition among buyers is low. On the other hand, interest rates charged by mortgage lenders are dropping, signalling these lower prices will not be around for long. Sellers are also still accepting liberal terms for the payment of purchase prices and interest rates on carrybacks are low.

All the economic attributes creating this favorable buyer's market are exactly the same factors suppressing the market value of the property the investor wishes to sell.

Thus, the investor must wait for the return of lower mortgage rates and investment yield expectations before he will be able to sell his property at a price obtainable in a seller's market.

The investor has **ample cash reserves** to buy properties in this market. However, he does not wish to permanently add more real estate to his investment portfolio at the expense of reduced cash reserves.

The investor knows he will be able to eventually sell the property he no longer wants, at the price he wants, even if the wait is two or three years.

When he does sell, the investor wants the profit to be exempt from taxes under Internal Revenue Code (IRC) §1031. However, he is uncertain whether he can qualify for the profit exemption unless he first sells the real estate he no longer wants.

Here, the investor does not need to first sell his property, or even concurrently sell or exchange it for replacement property, to qualify under the §1031 profit tax exemption. The investor may first **fund** the purchase of a replacement property he locates, however, the replacement property must be acquired by an **interim owner**. Then, the investor may later sell his property and use the sales proceeds to buy out his interim owner, an arrangement called a *reverse like-kind exchange* by the Internal Revenue Service (IRS).

Since the sell-buy chronology of the typical §1031 reinvestment is "reversed," no sales proceeds will be available to fund the purchase of the replacement property to be acquired by the interim owner selected by the investor.

Thus, before an investor can consider embarking on a reverse exchange, the investor must have **adequate cash reserves** to fund the purchase and carrying costs of the replacement property.

Some **economic factors** might induce a real estate investor who has sufficient cash reserves to control the acquisition of a replacement property at a fixed price. Those factors include:

- *declining interest rates* without a concurrent increase in prices;

- *increasing willingness of lenders* to extend credit;

- a *bear market for sellers* in response to government recessionary policy pressures or the local economy;

- anticipated *future inflation* that will reduce the purchasing power of cash reserves; and

- *future appreciation* of a property's value due to the demographics of its location.

The investor must take care to avoid holding title at the same time to both the property he intends to sell and the replacement property, called *concurrent ownership*.

Concurrent ownership prohibited

An individual is the owner and operator of a business, occupying nonresidential property as a tenant. He would like to own the real estate his business now rents.

What the businessman would like to do to acquire the property is exchange residential rental units he now owns for his landlord's property. The equity in the units is nearly equal to the landlord's equity. However, while the landlord is willing to sell, he is not willing to accept the units in exchange for any part of the price.

Thus, if the businessman is to retain his cash reserves, he must sell his units to produce the funds needed to purchase the nonresidential property he now occupies.

The businessman makes an offer to buy the landlord's nonresidential property on terms consisting of cash to the existing loan. Closing is contingent on the sale of the residential units so he may qualify for the profit tax exemption under IRC §1031.

In response, the landlord counters, offering to sell without the contingency that the businessman first sell his property. The businessman accepts the counteroffer, which commits him to use his cash reserves if the units do not first sell.

The purchase agreement includes provisions stating:

- the parties will cooperate in a §1031 transaction [See **first tuesday** Form 159 §10.6]; and

- the businessman reserves the right to assign his purchase rights and change the vesting to a substitute buyer prior to closing. [See **first tuesday** Form 159 §10.6]

The businessman's intent is to complete a §1031 reinvestment and avoid reporting taxes on the profit generated by the sale of his units.

However, before the rental property has been sold, the landlord makes a demand on the businessman to close escrow on the replacement property or he will cancel the purchase agreement since the date set for closing has passed.

Faced with losing the right to purchase the building he occupies, the businessman commits his cash reserves to fund the close of escrow and takes title to the property. He will merely replenish the cash advanced from the later sale of his rentals.

Does the businessman's transaction qualify for the §1031 profit tax exemption?

No! In order for the businessman's transaction to qualify for the §1031 exemption, he cannot **concurrently own both** the property to be sold and the replacement property. [**Bezdjian** v. **Commissioner** (9th Cir. 1988) 845 F2d 217]

To avoid concurrent ownership, the businessman must locate an **interim owner** to first acquire title and ownership to the replacement property he has agreed to buy, and do so directly from the landlord. The cooperation and assignment provisions in the purchase agreement permit the businessman to transfer his right to buy the property by assignment, to an interim owner.

The interim owner will close the purchase escrow on the replacement property by taking title in his own name. The interim owner will become the owner and operator of the property for whatever period of time it takes for the businessman to sell his property.

Designing the parking transaction

An income property investor owns an industrial building that is leased to a tenant who occupies the premises as his place of business. The tenant needs a larger and better facility to house his growing business.

A broker is retained by the investor to locate unimproved, vacant land at a location that will satisfy the tenant's needs in a new premises suitable for constructing improvements. The broker coordinates his efforts with the tenant. A parcel of land is located that will accommodate the construction of improvements, and the tenant agrees to lease it.

The investor acquires ownership of the vacant land. A planner and builder are retained to design and construct the improvements sought by the tenant. Approval for the issuance of a building permit is obtained and a construction loan commitment is arranged. A lease of the yet-to-be-built improvements is negotiated and entered into by the investor and the tenant.

Before originating the construction loan and taking out the building permit, the investor determines his finances require the sale of the industrial building presently occupied by the tenant. He again retains his broker. This time the broker is to locate a buyer for the property the tenant will be vacating on completion of the construction at the new location.

A prospective buyer is located who is willing to pay the cash price sought by the investor. Before entering into a purchase agreement with the prospective buyer, the investor inquires into the portion of the net sales proceeds he will retain after payment of profit taxes. The price includes a significant amount of profit since the investor's basis in the property to be sold is low in comparison to the price due to inflation, appreciation and depreciation deductions he has taken over several years of ownership.

To avoid the payment of profit taxes on the sale of the property to be sold, the investor retains an attorney and accountant who suggest the sale be structured as part of a §1031 reinvestment plan. A continuing investment in real estate will be established by the reinvestment of the sales proceeds in the construction of improvements on the vacant land the investor now owns.

Since the investor now owns both properties and cannot exchange them with himself, the investor is advised by his attorney to structure his §1031 tax avoidance and reinvestment plan in two steps.

As the first step, the investor transfers title of the vacant land to the buyer under a titleholding arrangement structured as a sale. The "price" for the land is set as the amount the buyer will pay for the property to be sold. The "price" for the vacant land is fully paid by executing a carryback note and trust deed in favor of the investor, secured by the vacant land conveyed to the buyer.

The carryback is a straight, noninterest-bearing, nonrecourse note that is due and payable when the buyer acquires title and possession of the property to be sold.

The investor reports a sale of the vacant land and pays taxes on the small profit resulting from the agreed-to sales price. At all times, the investor retains full control over the construction of improvements. The title will be reconveyed to the investor on completion of construction.

All documents that create a debt obligation and encumber the vacant land, such as loan documents, are nonrecourse and impose no liability on the buyer. The investor is authorized to act as the representative of the buyer for all aspects of construction and loan fund disbursements. All expenses, taxes, interest and other costs of ownership of the vacant land are paid by the investor directly. The buyer does not incur any liabilities since the investor is solely responsible for all costs of ownership and construction.

Further, if, for some reason, the buyer is held liable for any sums arising out of his holding title, the investor will indemnify the prospective buyer and hold him harmless by paying the sums due.

Thus, the buyer is not "out of pocket" at any time until he pays the agreed-to price for the property to be sold and concurrently receives title and possession. He also receives no gain or other economic benefit for holding title to the vacant land, other than the right to acquire ownership of the property to be sold on his payoff of the carryback note.

The second step in the related series of transfers is structured as an exchange of properties. The exchange agreement calls for the buyer to receive the property to be sold. On the buyer's return of title to the investor for the vacant land, the property to be sold is conveyed free of encumbrances. The buyer also pays off the carryback note he executed when he took title to the vacant land.

The payment of the principal amount of the carryback note is the only amount the buyer is obligated to pay in the entire series of activities. The amount of the note is the sales price of the property to be sold to the buyer.

The investor's broker expresses his concern that the investor:

- **already owns** the replacement property;

- is **retaining** all the rights and obligations of ownership to the replacement property;

- is merely **parking title** to the vacant land with the prospective buyer of the property actually being sold; and

- will still own the vacant land (with its newly constructed improvements) when the investor conveys the property he is selling.

Will this two-step transaction qualify as a §1031 transaction and exempt the profit on the sale of the investor's property?

No! The sale of the vacant land is not an arm's length sales transaction between the investor and the buyer. The *equitable ownership*, and thus the *beneficial ownership* of the vacant land, was never transferred to the buyer. Only naked title was transferred.

To effectively "sell" the vacant land, the transfer of title must include the transfer of the **economic functions of ownership**, such as the benefits and liabilities accompanying ownership of real estate. Here, no ownership was transferred, only the naked title was transferred. The investor at all times retained full control over all decisions concerning ownership activities, such as construction, financing, leasing, etc. More importantly, he remained **primarily responsible** for incurring all the risks and paying all the costs of ownership, construction and conveyancing.

Thus, the sale and reconveyance of the land as a two-step transaction collapses for lack of any **economic substance** to demonstrate an ownership of the vacant land had been transferred to the buyer. As a result, title was merely transferred under a **titleholding arrangement**, designed as a "parking transaction" to give the appearance that an exchange of properties was occurring.

At all times until the sale of his property, the investor remained the economic and beneficial owner of both properties. Accordingly, the §1031 exemption is disallowed since the investor was the concurrent owner of both properties. [**DeCleen** v. **Commissioner** (2000) 115 TC 457]

Here, the vacant land should have been initially purchased by an *interim owner*. An obvious interim owner the investor could have chosen would be the general contractor, who would construct the improvements, or an *unrelated person* (an uncontrolled entity or unrelated individual), such as the real estate broker. [See Chapter 1]

The investor could have **lent money** sufficient for the contractor or broker to purchase the land, pay for construction costs and carry the property until it could be conveyed to the investor.

The investor's acquisition of ownership would follow (or close concurrently with) the sale of his property. To coordinate the reinvestment, the net proceeds from the sale would be delivered to the contractor or broker who held title as the interim owner of the land. In turn, the contractor or broker would convey the improved land to the investor under their purchase agreement. On conveyance, they would pay off the loans from the investor used to buy and carry the investor's replacement property.

IRS recognized parking transactions

Sometimes it is a seller of replacement property being purchased who compels an investor to close escrow on the purchase before the investor is able to close escrow on the property he is selling. In this case, the investor must make **arrangements** to close escrow if he is to control the replacement property.

To close escrow on the purchase of the replacement property, the investor must use a **substitute buyer** in compliance with one of two types of *parking transactions* recognized by the IRS, to qualify the later sale of the investor's property for a §1031 exemption.

Under either type of parking transaction, the taxpayer will avoid his premature acquisition of the *beneficial ownership* of the replacement property before he closes escrow on the property to be sold. On the close of escrow, the

profit taken will qualify for the §1031 profit tax exemption. Then the investor will finally take title and ownership of the replacement property. [Revenue Procedure 2000-37 §3.02]

Parking transaction arrangements use one of two persons to avoid the investor's premature receipt of the beneficial ownership of the replacement property:

- an **interim titleholder**, also called an *exchange accommodation titleholder* by the IRS, who acts solely as the transitory holder of title, without the burden of operating obligations of beneficial ownership, under arrangements and time constraints that must be met absolutely as described by the IRS under the safe harbor rules; [Rev. Proc. 2000-37 §3.04] or

- an **interim owner**, who becomes the *beneficial owner* of the property, bearing the economic benefits and burdens of ownership and whose ownership is funded by loans and future advances made by the investor, and who ultimately resells the property to the investor under a purchase agreement. [IRS Revenue Ruling 82-144; Rev. Proc. 2000-37 §3.03]

Thus, an investor avoids being classified as the *beneficial owner* of the replacement property under either of these two parking arrangements.

If the investor is classified as the **beneficial owner**, it is considered that he has prematurely acquired the replacement property. Thus, he will not be able to couple the purchase with his sale to avoid reporting profit. The investor's beneficial ownership of both properties at the same time disqualifies the profit taken on the property sold from the §1031 exemption.

Interim titleholder procedures

Selecting the IRS **safe harbor procedures** for reverse exchanges automatically establishes the exchange accommodation titleholder as the *ben-*

eficial owner of the replacement property (even though the titleholder is an intermediary who in no way is an owner with the burdens and benefits of ownership). However, the safe harbor rules place a severe time constraint on the investor and a harsh penalty is imposed for the failure to close the transaction within the time constraints. [Rev. Proc. 2000-37 §4]

For example, after closing the purchase escrow on a replacement property under the safe harbor rules, an investor has **180 days** to close escrow on the sale of his property and complete the §1031 reinvestment plan. If the sale is not closed in time, he loses the right to ever acquire the replacement property in any §1031 reinvestment plan.

Thus, an investor who fails to sell his property within 180 days after title to replacement property is acquired in the name of the interim titleholder cannot complete his §1031 reinvestment plan. The investor will not be able to later couple the sale of his property with the purchase of the replacement property in a §1031 exchange and will have to pay profit taxes.

To purchase replacement property prematurely, before an investor's property to be sold has closed escrow under reverse exchange **safe harbor procedures**, a written agreement with the interim titleholder must be entered into, called a *qualified exchange accommodation arrangement* by the IRS.

A property is considered held in a QEAA if all of the following requirements are met:

1. Title to the replacement property (or a right to title under a California Civil Code §2985 land sales contract) is taken in the name of an individual or entity who is not the investor or *a disqualified person*, and who becomes the *exchange accommodation titleholder* or *interim titleholder*, and must have a federal tax number (for IRS tracking). [Rev. Proc. 2000-37 §4.02(1)]

2. The interim titleholder, on taking title, will retain title until it is transferred to the investor for a duration not to exceed 180 days, called a *qualified indicia of ownership*. [Rev. Proc. 2000-37 §4.02(1)]

3. The investor's intent for the property vested in the name of the interim titleholder is to acquire it as the *replacement property* in his §1031 reinvestment plan. [Rev. Proc. 2000-37 §4.02(2)]

4. The investor and the interim titleholder must enter into a written agreement (a qualified exchange accommodation agreement) **within five days** after the interim titleholder takes title to the replacement property. [Rev. Proc. 2000-37 §4.03(3)]

5. Title is held by the interim titleholder for the benefit of the investor in order for the investor to comply with §1031 requirements.

6. The investor and the interim titleholder report to the IRS the acquisition, holding and disposition of title, as required by the IRS to collect information from all participants for an audit.

7. The interim titleholder is considered the *beneficial owner* of the property for all federal income tax purposes and both the investor and the interim titleholder will report in their federal tax return the tax consequences. [Rev. Proc. 2000-37 §4.02(3)]

8. **Within 45 days** after the interim titleholder takes title to the replacement property, the investor **identifies** the property or properties, one or more of which the investor intends to sell as part of his §1031 reinvestment plan, (the identification to comply with the same rules in a delayed exchange). [Rev. Proc. 2000-37 §4.02(4); Rev. Regs. §1.1031(k)-1(c)]

9. **Within 180 days** after the interim titleholder takes title to the replacement property, the investor **takes title** to the replacement property on a conveyance by the interim titleholder. [Rev. Proc. 2000-37 §4.02(5)]

However, if the replacement property was **previously owned** by the investor at any time prior to the 180-day period before title to the property is transferred to the interim titleholder, the safe harbor rules do not apply. [Rev. Proc. 2000-37 §4.02 as modified by Rev. Proc. 2004-51]

Disregard of arms' length arrangements

The investor and the safe harbor interim titleholder are allowed to enter into numerous other arrangements during the period the title is "parked" with the interim titleholder. The arrangements, made without regard for the arms' length nature of the arrangements or the equitable use and ownership of the replacement property as established by state law, include:

- the investor may *guarantee* obligations incurred by the interim titleholder in the acquisition of the property, such as loan assumptions, purchase-assist loans or a carryback purchase-money note;

- the investor may *indemnify* the interim titleholder against any operating cost and expenses incurred by the interim titleholder in his care and maintenance of the property during the period he holds title and may use a hold harmless arrangement for reimbursing operating costs [Rev. Proc. 2000-37 §4.03(2)];

- the investor may make *loans or advances* as needed by the interim titleholder to cover such events as negative cash flow due to insufficient rental income to cover operating expenses, or the investor may *guarantee* the loans or advances when made by others to cover the negative cash flow [Rev. Proc. 2000-37 §4.03(3)];

- the investor may obtain possession of the property while title is held by the interim titleholder by entering into a *lease* [Rev. Proc. 2000-37 §4.03(4)];

- *property operations* may be taken over by the investor (or anyone else) as the property manager, supervisor of construction, the building contractor or provider of any other service with respect to the property [Rev. Proc. 2000-37 §4.03(5)]; and

- a *purchase agreement* to resell the property to the investor may be entered into between the interim titleholder and the investor, or they may enter into an option to purchase (call option) or an option to sell (put option), limited in their effectiveness to a 185-day expiration period for their performance after the interim titleholder takes title to the property. [Rev. Proc. 2000-37 §4.03(6)]

Risks imposed by use of safe harbor rules

By structuring the reverse exchange as a **titleholding arrangement** in compliance with the safe harbor rules, the investor exposes himself to the risk of losing his ability to acquire the replacement property as part of a §1031 reinvestment plan. The 180-day **warehousing constraints** require him to take title to the replacement property whether or not the property he intends to sell does sell.

Thus, the investor is unable to extend the time for his acquisition of the replacement property from the interim titleholder to a later date. As a result, after the 180-day period, the investor will be unable to acquire the warehoused property as §1031 replacement property.

The risks posed by the time constraints and the interim titleholder's acquisition of the replacement property may be small, and thus acceptable to an investor.

For example, a buyer has been located for the property an investor is selling. However, the replacement property must be acquired by the investor before he can close on his sale or he will lose the opportunity to buy it (or the price will increase).

Here, the safe harbor rules provide great flexibility in operating and developing the property during the 180-day period before closing out the §1031 reinvestment plan. Title to the replacement property may be taken in the name of the interim titleholder and the sales escrow on the property he is selling may be closed later.

However, failure to meet the five-day, 45-day and 180-day deadlines, as well as any failure to notify IRS (or enter into the requisite written agreements) when the replacement property has been "parked" under the safe harbor rules, will disqualify the profit on the property sold from the tax-exempt treatment of IRC §1031. [**Christensen** v. **Commissioner** (1996) TCM 1996-254]

Warehousing without constraints

To avoid holding title to both properties simultaneously, a reverse exchange may be structured to comply with general court-approved rules. An investor buying property under a purchase agreement or option, can **assign his right** to purchase the replacement property to an **interim owner**, an activity called *warehousing the property*.

For example, a broker who is experienced as a property manager is solicited by an investor to be the interim owner of incomeproducing replacement property the investor has agreed to buy under a purchase agreement. The broker agrees to be the **interim owner** of the replacement property until the investor's property is sold. [See Figure 1 accompanying this chapter]

The interim owner may be anyone except a *related person*, which excludes an immediate family member or a business controlled by the investor. [IRC §§267(b), 707(b); see Chapter 1]

Escrow closing instructions, including the investor's assignment to the interim owner of the right to buy the property, are prepared and agreed to by all.

The *assignment provision* in the purchase agreement permits a third party, such as the broker acting as the interim owner, to take title to the replacement property. [See **first tuesday** Form 159 §§10.6 and 13.3]

The interim owner will become the owner and landlord, collect rents, pay operating expenses, taxes, insurance and all other costs of ownership required under the leases.

The investor, to close the purchase escrow, **lends** the interim owner all the funds needed to purchase the replacement property. The loan is evidenced by a note signed by the interim owner, with or without a nonrecourse provision, called an *exculpatory clause*.

The investor also enters into a *future advances agreement* with the interim owner. By the agreement, the investor obligates himself to advance any additional funds the interim owner may need to cover cash flow deficiencies that may occur during the interim ownership of the replacement property.

Both the note and future advances agreement are **secured** by a trust deed on the property purchased. Thus, the investor is able to recover his advances from the property's value should the interim owner default. The trust deed used needs to reference both the note and the future advances agreement as secured by the property. [See **first tuesday** Form 450]

The interim owner usually is paid a fee for his cooperation and the risk of ownership he undertakes.

Any net spendable income generated by the property prior to resale to the investor also belongs to the interim owner. However, interest paid on the funds advanced by the investor may be paid out of the net spendable income available to the interim owner.

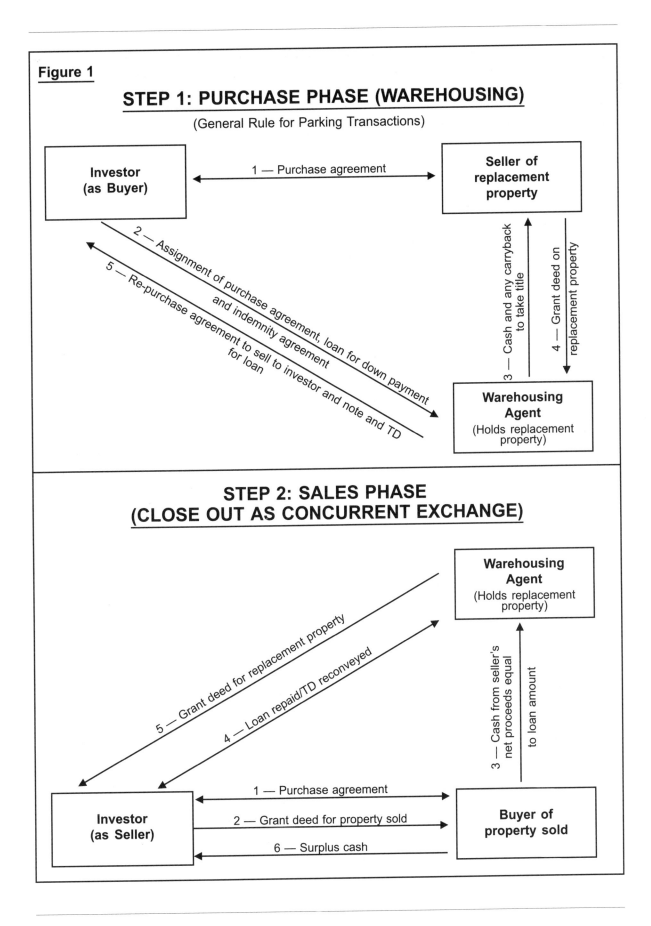

Figure 1

STEP 1: PURCHASE PHASE (WAREHOUSING)

(General Rule for Parking Transactions)

STEP 2: SALES PHASE
(CLOSE OUT AS CONCURRENT EXCHANGE)

A separate **purchase agreement** is entered into between the investor and the interim owner for the **resale** and **conveyance** of the replacement property to the investor. The purchase agreement assures the investor he has the right to acquire ownership of the replacement property when he is able to sell his property.

Occasionally, the interim owner's agreement to resell the property to the investor is secured by recording yet another trust deed on the replacement property, called a *performance trust deed*. Thus, the investor is assured the monetary value of his right to purchase the property under the purchase agreement will not be lost. [See **first tuesday** Form 451]

When the investor sells the property he is disposing of, the **net sales proceeds** are made payable and delivered to an escrow opened to purchase the replacement property from the interim owner, as would occur on any other purchase of a replacement property in a §1031 reinvestment.

The net sales proceeds fund the investor's down payment on his purchase of the replacement property under the purchase agreement with the interim owner.

From the down payment funds, the interim owner, now acting as the seller of the replacement property to the investor, pays off the *purchase-assist loan* made by the investor and any carrying costs advanced by the investor plus interest.

In turn, the investor reconveys the trust deed(s) he holds that secured the repayment of his advances as well as the interim owner's resale of the property to the investor.

The interim owner, through escrow, conveys the replacement property directly to the investor to complete the §1031 reinvestment plan. The ownership of the property by the interim owner ends.

Thus, the use of an interim owner, not a mere titleholder as under the safe harbor rules, allows replacement property to be bought and held for **however long it takes** to locate a buyer and close escrow on the property to be sold. Also, the replacement property will have been purchased when market prices were best for buyers.

Further, the property to be sold by the investor can be later sold during a period in which the market will allow the investor to demand and receive the highest price. The §1031 reinvestment plan is completed, and the profit taken on the property sold is exempt from taxes.

Deeding in a reverse exchange

Direct deeding between a seller and a buyer remains the common, most efficient and preferred method for transferring title. [See Chapter 16]

Sequential deeding of a property through intermediaries who are uninvolved in the beneficial ownership of the property can result in multiple escrow fees and other unnecessarily risky and burdensome activities. [Rev. Rul. 90-34; **Biggs** v. **Commissioner** (5th Cir. 1980) 632 F2d 1171]

In a reverse exchange, an investor can deed the property he is selling directly to the buyer. Also, title to the replacement property held by the interim owner does not need to be subjected to the chaos of sequential deeding by passing the title through others. The replacement property in a reverse exchange is deeded directly to the investor by the interim owner (who took ownership and possession from the prior owner of the property) to complete the §1031 reinvestment plan.

The sale of one property and the purchase of another property by the investor are treated as separate and unrelated transactions. However, to qualify for the §1031 profit tax exemption, he must comply with ancillary §1031 rules.

Section 1031 rules controlling reinvestments:

- limit the receipt of the investor's net sales proceeds;

- limit the time periods for identification and purchase of the replacement property in a delayed exchange, as well as the property to be sold in the case of a safe harbor reverse exchange;

- bar concurrent ownership by the investor of both the property sold and the replacement property; and

- bar receipt of interest on the net sales proceeds prior to acquisition of replacement property.

Chapter 24

Refinancing the property to be sold

This chapter discusses the seller's refinancing of the property to be sold or exchanged as part of or in contemplation of a §1031 reinvestment.

Within the §1031 plan or coincidental

An investor who receives *cash* on the sale of his property in a §1031 reinvestment plan must report profits on the sale, up to the amount of the cash he receives (and the value of any other cash items or net debt relief).

Cash received by the investor on the sale or exchange of his property **cannot be offset** by the investor's later execution of a purchase-money note or the assumption of a mortgage when he acquires replacement property. [Internal Revenue Code §1031(b)]

Any financing of the replacement property by the investor when he acquires it or at a later date, merely generates loan proceeds — whether invested in the property or used elsewhere. The net cash proceeds from the loan are neither income nor profit. Thus, funds borrowed by the investor on his purchase of the replacement property do not trigger the reporting of profit.

Refinancing prior to sale

Now consider an owner of investment real estate who wants to sell his property. The proceeds from the sale will be used to purchase other real estate for use in his business or as an investment.

New financing must be originated or be available to successfully market the property since it is presently encumbered with a loan for less than half its value.

To start the process of cashing out, the owner wants to refinance the property now. He will encumber the property with a loan for the maximum amount available, since long-term interest rates are near a cyclical low.

The owner believes the excess funds he will receive from refinancing his property will not be subject to profit or income taxes when received.

However, the listing broker advises the owner he should not refinance the property as part of his §1031 reinvestment plan. Excess funds from refinancing received by the owner are considered cash received on the sale in the §1031 transaction. Thus, the refinancing will trigger profit reporting up to the amount of the net proceeds received by the owner from the refinancing — even though the funds are received before the property is actually sold.

Will the net proceeds from refinancing originated in anticipation of a sale and received by the owner be considered **cash received on the sale** that cannot be later offset on the purchase of replacement property?

Yes! The excess funds received from refinancing were generated in **contemplation of a sale**. Thus, the funds constitute cash received on the sale of property in a §1031 reinvestment plan. The refinancing was part of the **marketing plan** to sell the property. More importantly, the excess funds are monies received prior to acquiring replacement property. Thus, profit on the owner's sale of the property must be reported up to the amount of the net loan proceeds received by the owner on the refinancing of the existing loan. [Revenue Regulations §1.1031(b)-1]

Even though the cash received from refinancing the property (which is then sold or exchanged) is offset financially by the owner's later execution of a purchase-money carryback note in part payment of the price paid for the replacement property, the cash was received before the replacement property was acquired and thus, profit will be reported up to the amount of cash received from the financing of the property in contemplation of a sale.

Refinancing unrelated to the reinvestment plan

Consider an investor who owns real estate and is confronted with meeting a final balloon payment on an $800,000 loan that encumbers the property.

Attempts to locate refinancing have so far been futile due to the type of property, its location and existing, tight mortgage credit.

The investor negotiates an option to extend the loan payoff date for one year. If exercised, the extension will require the investor to make a significant reduction in the principal on the loan and modify the note with an increase in the interest rate and monthly payments.

As an alternative in case of a failure to locate refinancing, the property is listed with a real estate broker for sale at $2,500,000, noting the buyer must obtain new financing.

The broker is informed the investor intends to buy replacement real estate with the proceeds of any sale that might be negotiated.

Continued efforts to refinance fail. Also, efforts to sell or exchange the property do not produce a buyer. The option to extend the due date on the note is exercised.

Prior to the extended due date, a $1,500,000 loan commitment is arranged. Before the loan processing is completed, the investor accepts an offer to purchase the property from a buyer located by the broker. The buyer will assume the refinanced loan to be recorded on the property by the investor.

The refinancing is recorded. The investor receives $700,000 in excess loan proceeds after paying off the old loan, which was due in a couple of months.

Now faced with taking a profit on the sale, arrangements are made to structure the sale as part of a §1031 reinvestment plan.

None of the net proceeds from the refinanced loan are impounded for use in the purchase of replacement property. The loan amount assumed by the buyer will be reported by the investor as **debt relief**. He will offset the debt relief by assuming an existing loan or originating a purchase-assist loan on the replacement property.

The buyer closes the sales escrow and takes title subject to the previously recorded refinancing.

Under mutual instructions to escrow, the net sales proceeds are disbursed by escrow to a §1031 trustee selected by the investor and appointed by the buyer to hold the funds. When the investor locates replacement property he will call for the §1031 trustee to fund his purchase of the property. [See Chapter 19]

Thus, the investor completes his plan to reinvest the cash proceeds from the sale into §1031 property.

Does the investor have to report profits on the sale up to the amount of **cash received** from refinancing the property he sold?

No! Here, the purpose for refinancing was entirely unrelated to the sale or plan to complete a §1031 reinvestment. The refinancing was not a part of the **integrated events** in the §1031 reinvestment plan set up by the investor for marketing the real estate's sale and the reinvestment of its equity in real estate to avoid profit reporting. [**Fredericks** v. **Commissioner** TCM 1994-27]

The refinancing was sought long before the investor listed or sold the property and was continually sought to properly finance his ownership of the investment. The refinancing was needed to meet the final balloon payment on the existing loan should a sale not occur or fail to close, and was not for the purpose of marketing the property.

The refinancing was brought about by conditions independent of the events surrounding the sale and reinvestment plan. Thus, the excess proceeds generated by the unrelated refinancing were not *cash received* on the sale of property in a §1031 reinvestment plan.

Other economic forces besides a refinance

Owners are often compelled to refinance or equity finance their investment or business property because of economic forces other than an impending due date for a loan secured by the property.

Consider an owner of §1031 property who seeks to refinance the loan on his property. The current interest rate for a new loan is a fixed rate that is significantly below the rate on his existing variable rate loan.

Soon after the property is refinanced and net loan proceeds are received by the owner, the property is listed with a broker, marketed and sold.

Before closing, the sale is restructured as part of a §1031 reinvestment plan. Here, the sale and reinvestment are unrelated to the refinancing. The refinancing was originated for an unrelated purpose, and was not part of the owner's integrated plan to sell and reinvest.

Another example of refinancing that is unrelated to a sale for §1031 tax avoidance includes owners who must refinance property with a large equity in order to use the equity as security to generate much needed cash to satisfy judgment liens, tax liens or loans with due dates that encumber other assets.

These reasons for refinancing exist without regard to the overlapping sale of the property, a sale superimposed on the refinancing by a §1031 reinvestment plan.

The refinancing would have occurred whether or not the sale took place.

SECTION F

Recap: §1031
Profit and Basis

Chapter 25

The §1031 profit and basis recap sheet

This chapter applies the §1031 concepts of capital offsets, cost basis and taxable profit experienced in a reinvestment plan by use of the §1031 Profit and Basis Recap Sheet.

Taxable profit on reinvestment

The tax objective of an investor in a §1031 reinvestment plan is to eliminate, or at least minimize, taxation of the profit realized on his sale of real estate. To meet this tax objective, the investor must **reinvest the capital** he had in the property sold in a replacement property in order to establish his *continued investment* in real estate.

What actually is "exchanged" in a §1031 transaction is the investor's capital investment in one parcel of real estate for an investment of capital in another property. In addition to the equity, loans also represent capital the investor has invested in the property.

Unencumbered property sold or exchanged for a reinvestment in unencumbered property of equal value is a perfect tax-free match of equities in properties. No adjustments are required for differences in loan amounts and equity values.

However, properties in §1031 reinvestment plans will have different values and most will be encumbered with differing loan amounts. These variables give rise to the need for capital adjustments that have tax consequences for the profit realized on the property sold or exchanged.

A tax analysis of a sale of §1031 property goes well beyond the mechanics of avoiding receipt of the sale's net proceeds and complying with time limitations and procedures for identification and acquisition of the replacement property.

For example, three capital events, some or all of which will occur on a sale, trigger the reporting of an equal amount of profit on the sale, unless offset. The **capital events** include:

- *existing debt relief* received by the investor on the sale of his property, consisting of the principal amount of secured or unsecured loans, whether paid off, taken over or formally assumed by the buyer of the property;

- *cash* or *carryback notes* received by the investor on the sale of his property; and

- *unqualified property*, also called *other property*, received by the investor in exchange for his property.

In reality, a §1031 transaction is just a sale of one property by an investor and his purchase of another. However, when consideration other than an equity in §1031 replacement property is received by an investor in his reinvestment, one or more of the three capital events has occurred. The dollar value of the amounts received by the investor will cause an equal amount of profit to be reported as taxable profit, unless the amounts are offset on the purchase of replacement property.

As long as an investor uses all the net proceeds from his sale (or his equity in exchange) to acquire replacement property with equal-or-greater debt *and* equal-or-greater equity than the debt and equity that existed in the property he sold, no profit reporting events occur. He has continued his investment in real estate by not withdrawing any capital and no debt reduction nor receipt of cash items occurred.

Conversely, if the investor "trades down" by acquiring property for a lesser price, a profit will be reported on the property sold (due to debt reduction or the receipt of cash items on the sale). The replacement property will have either lesser debt, lesser equity or both, than the property sold. [See Chapter 14]

The investor, on acquiring a lesser-valued replacement property, has **withdrawn capital** from the sale or exchange of his property in the form of either:

- *debt reduction*, also called *net debt relief* by the Internal Revenue Service (IRS) and more commonly called *mortgage boot*; or

- *cash*, *a carryback note* or *unqualified property*, also called *cash items and other property*, and more commonly called *cash boot*.

A broker's working tool

A §1031 Basis and Profit Recap Sheet is a checklist used by brokers to prepare a tax analysis of a proposed reinvestment for review with a client, an investor. As a checklist, the broker uses the Recap Sheet to **determine the tax consequences** of a potential §1031 transaction involving the acquisition of a particular replacement property. [See Form 354 accompanying this chapter]

The figures a broker calculates in the Recap Sheet regarding a potential replacement property should be reviewed with an investor before the investor makes an offer to purchase replacement property. By reviewing the contents of a prepared Recap Sheet, the investor can more fully understand the tax impact of acquiring a particular property, and better appreciate the tax benefits of maintaining a **continuing capital investment** in real estate.

The Recap Sheet demonstrates the tax consequences of acquiring one suitable property as opposed to a different property in consideration. By making a comparison between each replacement property, the broker

can minimize or eliminate reportable profit in a §1031 transaction. Selection of a replacement property among many suitable properties is influenced by optimal tax consequences.

If an investor has already agreed to sell his property, the Recap Sheet is used by enterprising brokers and agents to explain the tax benefits of **converting the sales transaction** into a §1031 reinvestment plan prior to closing. [See Chapter 19]

§1031 expertise includes accounting

Most brokers tend to know what type of real estate is referred to by the term "§1031 property." Also, brokers usually know how to determine values, balance equities in an exchange and escrow properties, whether the property is being bought or sold by the client.

However, when brokers discuss the tax consequences of §1031 reinvestments with investors, generally they are uncertain about how to anticipate and calculate the capital investment variables that generate profit reporting and taxes. The hesitancy to give tax advice arises out of the complications incurred when attempting to apply the variables that underpin §1031 accounting.

Thus, the broker who reviews the tax aspects of a transaction with an investor needs to know and understand the **accounting variables** involved in the transaction before he can fully assist the investor.

The **investment variables**, present in the ownership of real estate, that represent capital that can be withdrawn, created or transferred on the sale of one property or the acquisition of another and trigger the tax consequences for a §1031 reinvestment plan, include:

- the equities in both properties;

- existing loans;

- cash;

- carryback notes;

- unqualified property; and

- the remaining cost basis from the original investment.

The Recap Sheet

A broker uses a §1031 Profit and Basis Recap Sheet, called the Recap Sheet, to analyze the flow of invested, contributed or withdrawn capital his investor may experience when selling and buying properties in a §1031 reinvestment plan.

The **Recap Sheet** contains five sections. Of all the sections in the Recap Sheet, section 1 is the most critical. Section 1 nets out the existing debt and cash items to calculate the amount of capital withdrawn or added to the investment in the property sold. However, the broker and investor must complete all the sections to fully appreciate the contrasting tax consequences of a reportable profit versus a §1031 reinvestment.

Section 2 analyzes an investor's contribution of **unqualified properties** to acquire replacement property, such as personal property or dealer property held by a developer. The contribution of unqualified property produces a taxable profit or loss as though it had been sold for cash.

Section 3 calculates the *profit realized* on the sale, which sets the actual amount of profit taken by the investor in his §1031 reinvestment plan.

Section 4 calculates the *profit recognized* on the §1031 reinvestment, setting the portion of profit that will be reported and taxed.

Section 5 establishes the *cost basis* for the replacement property, needed to calculate the amount of the annual depreciation deduction available to the investor as the owner of the replacement property. When the depreciation deduction has been established, the investor can then analyze the property's annual reportable in-

come or loss from ownership and operations on an Annual Property Operating Data sheet (the APOD form). [See Chapter 26]

While the Recap Sheet determines how much of the profit on the sale will be reported due to the §1031 reinvestment, the Recap Sheet does not determine the amount of taxes an investor might pay.

The actual **tax payable** on the *recognized profit* reported on the sale, due to the withdrawal of capital, depends on the investor's adjusted gross income, itemized deductions and tax credits available to him, and the types of gains comprising the profit taken on the sale. [See **first tuesday** Form 351; see Chapter 6]

Off-form calculations for offsets

IRS Form 8824 is used to report the completion of a §1031 reinvestment plan. The form's checklist does not allow for the line-by-line off-setting of the various capital events flowing from the purchase of replacement property, comprised of existing debt, cash items and unqualified property. [See Chapter 27]

To properly report a §1031 reinvestment on IRS Form 8824, an investor must separate the existing loans he assumes on acquiring the replacement property from his analysis of any cash he contributes and any purchase-money note he executes to purchase the replacement property. Then he must net the **separately analyzed** capital withdrawals and contributions for the IRS **off form** by using a form such as the Recap Sheet. [See Form 354]

Debt relief and cash items

Cash, carryback notes, an investor's principal residence, dealer status properties, unsecured debt assumed and personal property involved in the investor's sale or purchase of property com-

§1031 PROFIT AND BASIS RECAP SHEET

Date _____, 20_____

USE: To be prepared to estimate reportable profit (§ 4.5) and basis (§ 5.5) in a proposed §1031 reinvestment plan. The form provides for a complete accounting for IRS 8824 off-form reporting.

Prepared by: _____

OWNER'S NAME: _____

PROPERTY SOLD/EXCHANGED: _____

_____

COMMENTS: _____

_____

REPLACEMENT PROPERTY: _____

COMMENTS: _____

1. NET DEBT RELIEF AND CASH ITEMS

Net existing debt:

1.1   Balance of debt(s) owner is **relieved** of on all property sold/exchanged . . . . + $_____

1.2   Balance of debt(s) owner **assumed** on §1031 property acquired . . . . – $_____

1.3   **Total net existing debt:** Enter the sum of 1.1 & 1.2 as either:

    (a)   **Net debt relief** (amount by which 1.1 exceeds 1.2) . . . . + $_____

    (b)   **Net debt assumed** (amount by which 1.2 exceeds 1.1) . . . . – $_____

Cash items received on close of the property sold:

1.4   Amount of cash **received** on sale (excluding prorations) . . . . $_____

1.5   Amount of carryback note **received** on sale . . . . $_____

1.6   Equity value in unqualified property **received** on sale . . . . $_____

1.7   **Total of cash items received on closing the property sold:** (The sum of 1.4, 1.5 & 1.6) . . . . + $_____

Net cash items received or transferred on close of the replacement property:

1.8   Amount of cash items **received** with replacement property (excluding prorations) . . . . + $_____

1.9   Amount of cash owner **contributed** (excluding prorations) . . . . . . $_____

1.10   Transactional costs **disbursed** at any time on either property (excluding prorations and loan payoffs) . . . . $_____

1.11   Amount of purchase-money notes **owner executed** in part payment for the replacement property . . . . $_____

1.12   Equity value of any unqualified property owner **exchanged** . . . . . $_____

1.13   Subtotal of cash items owner **transferred** (1.9 through 1.12) . . . . – $_____

1.14   **Total net cash items:** Enter the sum of 1.8 & 1.13 as either:

    (a)   **Net cash items owner received:** (amount by which 1.8 exceeds 1.13) . . . . + $_____

    (b)   **Net cash items owner transferred:** (amount by which 1.13 exceeds 1.8) . . . . – $_____

Netting all debt relief and cash items:

1.15   Enter net debt **relief** from 1.3(a) . . . . + $_____

1.16   Enter net cash items

    (a)   owner **received** from 1.14(a) . . . . + $_____

    (b)   owner **transferred** from 1.14(b) . . . . – $_____

1.17   Net debt relief and cash items, (1.15 & 1.16, but not less than zero) . . . . + $_____

1.18   Cash items received on sale from 1.7 . . . . + $_____

1.19   **TOTAL net money and other properties owner received:** (The sum of 1.17 and 1.18) . . . . + $_____

2. PROFIT/LOSS ON TRANSFER OF UNQUALIFIED PROPERTY

2.1 Market value of unqualified property owner transferred. . . . . . . + $_____

2.2 Remaining cost basis in unqualified property owner
transferred . . . . – $_____

2.3 **Total profit/loss on unqualified property owner transferred:** . . . . (+ or –) $_____

3. PROFIT REALIZED ON THE §1031 PROPERTY SOLD OR EXCHANGED
(before applying the §1031 exemption)
Consideration owner received:

3.1 Debt relief: Enter amount from 1.1 . . . . $_____

3.2 Market value of §1031 placement property owner acquired . . . . . $_____

3.3 Total cash items received from property sold:
Enter amount from 1.7 . . . . $_____

3.4 Total cash items received with replacement property:
Enter amount from 1.8 . . . . $_____

3.5 Total consideration owner received (3.1 through 3.4) . . . . + $_____

Consideration owner transferred:

3.6 Debt owner assumed: Enter amount from 1.2 . . . . $_____

3.7 Enter remaining cost basis in all §1031 properties
owner transferred . . . . $_____

3.8 Cash owner contributed: Enter amount from 1.9 . . . . $_____

3.9 Transactional costs disbursed: Enter amount from 1.10 . . . . $_____

3.10 Purchase notes owner executed: Enter amount from 1.11 . . . . . . $_____

3.11 Remaining cost basis in unqualified property owner transferred:
Enter amount from 2.2 . . . . $_____

3.12 Total consideration owner transferred (3.6 through 3.11) . . . . – $_____

3.13 **Total profits realized in §1031 property sold or exchanged:**
(3.5 less 3.12) . . . . (+ or –) $_____

4. REPORTABLE PROFIT/LOSS ON THE §1031 TRANSACTION

4.1 Total net debt relief and cash items owner receives:
Enter amount from 1.19, but not less than zero . . . . + $_____

(a) Carryback basis allocation: Amount by which 3.7
exceeds 1.1, but not more than the amount at 1.5 . . . . – $_____

4.2 Total profit/loss on unqualified property owner transferred:
Enter amount from 2.3 . . . . (+ or –) $_____

4.3 Subtotal: The amount of equity withdrawn:
(the sum of 4.1, (a) and 4.2) . . . . (+ or –) $_____

4.4 Total profits realized in §1031 property sold/exchanged:
Enter amount from 3.13 (But not less than zero) . . . . $_____

4.5 **Total reportable profit/loss:** (Enter lesser of 4.3 or 4.4) . . . . (+ or –) $_____

5. BASIS OF ALL PROPERTY(IES) RECEIVED

5.1 Debt relief. Enter amounts from:

(a) 1.3(a) Net debt relief . . . . – $_____

(b) 1.3(b) Net debt assumed . . . . + $_____

5.2 Cash items. Enter amounts from:

(a) 1.7 Cash items received on the sale . . . . – $_____

(b) 1.8 Cash items received on purchase . . . . – $_____

(c) 1.9 Cash contributed . . . . + $_____

(d) 1.10 Transactional cost disbursed . . . . + $_____

(e) 1.11 Purchase-money notes executed . . . . + $_____

5.3 Remaining cost basis in all property transferred.
Enter amounts from:

(a) 3.7 . . . . + $_____

(b) 3.11 . . . . + $_____

5.4 Reportable profit/loss. Enter amount from 4.5 . . . . (+ or –) $_____

5.5 **Basis of Replacement Property(ies) and cash items:**

(The sum of 5.1 through 5.4) . . . . $_____

(See Form 354.5 for allocation to cash items, multiple replacement properties and improvements.)

FORM 354   08-05   ©2006 **first tuesday**, P.O. BOX 20069, RIVERSIDE, CA 92516 (800) 794-0494

prise **cash boot**, called *money or other properties* by the IRS. Cash boot items are neither *mortgage boot* nor §1031 equities in like-kind property.

Loans existing on the property sold by the investor are part of his capital investment in that property. On a sale or exchange, the loan amounts constitute *debt relief*, called **mortgage boot**. The investor has been relieved of his commitment to maintain debt as part of his capital investment.

Thus, **debt relief** is a withdrawal of capital. Debt relief triggers the reporting of taxable (recognized) profit, unless the loan amounts are offset. Offsets include the investor's assumption of loans, contribution of cash or unqualified property or the execution of purchase-money paper to acquire the replacement property. [Revenue Regulations §1.1031(b)-1(c)]

Cash boot received by the investor on the sale of his property **cannot** later be offset in any way. Assuming loans, making an additional cash investment or executing a carryback note to purchase the replacement property do not offset an equivalent amount of capital withdrawals of cash items. Conversely, debt relief on a sale can later be offset on the purchase of a replacement property.

Two categories of boot

An investor acquires replacement property by the use of proceeds from a sale or the exchange of the equity in his property. All other **forms of capital** withdrawn or contributed by an investor in a §1031 reinvestment plan are inevitably classified for tax analysis as either:

- existing debt, called *mortgage boot*; or

- cash items and other property, called *cash boot*.

An analysis of the two categories of boot require existing loans to be separated from other items that do not qualify as like-kind property, before netting withdrawals and contributions. This process of separation is used to determine whether a **taxable profit** has been taken by the investor within each of the two categories of capital withdrawals.

For instance, the investor's **debt relief** from further responsibility for loan amounts encumbering the property he sold is a reduction in his capital investment of borrowed money and can later be offset if the investor either:

- **assumes or takes over loans** of an equal or greater amount that encumber the replacement property; or

- **contributes cash items** to purchase the replacement property, such as advancing cash, executing a carryback note, originating purchase-assist loans (cash) and exchanging other real estate or personal property that does not qualify as §1031 property.

Thus, the dollar amount or equity value of any **cash items** an investor contributes to his purchase of replacement property is a capital investment. The contributions will offset an equal amount of debt relief on the sale.

Conversely, and the economically illogical part, the investor cannot later offset the capital **withdrawal of cash** or a carryback note he receives on the sale of his property. Nor can the cash he withdraws on his purchase of the replacement property be offset by **assuming loans** on the replacement property, obligations that increase his capital investment to match the cash withdrawn.

For example, on the purchase of replacement property, the investor's **assumption** of a loan with a greater balance than the loan balance on the property the investor sold does not permit the difference in greater debt to spill over and offset cash received by the investor on closing out the §1031 reinvestment plan. [Rev. Regs. §1.1031(d)-2, Example 2]

Only cash items contributed or executed by the investor can be used to offset cash items received by the investor, and then only if the cash items are received on or after the date the replacement property is acquired. [See Form 354 §1.7]

Thus, loans existing on the property sold and loans assumed on the property purchased must first be netted out between themselves, separate from all cash, notes and other property considerations (cash items) withdrawn or contributed by the investor.

Netting existing debt

Under the **existing debt** section of the Recap Sheet, no profit on the sale is reported due to the investor's *debt relief* if:

- the investor assumes loans on his purchase of replacement property that have balances greater than the loan balances on the property he sold; or

- he makes other capital contributions toward his purchase of the replacement property.

However, if the loans on the property sold are greater in amount than the loans he assumes on the replacement property, *net debt relief* occurs. The investor has decreased his capital contribution to the investment in the form of reduced mortgage debt. Profit from the withdrawal of capital by reducing debt will be reported up to the amount of the net debt relief, unless it is offset by the investor's capital contribution of cash or unqualified property, his origination of purchase-assist financing or his execution of a purchase-money note to acquire the replacement property. [See Form 354 §§1.8, 1.9 and 1.10]

Of course, the profit to be reported on the **withdrawal of capital** due to failure to fully offset *net debt relief* by a contribution of cash items, is limited to the total *profits realized* on the property sold. [See Form 354 §§1.3(a), 1.14(b) and 3.13]

To analyze the netting process for **existing debt** on the respective properties, debt is classified as either:

- *debt relief*, representing loans taken over or paid off by others on all types of property the investor **sells** or **exchanges** in the §1031 reinvestment plan [See Form 354 §1.1]; or

- *debt assumed*, representing loans encumbering the replacement property that are taken over by the investor, and any unsecured loan the investor formally assumes. [See Form 354 §1.2]

For example, an investor sells property encumbered by a loan. His buyer takes over the loan or provides funds for the payoff of the loan.

The buyer agrees to become primarily responsible for making payments on the loan secured by the property the investor sold, and **debt relief occurs** for the investor. Thus, the investor has withdrawn capital he had invested in real estate in the amount of the unpaid loan balance he no longer owes.

Unless the debt relief is later offset by equal or greater loan amounts taken over or assumed by the investor on his purchase of the replacement property (or by the contribution of cash items to the purchase of the replacement property), the investor will have *net debt relief* to account for as taxable profit due to his permanent withdrawal of invested capital.

When an **unsecured debt** is taken over on the purchase of replacement property, it must be *formally assumed* to qualify and offset debt relief on the sale. A formal assumption is accomplished by a written agreement with the lender or the seller of the replacement property and imposes legal responsibility on the investor for payment of the unsecured loan. [See **first tuesday** Forms 431 and 432]

Netting cash items

Cash items include:

- cash withdrawn or invested by the investor;

- carryback notes either received by the investor on the sale of his property or executed by the investor to acquire the replacement property; and

- unqualified properties, also called *other property*, received by the investor on the sale or exchange of his property or contributed by the investor to acquire the replacement property.

Cash items are **withdrawn** or **contributed** by an investor when selling or buying real estate:

- to cover the difference between the equity in the property sold and the equity in the replacement property;

- to generate cash; or

- as a substitute for cash, such as the execution of a carryback purchase-money note or the origination of a purchase-assist loan to pay for part of the purchase price of property.

Cash items, like existing debt, both of which represent capital, are not §1031 property. They are cash boot. Cash, carryback notes, unqualified property and existing debt do not represent an equity in a §1031 property, which is the like-kind capital interest of the investor.

Cash items withdrawn by the investor **prior to acquiring** any replacement property cannot be offset. The premature receipt of cash items by the investor triggers the reporting of profit realized on the sale up to the value or face amount of cash items he withdrew. However, if the cash represents the premature receipt of interest accrued on the impounded net sales proceeds held by a §1031 trustee, all profits are taxed. [See Form 354 §§1.4 to 1.7, §1.18]

An investor will not report a profit due to his withdrawal of cash on or after he acquires a replacement property if the terms for purchase of the replacement property call for the investor to execute a purchase-money note or originate a purchase-assist loan for dollar amounts equal to or greater than the cash he receives. His continuing capital investment in the replacement property remains the same or is greater. He has merely restructured the form of his continued capital investment from equity to debt, called *recapitalization*.

A purchase-assist loan or a purchase-money note **originated by the investor** to buy the replacement property are cash items that also offset net debt relief resulting from the investor assuming a smaller loan on the replacement property. However, the reverse situation of debt assumed offsetting a cash withdrawal at any time is not allowed. [See Form 354 §1.17]

First account for §121 monies

On occasion, a rental property sold in a §1031 reinvestment plan has previously been occupied by the seller as his **principal residence** and is now occupied by a tenant, called a *sequential use* of property. Alternatively, the property might be currently occupied by the seller as his principal residence with part of the premises used and depreciated as either his home office space or a unit rented to a tenant, called a *mixed use property*. This mixed use occurs in the ownership of a one-to-four unit residential property or a single-family residence with a granny flat, maid's quarters, casita unit, etc.

Thus, in both a sequential use and mixed use situation involving a principal residence, the seller is entitled to an Internal Revenue Code (IRC) §121 $250,000 homeowner's **profit tax exclusion**. A seller qualifies if he has owned and occupied the premises as his *principal residence* for an aggregate of two years within five years prior to the close of the sale.

If the seller is entitled to the §121 exclusion on the mixed use property or the sequential use property he is now selling, he may first **withdraw cash** from the sales escrow up to the total amount of the exclusion. The cash withdrawal has no effect on his §1031 reinvestment of the balance of the sales proceeds in a replacement property.

Should the seller not withdraw the entire amount of the §121 exclusion, but only a portion of it, the entire amount is still excluded from the profit on the sale **before accounting** for the §1031 transactions. [Revenue Procedure 2005-14]

Thus, **§121 money**, being the amount of the exclusion from profit taxes, represents *after-tax dollars*, whether or not the amount is withdrawn or reinvested. In a §1031 reinvestment plan that involves the sale of the **present or prior principal residence** of the seller, the §121 exclusion is first fully accounted for before considering the application of the §1031 profit tax exemption to any cash and profit remaining.

The profit attributable to the §1031 portion of the property will include all the unrecaptured depreciation gains and any long-term capital gains remaining after the exclusion of §121 monies. Thus, the withdrawal of §121 money is not reflected on a §1031 Recap Sheet.

Conversely, if any portion or all of the §121 money is reinvested in the §1031 replacement property the seller acquires, the contribution of the §121 money, being after-tax dollars, is accounted for in the §1031 Recap Sheet as a **cash contribution**. [See Form 354 §1.9]

Cash contributions to the §1031

Cash advanced by an investor to sell or acquire properties will offset cash (and any unqualified properties) the investor might receive on or after he acquires ownership to the replacement property. [See Form 354 §1.13]

Cash invested includes all cash advanced by the investor in his effort to sell, buy or exchange any of the properties in the §1031 reinvestment plan, **excluding** prorations paid or received on either closing. [See Form 354 §§1.9 and 1.10]

Examples of **cash invested** by the investor include:

- cash advanced by the investor **to purchase** the replacement property [See Form 354 §1.9]; or

- cash advanced or sums accruing to the account of the investor that funded payment of the escrow **closing costs** for both the sale (or exchange) of his property and his purchase of replacement property, called *transactional costs*. [See Form 354 §1.10]

Cash does not include cash **paid by the buyer** of the investor's property (or the buyer's lender) that is **disbursed by escrow** to pay off loans encumbering the property sold by the investor.

Accordingly, the investor's use of cash funds deposited in his sales escrow by the buyer to pay off a loan does not constitute the receipt of cash by the investor. The funds were never available to the investor on demand. The buyer's funds used for the payoff are neither actually nor constructively received by the investor. Thus, the investor does not need to account for loan payoff funds deposited by the buyer or the buyer's lender. [**Garcia** v. **Commissioner** (1983) 80 TC 491]

However, loans paid off with funds from the buyer (or taken over by the buyer) are listed as **debt relief**. Any amount of debt relief not offset on the reinvestment is a withdrawal of capital. The withdrawal will be taxed as profit recognized on the sale, limited to the total profit realized on the sale. [**Barker** v. **Commissioner** (1980) 74 TC 555]

Carryback notes and purchase-assist loans

A note carried back and received by an investor on the sale triggers the reporting and taxing of profit. The amount of **profit in the principal** of a regular carryback note is based on the differences between the amounts of the property's cost basis and the existing debt on the property. Two situations in which an investor will pay profit taxes on a carryback include:

1. When the debt encumbering the property sold **exceeds** the amount of the property's cost basis, a situation called *mortgage-over-basis*, the **entire amount** of the carryback note becomes profit. No excess cost basis over debt exists to be allocated to the note.

2. When the basis in the property sold **exceeds** the amount of debt on the property, a situation called *basis-over-debt*, only a **portion of the amount** of the note's principal is profit. The excess basis over debt is allocated to the note. [See Form 355 §2; see Chapter 26]

Again, the amount of the carryback note received by the investor on his sale cannot later be offset. However, the investor can **avoid receipt** of the carryback note and the reporting of profit by causing the note (and trust deed) to be made payable to and delivered to the §1031 trustee as part of the investor's net proceeds from the sale. [See Chapter 20]

Carryback notes, sometimes called *purchase-money notes*, are occasionally unnecessarily structured as land sales contracts, and include all notes:

- **received by the investor**, secured or unsecured, in payment of the price received on the sale of his property [See Form 354 §1.5]; or

- **executed by the investor**, secured or unsecured, in part payment and as a contribution to the purchase price he is paying for the replacement property. [See Form 354 §1.11]

A purchase-money note executed by the investor to purchase the replacement property offsets an equal amount of cash received by the investor **on or after** the date he acquires the replacement property. [See Form 354 §§1.8 and 1.11]

Unqualified property: its basis and profit

Unqualified properties, called *other property* by the IRS, are properties exchanged that do not qualify as §1031 properties in a reinvestment plan. The investor might receive unqualified property on the sale of his property or he might contribute unqualified property toward the purchase of the replacement property. Unqualified properties can be either real estate or personal property. [See Form 354 §§1.6 and 1.12]

Examples of **unqualified properties** include:

1. The investor's **personal residence**, whether he acquires it in exchange for the property he sold, or exchanges his personal residence to purchase the replacement property, in which case he would first account for his individual §121 homeowner's exclusion of $250,000.

2. **Stocks, bonds** and **other certificates** of investments including an existing co-ownership interest in a real estate investment group. Co-ownership includes separate fractional interests in group investments vested in pass-through entities or as tenants in common (TIC) that, by vote, eliminate the unanimous approval of alienation rights. [See Chapter 12]

3. **Personal property** exchanged or received in exchange, unless it qualifies under the 15%-of-value incidental property rule or as §1031 property that can be exchanged for like-type personal property, such as trucks used in a business or furnishings in an apartment complex. [See Chapter 15]

4. **Inventory** and other **dealer status property**, real or personal. [See Chapter 9]

Unlike other cash items, such as cash and notes, **unqualified properties** do not have a dollar face value. Thus, the fair market value (price) of these properties must be established.

The investor's exchange of unqualified property he owns to purchase replacement property is treated as though the investor sold the unqualified property for an amount of cash equal to its value. Actually, the investor "sells" the unqualified property when he contributes it as an additional capital investment in the replacement property, equal to the value of the equity in the unqualified property contributed.

The investor's contribution of unqualified property is, in essence, a sale. Thus, the investor must report any profit that exists in the price and value he received for it. [See Form 354 §2]

If the unqualified property the investor contributes to purchase replacement property is encumbered by a loan, the investor's debt relief is accounted for as an existing debt. Not so for the treatment of debt that encumbers unqualified property the investor may receive on the sale or exchange of his property. [See Form 354 Instructions §§1.1 to 1.3]

Profit or loss on the contribution of unqualified property

Unqualified properties contributed by an investor as an additional capital investment to pay part of the purchase price of a replacement property are analyzed twice:

- once, to offset any net debt relief remaining from the property sold and any cash withdrawn on completion of the §1031 reinvestment plan [See Form 354 §§1.12 and 1.17]; and

- again, to report any profit or loss on the contribution of the unqualified property based on the value and price the investor received for it, as though the unqualified property had been separately sold for cash. [See Form 354 §2]

The second analysis is only concerned with unqualified properties the **investor contributes** as additional capital invested to purchase the replacement property. The purpose of the analysis is to set the profit or loss to be reported.

Even though the entire profit on the investor's sale might be exempt, the investor's contribution of unqualified properties toward the purchase of replacement property must be reported as a sale, along with its profit or loss.

The **profit or loss** on the investor's contribution of unqualified property is set as:

- the *price* or value of the unqualified property, as stated in the exchange or purchase agreement;

- the investor's remaining *cost basis* in the unqualified property. [See Form 354 §§2.1 to 2.3]

The profit or loss taken on the investor's contribution of unqualified property to purchase replacement property is again entered in the Recap Sheet to determine the overall profit or loss to be reported on completion of the §1031 reinvestment plan. [See Form 354 §4.2]

Conversely, the investor who accepts unqualified property in exchange for his property must report profits equal to the value of the **equity in the unqualified property** he received. No offset is allowed to avoid profit reporting (unless the investor somehow also advanced cash when he sold his property, such as transactional costs). [See Form 354 §§1.6 and 1.18]

Also, the price and value of the unqualified property received by the investor is included in the calculation of total profit realized on all aspects of the §1031 reinvestment plan. [See Form 354 §3.3]

Market value of unqualified property: priced or unpriced

The market values of properties actually exchanged between parties are arguably uncertain in amount. If no unqualified properties are received or contributed in exchange for the §1031 properties sold or acquired by the investor, then whether or not prices are placed on the §1031 properties is of no tax consequence.

The profit in an "exchange" of equities in §1031 properties is not taxed. Thus, the price given each property is of no concern.

However, when an equity in **unqualified property** is received or contributed by an investor, the investor should consider structuring the pricing of the §1031 properties to report profit based on the lowest justifiable value he can place on the unqualified property.

Typically, the prices set during negotiations for an exchange that includes unqualified property are all too often raised out of proportion to cash values.

As a result, the purchase or exchange agreement ends up stating the negotiated price as the value of the unqualified property. These written agreements will control the value of the unqualified property for tax purposes, although the price in the exchange could justifiably have been much lower, resulting in a much lower taxable profit.

Alternatively, unqualified property received on a sale or contributed to purchase a replacement property could be left *unpriced*. The value of the unqualified property can be left unstated, in what is called an **unpriced exchange**, for later reflection on its true value. Also left unpriced is the real estate exchanged and received for the unqualified property. [See Chapter 14, Example 5]

Hindsight, rather than negotiations, provides a better viewpoint from which to establish prices for setting reportable profits that will occur and be taxed.

Both sides in an actual exchange transaction that includes the transfer of any unqualified property, want the lowest justifiable price placed on it, since both sides will report a profit (or loss) in the exchange.

Total profits on the property sold or exchanged

The *profit realized* on the sale or exchange of any property is reported and taxed, called a *recognized gain*, unless a profit reporting *exemption* or *exclusion* exists. [Internal Revenue Code §1001]

IRC §1031 either fully or partially exempts the profit on the sale or exchange of like-kind properties from being reported and taxed.

In a **partial §1031 reinvestment**, the investor will end up reporting — *recognizing* — a portion of the profit he realizes on the sale. Here, the price paid for the replacement property is less than the price the investor received on his sale, called a "price trade-down" situation. [IRC §1031(b); see Chapter 14]

For example, the price received by an investor for the property he sold is greater than the price he paid for the replacement property. The difference between these prices in this trade-down situation will be the amount the investor will report as profits — limited of course by the total *profit realized* on the sale. [See Form 354 §3.13]

Reportable profit limited to the total profit

The Recap Sheet sets the actual amount of total profit on the sale or exchange of an investor's property, called *realized gain* by the IRS. The realized gain is the maximum amount of profit reportable. The realized gain includes any profit exempt from taxation in a §1031 reinvestment.

However, the portion of the profit taxed in a §1031 reinvestment plan, called *recognized gain* by the IRS, is the lesser of:

- the total profits the investor realizes (price minus basis) on the sale or exchange of the investor's property [See Form 354 §3.13]; or

- the total of the net existing debt and net cash items the investor receives (but not less than zero), **plus** any profit or loss on unqualified property the investor contributes toward the purchase of the replacement property. [See Form 354 §§ 1.19 and 2.3]

On the sale of a *mixed use property* comprised of the investor's principal residence and a separate unit or space on the property used as his home office or as a rental, the portion of the cost basis allocated to the home office or rental space (the §1031 like-kind portion of the property), for depreciation purposes is the §1031 cost basis carried forward to the replacement property.

The portion of debt relief allocated to the §1031 reinvestment is the same percentage figure used to originally allocate the property's basis to the depreciable portion of the property.

Profit reportable in the §1031 transaction

The tax reporting analysis for the property sold is concluded in the last section of the Recap Sheet. Here, the reportable profit or loss on the entire §1031 reinvestment plan is calculated.

No loss may be reported on a §1031 transaction unless the investor contributes unqualified property with a price and value below its remaining cost basis, in which case a loss was generated on its contribution.

The total reportable **profit or loss** on a §1031 reinvestment is the lesser amount of:

- the total *monies* (debt relief/cash items) and *unqualified properties* received by the investor after any credit for offsets [See Form 354 §4.3]; or

- the total *profits realized* on all property sold or contributed by the investor (in which case a reinvestment plan and the §1031 exemption are unnecessary). [See Form 354 §4.4]

In §1031 transactions where capital is not withdrawn by the investor through net debt relief or the receipt of cash items, neither profit nor loss may be reported on the §1031 property sold or exchanged by the investor. The profit or loss **implicitly accompanies** the cost basis carried forward from the property sold or exchanged to the replacement property, also called a "shifting of basis".

An example of **an unreportable loss** would be the sale of a property with a basis of $1,000,000 that has fallen in value to a current market price of $750,000 when the net proceeds of the sale are reinvested in §1031 property. Thus, a sale unaccompanied by a purchase of §1031 replacement property would produce a reportable loss of $250,000. [**Redwing Carriers, Inc.** v. **Tomlinson** (5th Cir. 1968) 399 F2d 652]

Chapter 26

Basis in the replacement properties

This chapter provides the §1031 formulas for setting the basis in a proposed replacement property so depreciation deductions and tax benefits can be estimated for a prospective buyer.

Setting the depreciation deduction

An investor enters into an agreement to sell real estate. Closing the sale is contingent on the investor's purchase of another property. The contingency is needed to accommodate the investor's completion of a §1031 reinvestment of his net sales proceeds.

The investor's broker locates what appears to be a suitable replacement property. An Annual Property Operating Data Sheet (the APOD form) is obtained to determine the economic feasibility of the property. [See **first tuesday** Form 353]

Taxwise, the APOD form is used to estimate the investor's yearly *reportable income* or loss from his annual operations and ownership. The estimate is based on the replacement property's income, expenses, loan interest payments and the depreciation deduction for one year.

The APOD form received from a listing agent should not contain a figure stating the property's annual depreciation. The amount of depreciation depends on the investor's cost basis. His basis will vary depending on whether the replacement property was acquired as an original purchase or with §1031 money as a reinvestment.

To prepare an estimate of the replacement property's reportable income or loss, the broker needs to enter the annual depreciation deductions on the APOD form.

To estimate the investor's tax consequences of owning the property, the broker should first prepare a **§1031 Profit and Basis Recap Sheet**. The Recap Sheet, in addition to identifying any reportable profits or losses on the property sold, sets the **cost basis** to be allocated to the replacement property. The cost basis is needed before the depreciation deduction can be calculated. [See **first tuesday** Form 354; see Chapter 25]

When the cost basis has been set on the Recap Sheet, the basis is then entered on the separate §1031 Basis Allocation Worksheet to allocate a portion of the cost basis to the property's *depreciable improvements*. The allocation of basis to improvements is based on the percentage of the replacement property's fair market value, represented by the value of the improvements. [See Form 354.5 accompanying this chapter]

The **depreciation deduction** allowed for one full year of ownership of the depreciable improvements is then calculated on the allocation worksheet and entered on the APOD form. The applicable 27.5-, 39- or 40-year depreciation schedule allows the investor to annually recover, as untaxed rental income, a portion of his capital investment in the property's improvements. [Internal Revenue Code §§168(c), 168(g)]

With the entry of the depreciation deduction on the APOD form, the estimated annual reportable operating income or loss for the proposed replacement property is set and presented to the investor.

When dealing with the tax aspects of a transaction, brokers need to remember that information about the investor's cost basis in his property, or the amount of his profit, performs no function in negotiations between the investor and the buyer of his property. Likewise, the inves-

§1031 BASIS ALLOCATION WORKSHEET

Replacement Property Depreciation Analysis
(Supplement to §1031 Recapitulation Worksheet Form 354)

DATE:_____, 20_____, at _____, California

Items left blank or unchecked are not applicable. References to forms includes their equivalent.

Prepared by: _____

Property sold or exchanged:_____

Replacement property: _____

Purpose: To determine the annual depreciation deduction to be entered on APOD **ft** Form 352 to set the after-tax return on property to be acquired.

1. **Cost basis** allocable between replacement property and cash items received:

    1.1   Enter the cost basis for all replacement properties as calculated on Form 354 at line 5.5 . . . . $_____
    (If no unqualified property or carryback note was received for the property sold, go to line 4.1)

2. Priority allocation of basis to installment **note carried back** on the property sold:

    2.1   Enter the **cost basis carried forward** from the property sold (as shown on **first tuesday** Form 354 at line 3.7) . . . . $_____

    2.2   Enter the **debt relief** on the property sold. . . . . (-)$_____

    2.3   **Cost basis of note:** If the amount of line 2.1 exceeds the amount of line 2.2, enter the difference, limited to the amount of the note (as shown on **ft** Form 354 at line 1.5) . . . . (-)$_____

3. Priority allocation of basis to **unqualified property received**:

    3.1   Enter the amount of the **equity** in the unqualified property received (as shown on **ft** Form 354 at line 1.6). . . . . (-)$_____

    3.2   Enter the amount of any **debt** which encumbers the unqualified property received. . . . . $_____

    3.3   **Cost basis for unqualified property:** Enter the total of line 3.1 plus 3.2 to set the cost basis in the unqualified property received in exchange for the property sold. . . . . $_____

4. Allocation of the remaining cost basis to **§1031 Replacement Property:**

    4.1   Enter the sum of line 1.1 minus lines 2.3 and 3.1 as the cost basis of all **§1031 Replacement Property** received. . . . . (=)$_____

    4.2   Allocation of basis between **two or more §1031 Replacement Properties:**

	Property 1	Property 2	
a. **Identification:** (Enter an identification for each §1031 property received)	_____	_____	
b. **Allocation for debt:** (Enter the amount of debt assumed on each property 1 and 2.) (Enter the total of the debts assumed on both properties.)	$_____	$_____	. . . . (-)$_____
c. **Basis to be allocated:** . . . . $_____ (Enter the amount at line 4.1 minus the total from line b.)			
d. **Equity valuation:** (Enter the **equity value** given each property 1 and 2.) (Enter the total value of the equities in both properties.)	$_____	$_____	. . . . = . $_____
e. **Equity ratios:** (Enter the percentage of each property's pro rata share of the total value of all equities from line d.)	_____%	_____%	= _____100%_____
f. **Allocation for equity:** (Enter the amount of each property's pro rata share of line c. based on line e. percentages.)	$_____	$_____	
g. **New cost basis:** (Enter the total of the amounts allocated to each property at line b. and f.)	$_____	$_____	

------------------------------ *PAGE ONE OF TWO — FORM 355* ------------------------------

5. Depreciable cost basis for **a single replacement property**:

    5.1   Enter the percent of the replacement property's market value represented by the market value of its improvements . . . . _____%

    5.2   **Depreciable Cost Basis:** Enter that portion of the basis at line 4.1 (or 4.2 g.) which represents the percentage of value attributable to improvements at line 5.1 . . . . $_____

6. Depreciation deduction from income for each year of ownership:

    6.1   **Depreciation Schedule:** Enter the number of years for recovery of the cost of improvements: . . . . ÷ _____ years
          (27.5 years for residential; 39 or 40 years for nonresidential)

    6.2   **Annual Depreciation Deduction:** Enter the result of dividing the depreciable cost basis at line 5.2 by the number of years at line 6.1 . . . . = $_____
          (Enter this amount on APOD ft Form 352 as the annual depreciation deduction for the replacement property)

FORM 355   11-04   ©2005 **first tuesday**, P.O. BOX 20069, RIVERSIDE, CA 92516 (800) 794-0494

tor's basis and profit is of no legal, financial or tax concern to the seller of the replacement property the investor will acquire. It is confidential information.

The basis and profit on any transaction are personal to the investor. Income tax matters are unrelated to the property's value and of concern only to the investor, his broker, other advisors of the investors and the taxing authorities.

Editor's note — This chapter discusses events requiring adjustments to the cost basis carried forward from the property sold. Section 5 of **first tuesday** *Form 354 brings together these adjustments to establish the cost basis allocable to the replacement property. Allocations of the newly established basis to cash items withdrawn by an investor or an allocation between two or more replacement properties, are calculated on a separate allocation worksheet form. [See Form 355]*

Estimating the basis

An entirely new basis and depreciation schedule are established for each replacement property an investor acquires in a §1031 reinvestment plan. The need for the amount of the new basis and the annual depreciation deduction should be anticipated by preparing estimates before the acquisition is negotiated.

The **basis** a broker estimates his investor would likely have in a proposed replacement property is calculated by use of the §1031 Recap Sheet as follows:

- **carry forward** the remaining cost basis in all types of properties sold or exchanged by the investor in the reinvestment plan [See Form 354 §5.3];

- adjust the cost basis carried forward for the **differences in existing debt** on the property sold and on the property purchased, and for the dollar amounts of cash items contributed or withdrawn [See Form 354 §§5.1 and 5.2];

- adjust the basis for **profit or loss** the investor will report on his contribution of personal property to his acquisition [See Form 354 5.4]; and

- the total is the **new cost basis** to be allocated between all types of properties received. [Revenue Regulations §1.1031(d)-1; see Form 354 §5.5]

To establish each replacement property's individual cost basis, **allocate the basis** between all properties and cash items received in the following order:

1. For any **carryback note received** by the investor, enter the dollar amount by which the basis carried forward exceeds the loan amount on the property sold (a *basis-over-mortgage* situation), limited to the amount of the carryback note. [See Form 355 §2]

2. For any non-§1031 **unqualified properties**, real or personal, received by the investor in exchange for his property, enter the dollar amount of the **equity** in the unqualified properties. [See Form 355 §3]

3. Any **remaining basis** is entered as the basis for the §1031 replacement property. [Rev. Regs. §1.1031(d)-1(c); see Form 355 §4.1]

In a further step, allocate the cost basis set for the replacement property between its land and improvements. The portion of the new cost basis **allocated to improvements** represents the amount of invested capital recoverable from rents by way of annual depreciation deductions. [Rev. Regs. §1.167(a)-5; Form 355 §5]

The applicable depreciation schedule (27.5-, 39- or 40-year) is used to calculate the annual depreciation deduction the investor may deduct from the property's net operating income. [See Form 355 §6]

Normally, an investor's **cost basis** in property is the price he paid to acquire it, plus the transactional costs he has capitalized. However, in a §1031 transaction, the cost basis for the replacement property is not based on the price paid for the replacement property.

The **price paid** for replacement property is comprised of the dollar amount of sales proceeds reinvested (or the equity exchanged) and loans assumed. Together, these amounts contain unreported profits the investor *realized* on the sale (or exchange) of his property.

The difference between the price paid for a replacement property and its cost basis on acquisition is the amount of unreported and untaxed **profit carried forward** from the property sold, called *nonrecognized gain* by the IRS. [See Form 354 §3.13]

Adjustments to the old basis

Property sold or exchanged by an investor has a **cost basis**, even if it is zero, whether the property is §1031 property or unqualified property (such as dealer property, the investor's principal residence or personal property).

The cost basis remaining in each property sold or exchanged by an investor in a §1031 reinvestment plan, whether §1031 property or unqualified property, is carried forward to establish the cost basis for the replacement property. [See Form 354 §5.3]

The basis in the replacement property is the result of accounting. The dollar amount reflects the investor's *continuing commitment* to an investment in real estate.

Capital adjustments are then made to the basis carried forward for the following items:

1. *Existing debt*: an increase or decrease to adjust for the difference between the loan amounts encumbering the property sold or exchanged and the loan amounts taken over on the replacement property. [See Form 354 §§1.3 and 5.1]

2. *Cash items*: a decrease for cash, carryback note and any unqualified property **withdrawn or received** by the investor at any time, and an increase for cash **contributed** by the investor, transactional costs paid on both the sale and purchase, any carryback notes executed by the investor and any unqualified property contributed to purchase the replacement property. [See Form 354 §§ 1.7 to 1.12 and 5.2]

3. *Profits reported*: an increase or decrease, respectively, for profits or losses reported and taxed on the property sold and on any unqualified property contributed by the investor to acquire the replacement property. [See Form 354 §§4 and 5.4]

The old basis carried forward, coupled with these adjustments, sets the cost basis to be allocated among all personal and real property purchased or acquired by the investor as part of the investor's §1031 reinvestment plan. [See Form 354 §5.5]

Existing debt and cash items affect basis

An investor will report profit he realizes on the sale of his property as the dollar amount of **debt relief** not offset by the assumption of loans or contribution of cash items on the purchase of replacement property. [See Form 354 §§1.3 and 4.1]

This **net debt relief** that is not offset is deducted from the basis carried forward to reflect the investor's reduction of his capital investment (represented by the debt). Conversely, any **profit reported** on the sale (due to the net debt relief) is added to the basis carried forward. [IRC §1031(d); Rev. Regs. §1.1031(d)-1(c); see Form 354 §§1.3 and 5.1]

Cash items include cash, carryback notes and unqualified properties, also called *money and other property* by the IRS.

As an adjustment to the cost basis carried forward, the value of the equity in each **cash item received** by the investor on the sale of his property or on his purchase of replacement property is deducted from the cost basis carried forward. The deduction represents a withdrawal of capital from the investment. [IRC §1031(d); see Form 354 §§5.2(a) and 5.2(b)]

Conversely, the amount of cash the investor **contributes** and notes he **executes** to purchase replacement property are added to the cost basis

carried forward. These additions to basis represent additional capital investment by the investor. [Rev. Regs. §1.1031(d)-2; see Form 354 §§5.2(c), 5.2(d) and 5.2(e)]

Contributing unqualified property

Unqualified property, called *other property*, contributed by the investor in exchange for the replacement property is also a *cash item*.

However, the accounting for unqualified property contributions is different from the accounting for the contribution of cash or the execution of a carryback note to acquire the replacement property.

Unqualified property owned by the investor has a cost basis (and possibly a taxable profit) in the hands of the investor.

The **market value** of the unqualified property contributed by the investor, less the remaining **cost basis** in that property determines any profit or loss taken on the contribution. (Price minus basis equals profit.) [See Form 354 §2]

Adjustments to the cost basis carried forward due to the investor's contribution of unqualified property include:

- any **existing debt** encumbering the unqualified property is entered as additional debt relief and reflects an adjustment to cost basis as a withdrawal of invested capital [Rev. Regs. §1.1031(d)-2; see Form 354 §§1.1, 1.3 and 5.1];

- the **cost basis** remaining in the unqualified property is added to the basis carried forward [See Form 354 §5.3(b)]; and

- the **profit** reported and taxed due to the contribution of the unqualified property is added to the cost basis carried forward. [Rev. Regs. §1.1031(d)-1(e); see Form 354 §§2.3, 4.2 and 5.4]

For example, an investor exchanges a $100,000 value in an airplane, which is unqualified property, in part payment for replacement property.

The contribution of the airplane is reported as a separate sales transaction. The airplane does not qualify as *like-kind property* for the §1031 profit tax exemption. Any profit or loss included in the price of the airplane is reported and taxed. [See Form 354 §§2.3 and 4.2]

As a contribution to the replacement property, both the basis and the reportable profit in the airplane are **added to the basis** carried forward. [See Form 354 §§5.3(b) and 5.4]

Any loan amount encumbering the airplane exchanged for the replacement property becomes a reduction in the basis under the process to offset debt. [See Form 354 §§1.1 and 5.1]

Priority allocation of the new basis

The Recap Sheet establishes the new basis that will be *allocated* among all types of properties acquired by an investor in a §1031 transaction: real or personal property, §1031 property, cash, carryback notes or unqualified property.

If a carryback note or unqualified property are not received by the investor on the sale of his property, the new basis is allocated in its entirety to the §1031 replacement properties acquired. [See Form 355 §4.1]

Conversely, the new basis must first be allocated to any carryback note or unqualified property received by the investor on the sale (or exchange) of his property. [IRC §1031(d); Rev. Regs. §1.1031(d)-1(c)]

A **note** the investor carries back on the sale (or exchange) of his property receives a priority **allocation of basis** under IRC §453 installment sale reporting rules for §1031 transactions. However, the allocation of basis to the installment note will only occur if the amount of the

remaining cost basis in the property sold is greater than the loan amounts that encumber it, a financial condition referred to as *basis-over-mortgage*.

For example, if the basis for a property sold is $300,000 and the debt on the property was the lesser amount of $200,000, the $100,000 difference is excess *basis-over-mortgage*. The excess amount is allocated to the carryback note. The allocation is limited to the amount of the note. [See Form 355 §2; see Chapter 13, Example 4]

As a result of this allocation, a **return of capital** (which is not taxed) is permitted by installment sale reporting in a partial §1031 reinvestment plan. The balance of the principal amount of the note is profit, taxable on a pro rata basis as principal is received on the note.

Unqualified property, such as a boat, car, plane, equipment, furnishings or a personal residence, is occasionally received by an investor "in trade" on the sale of his real estate. Any unqualified property acquired by the investor receives a **priority allocation** from the new cost basis for the value of its equity. [See Form 355 §3]

If the unqualified property acquired by the investor is encumbered, the dollar amount of the portion of the basis allocated to it is equal to its **equity value**. Added together, the debt on the unqualified property and the basis allocated to its equity become the cost basis in the unqualified property — the same cost basis as though a cash price had been paid for the unqualified property.

The basis remaining after all priority allocations becomes the basis for the §1031 replacement properties. [See Form 355 §4]

If only one §1031 replacement property is acquired to complete the §1031 reinvestment, it receives the remaining unallocated basis as its cost basis. [See Form 355 §4.1]

Basis allocation for two or more §1031 replacement properties

Occasionally, two or more §1031 replacement properties are acquired by an investor to complete a §1031 reinvestment. The new cost basis is allocated between the replacement properties based on the **price paid** for each — but only if the replacement properties are free of any loans, an unlikely event. [IRS Revenue Ruling 68-36]

One of two situations arises affecting allocations of the basis when two or more replacement properties are acquired:

- the multiple replacement properties are **unencumbered** with no debt to be taken over by the investor; or

- one or more of the multiple replacement properties is **encumbered** by debt to be taken over by the investor. [Rev. Rul. 68-36]

The allocation of basis among multiple replacement properties is different than the **further allocation** of each property's new basis to its land and improvements. Future depreciation deductions are based solely on the allocation to improvements.

Basis allocation among unencumbered replacement properties

Consider an investor who acquires two replacement properties to complete his §1031 reinvestment plan. The combined price paid for the two parcels purchased is the same as the price received for the property sold.

All properties bought and sold or exchanged are free of debt. Thus, the investor receives no debt relief and no debt is acquired. Also, no cash boot is involved.

Here, the basis carried forward for allocation between the two replacement properties will remain unadjusted, the same as the basis in the property sold. No adjustments for debt relief or cash items exist.

The **remaining basis** in the property sold by the investor is $600,000. Its sales price is $1,200,000. Both the property sold and the replacement properties are free and clear.

The price the investor pays for each of the replacement properties is $500,000 and $750,000, respectively, a total of $1,250,000, approximately the same total amount as the price received for the property he sold.

To allocate the cost basis between the two replacement properties, the investor must first determine the percentage of each replacement property's **pro rata share** of the total value of all §1031 replacement properties received in the reinvestment plan:

- $500,000 of $1,250,000 total for the first property received — a 40% allocation of the cost basis; and

- $750,000 of $1,250,000 total for the second property received — a 60% allocation of the cost basis.

Of the $600,000 cost basis to be allocated, $240,000 (40%) will go to the first property, and $360,000 (60%) will go to the second. [See Form 355 §4.2]

Finally, the basis allocated to each replacement property is further broken down and allocated between its land and improvements. The allocations will be based on the same ratio for each property's portion of the total price paid for the two properties. [See Form 355 §5]

Basis allocation among encumbered replacement properties

Usually, multiple replacement properties are encumbered and have different **loan-to-value** ratios. However, IRS regulations do not address basis allocation among multiple replacement properties that are encumbered, except that the allocation must occur.

Existing regulations allocate basis using **the equity** in free and clear replacement properties. It then follows that the total of the respective amounts of equity in each encumbered replacement property is **used to set** the percentage for the allocation of the adjusted basis to each property. Initially, there will be an allocation of basis to each property for the dollar amount of the loans assumed. [See Form 355 §4.2(e)]

To allocate basis among encumbered properties based on the value of each party's equity, an investor first allocates basis to each §1031 replacement property in the amount of the debt assumed on each property. [See Form 355 §§4.2(b) and 4.1]

The cost basis remaining after the priority allocation for debt is the "equity" basis that will be further allocated between the replacement properties. [See Form 355 §4.2(c)]

This remaining "equity basis" is allocated based on each property's **pro rata share** of the combined equities of all replacement properties. [See Form 355 §§4.2(c), 4.2(d) and 4.2(f)]

Finally, total the basis allocated to each property for loan amounts and equity valuations to set the basis in each of the replacement properties. [See Form 355 §§4.2(b), 4.2(f) and 4.2(g)]

Thus, the loan-to-value disparity between two or more replacement properties will not cause a highly leveraged property to have a disproportionately low basis compared to its loan amount — a result which would have occurred had the allocation been based on the value of each replacement property, rather than on the amounts of their debts and equities. [Rev. Rul. 68-36]

Chapter 27

IRS §1031 form handles cash defectively

This chapter discusses the deficiencies in IRS Form 8824 and reviews the use of off-form calculations to correctly report a §1031 reinvestment with a cash-back situation.

Netting the boot off form

Investors report their §1031 reinvestments on Form 8824 provided by the Internal Revenue Service (IRS). However, the content and instructions for Form 8824 are inadequate for the proper accounting of §1031 reinvestment plans involving the offset of *money* or *other property* received by an investor. [See Internal Revenue Service (IRS) Form 8824 accompanying this chapter]

Form 8824 fails to allow a line-by-line offset for cash items **received** and cash items **invested**, called a *multi-asset exchange* by the IRS. The IRS instructions are of little help since they do not provide either the formula or the calculations for handling cash. They do, however, instruct investors to attach their own statements, such as **first tuesday** Form 354, to IRS Form 8824 to show the offset of cash items.

To correctly report a §1031 reinvestment plan involving existing debt and cash items, situations common to most transactions, investors must themselves separate mortgage boot from cash boot items and net them **off form**.

IRS instructions accompanying Form 8824 for netting cash items appear under the heading of "reporting of multi-asset exchanges." An investor who **contributes** and **receives** various cash items on the completion of his §1031 reinvestment, must be advised these "multi-asset" instructions apply.

Further, the instructions merely state the investor must provide an **off-form statement** showing the *realized gain* and *recognized gain*, which is the profit (realized) on the sale of his property versus the profit reported and taxed (recognized) on the sale.

Separate analysis required

Off-form analysis is required when the investor executes a purchase-money note and receives cash back as part of the terms for the purchase of the replacement property.

Form 8824 lacks a subsection to offset and net out the cash items contributed and received **on completion** of the reinvestment plan. Cash received on completion of the §1031 reinvestment is entered at line 15, but is **not offset** at any point in the form by:

- **other property** contributed to purchase the replacement property [**Redwing Carriers, Inc.** v. **Tomlinson** (5th Cir. 1968) 399 F2d 652]; or

- **notes executed** to purchase the replacement property, called *carryback paper*. [**Feldman** v. **Commissioner** (1930) 18 BTA 1222]

Thus, any cash withdrawn on completion of a §1031 reinvestment is listed at line 15 and becomes reportable profit at line 20, unless the off-form analysis occurs. Off form, the cash withdrawn is offset by the contribution of other property or the execution of a note to purchase the replacement property. [See IRS Form 8824]

For example, an investor sells §1031 real estate for a price of $500,000. The property has an existing encumbrance of $300,000 and a net equity of $200,000. The buyer pays cash for the equity and assumes or refinances the existing loan.

The replacement property located to complete the investor's §1031 reinvestment plan is priced at $600,000, with an existing encumbrance of $200,000 and a net equity of $400,000. [See **first tuesday** Form 354 §1.2]

The investor knows all his profit on the sale will qualify for the §1031 exemption from taxes if he purchases replacement property with equal-or-greater equity and equal-or- greater debt to complete the reinvestment.

However, since the existing debt on the replacement property is $100,000 short of being equal to his debt relief on the property sold, the investor must resort to the contribution (or execution) of cash items to offset the net debt relief. The terms negotiated to purchase replacement property with a greater price than the property sold will create the necessary offsets.

The investor has control over the $200,000 cash from the property sold, which is available for a down payment on the $400,000 equity in the replacement property.

However, the investor also wants to withdraw $100,000 in cash on the closing of the purchase escrow.

The seller of the replacement property is willing to carry back a note for the balance of his equity after a $100,000 (17%) down payment.

The investor negotiates the purchase of the replacement property for a price of $600,000 payable on the following terms:

- a down payment of $100,000;

- the takeover of the $200,000 existing loan; and

- execute a carryback note for $300,000.

Thus, $100,000 in cash from the net proceeds of the investor's sale will remain unused when he closes escrow on the purchase of the replacement property. These funds will have been deposited into the purchase escrow for the investor's account and released to the investor on closing the purchase escrow for the replacement property.

The $300,000 carryback note executed by the investor to purchase the replacement property accomplishes the financial and tax objectives sought by the investor, including:

- payment of the balance remaining on the purchase price after the down payment and assumption of the existing debt;

- offset of the remaining $100,000 net debt relief on the property sold (mortgage boot); and

- offset of the $100,000 cash received by the investor on or after the close of escrow for his purchase of the replacement property. [See Form 354 §§1.14 to 1.18]

If the investor or his accountant completes IRS Form 8824 under instructions for lines 15 through 18, failing to go off form to net the existing debt and cash items, the result will be an **over-reporting of profits** by $100,000. [See IRS Form 8824]

IRS Form 8824 now instructs investors to complete offset calculations off form in situations where cash is involved in the reinvestment. If the investor does not go off form to do those calculations, he would have to report profits on the $100,000 cash received since Form 8824 does not account for an offset by a cash item contributed to purchase replacement property.

For example, on Form 8824, the $100,000 **cash received** is entered at line 15. The $300,000 **carryback note given** to buy replacement property would be entered at line 18 as a cash item invested. However, line 18 only adds the note amount as a contribution to the cost basis in the replacement property.

The investor can withdraw cash or cash items on or after acquisition of replacement property and still avoid reporting profit on the property sold.

Form **8824**	**Like-Kind Exchanges**	OMB No. 1545-1190

Form **8824**

Department of the Treasury
Internal Revenue Service

Like-Kind Exchanges

(and section 1043 conflict-of-interest sales)

▶ **Attach to your tax return.**

OMB No. 1545-1190

2005

Attachment
Sequence No. **109**

Name(s) shown on tax return

Identifying number

Part I **Information on the Like-Kind Exchange**

Note: *If the property described on line 1 or line 2 is real or personal property located outside the United States, indicate the country.*

1 Description of like-kind property given up ▶ ....

2 Description of like-kind property received ▶ ....

3 Date like-kind property given up was originally acquired (month, day, year) . . . . . . | **3** | / / |

4 Date you actually transferred your property to other party (month, day, year) . . . . . . | **4** | / / |

5 Date like-kind property you received was identified by written notice to another party (month, day, year). See instructions for 45-day written notice requirement . . . . | **5** | / / |

6 Date you actually received the like-kind property from other party (month, day, year). See instructions | **6** | / / |

7 Was the exchange of the property given up or received made with a related party, either directly or indirectly (such as through an intermediary)? See instructions. If "Yes," complete Part II. If "No," go to Part III . . . ☐Yes ☐No

---

Part II **Related Party Exchange Information**

8 | Name of related party | Relationship to you | Related party's identifying number |
|---|---|---|

Address (no., street, and apt., room, or suite no., city or town, state, and ZIP code)

9 During this tax year (and before the date that is 2 years after the last transfer of property that was part of the exchange), did the related party directly or indirectly (such as through an intermediary) sell or dispose of any part of the like-kind property received from you in the exchange? . . . . ☐Yes ☐No

10 During this tax year (and before the date that is 2 years after the last transfer of property that was part of the exchange), did you sell or dispose of any part of the like-kind property you received? . . . . ☐Yes ☐No

*If both lines 9 and 10 are "No" and this is the year of the exchange, go to Part III. If both lines 9 and 10 are "No" and this is **not** the year of the exchange, stop here. If either line 9 or line 10 is "Yes," complete Part III and report on this year's tax return the deferred gain or (loss) from line 24 **unless** one of the exceptions on line 11 applies.*

11 If one of the exceptions below applies to the disposition, check the applicable box:

a ☐ The disposition was after the death of either of the related parties.

b ☐ The disposition was an involuntary conversion, and the threat of conversion occurred after the exchange.

c ☐ You can establish to the satisfaction of the IRS that neither the exchange nor the disposition had tax avoidance as its principal purpose. If this box is checked, attach an explanation (see instructions).

For Paperwork Reduction Act Notice, see page 5.   Cat. No. 12311A   Form **8824** (2005)

Name(s) shown on tax return. Do not enter name and social security number if shown on other side. | Your soc

Part III Realized Gain or (Loss), Recognized Gain, and Basis of Like-Kind Property Receive

Caution: If you transferred **and** received **(a)** more than one group of like-kind properties or **(b)** cash or other (no see **Reporting of multi-asset exchanges** in the instructions.

Note: Complete lines 12 through 14 **only** if you gave up property that was not like-kind. Otherwise, go to

12	Fair market value (FMV) of other property given up	**12**	
13	Adjusted basis of other property given up	**13**	
14	Gain or (loss) recognized on other property given up. Subtract line 13 from line 12. Report the gain or (loss) in the same manner as if the exchange had been a sale		**14**

Caution: If the property given up was used previously or partly as a home, see **Property used as home** in the instructions.

15	Cash received, FMV of other property received, plus net liabilities assumed by other party, reduced (but not below zero) by any exchange expenses you incurred (see instructions)	**15**
16	FMV of like-kind property you received	**16**
17	Add lines 15 and 16	**17**
18	Adjusted basis of like-kind property you gave up, net amounts paid to other party, plus any exchange expenses **not** used on line 15 (see instructions)	**18**
19	**Realized gain or (loss).** Subtract line 18 from line 17	**19**
20	Enter the smaller of line 15 or line 19, but not less than zero	**20**
21	Ordinary income under recapture rules. Enter here and on Form 4797, line 16 (see instructions)	**21**
22	Subtract line 21 from line 20. If zero or less, enter -0-. If more than zero, enter here and on Schedule D or Form 4797, unless the installment method applies (see instructions)	**22**
23	**Recognized gain.** Add lines 21 and 22	**23**
24	Deferred gain or (loss). Subtract line 23 from line 19. If a related party exchange, see instructions	**24**
25	**Basis of like-kind property received.** Subtract line 15 from the sum of lines 18 and 23	**25**

Part IV Deferral of Gain From Section 1043 Conflict-of-Interest Sales

Note: This part is to be used **only** by officers or employees of the executive branch of the Federal Goven nonrecognition of gain under section 1043 on the sale of property to comply with the conflict-of-interest requ can be used **only** if the cost of the replacement property is more than the basis of the divested property.

26	Enter the number from the upper right corner of your certificate of divestiture. (**Do not** attach a copy of your certificate. Keep the certificate with your records.) ▶	_____

27 Description of divested property ▶ ....

28 Description of replacement property ▶ ....

29	Date divested property was sold (month, day, year)		**29**
30	Sales price of divested property (see instructions)	**30**	
31	Basis of divested property	**31**	
32	**Realized gain.** Subtract line 31 from line 30		**32**
33	Cost of replacement property purchased within 60 days after date of sale	**33**	
34	Subtract line 33 from line 30. If zero or less, enter -0-		**34**
35	Ordinary income under recapture rules. Enter here and on Form 4797, line 10 (see instructions)		**35**
36	Subtract line 35 from line 34. If zero or less, enter -0-. If more than zero, enter here and on Schedule D or Form 4797 (see instructions)		**36**
37	**Deferred gain.** Subtract the sum of lines 35 and 36 from line 32		**37**
38	**Basis of replacement property.** Subtract line 37 from line 33		**38**

General Instructions

Section references are to the Internal Revenue Code unless otherwise noted.

Purpose of Form

Use Parts I, II, and III of Form 8824 to report each exchange of business or investment property for property of a like kind. Certain members of the executive branch of the Federal Government use Part IV to elect to defer gain on conflict-of-interest sales.

Multiple exchanges. If you made more than one like-kind exchange, you may file only a summary Form 8824 and attach your own statement showing all the information requested on Form 8824 for each exchange. Include your name and identifying number at the top of each page of the statement. On the summary Form 8824, enter only your name and identifying number, "Summary" on line 1, the total recognized gain from all exchanges on line 23, and the total basis of all like-kind property received on line 25.

When To File

If during the current tax year you transferred property to another party in a like-kind exchange, you must file Form 8824 with your tax return for that year. Also file Form 8824 for the 2 years following the year of a related party exchange (see the instructions for line 7 on page 4).

Like-Kind Exchanges

Generally, if you exchange business or investment property solely for business or investment property of a like kind, no gain or loss is recognized under section 1031. If, as part of the exchange, you also receive other (not like-kind) property or money, gain is recognized to the extent of the other property and money received, but a loss is not recognized.

Section 1031 does not apply to exchanges of inventory, stocks, bonds, notes, other securities or evidence of indebtedness, or certain other assets. See section 1031(a)(2). In addition, section 1031 does not apply to certain exchanges involving tax-exempt use property subject to a lease. See section 470(e)(4).

Like-kind property. Properties are of like kind if they are of the same nature or character, even if they differ in grade or quality. Personal properties of a like class are like-kind properties. However, livestock of different sexes are not like-kind properties. Also, personal property used predominantly in the United States and personal property used predominantly outside the United States are not like-kind properties. See Pub. 544, Sales and Other Dispositions of Assets, for more details.

Real properties generally are of like kind, regardless of whether they are improved or unimproved. However, real property in the United States and real property outside the United States are not like-kind properties.

Deferred exchanges. A deferred exchange occurs when the property received in the exchange is received after the transfer of the property given up. For a deferred exchange to qualify as like-kind, you must comply with the 45-day written notice and receipt requirements explained in the instructions for lines 5 and 6.

Multi-asset exchanges. A multi-asset exchange involves the transfer and receipt of more than one group of like-kind properties. For example, an exchange of land, vehicles, and cash for land and vehicles is a multi-asset exchange. An exchange of land, vehicles, and cash for land only is not a multi-asset exchange. The transfer or receipt of multiple properties within one like-kind group is also a multi-asset exchange. Special rules apply when figuring the amount of gain recognized and your basis in properties received in a multi-asset exchange. For details, see Regulations section 1.1031(j)-1.

Reporting of multi-asset exchanges. If you transferred and received (a) more than one group of like-kind properties or (b) cash or other (not like-kind) property, do not complete lines 12 through 18 of Form 8824. Instead, attach your own statement showing how you figured the realized and recognized gain, and enter the correct amount on lines 19 through 25. Report any recognized gains on Schedule D; Form 4797, Sales of Business Property; or Form 6252, Installment Sale Income, whichever applies.

Exchanges using a qualified exchange accommodation arrangement (QEAA). If property is transferred to an exchange accommodation titleholder (EAT) and held in a QEAA, the EAT may be treated as the beneficial owner of the property, the property transferred from the EAT to you may be treated as property you received in an exchange, and the property you transferred to the EAT may be treated as property you gave up in an exchange. This may be true even if the property you are to receive is transferred to the EAT before you transfer the property you are giving up. However, the property transferred to you may not be treated as property received in an exchange if you previously owned it within 180 days of its transfer to the EAT. For details, see Rev. Proc. 2000-37 as modified by Rev. Proc. 2004-51. Rev. Proc. 2000-37 is on page 308 of Internal Revenue Bulletin 2000-40 at *www.irs.gov/pub/irs-irbs/irb00-40.pdf*. Rev. Proc. 2004-51 is on page 294 of Internal Revenue Bulletin 2004-33 at *www.irs.gov/irb/2004-33_IRB/ar13.html*.

Property used as home. If the property given up was owned and used as your home during the 5-year period ending on the date of the exchange, you may be able to exclude part or all of any gain figured on Form 8824. For details on the exclusion (including how to figure the amount of the exclusion), see Pub. 523, Selling Your Home. Fill out Form 8824 according to its instructions, with these exceptions:

1. Subtract line 18 from line 17. Subtract the amount of the exclusion from the result. Enter that result on line 19. On the dotted line next to line 19, enter "Section 121 exclusion" and the amount of the exclusion.

2. On line 20, enter the smaller of:
   a. Line 15 minus the exclusion, or
   b. Line 19.
   Do not enter less than zero.

3. Subtract line 15 from the sum of lines 18 and 23. Add the amount of your exclusion to the result. Enter that sum on line 25.

Property used partly as home. If the property given up was used partly as a home, you will need to use two separate Forms 8824 as worksheets—one for the part of the property used as a home and one for the part used for business or investment. Fill out only lines 15 through 25 of each worksheet Form 8824. On the worksheet Form 8824 for the part of the property used as a home, follow steps (1) through (3) above, except that instead of following step (2), enter the amount from line 19 on line 20. On the worksheet Form 8824 for the part of the property used for business or investment, follow steps (1) through (3) above only if you can exclude at least part of any gain from the exchange of that part of the property; otherwise, complete the form according to its instructions. Enter the combined amounts from lines 15 through 25 of both worksheet Forms 8824 on the Form 8824 you file. Do not file either worksheet Form 8824.

More information. For details, see Rev. Proc. 2005-14 on page 528 of Internal Revenue Bulletin 2005-7 at *www.irs.gov/irb/2005-07_IRB/ar10.html*.

Additional information. For more information on like-kind exchanges, see section 1031 and its regulations and Pub. 544.

Specific Instructions

Lines 1 and 2. For real property, enter the address and type of property. For personal property, enter a short description. For property located outside the United States, include the country.

Line 5. Enter on line 5 the date of the written notice that identifies the like-kind property you received in a deferred exchange. To comply with the **45-day written notice requirement,** the following conditions must be met.

1. The like-kind property you receive in a deferred exchange must be designated in writing as replacement property either in a document you signed or in a written agreement signed by all parties to the exchange.

2. The document or agreement must describe the replacement property in a clear and recognizable manner. Real property should be described using a legal description, street address, or distinguishable name (for example, "Mayfair Apartment Building").

3. No later than 45 days after the date you transferred the property you gave up:

a. You must send, fax, or hand deliver the document you signed to the person required to transfer the replacement property to you (including a disqualified person) or to another person involved in the exchange (other than a disqualified person), or

b. All parties to the exchange must sign the written agreement designating the replacement property.

Generally, a disqualified person is either your agent at the time of the transaction or a person related to you. For more details, see Regulations section 1.1031(k)-1(k).

Note. If you received the replacement property before the end of the 45-day period, you automatically are treated as having met the 45-day written notice requirement. In this case, enter on line 5 the date you received the replacement property.

Line 6. Enter on line 6 the date you received the like-kind property from the other party.

The property must be received by the earlier of the following dates.

● The 180th day after the date you transferred the property given up in the exchange.

● The due date (including extensions) of your tax return for the year in which you transferred the property given up.

Line 7. Special rules apply to like-kind exchanges made with related parties, either directly or indirectly. A **related party** includes your spouse, child, grandchild, parent, grandparent, brother, sister, or a related corporation, S corporation, partnership, trust, or estate. See section 1031(f).

An exchange made **indirectly** with a related party includes:

● An exchange made with a related party through an intermediary (such as a qualified intermediary or an exchange accommodation titleholder, as defined in Pub. 544), or

● An exchange made by a disregarded entity (such as a single member limited liability company) if you or a related party owned that entity.

If the related party (either directly or indirectly) or you dispose of the property received in an exchange before the date that is 2 years after the last transfer of property from the exchange, the deferred gain or (loss) from line 24 must be reported on your return for the year of disposition (unless an exception on line 11 applies).

If you are filing this form for 1 of the 2 years following the year of the exchange, complete Parts I and II. If both lines 9 and 10 are "No," **stop.**

If either line 9 or line 10 is "Yes," and an exception on line 11 applies, check the applicable box on line 11, attach any required explanation, and **stop.** If no line 11 exceptions apply, complete Part III.

Report the deferred gain or (loss) from line 24 on this year's tax return as if the exchange had been a sale.

An exchange structured to avoid the related party rules is not a like-kind exchange. Do not report it on Form 8824. Instead, you should report the disposition of the property given up as if the exchange had been a sale. See section 1031(f)(4). Such an exchange includes the transfer of property you gave up to a qualifed intermediary in exchange for property you received that was formerly owned by a related party if the related party received cash or other (not like-kind) property for the property you received, and you used the qualified intermediary to avoid the application of the related party rules. See Rev. Rul. 2002-83 for more details. You can find Rev. Rul. 2002-83 on page 927 of Internal Revenue Bulletin 2002-49 at *www.irs.gov/pub/irs-irbs/irb02-49.pdf.*

Line 11c. If you believe that you can establish to the satisfaction of the IRS that tax avoidance was not a principal purpose of both the exchange and the disposition, attach an explanation. Generally, tax avoidance will not be seen as a principal purpose in the case of:

● A disposition of property in a nonrecognition transaction,

● An exchange in which the related parties derive no tax advantage from the shifting of basis between the exchanged properties, or

● An exchange of undivided interests in different properties that results in each related party holding either the entire interest in a single property or a larger undivided interest in any of the properties.

Lines 12, 13, and 14. If you gave up other property in addition to the like-kind property, enter the fair market value (FMV) and the adjusted basis of the other property on lines 12 and 13, respectively. The gain or (loss) from this property is figured on line 14 and must be reported on your return. Report gain or (loss) as if the exchange were a sale.

Line 15. Include on line 15 the sum of:

● Any cash paid to you by the other party,

● The FMV of other (not like-kind) property you received, if any, and

● Net liabilities assumed by the other party—the excess, if any, of liabilities (including mortgages) assumed by the other party over the total of (a) any liabilities you assumed, (b) cash you paid to the other party, and (c) the FMV of the other (not like-kind) property you gave up.

Reduce the sum of the above amounts (but not below zero) by any exchange expenses you incurred. See the example on this page.

The following rules apply in determining the amount of liability treated as assumed.

● A recourse liability (or portion thereof) is treated as assumed by the party receiving the property if that party has agreed to and is expected to satisfy the liability (or portion thereof). It does not matter whether the party transferring the property has been relieved of the liability.

● A nonrecouse liability generally is treated as assumed by the party receiving the property subject to the liability. However, if an owner of other assets subject to the same liability agrees with the party receiving the property to, and is expected to, satisfy part or all of the liability, the amount treated as assumed is reduced by the smaller of (a) the amount of the liability that the owner of the other assets has agreed to and is expected to satisfy or (b) the FMV of those other assets.

Line 18. Include on line 18 the sum of:

● The adjusted basis of the like-kind property you gave up,

● Exchange expenses, if any (except for expenses used to reduce the amount reported on line 15), and

● Net amount paid to the other party—the **excess,** if any, of the total of (a) any liabilities you assumed, (b) cash you paid to the other party, and (c) the FMV of the other (not like-kind) property you gave up **over** any liabilities assumed by the other party.

See Regulations section 1.1031(d)-2 and the following example for figuring amounts to enter on lines 15 and 18.

Example. A owns an apartment house with an FMV of $220,000, an adjusted basis of $100,000, and subject to a mortgage of $80,000. B owns an apartment house with an FMV of $250,000, an adjusted basis of $175,000, and subject to a mortgage of $150,000.

A transfers his apartment house to B and receives in exchange B's apartment house plus $40,000 cash. A assumes the mortgage on the apartment house received from B, and B assumes the mortgage on the apartment house received from A.

A enters on line 15 only the $40,000 cash received from B. The $80,000 of liabilities assumed by B is not included because it does not exceed the $150,000 of liabilities A assumed. A enters $170,000 on line 18—the $100,000 adjusted basis, plus the $70,000 excess of the liabilities A assumed over the liabilities assumed by B ($150,000 - $80,000).

B enters $30,000 on line 15—the excess of the $150,000 of liabilities assumed by A over the total ($120,000) of the $80,000 of liabilities B assumed and the $40,000 cash B paid. B enters on line 18 only the adjusted basis of $175,000 because the total of the $80,000 of liabilities B assumed and the $40,000 cash B paid does not exceed the $150,000 of liabilities assumed by A.

Line 21. If you disposed of section 1245, 1250, 1252, 1254, or 1255 property (see the instructions for Part III of Form 4797), you may be required to recapture as ordinary income part or all of the realized gain (line 19). Figure the amount to enter on line 21 as follows:

Section 1245 property. Enter the smaller of:

1. The total adjustments for deductions (whether for the same or other property) allowed or allowable to you or any other

person for depreciation or amortization (up to the amount of gain shown on line 19), or

2. The gain shown on line 20, if any, plus the FMV of non-section 1245 like-kind property received.

Section 1250 property. Enter the smaller of:

1. The gain you would have had to report as ordinary income because of additional depreciation if you had sold the property (see the Form 4797 instructions for line 26), or

2. The larger of:

a. The gain shown on line 20, if any, or

b. The excess, if any, of the gain in item (1) above over the FMV of the section 1250 property received.

Section 1252, 1254, and 1255 property. The rules for these types of property are similar to those for section 1245 property. See Regulations section 1.1252-2(d) and Temporary Regulations section 16A.1255-2(c) for details. If the installment method applies to this exchange:

1. See section 453(f)(6) to determine the installment sale income taxable for this year and report it on Form 6252.

2. Enter on Form 6252, line 25 or 36, the section 1252, 1254, or 1255 recapture amount you figured on Form 8824, line 21. Do not enter more than the amount shown on Form 6252, line 24 or 35.

3. Also enter this amount on Form 4797, line 15.

4. If all the ordinary income is not recaptured this year, report in future years on Form 6252 the ordinary income up to the taxable installment sale income, until it is all reported.

Line 22. Report a gain from the exchange of property used in a trade or business (and other noncapital assets) on Form 4797, line 5 or line 16. Report a gain from the exchange of capital assets according to the Schedule D instructions for your return. Be sure to use the date of the exchange as the date for reporting the gain. If the installment method applies to this exchange, see section 453(f)(6) to determine the installment sale income taxable for this year and report it on Form 6252.

Line 24. If line 19 is a loss, enter it on line 24. Otherwise, subtract the amount on line 23 from the amount on line 19 and enter the result. For exchanges with related parties, see the instructions for line 7 on page 4.

Line 25. The amount on line 25 is your basis in the like-kind property you received in the exchange. Your basis in other property received in the exchange, if any, is its FMV.

Section 1043 Conflict-of-Interest Sales (Part IV)

If you sell property at a gain according to a certificate of divestiture issued by the Office of Government Ethics (OGE) and purchase replacement property (permitted property), you may elect to defer part or all of the realized gain. You must recognize gain on the sale only to the extent that the amount realized on the sale is more than the cost of replacement property purchased within 60 days after the sale. (You also must recognize any ordinary income recapture.) Permitted property is any obligation of the United States or any diversified investment fund approved by the OGE.

 If the property you sold was stock you acquired by exercising a statutory stock option, you may be treated as meeting the holding periods that apply to such stock, regardless of how long you actually held the stock. This may benefit you if you do not defer your entire gain, because it may allow you to treat the gain as a capital gain instead of ordinary income. For details, see section 421(d) or Pub. 525.

Complete Part IV of Form 8824 only if the cost of the replacement property is more than the basis of the divested property and you elect to defer the gain. Otherwise, report the sale on Schedule D or Form 4797, whichever applies.

Your basis in the replacement property is reduced by the amount of the deferred gain. If you made more than one purchase of replacement property, reduce your basis in the replacement property in the order you acquired it.

Line 30. Enter the amount you received from the sale of the divested property, minus any selling expenses.

Line 35. Follow these steps to determine the amount to enter.

1. Use Part III of Form 4797 as a worksheet to figure ordinary income under the recapture rules.

2. Enter on Form 8824, line 35, the amount from Form 4797, line 31. Do not attach the Form 4797 used as a worksheet to your return.

3. Report the amount from line 35 on Form 4797, line 10, column (g). In column (a), write "From Form 8824, line 35." Do not complete columns (b) through (f).

Line 36. If you sold a capital asset, enter any capital gain from line 36 on Schedule D. If you sold property used in a trade or business (or any other asset for which the gain is treated as ordinary income), report the gain on Form 4797, line 2 or line 10, column (g). In column (a), write "From Form 8824, line 36." Do not complete columns (b) through (f).

Paperwork Reduction Act Notice. We ask for the information on this form to carry out the Internal Revenue laws of the United States. You are required to give us the information. We need it to ensure that you are complying with these laws and to allow us to figure and collect the right amount of tax.

You are not required to provide the information requested on a form that is subject to the Paperwork Reduction Act unless the form displays a valid OMB control number. Books or records relating to a form or its instructions must be retained as long as their contents may become material in the administration of any Internal Revenue law. Generally, tax returns and return information are confidential, as required by section 6103.

The time needed to complete and file this form will vary depending on individual circumstances. The estimated burden for individual taxpayers filing this form is approved under OMB control number 1545-0074 and is included in the estimates shown in the instructions for their individual income tax return. The estimated burden for all other taxpayers who file this form is shown below.

Recordkeeping . . . . 1 hr., 38 min.

Learning about the law or the form . . . . . . 27 min.

Preparing the form . . . . . 59 min.

Copying, assembling, and sending the form to the IRS . . 33 min.

If you have comments concerning the accuracy of these time estimates or suggestions for making this form simpler, we would be happy to hear from you. See the instructions for the tax return with which this form is filed.

A reportable profit (or loss) does not occur in a §1031 transaction if cash is withdrawn concurrent with the execution of a carryback note or contribution of any cash item (such as a boat or plane) toward the purchase of the replacement property.

In economic, legal and tax terms, the cash withdrawn by the investor on his purchase of the replacement property **constitutes a loan**. The loan is evidenced by a note executed by the investor in part payment for the replacement property or by the origination of a loan encumbering the property. Thus, the investor received cash and real estate in exchange for executing the note or originating the loan.

To correctly reflect the unreported profits transferred into the replacement property, the owner must prepare and attach an accounting, such as **first tuesday** Form 354, to his IRS Form 8824, in lieu of filling in lines 12 through 18. The computations from §§ 4.4 and 4.5 of Form 354 are then transferred to lines 19 and 20 of the IRS Form 8824, leaving lines 12 through 18 blank, except to note the off-form accounting.

Editor's note — A boat or plane "added" to acquire the replacement property may have a profit, which must be reported. [See Form 354 §1.11 and §2.3]

Also, any amount paid for improvements made after acquiring ownership of the replacement property will be added to the basis in the replacement property. However, the costs incurred for improvements completed after ownership is acquired cannot be included in the §1031 accounting. [See Chapter 15]

Cash reinvested or borrowed

An investor intending to complete a §1031 transaction receives cash (deposited into his checking account) for his equity in the property he sold. However, he reinvests only part of the cash to purchase the replacement property. The terms for the purchase of the replacement property include the investor's execution of a carryback note of equal or greater amount than the cash withdrawn on the sales leg.

The investor claims the cash withdrawn from the sale of his property is later (within the 180-day limitation) offset by the note (a cash item) he executed to purchase the replacement property and complete his §1031 reinvestment plan.

The investor believes all steps in a §1031 reinvestment plan — including the receipt of cash from the property sold — must be viewed as one transaction in order to complete the exchange.

However, a §1031 reinvestment plan is completed only when cash received from a sale is **reinvested** to purchase replacement property and actual and constructive receipt is avoided. Thus, any cash withdrawn by the investor from the sales proceeds prior to acquiring replacement property causes profits of an equal amount to be reported. [**Behrens** v. **Commissioner** (1985) TCM 1985-195]

While *Behrens* correctly denied the investor's profit exemption on cash withdrawn, it applied the wrong rule in its decision. The court failed to address the IRS rule that states cash acquired in a §1031 reinvestment plan may not be offset under any circumstances by the assumption of debt on a replacement property.

In *Behrens*, the carryback note created to purchase the replacement property was improperly classified as **existing debt** assumed by the investor.

However, debt created is not an existing loan. Thus, the carryback note executed by the investor is not mortgage boot. Created debt cannot be assumed (or guaranteed) by the person creating it. Creation of a purchase-money debt and assumption of an existing loan are not considered the same in a §1031 reinvestment.

The carryback note should have been classified as debt originated by the investor, making it a cash item. While existing debt assumed can never offset cash received, the investor's execution of a carryback note does offset cash. However, a carryback note, does not offset cash the investor received before he acquired ownership to the replacement property. Thus, *Behrens* correctly denied the profit exemption, but for the wrong reasons.

A carryback note is debt arranged in a credit or installment sale, not a loan assumed. A carryback note is a cash boot item, not mortgage boot consisting of existing debt, whether assumed or not. [**Mitchell** v. **Commissioner** (1964) 42 TC 953]

When to withdraw cash

Although all steps in a §1031 transaction must be viewed as one, cash withdrawn prior to the purchase of replacement property constitutes an actual receipt of sales proceeds.

Any cash actually or constructively received in a §1031 transaction prior to acquiring replacement property (and creating a carryback note) triggers the reporting of an equal amount of profit. [Revenue Regulations §1.1031(b)-1(a)]

To avoid the actual or constructive receipt of cash prior to acquiring ownership of the replacement property, all cash items derived from the sale of property in a §1031 transaction must at all times be placed beyond the investor's **immediate legal access** until he acquires ownership of the replacement property.

Then, on his acquisition of a replacement property, an investor may withdraw cash concurrent with the purchase of the replacement property.

Cash withdrawn concurrent with the creation of carryback paper on the purchase of the replacement property constitutes the equivalent of **loan proceeds**, a tax-free event that is not part of the basis in the replacement property.

Since the amount of the cash withdrawn is not part of the basis in the replacement property, the **interest paid** on the cash portion of the carryback note may not be deducted from rental income on the replacement property. That portion of the interest, attributable to the cash withdrawn and used elsewhere, is deducted from rental income on another property purchased with cash withdrawn. [Feldman, *supra*]

Glossary

A glossary of IRS terminology.

A

Actual or constructive receipt:

Obtaining a portion or all of the sales proceeds and using the *economic benefits* of the sales proceeds prior to acquiring ownership of the replacement property in a delayed §1031 reinvestment plan. Receipt of all the sales proceeds, even temporarily, before acquiring the replacement property nullifies the use of the §1031 exemption since a *sale of property* has occurred. Conversely, receipt of only a portion of the sales proceeds before acquiring replacement property qualifies as a partial §1031 exchange. Receipt of the sales proceeds by an investor under a purchase agreement and escrow instructions in a sale that has not yet closed, can be fully avoided by amending the escrow instructions and obligating escrow to deliver the proceeds to a person other than the investor on closing, such as a trustee established by the buyer under a provision to cooperate, or an intermediary under the safe harbor rules [Revenue Regulations §§1.1031(k)-1(f), 1.1031(k)-1(g); **Alderson** v. **Commissioner (9th Cir. 1963) 317 F2d 790; Barker** v. **Commissioner** (1980) 74 TC 555; **Biggs** v. **Commissioner** (5th Cir. 1980) 632 F2d 1171]

D

Deferred exchange:

The sale and transfer of one or more properties under purchase agreement provisions and amended escrow instructions allowing for the investor to later identify and reinvest the sales proceeds to acquire ownership of a replacement property within the 180-day *exchange period*, without receipt of the sales proceeds prior to acquiring a replacement property. A portion of the sales proceeds can be received at any time without disqualifying the sale's profit from partial exemption under Internal Revenue Code (IRC) §1031(b). [Rev. Regs. §1.1031(k)-1; **Starker** v. **United States** (9th Cir. 1979) 602 F2d 1341]

Direct transfers:

Also called *direct deeding* of property; available for use only under the *general rule* for avoiding receipt of money, not the *safe harbor procedures* for avoidance. The conveyance of title and ownership directly to the cash buyer of a property. No facilitator, intermediary or other strawman are sequentially involved in the conveyancing of either the property sold or the replacement property. [IRS Revenue Ruling 90-34; **W. D. Haden Co.** v. **Commissioner** (5th Cir. 1948) 165 F2d 588]

Disqualified persons:

A *disqualified person* is not allowed to participate in two situations that arise in a delayed §1031 reinvestment. One situation involves the person who may receive the 45-day identification notice from the investor in all delayed reinvestments not completed within 45 days after closing the sale of the property to be sold. The other situation involves the person who may be the *intermediary* when the investor elects to use the safe harbor sequential deeding procedures to avoid receipt of the sales proceeds. *Disqualified persons* include the investor's employees, attorney, accountant, investment banker or broker or real estate broker or agent who, within two years prior to closing the sale, rendered services to the investor unrelated to §1031 reinvestment plans. Relatives of the investor and entities in which the investor or other disqualified persons hold more than a 10% ownership interest are also *disqualified persons*.

E

Economic benefit:

An investor's use of the proceeds from a sale that are held by a §1031 trustee or an intermediary. To receive the net sales proceeds on demand or on demand following a notice and to pledge, collaterally assign, borrow against or otherwise hypothecate the proceeds prior to acquiring ownership of replacement property. An investor's use of the economic benefits disqualifies the reinvestment plan for the §1031 exemption. The right of an investor to receive the interest on the proceeds is not constructive receipt of the funds, but actual receipt of any interest before acquiring replacement property is treated as receipt of the entire sales proceeds and will disqualify the reinvestment.

Exchange:

The sale of one or more properties owned by an investor and the investor's purchase of replacement property, concurrently or after a delay, without the investor first receiving all of the net proceeds of the sale prior to their reinvestment. Also called a §1031 transaction, whether it is an actual exchange of properties or a sell-then-buy reinvestment plan. An *exchange* also occurs under IRC §1031(b) if a portion but not all of the proceeds from a sale are received by the investor prior to his acquiring ownership of the replacement property. [Rev. Regs. §1.1031(k)-1; Rev. Rul. 77-297; **Carlton** v. **United States** (5th Cir. 1967) 385 F2d 238]

Exchange agreement:

A purchase agreement containing a §1031 cooperation provision and amended escrow instructions that redirect cash sales proceeds on closing to a person other than an investor, and re-route the money for use in the investor's purchase of replacement property. Also, any reinvestment plan consisting of all the contractual arrangements between the investor and the buyer of his property, including purchase agreements and amended escrow instructions that, on the close of the sales escrow, establish the investor's right to concurrently or later acquire the rights to ownership of yet-to-be-identified replacement property, accommodated by the buyer's promise to cooperate with the investor. [Biggs, *supra*]

I

Intermediary:

Also called a *qualified intermediary* by the Internal Revenue Service (IRS). An individual or entity, other than an investor or a *disqualified person*, who acts as the strawman under the alternative safe harbor procedures available as an election by an investor to avoid receipt of the sales proceeds from the property he sold, used when a buyer is unwilling to cooperate. Unlike a §1031 trustee, an intermediary acts under the safe harbor rules of sequential deeding to avoid receipt of the sales proceeds to be reinvested in a replacement property. Both the intermediary and the §1031 trustee act as **conduits** through which the cash proceeds from the investor's sale flow before funding the purchase of a replacement property.

Interest:

Money earned by accrual on the net sales proceeds during the delay in a reinvestment, following the close of escrow on a cash sale and until the close of escrow on the purchase of the replacement property when the interest may first be received. The investor is entitled to receive the interest and must report it as income. [Rev. Regs. §§1.1031(k)-1(g)(5), 1.1031(k)-1(h); Starker, *supra*]

P

Purchase of property:
The acquisition of ownership to a replacement property by the use of funds delivered to and received by the investor as proceeds from a sale of his property, no matter the duration of time the investor held the funds before reinvestment. As a matter of commercial reality, the purchase of property by an investor occurs in nearly all §1031 reinvestment plans when the investor enters into a purchase agreement and escrow instructions to acquire replacement property by the use of the sales proceeds held by a §1031 trustee or intermediary. [Barker, Carlton and Alderson, *supra*]

Q

Qualified intermediary:
See *Intermediary*.

R

Receipt of money:
A condition that arises in a cash sale of an investor's property when the proceeds of the sale are delivered to the investor on close of escrow, or when the proceeds are legally available for the investor to immediately draw on demand or on demand following notice. When the investor actually receives the *beneficial use* of the proceeds. [Rev. Regs. §1.1031(k)-1(f); Rev. Rul. 77-297; Alderson and Barker, *supra*]

Reinvestment in property:
The use of cash proceeds received by an investor from a sale to fund the purchase of replacement property. The common application is to shift the equity in the property sold into the equity in a replacement property by any means, provided the investor does not first receive the cash proceeds of the sale. [Rev. Regs. §1.1031(k)-1(a)]

Relinquished property:
The IRS term for the property sold that was owned by the investor, whose sale provided the cash funds the investor reinvested in replacement property. The IRS also refers to the property sold by the investor as the **property transferred**.

S

Safe harbors rules:
A highly detailed procedure for avoiding receipt of the sales proceeds from a sale, established by the IRS in §1031 deferred exchange regulations so an investor may elect to use it as an alternative to the *general rules* for avoiding receipt of the sales proceeds. The §1031 safe harbor regulations call for the use of a **strawman**, called an *intermediary*, to act as a transitory titleholder in a contractually formalistic series of additional steps in a reinvestment plan, each with no legal consequence or economic significance. The safe harbor rules are designed solely to place a strawman between an investor and both the buyer of the property sold and the seller of the replacement property by engaging in sequential contracting and conveyancing through the intermediary, giving a sale and purchase the appearance of an actual two-party exchange. [Rev. Regs. §1.1031(k)-1(g); **Gregory** v. **Helvering** (1935) 293 US 465]

Sale of property:

Receipt of money by an investor on the close of escrow for a cash sale of his property, before he acquires ownership of replacement property and in the **full amount** of all the net proceeds of the sale, called a "cash-out sale". It is a receipt that disqualifies the sale for the profit tax exemption under IRC §1031(a). However, the receipt of a portion, but not all, of the net sales proceeds prior to acquiring ownership of the replacement property is not a *sale of property*, but instead, is a withdrawal of capital on the reinvestment. A withdrawal of capital requires profit to be reported on the sale up to the amount of the cash received as a partial §1031 reinvestment. In practice, entering into a purchase agreement for the sale of property on cash terms is usually essential to the investor's purchase of the replacement property in a §1031 reinvestment. [Rev. Regs. §1.1031(k)-1(f)(1); Carlton, *supra*]

Case Index

California Codes

Federal Codes

D